Henri Mercier

AND THE AMERICAN
CIVIL WAR

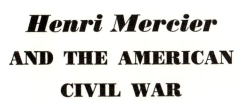

Henri Mercier
AND THE AMERICAN
CIVIL WAR

By
Daniel B. Carroll

Princeton University Press
Princeton, New Jersey

1971

Publication of this book has been supported by a
subvention from the Institut français de Washington,
the Gilbert D. Chinard prize awarded to the manuscript in
1968 by the Society for French Historical Studies.

This book has been composed in Linotype Caledonia
Printed in the United States of America
by Princeton University Press,
Princeton, New Jersey

To Lorie

Contents

XI. A SEA OF TROUBLES

XII. LAST WEEKS AND RETURN

Preface

In the great history of human groups, of man's identification with units beyond the family, few events have been more weighty than the American Civil War. What is an American? Is the South the home of a nationality and should it be a nation? Should loyalty to Virginia press harder on the conscience than loyalty to the United States? Such questions received answers of a sort from the war. Others, while not answerable in a final sense, were plumbed more deeply as the suffering went on: What does the word "American" mean for the rights of man? From first to last it was a business of defining "American," and in this work the great ethnic question was at once a puissant cause and formidable effect of the war: Must a man be white to be a fully endowed American?

European observers gave various answers to such questions, answers of considerable moment and interest. Participation brings its own depth of understanding, but the outsider, detached and reflective, is always worth hearing. Henri Mercier was such an observer, and his comments are valuable for the light they throw on the great events of his time. But he was more. As the representative of a great power, he drew conclusions which were a matter of life or death for the United States—and for the Confederacy. Some who have touched upon Mercier's role have argued that those conclusions were prejudicial to the United States. Such generalizations are inevitable when a subject is so little known as this one, and English-language authors have been sometimes content to let England stand for Europe in the diplomatic story of the Civil War. I hope that this study will help to redress that imbalance and to recover for Henri Mercier the important place on stage which his contemporaries recognized as his.

I have accumulated an enormous debt of gratitude during the time this study was in progress. My thanks go first of all to Professor Lynn M. Case of the University of Pennsylvania for his generous help and encouragement. Like Dr. Case, Professor Warren F. Spencer of the University of Georgia has allowed me to consult sources which he had obtained on film for his own work: these have been extremely helpful, and I am most grateful. The scores of American and French librarians, archivists, and other scholars who have answered my requests for help will understand, I am sure, if their names are not catalogued here, but I deeply appreciate their kind and professional assistance. I am especially appreciative of permissions accorded me, in letters from a succession of Quai d'Orsay staff members, to have documents filmed. My debt to private individuals is equally great, especially to M. Jean Le Cour Grandmaison, Dom Maur Le Cour Grandmaison, O.S.B., M. Franck Mähler-Besse, and most especially to Madame Henri Mähler-Besse for friendship, help, and films of family documents of her great-grandfather, Henri Mercier. The following were kindly helpful in my effort to follow Mercier's activities and whereabouts: Mr. John Beverley Riggs; Mrs. Henry J. Spitzer of Lostant, Illinois; and Mr. and Mrs. David E. Finley of Washington. I am extremely grateful too to my friends Mrs. Bess Polkowski and Mrs. Florence Collins, who prepared the manuscript. Thanks go to the administration of Villanova University for a generous grant, and to my chairman, Professor Joseph R. George, Jr. Finally, I thank most sincerely the administrators of the Gilbert D. Chinard trust, the Society for French Historical Studies, the Institut français de Washington, and the prize committee which selected this work for its award in 1968. I am especially grateful to Professor Frances S. Childs and Professor Ambrose Saricks for their subsequent encouragement and helpful criticisms. My thanks for help and criticism go also to Mr. Sanford G. Thatcher and Mrs. Martyn Hitchcock of Princeton University Press.

Speaking of one's family in a preface must always be an inadequate undertaking. Francis M. and Elizabeth E. Carroll and Gertrude A. Donahue—my father and mother and my aunt—have gone on before me and know the depth of my gratitude. Other, younger folk have also been a happy part of this book's composition though they are not yet fully aware of it; thanks, then, to each of our six children. Most especially does Dolores Anne Carroll receive a husband's loving, grateful dedication.

Villanova, Pennsylvania
November 18, 1970

A Note on Sources

THE American career of Henri Mercier has suffered at historians' hands from cursory treatment and from the easy summation such treatment usually constructs. According to this, Mercier was influenced by his Southern friends; he represented a government which wanted American scission as an aid to its Mexican policy; he made a trip to Richmond in 1862; he tried to end the war on the basis of Southern independence; he went home. The comparatively scant published documents and memoirs of which the early accounts were compounded are of course part of the explanation for this unhappy situation. *Foreign Relations of the United States*, the continuing work in which the State Department publishes select diplomatic documents, contains, for example, the opinion of Secretary of State William H. Seward that Mercier sympathized with the South because he had made friends with prominent Southerners in 1860.[1] Supplementary American printed collections include the Confederate state department set edited by James D. Richardson, containing, for instance, Judah P. Benjamin's version of what Mercier said in Richmond, and the well-known series put out by the War and Navy Departments of the United States.[2]

[1] See, for example, Seward to Dayton, Washington, Jan. 4, 1864, no. 452, *Papers Relating to Foreign Affairs Accompanying the Annual Message of the President, 1864*, III (Washington: U.S. Government Printing Office, 1865), 15-16. Though the early volumes of this series appeared under a variety of titles, it is generally known as *Foreign Relations of the United States* and will hereafter be cited as *For. Rel. U.S.*

[2] *A Compilation of the Messages and Papers of the Confederacy, Including the Diplomatic Correspondence, 1861-1865*, ed. James D.

Documents of the French foreign office published in this period may be found in *Documents diplomatiques*, known as the *Yellow Books* (*Livres jaunes*). Of much greater importance are the seven letters from Thouvenel to Mercier in the collection of private correspondence which Louis Thouvenel, the minister's son, published in 1889. The correspondence in the British *Sessional Papers* is more full than the French series, and the comments by the British minister, Lord Lyons, upon his French colleague's actions are of value; of even greater value are the Lyons dispatches reproduced in Lord Newton's biography.[3]

Setting aside the occasional stories about Mercier carried in American newspapers and journals, the earliest accounts of his doings appeared in the many published memoirs to which the Civil War gave birth. William H. Seward did not write his autobiography, but the books published by his son and secretary, Frederick W. Seward, are of prime interest. Brief references to Mercier can also be found in the diaries and memoirs of such contemporaries as John Bigelow, the American consul in Paris, and Adam Gurowski, the eccentric refugee count and State Department translator. Mercier's 1861 trip throughout the North and behind Confederate lines has been well covered in the two accounts published at the time by Camille Ferri-Pisani and Maurice

---

Richardson (hereafter cited as Richardson), 2 vols. (Nashville: U.S. Publishing Co., 1905); *The War of the Rebellion: A Compilation of the Official Records of the Union and Confederate Armies* (hereafter cited as *ORA*), 70 vols. (Washington: U.S. Government Printing Office, 1880-1920); *Official Records of the Union and Confederate Navies in the War of the Rebellion* (hereafter cited as *ORN*), 30 vols. (Washington: U.S. Government Printing Office, 1894-1927).

[3] *Documents diplomatiques* (hereafter cited as *LJ*) (Paris: Imprimerie Impériale, 1859-1868); *Le secret de l'Empereur*, ed. L. Thouvenel, 2 vols. (Paris: Calmann Lévy, 1889); *British Sessional Papers, House of Commons*, ed. Edgar L. Erickson for the microprint edition; Lord Newton, *Lord Lyons: A Record of British Diplomacy*, 2 vols. (London: Edward Arnold, 1913).

Sand, both members of Prince Napoleon's entourage; the Prince's own diary of the trip was published in 1933. All three accounts contain descriptions and evaluations of Mercier.[4]

The standard nineteenth-century histories of the Civil War and of the Second Empire, as well as the biographies of relevant leading figures, contain such sparse references to Mercier that they may be passed over in this brief review. In the first quarter of this century, however, there appeared, in addition to Newton's biography of Lyons, the work of Ephraim D. Adams on *Great Britain and the American Civil War*, with its comparatively full treatment of Mercier's activities in the early stages of the war and during his Richmond trip. Several articles by Charles Francis Adams, Jr., son of the Civil War minister to Great Britain and president of the Massachusetts Historical Society, are also of more than ancillary interest. These efforts testify quite amply to the preoccupation of historians with the role of Great Britain. Frank L. Owsley's *King Cotton Diplomacy* is still of basic importance wherever the Confederacy enters the story directly. The work by Donaldson Jordan and Edwin J. Pratt, *Europe and the American Civil War*, contains an entire section on the continent by Pratt. It is

[4] Frederick W. Seward, *Seward at Washington as Senator and Secretary of State*, 2 vols. (New York: Derby & Miller, 1891), and *Reminiscences of a War-Time Statesman and Diplomat, 1830-1915* (New York: G. P. Putnam's Sons, 1916); John Bigelow, *Retrospections of an Active Life*, 5 vols. (New York: Baker & Taylor Co., 1909-1913); Adam Gurowski, *Diary*, 3 vols. (vol. I, Boston: Lee & Shepard, 1862; vol. II, New York: Carleton, 1864; vol. III, Washington: W. H. & O. H. Morrison, 1866); Camille Ferri-Pisani, *Prince Napoleon in America, 1861* (Bloomington: Indiana University Press, 1959), a translation of *Lettres sur les États-Unis d'Amérique* (Paris: L. Hachette et cie., 1862): references here are to the 1959 publication; Maurice Sand, *Six mille lieues à toute vapeur* (Paris: Michel Lévy Frères, 1862); "Voyage du Prince Napoléon aux États-Unis, 1861," ed. Ernest d'Hauterive, *Revue de Paris*, XL (15 Sept. and 1 Oct. 1933), 241-72 and 547-87.

concerned more with European reaction than with diplomacy in Washington, however, and is completely without value so far as Mercier is concerned. The authors were not able to use the archives of the French foreign office, and we may question their assertion that "there are printed works which throw enough light on the opinions of the Emperor and his circle to enable us to form an accurate estimate of the character and development of French policy."[5]

C. F. Adams, Jr., seemingly more meticulous than Jordan and Pratt were to be, tried as early as 1914 to gain admittance to the preeminent source for any sensible study of Mercier: the archives at the Quai d'Orsay. He wrote to his friend James Hazen Hyde and asked him to sound out the ministry about Mercier's dispatches to the foreign ministers, Thouvenel and Drouyn de Lhuys: "Only the least material portions of them were published in the French 'Yellow Book' of the period. Otherwise, I do not know that they have been used at all."[6] Hyde found his way "absolutely blocked," and added confidentially that "Mr. M's letters are rather hostile to the North and very much in favour of the rebels and therefore no one is very anxious to have them published." The year 1914 was apparently not the time for the French foreign office to take unnecessary chances with American public opinion. In fact, the decision to classify Mercier's letters can be traced back to Jules Jusserand him-

---

[5] E. D. Adams, *Great Britain and the American Civil War*, 2 vols. (London: Longmans, Green & Co., 1925). Among the works of Charles Francis Adams, Jr., see esp. "The Negotiation of 1861 Relating to the Declaration of Paris of 1856," *Massachusetts Historical Society Proceedings*, XLVI (October 1912), 23-84, and "A Crisis in Downing Street," *ibid.*, XLVII (May 1914), 372-424; Donaldson Jordan and Edwin J. Pratt, *Europe and the American Civil War* (Boston: Houghton Mifflin Co., 1931), p. 288.

[6] Adams to Hyde, Washington, 6 Jan. 1914, New York Historical Society, New York, Papers of James H. Hyde.

self, the French ambassador in Washington from 1902 to 1925.[7]

Fortunately time not only heals all wounds but calms all apprehensions; the French as well as the American materials are now available. Relevant papers of the United States Department of State are lodged at the National Archives in Washington and are readily available on microfilm. They divide into four basic categories, namely, diplomatic and consular instructions to American representatives abroad, diplomatic dispatches from American ministers, notes to foreign legations in Washington, and notes from those legations to the secretary of state. But far more significant than the United States papers are the documents of the French foreign ministry, sources which have with few exceptions been unused till now in Mercier's regard. The basic set of dispatches to and from Paris is in the *Correspondance politique* section of the foreign ministry archives, but the private correspondence between Mercier and Thouvenel in the *Papiers Thouvenel* section of *Mémoires et documents* is even more revealing. Mercier's private dispatches to Drouyn de Lhuys, on the other hand, are found in the *Correspondance politique* along with the official correspondence. In fact these dispatches, while they normally treat more sensitive areas than the official correspondence and sometimes contain Mercier's extended reflections, are altogether less personal than Mercier's private letters to Thouvenel. Finally there is valuable additional information in the *Correspondance commerciale* and *Correspondance politique des consuls* at the Quai d'Orsay.[8]

[7] Hyde to Adams, copy, Paris, 24 Jan. 1914, *ibid.* An appendix to this letter contains a statement by a Monsieur Piccioni at the foreign office, including the reference to Jusserand.

[8] Correspondence of the U.S. Department of State, Washington (hereafter cited as State Dept. Corres.), Diplomatic and Consular Instructions, France (hereafter cited as France, Instructions); Diplomatic Despatches, France (hereafter cited as France, Dispatches);

Previous work with the French documents in areas which embrace the work of Henri Mercier includes most significantly the articles by Lynn M. Case on Franco-American relations in 1861 and by Warren F. Spencer on events in 1863. They have climaxed their work in this field with the recent and indispensable *The United States and France: Civil War Diplomacy*. The doctoral dissertation of Richard Korolewicz-Carlton, "Napoléon III, Thouvenel et la guerre de sécession," is also important. His somewhat venturesome judgments of Henri Mercier will be placed under scrutiny in due course.[9]

One additional interesting source of information about Mercier's life in Washington is the papers of the banker and philanthropist William W. Corcoran at the Library of Congress. Corcoran, a Southern sympathizer, lived in Paris during the second half of the war with his daughter and son-in-law, George Eustis, secretary to John Slidell. Mercier lived in Corcoran's Washington house from the fall of 1862 until his return to France at the end of 1863. Throughout that time Corcoran's secretary, Anthony Hyde, wrote weekly reports on business and personal matters to his

---

Notes to Foreign Legations, France; Notes from Foreign Legations, France.

Archives du Ministère des Affaires étrangères, Paris, Correspondance politique, États-Unis (hereafter cited as AMAE, CP, E-U); Mémoires et documents (hereafter cited as MD), Papiers Thouvenel; Correspondance commerciale; Correspondance politique des consuls.

[9] See esp. Lynn M. Case, "La sécession aux États-Unis, problème diplomatique français en 1861," *Revue d'histoire diplomatique*, LXXVII (1963), 290-313, and "La France et l'affaire du 'Trent'," *Revue historique*, CCXXVI (1961), 57-86; Warren F. Spencer, "Drouyn de Lhuys et les navires confédérés en France, l'affaire des navires d'Arman, 1863-1865"; *Revue d'histoire diplomatique*, LXXVII (1963), 314-41; Lynn M. Case and Warren F. Spencer, *The United States and France: Civil War Diplomacy* (Philadelphia: University of Pennsylvania Press, 1970); Richard Korolewicz-Carlton, "Napoléon III, Thouvenel et la guerre de sécession" (doctoral thesis, University of Paris, 1951).

chief. These reports are a unique check not only upon Mercier's whereabouts but also on some of his personal problems.[10]

Finally there are the documents which have already been noted from the archives of the Le Cour Grandmaison family. They consist of copies or first drafts of private letters from Mercier to Thouvenel, Drouyn de Lhuys, and in one case, Prince Napoleon. For most of them, counterpart final versions may be found in the foreign ministry archives, but even so, a comparison of first with second versions can sometimes give an insight into Mercier's thinking which we would not otherwise have.[11]

No general study of Mercier's work in Washington has ever been attempted, and until recently, full French documentation has been impossible. This latter fact has foreclosed the drawing of any but the most sketchy picture. The results have been those cursory treatments in quick clichés which must be the fate of every unstudied historical figure. Now, with more information at our command, we may tell the story more fully.

[10] Library of Congress, Washington, Papers of William W. Corcoran.

[11] Archives of the Le Cour Grandmaison family, Dordogne, France, Papers of Henri Mercier.

Henri Mercier

AND THE AMERICAN
CIVIL WAR

CHAPTER I

Background

In the year 1860, the position of envoy extraordinary and minister plenipotentiary of Emperor Napoleon III to the government of the United States was a post of limited importance and even less desirability. It was accepted as such, with reluctance and resignation, by the subject of this study.

For over a generation relations between the United States and France had been at ebb tide, receding quietly from the points of high excitement which had been reached in the eras of revolution, Federalists, and Virginia dynasty, of Louis XVI and Napoleon I. No action of France in 1860, it seemed, could equal in vital importance the midwife's help which had attended America's birth. Nothing could furnish raw material of such historical importance as the purchase of Louisiana. Seemingly no threat of French intervention could stimulate another Monroe Doctrine. Henri Mercier, certainly, could not anticipate even the clouded historical eminence of a Citizen Genet as a result of his stay in the New World. To a rising young diplomat, Washington in 1860 was at best a shaky rung on the ladder of career: a thing to be touched lightly, used, and transcended.

For the United States, whose main preoccupations were expansion and sectional tension, France had become a sort of minor irritant, an imperial monarchy whose friendship with Great Britain and dabbling in Latin America could annoy the expanding republic but not threaten her life. For

3

France, whose main preoccupation was Italy, the United States was no longer the great counterweight, the balancing force against Britain, which she had been in Bourbon policy. The completion of Italian unification, the inauguration of the Cobden-Chevalier commercial treaty, the concern in England about France's naval growth and her annexation of Savoy and Nice: these were what mattered at the Quai d'Orsay in 1860.

In the Western Hemisphere the government of France had long since established an entente with Great Britain, a working relationship which had, for example, helped deny Cuba to Washington, though it could not do the same for Texas. What it might do if a Republican won the presidential election of 1860 was a question of no immediate worry in Paris in the early months of the year, though such concern would grow as the year wore on.

Henri Mercier could gain some hint of the sort of work which lay ahead by reviewing the actions of his predecessor, Count Eugène de Sartiges, who served in Washington through most of the 1850's. Sartiges worried much about the bumptious expansionism and ideological aggressiveness of the Yankees. In 1853 and 1854 he had warned Washington of what Britain and France might do if America tried to annex Hawaii; his own recommendation to Paris was an Anglo-French protectorate for the islands. Again in 1854 he had helped block an offer of United States mediation in the Crimean War, an offer surrounded with portentous talk about Russo-American cooperation against the Anglo-French front. By the end of the decade the exciting possibility of a sectional rupture appeared. Sartiges thought it would mean war. In the year between Sartiges' departure and Mercier's arrival, the French chargé in Washington was Viscount Jules Treilhard. He too foresaw the possibility of a civil war and thought it would be of vast international significance. And if that were so, it might matter a great deal what kind of man was coming to America to represent the imperial government.[1]

Looking at it in personal terms, Sartiges as early as 1857 had had some thoughts about his successor. "Six years of studying liberty in this country," he wrote, "where the law protects the rogue and the honest man has to look out for himself, are enough for *my* political education; replace me with some retarded statesman so he can begin his."[2]

HENRI MERCIER IN 1860

The statesman to whom this unique educational opportunity would be offered was born Édouard Henri Mercier on 24 September 1816 in Baltimore, Maryland, where his father was serving as Louis XVIII's consul. The Mercier family was of the upper bourgeoisie and noted among its more interesting forbears the nurse of Louis XV, a lady whose influence at Versailles had enabled her to marry off her children well. Marie-Philippe, the consul, had been a prefect in Jerome Bonaparte's Westphalia before coming to America. His wife, Henri Mercier's mother, was Henriette Adèle Leroy.[3]

Mercier was educated in Europe after the family's return there, most notably at the international school of Rodolphe Töpffer in Switzerland. His mother Henriette is remembered as a lady of charm who conducted a famous salon during the Orleans period, frequented by the Russian min-

[1] For a good summary of Franco-American relations from Jackson to Grant, see Henry Blumenthal, *A Reappraisal of Franco-American Relations, 1830-1871* (Chapel Hill: University of North Carolina Press, 1959).

[2] Sartiges to Conneau, n.p. [Washington], 28 June 1857, *Papiers et correspondance de la famille impériale*, 2 vols. (Paris: Librairie L. Beauvais, 1872), I, 350-51.

[3] In addition to biographical information obtained from Dom Maur Le Cour Grandmaison, there are a few useful biographical facts in *The Titled Nobility of Europe: An International Peerage*, ed. Marquis of Ruvigny (London: Harrison & Sons, 1914), p. 1004.

ister Prince Menshikov among other notables. Thus influenced and aided from both sides of his family, Mercier must have come quite easily to the decision to follow a career in government service. At the age of twenty-three he was sent to Mexico as unpaid attaché, and he filled out the 1840's as apprentice and journeyman diplomat in Madrid, Lisbon, and St. Petersburg.

The revolution of 1848, the coup of 1851, and the change of Louis Napoleon's title in 1852 advanced rather than stunted Mercier's career. He attained the rank of minister in 1852 as the prince-president's man in Dresden, and in 1854 he was promoted to the Athens legation. It was here in the East, during the sensitive period of the Crimean War, that a friendship, born in Madrid ten years earlier, grew between Mercier and his counterpart in Constantinople, Édouard Antoine Thouvenel.

Henri Mercier was a complicated man, perhaps more than normally so. His tone and temperament were active, outgoing, and generally optimistic, but his correspondence shows signs of sourness as well as laughter and wit. While given to large reflection, to economic, political, and socio-historical theorizing, his fine mind was quick about current matters, and he wanted to be up and doing. Traveling companions attest his uncomplaining good humor, but this was the positive satisfaction of the good traveler, not the serenity of slack nerves: Mercier was an intense, perhaps even mercurial, person. And he did know how to complain, as his superior Édouard Thouvenel had better reason to know than anyone else. The kind of heart-on-the-sleeve letters which passed from Stockholm and Washington to this old friend at the Quai d'Orsay betray a genuine, emotional nature, normally kept in check for official business, but apt to try the imprudent. Mercier was not reticent by nature, only by training, and Thouvenel had to worry about his rashness more than once.

6

At once hearty and discriminating, Mercier was famous as a host and a good companion in conversation; among those he met in America, several became his friends; he made no personal enemies. His appreciation of the good life and aristocratic preferences about ceremony were tempered by a mature detachment, for he was willing to "rough it." A man of the middle class, he was profoundly distrustful of democracy; he respected titles; and he valued order in society. His admiration for Napoleonic rule was deep and genuine, and in 1870 it was to cost him his career.

Mercier was above average in height, physically robust and athletic. In a photograph taken in February 1862 by Mathew Brady, he appears a few years younger than his actual forty-five. His large, longish head and dignified Roman nose are kept from being pompous by a half-closed right eye, the whole giving an impression of annoyance or suspicion. Thick, dark hair, thinning at the forehead, descends on either side into long sideburns and a handlebar moustache, without a beard. As posed, left hand gripping his vest pocket, he appears unheroically formal. The picture does not exactly mirror the man.[4]

In June of 1856, Mercier married Cécile-Élisabeth Philibert Benoît de Lostende, a young lady of aristocratic line-

[4] This picture is part of an illustrated article on "The Diplomatic Corps in Washington," *Harper's Weekly*, 22 Feb. 1862. The accompanying text betrays the uninspired journalism of the period where any except the British minister were concerned: "The other Ministers—M. Mercier, who represents France; Baron Stoeckel [*sic*], who represents Russia; and Baron Von Gerolt, who represents Prussia, have not as yet filled any prominent place in history. At Washington they are popular, and widely known. . . . M. Mercier is famous for his hospitalities; his dinners are the best in Washington, and he is not sparing of them." For Mercier's height, see the photograph taken of Seward and the diplomatic corps at Trenton Falls, New York, in *ibid.*, 19 Sept. 1863, and the one in F. W. Seward, *Seward at Washington*, II, facing 188; Mercier is the second figure to Seward's right. The character description above is the author's estimate, derived partly from an acquaintance with Mercier's correspondence.

7

age whose father, Baron Grégoire Benoît de Lostende, was one of the last to be given a title by Charles X. (This title would eventually pass to Mercier in 1867: after his father-in-law's death he became Baron Mercier de Lostende.) The couple established themselves in Stockholm in 1857 where Mercier served for two and a half years as minister of Napoleon III. Here his first child, Madeleine, was born; Cécile-Élisabeth's delicate health gave the new father some concern, but mother and child did nicely. It was also in Stockholm, in the winter of 1859, that Mercier received in quick succession two remarkable pieces of news, one bad, the other good: he would have to leave the civilized legations of Europe and go to the United States; there he would execute the orders of his friend Thouvenel, who had just been named minister of foreign affairs.

Mercier wrote to congratulate him, praising the choice, disavowing any intention to flatter, and calling attention to his own sorry prospects:

> This distant, fruitless assignment could not possibly be suitable for me in any way: it runs counter to my feelings, my interests, my tastes, my hopes; it deprives me of every advantage my experience and knowledge of personalities could bring to the diplomatic service. . . . I am thunderstruck, and I have been thrown into a gloom which I hide as best I can but from which only your promotion to the ministry can rescue me.

The special close relationship which existed between Thouvenel and Mercier is apparent from the whole thrust of this uninhibited outburst; it is a factor which must be given due weight when we come to assess the correspondence they shared in the years ahead about things American.[5]

[5] Mercier to Thouvenel, Stockholm, 8 Jan. 1860, Archives Nationales, Fonds Thouvenel (microfilm) 255 AP 3.

Thunderstruck as he was, Mercier still prepared to return to the country of his birth. Last-minute ceremonial business made it necessary for him to stay in Stockholm briefly while Madame Mercier and Madeleine went home for a short vacation. He entrusted them to Thouvenel's hospitality:

> As soon as she recovers from her trip, my wife will present her respects to Madame Thouvenel. Make her welcome, I beg you, and let her bring her pretty little Swedish girl to play with your two Turkish gallants. ... You are lucky to be in a climate where you can allow children to play outside.[6]

Mercier joined his family about the middle of May. While he was in Paris for pretrip conferences, he frequently met Charles J. Faulkner of Virginia, whom President Buchanan has recently sent to replace John Y. Mason as the United States minister to France. Faulkner was favorably impressed with Mercier: "He is a gentleman of considerable experience in diplomatic life, of a frank and manly disposition, and impressed with sentiments of high admiration of our country and its institutions."[7] Those sentiments of high admiration for the "distant and fruitless" country to which he had been sentenced came readily to the professional diplomat. In all the three and a half years' record which Mercier left in America, there is no evidence that any American knew the extent of his discomfort.

Mercier's worry must have increased considerably when he learned that Cécile-Élisabeth was expecting their second child. Her health was never good, or at least she thought

[6] Mercier to Thouvenel, n. p. [Stockholm], 14 April 1860, AMAE, MD, Papiers Thouvenel, XIII, 338-40.

[7] Faulkner to Cass, Paris, 19 June 1860, State Dept. Corres., France, Dispatches, XLVII, no. 29.

not, and hypochondria could have the same depressing effect on her husband's outlook as physical trouble. The unhappy little family took passage on 20 June 1860, aboard the Cunard liner *Adriatic*. The seas ahead were rough in both a metaphorical and a literal sense.

CHAPTER II

Last Days of the Old Republic

MERCIER'S FIRST IMPRESSIONS

THE *Adriatic* reached New York on the evening of Saturday, 30 June. Newspapers noted laconically the presence of the French minister, but were more taken with the new mammoth liner *Great Eastern*, which had preceded the *Adriatic* by only two days, and with the news from Europe of Garibaldi's "further successes" against the Kingdom of the Two Sicilies. Mercier left his wife and daughter in New York and went immediately to Washington to meet Treilhard and to present himself to the government.[1]

The coincidence of dates made Mercier the central foreign figure at what might have been the last celebration of Independence Day by a united American nation. At noon on a hot, rainy 4 July, he was presented to the self-styled Old Public Functionary, James Buchanan. The presentation was made by Acting Secretary of State William Henry Trescot, who would be in Richmond within the year, along with many other of Buchanan's friends and aides.

Predictably, the president noted the significance of the date and delivered the usual platitude about France being America's oldest ally. No difficulty between the two countries could be foreseen, and he stood ready to intercept and smooth the unforeseen. Mercier found the president's cordiality a compensation for the lack of White House cere-

[1] *New York Times*, 2 July 1860; *National Intelligencer* (Washington), 3 July 1860.

11

mony. In his report he told Thouvenel that since the other diplomats were fleeing the Washington heat, he too would leave and would take the opportunity to visit important cities and familiarize himself with the country.[2]

Mercier's actual itinerary, however, was somewhat different. He was in New York, undoubtedly to be with his family and attend to details of moving, from 9 to 13 July, and he was back in Washington four days later. His activities were a hodgepodge of trivia and gravia, from seeing his brandy and cigars safely into the country to meditating on the American sectional tensions.

Among the substantive matters which Mercier had to address this early, the interests of Britain and France in Mexico stand out. There the liberal, anticlerical revolt of Benito Juárez against the Miramon government was well advanced, and in fact Juárez had been extended American recognition. In July, Mercier's British colleague Lord Lyons presented an invitation for the United States to join England and France in approaching both sides; the Mexicans would then elect a national assembly which would reconcile the factions enough to end the war. The Anglo-French entente was again at work, and in fact a similar proposal had already emanated from Paris and been relayed fruitlessly to the State Department before Mercier's arrival. James Buchanan, however, with his longstanding hope of American domination in Mexico and the Caribbean, was the last man to tie the United States to a European initiative there. Mercier predicted correctly that the British démarche would be rejected as the French had been.[3]

[2] Mercier to Thouvenel, Washington, 5 July 1860, AMAE, CP, E-U, 123: 299-302, no. 1. See also *New York Times*, 6 July 1860 and *Courrier des États-Unis* (New York), 7 July 1860.

[3] Mercier to Thouvenel, Washington, 19 July 1860, AMAE, C-P, E-U, 123: 304-06, no. 2; Faulkner to Cass, Paris, 30 July 1860, State Dept. Corres., France, Dispatches, XLVII, no. 39.

As yet, of course, the problem of Mexico was not central to the main issue, the sectional issue, which was pregnant with possibilities in foreign relations. From his first dispatch to his last, Mercier probed and expounded this issue, but his earliest thinking was not set against the sultry, cluttered background of Washington. Mercier had thought of traveling in August and September to make soundings in various American cities. Instead, he went to Newport.

For a generation now, this pretty seaside town had been a summer retreat for affluent Americans, mostly from the South. In the early days accommodations had been meager enough, but the 1850's saw something of a building boom, and some New Englanders had taken notice of their local treasure. A Newport festival was held in 1859 to advertise the town, and many former residents returned for the climactic celebration that August. Culturally and intellectually it was a moneyed, Southern milieu in which the Merciers were to receive their American initiation.[4]

Mercier had already found time to tell Thouvenel about the Democratic conventions, the Charleston and Baltimore schism which had both Stephen Douglas and Vice-President Breckinridge running as Democrats. He noted that because of this, chances were good for a Republican victory, perhaps through a vote in the House. Still, it was too early for weighty judgments:

> I am far too ignorant of things in this country to form independent opinions about the importance of this or that candidate for the political future of the American government. Moreover, if I can credit the judgment of various well-informed people, this importance will be far less than one would conclude from the intensity of each party's support for its candidate. It would seem

[4] W.P.A. authors, *Rhode Island: A Guide to the Smallest State* (Boston: Houghton Mifflin Co., 1937), pp. 211-12.

that whoever the new president is, he will face ob-
stacles which will greatly limit his independence of
action.[5]

The atmosphere of Newport, however, its relaxations and
undoubtedly its conversations, disposed Mercier to greater
expansiveness. There were three parties, he noted, Republican, Democratic, and "*les* Know Nothing," dividing principally along lines of free state, slave state, and opposition
to immigrants. (It is doubtful that the Bell–Everett Constitutional Union party would have accepted the "Know
nothing" description in 1860, if only because Fillmore and
his American party had lost so badly in 1856. Mercier's
blunt description of them, however, reflecting the things
he heard in Newport, suggests that the Bell–Everett party
was not quite the sweetly reasonable faction it has sometimes been described.)

Slavery, he continued, was the main issue of the campaign, but only the insignificant abolitionist sect was willing to sunder the Union in the name of human freedom.
The interests and prejudices of the rest, North as well as
South, would check the abolitionists. "The real thing at
stake in the fight over slavery is simply control of the Senate,
control which involves a dominating influence in the federal government." The southern states had had this control
in the past; they were demanding slavery in the territories
and the future admission of more slave states. On the other
hand, it was wisely bruited that climate would be the real
determinant of slavery's growth or decline, whatever the
parties might wish to see happen.

The Republican party, Mercier went on, wished to forbid
slavery in the territories. Who was the leader of this party?

It is surprising that Mr. Seward did not receive the
nomination, for he is undoubtedly the head of the party,

---

[5] Mercier to Thouvenel, Washington, 19 July 1860, AMAE, CP, E-U,
123: 304-06, no. 2.

14

but apparently it is his recognized preeminence which has led people to prefer a relative unknown like Mr. Lincoln, whose background excites neither anger nor jealousy, and whose humble origins appeal to the masses.

Among the rest, Mercier continued, Bell was seeking mainly to preserve the Union; Douglas wanted the territories to make their own decisions on slavery; Breckinridge was for protection everywhere of property rights in slaves. At this point Mercier tended to equate Democrats with Southerners, and he reported that they were threatening secession if Lincoln were elected, but that the best-informed people discounted this as campaign hyperbole and thought the South would submit, albeit with some grumbling. A realignment of parties might ensue, with all moderates coming together. "This country is too used to governing itself for the election of a president to make any vital difference, despite the apparently broad powers of the office, and if you dig deeply enough, you discover that political jobs are the principal objects of the politicians." In America better-off people disdained public office, leaving the government to the less scrupulous.[6]

It is obvious that this report is somewhat heterogeneous, its ingredients partly immiscible. According to Mercier, slavery was the big issue; but not really, for climate would determine where and how it spread, and politicians were in any case more interested in jobs and in control of the Senate. Mercier's thoughts about the Democratic party compounded the confusion; in an understandable effort at simplification, he argued that in general "the Democrats," i.e., Breckinridge *and* Douglas, represented the tendencies of the slave states. This, of course, would have been astounding news to the Douglas managers. There is this much truth

[6] Mercier to Thouvenel, Newport, 14 August 1860, *ibid.*, fol. 309-15, no. 3.

in it: the South might well have swallowed Douglas' election without seceding, a compliment they were unwilling to pay Lincoln. Mercier was wrong on that last point and discounted the danger of secession in the event of Lincoln's victory.

The Autumn of James Buchanan

Henri Mercier returned in September to a Washington whose social life, appearance, and very name were charged with dramatic portent in this fall and winter of discontent, 1860-1861. The unfinished, tentative streets and buildings reflected both the newness and the peril of the great experiment in republican democracy. There was little in all this to soften Mercier's disgust at being where he was.

Gas lamps, which had been installed seven years back, were of some use, but offered only a pale reflection of Paris, and only a small check to the brigandage which had upset Sartiges. "Riot and bloodshed are of daily occurrence," a Senate report had cried,[7] and if the Merciers never witnessed such horrors, it was bad enough to be near them. Unpaved thoroughfares of dirt still told the visitor from Europe that he was at the perimeter of civilization's clearing. And down the dusty expanse of Pennsylvania Avenue, ministers from Europe and other residents of the White House neighborhood could see the most confounding symbol of all—a half-finished Capitol whose gaping, open rotunda meant hope or destruction as the mood happened to strike the viewer.

Except for business and official pleasure, however, the Merciers could avert their eyes from Washington to whatever extent their sensibilities required. Their home for almost two years was on the heights of Georgetown, the same lovely house which Sartiges had occupied during his tenure.

---

[7] Quoted in Constance McLaughlin Green, *Washington, Village and Capital, 1800-1878* (Princeton: Princeton University Press, 1962), p. 215.

Set on the southwest corner of the present 30th and "R" Streets, it was a cottage of brick and wood surrounded by trees and a garden. Visitors were apt to admire the "peaceful and luxurious landscape," and Prince Napoleon himself pronounced the view superb. Directly opposite was Oak Hill cemetery, studded with flowering bushes in springtime and flaming oaks in fall, a contemplative expanse whose gabled gatehouse was across the street from the legation. Inside the cemetery a tasteful Doric temple marked the remains of Louise Corcoran, wife of William W. Corcoran, the cemetery's chief benefactor, and contrasted pleasantly with the Gothic Revival chapel by James Renwick, architect of the Smithsonian Institution and St. Patrick's Cathedral in New York.[8]

It was Thomas Beall, original owner of all of Georgetown Heights, who had sold the 30th and "R" site in 1798 to Dr. William Craik, the physician who attended George Washington in his last illness. The property passed to David Peter, who built the house in 1808 and named it "Peter's Grove," a name changed in the 1830's to "Carolina Place" when it was owned by Congressman John Carter of South Carolina. It seems later to have become the property of Elisha Riggs, Jr., of the famous banking family. The house was occupied by three notable diplomats, starting with the British minister John F. Crampton. In the 1850's it was rented by Count Sartiges, whose frequent and lavish dinners were a brilliant feature of capital society.[9]

[8] Camille Ferri-Pisani, *Prince Napoleon in America, 1861* (Bloomington: Indiana University Press, 1959), p. 92; Prince Napoleon's diary, p. 256. The author is indebted for information on Mercier's residences to Mr. John Beverley Riggs of Wilmington, Del. For Oak Hill cemetery see *A Guide to the Architecture of Washington, D.C.*, ed. Hugh Newell Jacobsen (New York: Frederick A. Praeger, 1965), pp. 136-37.

[9] Grace Dunlop Ecker, *A Portrait of Old George Town* (Richmond, Va.: Dietz Press, 1951), pp. 288-89; Virginia Clay-Clopton, *A Belle of the Fifties* (New York: Doubleday, Page & Co., 1905), p. 30.

In fact the growing political tension had dampened Washington's social life to the extent that "when belles met they no longer discussed furbelows and flounces, but talked of forts and fusillades."[10] Washington, to a large extent, was a Southern city: its society, especially in the Buchanan period, was dominated by secessionist and moderate Democrats, mostly from the deep South and the border states. In Newport and now in the capital, the American whom Mercier met, who taught him his lessons in constitutional freedom and states' rights, who influenced his view of Negro slavery, was a different sort of person from the American who would try to reeducate him in 1861-1863. In this sense, a sense which needs refined and subtle examination, the old cliché about Mercier's "Southern friends" and their influence upon his reports to Paris can partially be sustained. When Mercier speaks of "enlightened sources," it is more probably a William Corcoran he has in mind, not a Thaddeus Stevens or a Charles Sumner.

Of all the private individuals whom Mercier knew in America, none is more important than William W. Corcoran, one of Washington's most affluent, beneficent, and socially prominent citizens. A native of Georgetown, he had begun his career in the era of James Madison with a small dry-goods business. By Polk's time he was a wealthy banker and investment broker, and he financed the Mexican War almost single-handedly. In 1854, still in his fifties, he had retired from the firm, leaving it to the sole management of his partner, George W. Riggs, and had since devoted himself to patronizing artists and financing political moderation. He was high in the counsels of the Democratic party, especially during Buchanan's administration. In 1856 he had swelled the war chest which helped Buchanan defeat Fremont, and the president-elect had stayed in his palatial home before the inauguration ceremony. His friends were

[10] Clay-Clopton, p. 138.

the national leaders of the next four years: President Buchanan, Chief Justice Roger B. Taney, Secretary of the Treasury Howell Cobb, General Winfield Scott, senators like John Slidell, Judah P. Benjamin, Jesse D. Bright, and Robert Toombs—men of substance, of tender constitutional principles but little sensitivity to human slavery, of limited passion for preserving the national Union.

As the capital's most cosmopolitan and distinguished host, Corcoran made it his business to know the diplomatic corps. Many of them rented houses from him, and they were frequent partakers of his terrapin and Johannesberg. He gave weekly dinners and managed each session to include half of Congress among his guests.[11]

Another influential Washingtonian was Corcoran's former partner, George Washington Riggs. Forty-seven years old in 1860, Riggs was at the height of his financial power, banker to the community and owner of much of its real estate. He entertained brilliantly at his "I" Street home. The Riggs family remained friendly with Corcoran despite the dissolution of the partnership, and Corcoran even stayed at the Riggs's summer house in Newport. Unlike Corcoran, however, George Riggs was flexible enough to survive into the Republican era, and despite attacks from red-hot critics like Count Gurowski, he remained a Washington fixture

[11] For Corcoran's role as host and friend of Southerners and moderates, see Margaret Leech, *Reveille in Washington* (New York: Harper & Bros., 1941), p. 25, and Clay-Clopton, *Belle of the Fifties*, pp. 120-21. For his position in the Democratic party, see Roy F. Nichols, *The Disruption of American Democracy* (New York: Macmillan Co., 1948), p. 46. For his friendship with Buchanan see also Ben: Perley Poore, *Perley's Reminiscences of Sixty Years in the National Metropolis*, 2 vols. (Philadelphia: Hubbard Bros., 1886), I, 508. Striking indications of Corcoran's political connections abound in the Corcoran papers at the Library of Congress. See, for instance, Scott to Hodge, 29 Oct. 1860, a copy of General Scott's famous "Views" about the legal and military situation regarding secession. Corcoran's copy is marked "Show these papers to my friend W. W. Corcoran W. S."

during the Civil War. His sympathies were Democratic and moderate, if not pro-Southern; in 1860 he had played a key financial role in the Breckinridge campaign. His brother Lawrason was married to a daughter of Jesse D. Bright of Indiana, vulgarian speculator and friend of Southerners, who lived across the street from Mercier in Georgetown. After the war Riggs's daughter Catherine married Louis de Geofroy, first secretary of the French legation under Mercier.[12]

Mercier's friendship with yet another pro-Southern family must be recorded here, the famous Ridgelys of Hampton, Maryland, near Mercier's own birthplace of Baltimore. One young member of the family, the early twentieth-century ambassador Henry White, remembered that the Merciers had spent a summer at Hampton:

> I remember the Minister used to pay long visits to Washington and return to Hampton in the afternoon, saying that he had had interesting interviews with Mr. Lincoln or Mr. Seward. Unfortunately, I was too young then to appreciate the interest which was to be derived from Baron Mercier's accounts; but I do recollect that it became a great nuisance for our Grandfather Ridgely to send him constantly to the station in Baltimore.[13]

Though Mercier undoubtedly visited with the Ridgelys in Newport, it was at Hampton, with its famous cupola and

[12] Nichols, *Disruption*, pp. 4-5, 337-38; for a description of the "I" Street house and other interesting biographical information, see the section "George W. Riggs (1813-1881)" in the anonymous, untitled, and undated typescript in Library of Congress, Washington, Riggs Family Papers.

[13] White to William Hepburn Buckler, Lenox [Mass.], 31 Aug. 1925, quoted in Allan Nevins, *Henry White, Thirty Years of American Diplomacy* (New York: Harper & Bros., 1930), pp. 12-13, n. 4.

For a description and picture of Hampton see John H. Scarff, " 'Hampton,' Baltimore County, Maryland," *Maryland Historical Magazine*, XLIII (June 1948), 96-107.

its gardens and rolling lawns, that he had his chief experiential contact with the affluent, graceful culture of the "slavocracy." Henry White remembered that his grandfather Ridgely heard the news of First Bull Run with marked satisfaction, and as the war progressed, with the slaves scattered and social life constricted, Grandmother Ridgely's asperity against Washington reached the point of mental illness. Perhaps Mercier never saw, as White did, a slave boxed on the ears; perhaps he was absent the day his friends shaved off the hair of an impertinent slave girl. But the Ridgelys reflected a culture which could do such a thing without tears or nausea, and so far as we know, Mercier was neither more nor less sensitive than the average white American in matters of this kind.

In addition to his neighbor Jesse Bright, Mercier met many congressional leaders that first season, though for the most part we are left to infer this from mutual friends such as Corcoran. John Slidell and Judah P. Benjamin of Louisiana would both play crucial parts in Franco-Confederate relations. Both met Mercier in 1860; both were friends of Corcoran; both had helped Bright in working against Stephen Douglas at the 1856 Cincinnati convention. They succeeded in nominating Buchanan but would later turn on him as a Unionist. Mercier met Douglas too, and in fact liked him better than he did Slidell, whom he sized up as one who "passes for an able man, is very energetic, but without scruple and not a very good character."[14]

The executive branch, of course, held up its end of Washington's social life. Assisted by his niece Harriett Lane, the bachelor president generally gave two dinners weekly, one informal and small, for close friends like Howell Cobb and George Riggs, the other for forty or so justices, senators, diplomats, and the like. Other active hostesses

[14] Mercier to Thouvenel, New York, 29 Sept. 1861, AMAE, MD, Papiers Thouvenel, XIII, 406-09.

included Kate Thompson, wife of Secretary of the Interior Jacob Thompson of Mississippi, and Mrs. Howell Cobb, wife of Corcoran's friend and Buchanan's "prime minister," the secretary of the treasury. Cobb was remembered as a jolly Falstaffian who, despite his coolness toward slavery, left the cabinet after Lincoln's election and appeared later as chairman of the Confederate convention in Montgomery.[15]

The secretary of state when Mercier first entered Washington society was the venerable Lewis Cass, an old Jacksonian whose service to his country had run the gamut from secretary of war through minister to France, senator from Michigan, and Democratic presidential nominee. In 1847 Cass had made the first clear statement of the popular sovereignty doctrine, which would have left it to the people of the territories to decide for or against slavery. As with Stephen Douglas, so with Cass: the presence or absence of slavery meant far less than the keeping of the Union. Cass had retired from strenuous activity as secretary of state, for Buchanan was his own foreign minister; Cass's chief function was to be respectable and to remind people of the government's historical link with Andrew Jackson. Such individual diplomatic ideas as he had, his anti-British prejudice for instance, were apt to be of indifference to Buchanan.[16]

When Cass resigned, criticizing the president for not doing enough to defend the South Carolina forts, Buchanan

[15] Clay-Clopton, p. 30.

[16] Philip Shriver Klein, *President James Buchanan, A Biography* (University Park: Pennsylvania State University Press, 1962), p. 357; Lewis Einstein, "Lewis Cass," *The American Secretaries of State and Their Diplomacy*, vi, ed. Samuel F. Bemis (New York: Alfred A. Knopf, 1928), 297-300. Klein's reference to Cass's indolence is borne out by Faulkner's complaint from Paris: despite his fifty-two dispatches to Washington, he had heard very little from the secretary (Faulkner to Buchanan, Paris, 1 Sept. 1860, Historical Society of Pennsylvania, Philadelphia, Papers of James Buchanan).

put in his unkempt, emotional attorney general, Jeremiah Black, to fill out the four remaining months. Again it was not for any advice he might give about foreign affairs that the president named Black. Domestic friction had all but obliterated foreign problems; no important developments came across Black's desk.[17]

The diplomatic corps were always the most colorful and distinctive feature of Washington society. Most of them lived in a sort of cluster near the White House, several in houses rented from Corcoran. Baron von Gerolt of Prussia, a particular friend of Corcoran, lived at 15th and "H" Streets, while the address of Don Gabriel Garcia y Tassara of Spain was given as "Corcoran's Row, 'I' Street." Édouard de Stoeckl of Russia was a fixture when Mercier arrived, and remained after the war to sell Alaska. Others included Chevalier Hülsemann of Austria, a veteran whose jousts with Yankee diplomacy went back to Daniel Webster and the mid-century liberal-nationalist revolts; Chevalier Bertinatti of Sardinia, soon to be Italy; and Rudolph Schleiden of Bremen.[18]

Mercier's most important colleague, in personal and professional terms, was Richard, Lord Lyons, the British minister. His stiff, formal dinners were a staple of Washington life, and his bachelor status entered the calculations of more than one designing matchmaker. Lyons's Washington career is central to any consideration of Mercier's work and will unfold as this story unfolds. Both men were professionals of long training, both fairly young for their positions,

---

[17] Philip Gerald Auchampaugh, *James Buchanan and His Cabinet on the Eve of Secession* (Lancaster, Pa.: Lancaster Press, 1926), p. 72; Roy F. Nichols, "Jeremiah Black," in Bemis, *American Secretaries of State*, vi, 387-94.

[18] A valuable list of the 1860 diplomatic corps, dated 26 Nov. 1860, complete with addresses, may be found in Library of Congress, Washington, Buchanan-Johnston Papers, Papers of Harriet Lane Johnston, i, 1558-63.

both agents of the entente. After 1865 Lyons was named ambassador to Napoleon III, and he stayed in Paris well into the period of the Third Republic (the period of Mercier's premature retirement), till 1886, when Mercier died, and Lyons, one year from death himself, was offered and refused the post of foreign secretary. In Washington the stolid, prudent Englishman was a complement to Mercier's chancy flamboyance. The two worked well together for the most part, so well that Lyons would later recall the Civil War period as a time of exceptional harmony with his French counterpart.[19]

In October, Buchanan's own state, Pennsylvania, chose her governor, Andrew Gregg Curtin of the pro-Lincoln People's Party; the future reality of Abraham Lincoln in the White House now had to be faced by even the most sanguine of his opponents. Mercier, reflecting the shift toward gloom among his Washington acquaintances, began to sound warnings about secession. "I must say . . . that knowledgeable people, who some time ago had no fear of arrangements which they thought were a mere political maneuver to frighten the North, are beginning to take them very seriously."[20] It was more than a question of slavery as such: the South had evolved a wholly different way of life, a sort of nationality of its own based upon slavery, agriculture, and free trade. If Lincoln tried hard enough, Mercier thought, he might be able to calm passions, but news just in from South Carolina made it certain that there would be at least a temporary secession.[21]

[19] Clay-Clopton, pp. 139-41; Lord Newton, *Lord Lyons: A Record of British Diplomacy* (London: Edward Arnold, 1913), I, 1-2, 156.

[20] Mercier to Thouvenel, Washington, 22 Oct. 1860, AMAE, CP, E-U, 123: 345-52, no. 7.

[21] Mercier to Thouvenel, Washington, 8 Nov. 1860, *ibid.*, fol. 360-64, no. 9.

As Cobb, Thompson, and other cabinet Southerners prepared to resign and to assist their new "nationality" toward
its political sovereignty, the president wrestled with the
impossible problem. He wanted to call a convention and
let it decide whether the old constitution could be bent to
weather the storm. And maybe if Georgia could be placated,
the dissolution might yet be contained.

Mercier saw that Southern moderates like Alexander
Stephens of Georgia were having difficulty being heard.
Some secessionists were even saying that France and Britain
would aid the new Southern government in order to guarantee themselves a supply of cotton. Such sanguine hopes,
would, Mercier thought, be contradicted by events, but
they were more favorably heard than Stephens' sensible
views. Meanwhile, the continuing financial crisis gave hope
to Mercier's informants that the North would yield enough
to save the situation; perhaps when Congress met in December the picture would be clearer.[22]

Mercier established his credentials as an observer by
launching predictions of Southern secession early on.[23]
Against this must be set his occasional hedging against the
future by phrasing his dispatches in a kind of dialectic of
opposites. From Mercier, however, the French government
knew about as much as anyone in Washington at the end
of November: secession was probable, but Unionists might
yet yield enough to stave it off.

22 On the financial crisis, which failed to move Lincoln to any
public statement of reassurance to the South, see Allan Nevins, *The
Emergence of Lincoln*, 2 vols. (New York: Charles Scribner's Sons,
1950), II, 336.

23 See Lynn M. Case, "La sécession and États-Unis, problème diplomatique français en 1861," *Revue d'histoire diplomatique*, LXXVII
(1963), 295, and Richard Korolewicz-Carlton, "Napoléon III, Thouvenel et la guerre de sécession" (doctoral thesis, University of Paris,
1951), p. 8.

MERCIER AND THE BUCHANAN POLICIES

Meanwhile, the president was proceeding to his message to Congress of 3 December, his answer to the overwhelming question of the moment: would the lame-duck government do anything to stop secession? In the third week of November, he previewed his statement for a group of Southerners at the White House. He agreed entirely that the North must rectify the wrongs it had done the South, but he flatly denied that secession was a right, and he predicted that the West would not quietly tolerate the mouth of the Mississippi's being transferred to a "foreign power." From Attorney General Black he got the opinion that although secession was not legal, the federal government could use force only to protect its property and enforce court decrees on individuals, not to oppose the united will of a state. The shape of Buchanan's strange view was thus determined: the South could not legally secede; the Union could not legally stop her from doing so.[24]

Mercier knew by the end of the month the general tenor of Buchanan's message. He knew also that the president would probably ask Congress to call a national convention to guarantee Southern rights, and in the optimistic phase of Mercier's dialectic, this move seemed to give hope of saving the Union. His shrewd assessment of Buchanan—helped, certainly, by the remarks of mutual friends—even discerned the Jacksonian connections of the old man's Unionism. "Mr. Buchanan," he wrote, "in the midst of this turbulent ordeal, seems in great difficulty over his message to Congress. By background he is a Democrat, but he is a man of the North, and like all his generation, he has a strong devotion to the Union."[25] Whatever insight this ob-

---

[24] Klein, *President James Buchanan*, p. 361; Auchampaugh, *James Buchanan*, p. 134.

[25] Mercier to Thouvenel, Washington, 26 Nov. 1860, AMAE, CP, E-U, 123: 370-78, no. 11.

servation on American generations may show, Mercier's alertness should be judged against the background of his own personal distractions and the advent of yet another generation: his first son, Maurice Henri, was born on 1 December.

The foreign policy section of Buchanan's message was understandably meager and totally overshadowed by the pressing domestic strife. There was almost nothing to be said about France, beyond a gracious compliment to her courts for accepting the principle that naturalized American citizens were not subject to French military conscription. "With France, our ancient and powerful ally, our relations continue to be of the most friendly character."[26] The section on Mexico and Central America was, as usual with Buchanan, expansionist, and it included a proposal to buy Cuba from Spain. But the old cosigner of the Ostend Manifesto did not say everything that was in his mind. Years later, in a passage made sharper, perhaps, by hindsight, Buchanan had this to say about France:

> The President did not apprehend interference in Mexico from any European sovereign except the Emperor of the French. It was his known policy to seek new colonies for France. . . . Besides, he had previously directed his attention in a special manner to Central America.[27]

Mercier knew nothing of these suspicions, if indeed Buchanan really entertained them as early as this. In any case, as Lincoln and Seward would discover soon enough, there was little which a broken America could do even should such a challenge arise.

Mercier was most struck by the president's lack of focus,

[26] Quoted in *National Intelligencer* (Washington), 5 Dec. 1860.
[27] James Buchanan, *Mr. Buchanan's Administration on the Eve of the Rebellion* (New York: Appleton, 1866), p. 276.

a reflection of the government's confused state and of its lame-duck character. Then too, Mercier thought, Buchanan was taking a soft line for fear of provoking the South into forming a confederacy. On balance, the message would probably worsen rather than help the situation:

> That situation, Mr. Minister, is becoming so grave as to merit Your Excellency's serious attention. In fact, nine of every ten members of Congress I ask are convinced that the Union will not survive the ordeal it is undergoing. It is especially the Southerners who seem to have decided to push things to extremes. . . . One can scarcely stop Christians, who live under a government of freedom, from hating slavery—even though they would be without pity for the slave—or from trying to make their views prevail. And neither can one stop those who profit directly from slavery from seeing good in it and trying to maintain it.[28]

Lewis Cass sent in his resignation as secretary of state on 12 December, blaming Buchanan for not doing enough to protect the forts in Charleston harbor. It was especially galling to the president to experience this attack from the left flank, with his right so heavily bombarded by his Southern friends. In fact he knew that conservative Northern opinion was now his only mainstay. As noted earlier, he named Jeremiah S. Black to the State Department for the limping remainder of the old regime.[29]

Mercier found the coming political break a natural outgrowth of America's constitutional weakness and of her two most degraded institutions, democracy and slavery. Dissolu-

[28] Mercier to Thouvenel, Washington, 7 Dec. 1860, AMAE, CP, E-U, 123: 385-90, no. 14. See also Lynn M. Case and Warren F. Spencer, *The United States and France: Civil War Diplomacy* (Philadelphia: University of Pennsylvania Press, 1970), pp. 20-21.

[29] Einstein, "Lewis Cass," *American Secretaries of State*, VI, 384; Cass to Buchanan, Washington, 12 Dec. 1860, Buchanan Papers.

tion proved the inherent weakness of the American experiment; indeed a nation so conceived and so dedicated could not long endure:

> In these facts we see a sure proof that the American system is no longer running smoothly and that the disease germs which it harbors in its head, especially slavery and universal suffrage, are spreading everywhere without check and have taken a course which puts it at the mercy of the first accident.

Lincoln's election, he thought, was that accident. But— and here Mercier's dialectic appears again, a confusion understandable in such an unsettled transitional period— American strength and practicality were such that the anarchy would probably not last long.

Senators Slidell and Benjamin had told him recently that Lincoln's election was the chance the South needed to dissolve the Union. The seven or eight Southern states would then form a provisional government to negotiate with the other states. If all went well, said the senators, only New England would stay out of the new confederation, and she in turn could then unite with Canada. Mercier thought this idea more economically and politically sensible than the plan for a confederation exclusively composed of slave states.[30]

While Mercier's bland acceptance of this wild surmise may connote a weak grasp of alternatives, he can scarcely be too heavily blamed for not being able, in these chaotic weeks, to see the future's shape more plainly. As each development appeared, he reported it accurately and discussed its possible implications. In this way the final secession of South Carolina on 20 December, the arrival of com-

---

[30] Mercier to Thouvenel, Washington, 17 Dec. 1860, AMAE, CP, E-U, 123: 394-402, no. 15. See also Blumenthal, *Franco-American Relations*, p. 140, and Case and Spencer, p. 22.

missioners from that state in Washington, Major Anderson's regrouping of forces on Sumter, the resignation of Floyd from the War Department, and the hapless efforts of the House and Senate special committees to save the situation— all passed under Mercier's review. By year's end he was again sure that the Union had seen its last. "The American Union is in its death agony," he said, "and in all probability will not survive the Buchanan administration by so much as a day. It is no longer a question of whether the break will come, but how."[31]

Mercier was far from being unique in the shifting character of his reports. Politicians, editorialists, business leaders, and others shifted in like fashion, and the total picture of all their views was one of bewildering confusion. Philosophies of what *should* happen were as varied as predictions of what *would* happen. There were secessionists and Unionists; there were Unionists who, like the president, held coercion of secession wrong; there were even Unionists who held secession legal though inadvisable; there were secessionists who wanted immediate action, secessionists who wanted to wait until the inauguration, secessionists who wanted their states to act only if the new administration used force. Each observer's philosophy tended to color his predictions, but even a determinedly antislavery man like Charles Eliot Norton, the famed New England editor, held war to be "most likely" on 17 December, then two months later thought it was only a "remote possibility." As one historian has put it, "Such was the confusion, North and South, that conscientious men, torn between hope and despair, anger and conciliation, caution and impatience, changed in mood from day to day."[32]

[31] Mercier to Thouvenel, Washington, 31 Dec. 1860, AMAE, CP, E-U, 123: 411-17, no. 17.

[32] Nevins, *The Emergence of Lincoln*, II, 340, where the Norton quotation may also be found.

And so it went, into the year of agony, a crisis which many Americans felt, as did the French minister, was indeed an agony of death for the United States of America. The very atmosphere of the president's New Year's reception must have seemed appropriate to the diplomats present, studded as it was with elderly gentlemen about to pass from the scene: Buchanan, General Scott, Chief Justice Taney. In the city, each week saw some further wrenching change as the old order passed and the Republicans arrived:

Vehicles lumbered on their way to wharf or station filled with the baggage of departing Senators and Members. The brows of hotel-keepers darkened with misgivings. . . . In the strange persons of the politicians, already beginning to press into the capital, there was little indication that these might prove satisfactory substitutes for us who were withdrawing.[33]

Still there was a strong conciliatory current in the North; Mercier reported that New York was again the source of peace efforts and was even sending a commission of leading citizens to Washington to propose a compromise. This would be similar to the plan of Senator Crittenden of Kentucky, who on 3 January suggested the unprecedented technique of a national referendum for his own compromise, a complicated plan which would guarantee territorial slavery south of latitude 36°30′ by constitutional amendment. Meanwhile, could Virginia be saved for the Union? Perhaps, Mercier thought, the secessionists would establish solidarity among all the slave states by creating some sort of overwhelming crisis, "by an attack against Fort Sumter, for example."

On 6 January, Mercier had had an interesting talk with the retired secretary of state, Lewis Cass—a talk which

---

[33] Clay-Clopton, p. 151.

suggests the force of Northern, and even Unionist, views on the decisions, present and future, of the French minister:

> Yesterday I had a long conversation with General Cass, and with a tone of saddest conviction he said: "Those who think the Union can be saved are very foolish; those who think it can be broken without a civil war are even more foolish; but the most foolish of all are those who imagine that once broken, it can ever be put back together." Among the people I meet, I admit there would be very few who would see anything else in these words except an expression of despair from an aged patriot who sees the structure which he has spent his life building, beginning to crumble. The confidence of Americans in the future remains strong, and they should be congratulated for that; but nonetheless, the opinion given by General Cass seems to me the soundest I have yet heard.[34]

It is questionable how much time Thouvenel had had to appreciate the wealth of American information which Mercier was sending to Paris. Despite the importance of the material, no immediate decision of any crushing importance had to be taken. Meanwhile, the fall of 1860 had seen Garibaldi's conquest of Naples, Cavour's invasion of the Papal States, and the plebiscites in Sicily and Naples which favored annexation to Piedmont. The continuing close involvement of France in these events, especially her protection of Rome and the Patrimony, was naturally uppermost in the counsels of the foreign office. In addition, French troops were still in Syria, ostensibly to prevent further massacres such as had taken place the previous year, and this too was roiling relations with Great Britain.[35]

[34] Mercier to Thouvenel, Washington, 7 Jan. 1861, AMAE, CP, E-U, 124: 8-11, no. 19. See also Case and Spencer, p. 23.

[35] So bad was this situation that Napoleon III was reported to have told the Austrian ambassador, "I desire and will make every

By the beginning of the new year Thouvenel was well aware of Mercier's opinion that the Union would break, and he had before him the complete American story down to early December, including the gentle hint that "the situation, Mr. Minister, is becoming so grave as to merit Your Excellency's serious attention." Yet he had no advice or guidance of any major import to give to his minister in Washington.[36]

THE IMPENDING CRISIS

Southern resignations from the cabinet and the inherent logic of the Unionist position moved the administration toward a firmer stance in January as South Carolina and other slave states proved intransigent. In his message to Congress of 8 January, Buchanan appealed to all Americans "to declare in their might that the Union must and shall be preserved by all constitutional means."[37] Already he had sent the unarmed *Star of the West* to reinforce Major Anderson at Fort Sumter, only to see it forced back by South Carolina's guns. Conflicting moves continued into early February when two important conventions met and crossed purposes. In Montgomery, delegates from South Carolina, Louisiana, Georgia, Alabama, Mississippi, and Florida met to begin writing a fundamental law for the new confederation. In Washington a Peace Convention of twenty-one

---

sacrifice to maintain friendly relations with England, but if public opinion in France, which, however, I will do my best to control, should render a rupture necessary, I will make war on England with such vigour and such means as shall at once put an end to the affair." (Lord Cowley, *Secrets of the Second Empire*, ed. F. A. Wellesley [New York: Harper & Brothers, 1929], p. 215).

[36] Mercier to Thouvenel, Washington, 7 Dec. 1860, AMAE, CP, E-U, 123: 385-90, no. 14; Thouvenel to Mercier, Paris, 24 Jan. 1861, *ibid.*, 124: 37-38, no. 3.

[37] Quoted in J. G. Randall and David Donald, *The Civil War and Reconstruction*, 2nd ed. (Boston: D. C. Heath & Co., 1961), p. 154.

states met under the chairmanship of ex-President John Tyler and spent three weeks bringing forth a compromise proposal similar to Crittenden's.

In the circumstances it is not surprising that Mercier's predictions continued to leave room for peace or war, Union or dissolution. He of course thought well of Senator Crittenden's proposal to guarantee slavery in territories south of the Missouri Compromise line, and he was impressed by the conciliatory direction of Senator Seward's speeches: in the senate chamber Crittenden had bowed his white head and wept when Seward offered to support an unamendable constitutional amendment which would prevent federal interference with slavery in the states. But Mercier saw that it was passion which ruled at the moment, and Crittenden's plan, since it sprang from reason, had little chance of success in his opinion.[38]

Mercier had a chance to talk things over with Crittenden and other prominent moderates at two dinners, one about 30 January at the home of Senator Stephen A. Douglas, and the other about 9 February at Mercier's Georgetown residence.[39] The Douglas affair, a large party, included Crittenden, Seward, and Justice John A. Campbell, who would

[38] Albert D. Kirwan, *John J. Crittenden: The Struggle for the Union* (Lexington, Ky.: University of Kentucky Press, 1962), pp. 397-98; Mercier to Thouvenel, Washington, 20 Jan. 1861, AMAE, CP, E-U, 124: 32-35, no. 21.

[39] Much of the following account is based on Henry G. Connor, *John Archibald Campbell, Associate Justice of the United States Supreme Court, 1853-1861* (Boston: Houghton Mifflin Co., 1920). Connor gives the date as "February, 1861" and quotes at length from Justice Campbell's memorandum which calls it "a dinner by Senator Douglas to the French Minister Mercier." Mercier, in a dispatch dated 1 February, mentions "dining the other day at Mr. Douglas'," and in another note, 11 February, says that a few senators "dined the other day at my house." See Connor, p. 116; Blumenthal, *Franco-American Relations*, p. 123: Korolewicz-Carlton, p. 8; Mercier to Thouvenel, Washington, 1 Feb. 1861, AMAE, CP, E-U, 124: 39-47, no. 22; Mercier to Thouvenel, Washington, 11 Feb. 1861, *ibid.*, fol. 53-60, no. 23; Case and Spencer, pp. 24-25.

serve in a few weeks as Seward's go-between with the Confederate commissioners in Washington.

The "Little Giant" himself was at his best in this last year of his life. Having campaigned hopelessly for president in the middle ground of compromise, he devoted the anticlimax of his career to working out formulas for saving the Union, trying to make his old rival's accession to the presidency as smooth as possible, and vigorously supporting him during the spring crisis. His wife, the former Addie Cutts, was an accomplished linguist, and the Douglases had long been popular entertainers. We are left to speculate whether this dinner, at which Mercier was guest of honor, was a planned gathering of moderate men, some sort of attempt to sound out French opinion or to impress it with Unionist sentiment, or merely a social coincidence. Mercier's reciprocal function in the second week of February was a smaller affair which included Douglas, Seward, and Crittenden, and was certainly intended in part as a source of ideas and information for relaying to Paris.

At Douglas's dinner, an orgy of Unionism and reason, Seward urged all the company to fill their glasses and drain them dry: "Away with all parties, all platforms, all previous committals, and whatever else will stand in the way of restoration of the American Union." Justice Campbell, a Southern man, allowed that slavery was, after all, only a transitory institution and that in the last ten years fewer than thirty slaves had been brought into the New Mexico territory, hardly a matter worth the tearing of the Union. Seward responded that he agreed, but that he might not be in a position to influence events.[40] Mercier himself felt that the problem was much deeper than a mere adjustment of slavery and that the Union would not survive unscathed.[41]

[40] Connor, *John Archibald Campbell*, p. 118.
[41] Mercier to Thouvenel, Washington, 1 Feb. 1861, AMAE, CP, E-U, 124: 39-47, no. 22.

By the eleventh the picture seemed a bit brighter: the Peace Convention was hard at work, and in Virginia secessionists lost out in the election to a state convention. Northern moderates again were raising hopes, and Mercier was not entirely sure they would fail:

> There is certainly in this combination of factors at least some matter for illusion, but I don't know whether it is enough to justify the supreme confidence which the current heads of the Unionist cause, Senators Seward, Douglas, and Crittenden, recently evidenced to me. These three gentlemen were my guests the other day in a small, intimate dinner party. In the course of a free-wheeling conversation they told me that if I had written my government that the Union would be dissolved, I should quickly reverse myself, for the majority of the people who run things here want to preserve the Union and are well able to do so.

Mercier again was not overly impressed. He noted to Thouvenel that seven states with four million people had already seceded and that the border states were strongly opposed to any federal use of force. Moreover, the much-bruited constitutional amendment guaranteeing territorial slavery was a direct contradiction of the basic Republican position: "There is agreement now on the aim—the Union, and it is natural that men come together with conciliatory feelings. But when it comes to translating those feelings into action, the difficulty begins, and it could turn out to be insurmountable."[42]

There were those in the North, of course, who actually wanted a rupture as much as Southern secessionists: the abolitionist "church" as Mercier styled them. But most

[42] Mercier to Thouvenel, Washington, 11 Feb. 1861, *ibid.*, fol. 53-60, no. 23.

Northerners, he thought, were more interested in economic prosperity:

> Doubtless the abolitionist doctrines flatter their natural inclinations, but surely not to the point of making them forget their interests. Moreover, the black race is the object of such prejudice that one can say without too much exaggeration that if the Negro were a domestic animal in the South, in the North he would be an unclean animal. They are certainly not about to kill the goose that lays the golden eggs for a principle; but it still remains to know how to save the Union with things having gone as far as they have, and on this point there is no agreement.

Mercier felt, at base, that the American constitution was simply not equal to the strains which American life and development were subjecting it to, and that it could not reconcile "the needs, the interests, and the passions of a population which has not been able to develop so phenomenally without losing a great part of its homogeneity." American prosperity was indeed great, he continued, but this very richness had helped to weaken the machinery of government and the mores of the people:

> Every revolution, in effect, reacts against the ruler of the moment; in America this ruler is the populace, and its despotism even has a name—it is called "Mobocracy." . . . There is only one way to combat mobocracy: strengthen authority. I know that it is not easy to discover the elements necessary for such a change, but if struggles become necessary to produce them, these struggles will inevitably occur.[43]

[43] Mercier to Thouvenel, Washington, 1 Feb. 1861, *ibid.*, fol. 39-47, no. 22.
Korolewicz-Carlton pursues the thesis that Mercier's prejudices against popular government colored his reports to Paris and served

It was in this context, in discussing America's prosperity and the imminent revolutionary change which would be accompanied by struggle, that Mercier noted the opinion of Seward and other guests that "a good war would have been the best way to prolong the life of the Union." Since Mercier did not elaborate on this, it is difficult to know whether it was a foreshadowing of Seward's policy of 1 April: the policy of entering a foreign war in order to pull domestic, sectional factions together. What is apparent from the way Mercier picks up and drops the subject is its relative unimportance: casual, relaxed dinner talk got around to the point that a nation in domestic trouble might start a war to pull itself together.

Such a thought was hardly original with Seward, nor did it appear for the first time in 1861. To a president like Buchanan, for example, with his penchant for adventures in Latin America and his dedication to the Union, it was the merest adding of two and two to see foreign affairs as an aid to domestic unity. Lincoln, after his election, was also urged to see them that way, and Seward especially was widely quoted in these winter months as toying with bel-

---

to encourage Napoleon III's own anti-Union bent. Thouvenel, in this scenario, tried to counter the influence of his minister and his sovereign by holding out against diplomatic recognition of the South.

Mercier, says Korolewicz-Carlton, was an accurate reporter of events, but "he does not exhibit the same objectivity in describing the personalities and value of the government to which he was accredited, and he obviously lets his aristocratic sympathies and disdain for all popular government influence him" (Korolewicz-Carlton, pp. 9-10).

We can assay this thesis better as we go along, but to single out such passages as the one quoted above to prove that Mercier was more "aristocratic" than other Europeans seems a bit forced. In fact his views were the views of most literate and influential Europeans of his day. Such Europeans, while evaluating American democracy in a way that was not Abraham Lincoln's way, would nevertheless agree with him that the American crisis of the 1860's was a test of democracy's viability.

licose notions. The fact, therefore, that Douglas's dinner guests could speak of "a good war" was not, in this framework, an earth shaking piece of news.[44]

Other matters of greater ultimate importance were adumbrated in these preinauguration weeks, noted by Mercier, and submitted to Paris for reflection. Already in the third week of January he mentioned the possibility of a Northern blockade of Southern ports and concluded that such a move would surely precipitate civil war.[45]

In addition, the Morrill tariff of 1861 was in the legislative mill at this time and actually passed on 20 February. Its schedules, while moderate, were a considerable increase over the low duties of the 1857 act. Lyons was particularly concerned and drew a bleak picture of the future, which Mercier relayed home:

> "We therefore are threatened," he told me, "with finding ourselves stopped by a Northern blockade—in the South by ships, in the North by the tariff—and we must therefore take precautions." I suppose also that the confederation of the South, as soon as her provisional government is organized, will quickly send agents to Europe to announce her existence to the various courts and seek recognition.[46]

[44] Mercier to Thouvenel, Washington, 1 Feb. 1861, AMAE, CP, E-U, 124: 39-47, no. 22. For the advice to Lincoln, see the enclosure in James W. Taylor to Buchanan, St. Paul, 27 Nov. 1860, Buchanan Papers. For reports similar to Mercier's remarks, see Lyons to Russell, Washington, 7 Jan. 1861, Newton, *Lord Lyons*, I, 30, and Lyons to Russell, Washington, 4 Feb. 1861, in C. F. Adams, Jr., "The British Proclamation of May, 1861," *Massachusetts Historical Society Proceedings*, XLVIII (1915), 217-19; Ralph Haswell Lutz, "Rudolf Schleiden and the Visit to Richmond, April 25, 1861," *Annual Report of the American Historical Association for the Year 1915* (Washington: U.S. Government Printing Office, 1917), pp. 207-22.

[45] Mercier to Thouvenel, Washington, 20 Jan. 1861, AMAE, CP, E-U, 124: 32-35, no. 21.

[46] Mercier to Thouvenel, Washington, 11 Feb. 1861, *ibid.*, fol. 53-60, no. 23.

Here was another hint of the future, the problem of recognition. Mercier, who three months earlier had signaled his great prudence to Thouvenel in this sensitive area, apparently forgot himself at least once in February. Senator L. T. Wigfall of Texas recorded it this way in a letter to Leroy P. Walker, soon to be Confederate secretary of war:

> The French minister stated Saturday in our cloak room that the Emperor would at once recognize your Government. He understands the present treaties to be still existing between his Government and the seceding States, and said that, when officially informed that they were disposed to carry the stipulations out, no difficulty would be made as to the mere agent through which they may hereafter act.[47]

So now the federal government was a "mere agent" for the states, even in matters of foreign relations. If Wigfall reported Mercier's thought accurately, the French minister was indeed applying a peculiarly Southern interpretation of the constitution.

There is one further foreshadowing of great interest which should be noted. Several times in the coming months and years, Mercier would suggest to his government that the American bloodbath might be stopped by getting both sides to agree to a sort of Mississippi customs union, a common market of Confederate and Union states. The South could have her independence, the North could have her tariff protection and industrial growth, and people could stop killing one another. It is possible that Mercier derived

[47] Wigfall to Walker, Washington, 11 Feb. 1861, *ORA*, 1st ser., LIII, 123-24. Mercier may have been influenced in his thinking by Lyons. At about the same time as the cloakroom incident, he reported to Thouvenel that Lyons thought British recognition would come quickly (Mercier to Thouvenel, Washington, 11 Feb. 1861, AMAE, CP, E-U, 124: 53-60, no. 23).

his idea from someone in the confidence of Stephen Douglas. Ever since his European tour of 1853, Douglas had been much impressed with the German *Zollverein*; on the eve of the Civil War, but only within the circle of his private friends, he elaborated its possibilities for saving lives in America.[48]

William Henry Seward, as he approached his sixtieth birthday, had good claim to that title, "most influential leader of the Republican party," which Mercier and others so liberally bestowed upon him. Six years earlier he had led the scattered remnants of the Northern Whigs into the new Republican alliance; the nominations of Fremont in 1856 and of Lincoln in 1860 were as much tributes to his political importance as rejections. It was assumed he would heavily influence and perhaps even direct the incoming administration.

This being so, Mercier was fortunate that Seward was in Washington, as senator from New York, all during the transitional period in early 1861. The two men met at least a few times socially. In the years ahead the French minister would learn that Seward was first and last an iron-willed American nationalist. He would occasionally send to Paris angry accounts of what he considered the secretary's bumptious, intractable, histrionic determination to preserve the Union. The relationship between the two, born in curiosity in these preinauguration weeks, would move irregularly through detestation and admiration to something like real friendship at the end.

As we have seen, Mercier at first assessed Seward as an enormously powerful Republican whose inclination to com-

[48] George Fort Milton, *The Eve of Conflict: Stephen A. Douglas and the Needless War* (Boston: Houghton Mifflin Co., 1934), pp. 540-41. Mercier mentioned Douglas, but only as a supporter of the common market, not as his source (Mercier to Thouvenel, Washington, 7 Nov. 1861, AMAE, CP, E-U, 125: 186-97, no. 68).

promise was a vital factor working for peace and union. Mercier was in the senate gallery on Saturday, 12 January, as Seward spoke for two hours in favor of conciliation and brought tears to the eyes of John J. Crittenden. After blaming secessionist-minded politicians for the country's trouble and calling on all to credit Lincoln's moderation, Seward seconded the call for a national convention to guarantee slavery in states where it existed (though not, of course, in territories). Mercier was not too much excited: "The speech, truly outstanding for its dignity of style and loftiness of ideas, and the one most attentively listened to, from beginning to end, of all those given during this debate, did not, however, produce a very lively impression." It gave away too much to suit Republican intractables and not enough to suit the Southerners.[49]

Nor was Mercier especially impressed by anything the president-elect had to say in these troubled weeks. Demonstrations provoked by Lincoln's progress from Springfield to Washington failed to break down his careful reserve; the country and the diplomats had yet to learn what his precise policy would be toward the South. Mercier wondered whether this reserve sprang from confusion or from calculation:

> I must state that in general one gets a very poor opinion of Mr. Lincoln. People note that he has made politics only one of the secondary occupations of his busy life; . . . that his embarrassment at having come

[49] Mercier to Thouvenel, Washington, 14 Jan. 1861, AMAE, CP, E-U, 124: 12-21, no. 20. Mercier complained of "the garbled voice of the speaker," a remark which may reflect the listener's limited command of spoken English as much as Seward's throaty enunciation. In his evaluation of the speech, Mercier was influenced to some extent by unnamed Americans, persons claiming to know Seward's views. For Seward's idea that after a period of secession he might become the architect of reunion, see Nevins, *The Emergence of Lincoln*, II, 400.

onto the stage where the fortunes of political struggle have called him to play the leading role, should actually become so much worse that agreement has already begun to break down among those who can be called the authors of his election.

Mercier judged that Lincoln was strong, but not great:

> For myself, Mr. Minister, when I look at Mr. Lincoln's background, I am inclined to see one of those American types characterized by energy and strong will, who in difficult circumstances must display so much more stubbornness that qualities of mind are not always up to those of character. . . . I would not be surprised, therefore, if at the present hour his decision were not already made but that he has not yet judged it opportune to unmask himself completely.[50]

Mercier, then, at a time when he had not yet met Abraham Lincoln, was no more successful than most of his contemporaries, American or foreign, in discerning the charismatic greatness behind the country-lawyer exterior. Mercier at least credited Lincoln with courage and tenacity, but not with largeness of vision. In balance, however, the French foreign office was well served by this report, an analysis which quite correctly had Lincoln more anxious than Seward to protect Fort Sumter.

Lincoln arrived in Washington in the last week of February under circumstances which emphasized his seeming lack of dignity and style. Word of a Baltimore murder plot had been rushed to him in his Philadelphia hotel by Senator Seward acting through his son, Frederick W. Seward. Reluctantly Lincoln agreed to cancel a scheduled reception in Baltimore and, in effect, to sneak through the city and

---

[50] Mercier to Thouvenel, Washington, 18 Feb. 1861, AMAE, CP, E-U, 124: 62-68, unnumbered [no. 24].

into Washington. Mercier apparently got the story from a prejudiced source; as he told it, Lincoln was afraid of some insult or scandalous incident, and the main effect of his decision was to inconvenience people in Baltimore. Mercier remained skeptical about the president-elect's capability and drew a sharp contrast for Thouvenel between Lincoln and Jefferson Davis, the provisional president of the Southern government—soldier, administrator, senator, not unknown and inexperienced like Lincoln.[51]

On the last weekend of the old regime, Mercier, settling into a definite, repeated, and quite accurate estimate of events, summed up: "Despite assurances from Mr. Seward, all the indications are that dissolution will go forward; the only areas open to question are how and at what cost." He also filled in his unflattering portrait of Abraham Lincoln:

> In my view he might be one of those Yankee types: good Christians, good patriots, but trusting no one, going their own way, scarcely knowing how to pull back. He and his wife seem like a real family of western farmers, and even in this country, where one has no right to be fastidious, their common manners and their ways expose them in unfortunate fashion to ridicule.[52]

All in all, by the eve of Lincoln's inauguration the French government had an accurate and complete picture of American developments. Though the portraits of Lincoln had not yet arrived, the basic, critical situation as sketched by Mercier was there for Thouvenel and the emperor to contemplate: the American federal Union was in process of disintegration; efforts to shore it up were still going for-

[51] Mercier to Thouvenel, Washington, 25 Feb. 1861, *ibid.*, fol. 73-80, no. 25.
[52] Mercier to Thouvenel, Washington, 1 March 1861, AMAE, MD, Papiers Thouvenel, XIII, 350-55.

ward but would probably fail; such corollary problems as blockade and recognition would have to be faced quite soon.

Thouvenel, who at the time had everything of Mercier's up to his dispatch of 11 February, expressed the usual thanks for a good job of reporting. But as to action, or even policy, that would have to wait upon events: "At present I can but follow their progress attentively and must, as you realize, await the decisive climax, if there is one, in order to send you instructions which would take into account a radical change in the constitutional bonds now existing between the Northern and Southern states of the Union."[53]

Europe, then, would wait together with America: wait for Monday, 4 March, for the inauguration and for whatever might lie beyond.

[53] Thouvenel to Mercier, Paris, 4 March 1861, AMAE, CP, E-U, 124: 88, no. 5.

CHAPTER III

Maneuvers and Positions

MARCH TO SEPTEMBER 1861

BEFORE THE WAR

THE morning of 4 March was cloudy and raw in Washington. Something like a normal inauguration crowd was milling about the city, and thirty thousand eventually gathered before the Capitol to witness the transfer of power. Inevitably the threat of violence hung in the air, and General Scott had moved in with a large force of regulars supported by volunteer companies; they were collected on "G" Street, commanding New York Avenue and the Treasury Building, and at Long Bridge. One witness thought that "all preparations seemed more fitting for the capital of Mexico than that of these United States."[1]

Mercier, of course, was part of the colorfully bedecked diplomatic corps which always lent a dash of Old World splendor to these republican occasions. He noted the troops, without any Mexican allusions, and the fact that Buchanan stopped at Willard's Hotel for Lincoln, the two then riding together to the Capitol in a simple gesture of political good order. In the Senate chamber, Mercier, Lyons, and the others took their places behind the senators for the swearing-in of Hannibal Hamlin as vice-president. Mercier noted

[1] T. C. De Leon, *Belles, Beaux, and Brains of the 60's* (New York: G. W. Dillingham Co., 1909), p. 42. See also Milton, *Eve of the Conflict*, p. 547, and Allan Nevins, *The War for the Union*, 2 vols. (New York: Charles Scribner's Sons, 1959-1960), I, 4.

that the Senate had been in session all night—the session of 3 March going on almost till noon—but he seems not to have realized that the Crittenden compromise had been the last subject of debate.

At 1:00 the Supreme Court entered the Senate chamber, followed by Buchanan and Lincoln, arm in arm as Mercier noted it; the representative of the Second Empire was at least slightly impressed by the Republic's ability to manage a presidential succession. After Hamlin had been sworn in, a procession formed and moved to the steps outside. There a badly shaking Roger B. Taney swore in the Western farmer; there Stephen Douglas held the new president's hat as he spoke. Mercier later described the undecorated platform over the Capitol steps, the covered tribune at which Lincoln delivered his speech, his loud voice, and above all the lack of gorgeous display:

> Americans call this lack of ceremony republican simplicity, as if simplicity forbade good form and the dignified bearing which commands respect. This so-called simplicity, moreover, is totally out of harmony with the marble and gilt of a monument erected with the pretension that when it is finished, it will surpass in richness every other modern building. It's as if one wanted to inaugurate a Quaker in a basilica. It is true that the fate of this monument, a new Tower of Babel, may be only to witness to future generations the bold presumption of those who conceived its design. In sum, the impression which all these contrasts leaves is that of a greatness vainly sought, a diminished power which no more holds the place which befits it.

What Mercier heard in Lincoln's first inaugural address was what most others heard, an eloquent but vague plea for the Union: "Can aliens make treaties easier than friends can make laws?" No bugles, no pennants, no rabbits in the hat. Like others, Mercier missed any clear statement of policy on secession and a national convention. Lincoln contented himself with noting that circumstances favored a convention; he forswore invasion and the use of force, except to hold federal property. Mercier failed to notice the significant omission of any plan to reclaim forts already in Confederate hands.

From this time on, Mercier had no more derogatory characterizations of Abraham Lincoln to offer—perhaps because he had said it all already, perhaps because his dealings were almost totally with the secretary of state; but perhaps too, because he had finally met the president and heard him speak. There was a diplomatic reception at the White House on Thursday, the seventh. Meanwhile, the new cabinet was being formed. Mercier singled out the two most important names: Salmon P. Chase at the treasury and William H. Seward at state, Chase the intransigent and Seward the moderate.[2]

The month of March 1861 was the one in which William H. Seward, with considerable justification, thought that he was running the country. The president had not laid out any clear blueprint or list of options; there was ample precedent in American history for the kind of moderator-president which Lincoln apparently would be; and the biographies of the Illinois ex-congressman and the New York ex-governor and senator seemed to indicate clearly that the state department should be the locus of decision-making.

[2] Mercier to Thouvenel, Washington, 7 March 1861, AMAE, CP, E-U, 124: 89-95, no. 27. See also Kirwan, *John J. Crittenden*, 421; Allen Johnson, *Stephen A. Douglas: A Study in American Politics* (New York: Macmillan Co., 1908), p. 464; *National Intelligencer* (Washington), 5 and 9 March 1861. For other French thought on the unfinished Capitol, see Serge Gavronsky, *The French Liberal Opposition and the American Civil War* (New York: Humanities Press, 1968), pp. 58-59.

It was Seward, not Lincoln, whom General Scott addressed on inauguration eve, listing permitted, peaceful secession as a thinkable program for the new government. Seward showed the letter around town as a kind of credential and as a prop to strengthen the peace party.

In Virginia, where the key to the future seemed to be held, a state convention was still in session, still undecided. In Washington two representatives of the Montgomery "government" had come to bargain—Martin J. Crawford and John Forsyth; later in the month they were joined by A. B. Roman. Given time, the federal government might be able to call a national convention, manipulate a settlement, muddle through. But in Charleston harbor Anderson and his men needed food, and time was limited to just this one month of March.[3]

Despite his pledge of nonabandonment given in the inaugural address, the president was willing to consider evacuating Sumter. Fort Pickens at Pensacola, Florida, on the other hand, seemed easier to hold, and Lincoln ordered its reinforcement on 12 March. Perhaps, then, he could redeem his pledge at Pickens and still follow the advice of Seward and other cabinet members, given on 14 March, not to risk war over Fort Sumter. Meanwhile the Montgomery commissioners were trying unsuccessfully to meet personally with the secretary of state.[4]

Mercier as early as the first of the year had specifically singled out Sumter as a tinderbox. Now he underlined this: if the government were to abandon the fort, it could counteract the bad impression only by using warships to collect duties outside the Gulf ports, or perhaps by a blockade. Lincoln, he thought, would have to convoke a special ses-

[3] Nevins, *The War for the Union*, i, 39-40.

[4] John Nicolay and John Hay, *Abraham Lincoln, A History*, 10 vols. (New York: Century Co., 1890), iii, 399-403; Randall and Donald, *Civil War and Reconstruction*, pp. 172-73.

sion of Congress and try, as Buchanan had, to slough off his responsibilities onto the legislative branch; either that, or let the seceded states alone while a national convention gave tempers a chance to cool. Fear of civil war, he judged, would hold the Southern states together; remove that fear, and they might one day rejoin the Union. It is possible that Seward himself was the source of some of these pacific ideas.[5]

Seward's audacious, even frenzied, efforts to keep the peace came to the attention of the diplomatic corps in a striking way. On Sunday morning, 24 March, the Russian minister Stoeckl called upon A. B. Roman of the Montgomery delegation and pressed him to credit Seward's protestations of peace. The secretary, said Stoeckl, wanted to meet with Roman by chance, "over a cup of tea" at the Russian legation. Subsequently, Seward decided not to go through with this risky plan. Perhaps it was bad enough already that the Russian minister was privy to a delicate matter of which the president of the United States presumably was unaware.

Writing the next day, Mercier thought that this teatime tryst was still on. He was fully cognizant, of course, that Seward was trying hard to satisfy the demands put forward by the commissioners in a letter they had sent him. "Mr. Seward did not think it right to answer this message directly, but he has made his views known to the commissioners indirectly, and they have let him know that his per-

[5] Mercier to Thouvenel, Washington, 17 March 1861, AMAE, CP, E-U, 124: 105-12, no. 27 *bis*. By this time Mercier knew of Thouvenel's instructions that French diplomats begin distinguishing in their dispatches between what was publishable and what was not. Sensitive material should be relegated to dispatches numbered the same as publishable letters so as to keep the numbering of the latter consecutive (Thouvenel to Mercier, Paris, 2 Feb. 1861, *ibid.*, fol. 49-50, no. 4, circular). Thus Mercier wished to withhold from publication this dispatch of 17 March, no. 27 *bis*; no. 27 had been dated 7 March.

sonal dispositions are no less peaceful than those of the Montgomery government." The commissioners wanted assurances that all thought of force would be abandoned, and Seward, "to discuss this subject has arranged without his colleagues' knowledge, a secret interview with one of them." There, Mercier stated, the affair rested, and he thought there was every reason to hope matters would not end in an outbreak. Mercier noted that moderate opinion was again growing, but on the other hand the Montgomery government seemed secure enough to him, and the South seemingly no longer needed a civil war in order to unify itself.[6]

In this week the Southern commissioners were able to report favorably on the diplomats' attitudes. Lyons, they said, had told a friend (Corcoran) that the option of British diplomatic recognition of the Confederacy should be kept open. Stoeckl, according to the commissioners, openly suggested to Seward that the United States recognize the Confederacy, for Europe would certainly do so. Mercier, it would appear, was either more reserved or less deeply plumbed: he said merely that as the present truce went on, France would probably follow the lead of the United States regarding acceptance of the Confederacy.[7]

On Monday evening, 25 March, Lyons gave a dinner for the cabinet and his fellow diplomats. Seward took the occasion to think out loud some of the "thoughts" he would later submit "for the president's consideration." The secretary, speaking quite loudly, talked very tough to Stoeckl, Lyons, and Mercier:

[6] Mercier to Thouvenel, Washington, 25 March 1861, *ibid.*, fol. 113-20, no. 28; Samuel Wylie Crawford, *The Genesis of the Civil War: The Story of Sumter, 1860-1861* (New York: Charles L. Webster & Co., 1887), p. 334. Mercier later realized that Seward never did meet with Roman (Mercier to Thouvenel, Washington, 29 March 1861, AMAE, CP, E-U, 124: 121-29, no. 29).

[7] Crawford, pp. 335-36.

After dinner Mr. Seward quizzed us, Lord Lyons, Stoeckl (the Russian) and me, about our commercial relations with the South, and on this subject he treated us to the most ridiculous and uncalled for boasts, for instance, that the best thing that could happen to America right now would be for Europe to get involved in some way in her affairs, and that if the Union were dissolved, not a government in Europe would remain standing. He had drunk quite a bit, which parenthetically he does quite often, and the tone of his words probably showed the effects of it, but *in vino veritas*.

Lyons was so embarrassed that he "took a natural opportunity of turning as host, to speak to some of the ladies in the room." Upon reflection the British minister concluded that the "violent party" was now gaining the upper hand in the cabinet.[8]

It is apparent, then, that for some days before 1 April, Seward's pugnacity toward Europe had been building up again. On Thursday the president gave his first state dinner. In the course of the evening he called his cabinet into a separate room and agitatedly told them that General Scott had just advised giving up Pickens as well as Sumter. Scott, of course, was close to Seward; his advice was thought to reflect the secretary's, and Lincoln regarded it as craven. The next day, at the official meeting of the cabinet, Seward hardly dared to speak. He now counseled that Sumter be abandoned but Pickens and the Texas forts be defended "at every cost." Only Caleb Smith, secretary of the interior,

[8] Mercier to Thouvenel, Washington, 26 March 1861, AMAE, MD, Papiers Thouvenel, XIII, 368-70; Lyons to Russell, Washington, 26 March 1861, Newton, I, 32-34.

Mercier's private letter, which he penned in his own indescribable hand, was misfiled in the Papiers Thouvenel as if it had been dated 26 May 1861. Since Mercier makes current allusions in it to events which transpired in late March, his "mars" was probably misread as "mai."

joined Seward in writing off Sumter. March, the month of Seward's "presidency," was over.[9]

In speaking of a "violent party" in the cabinet which was now in the ascendant, Lyons had meant violent toward Europe; he thus blurred a bit the distinction between Europe and the American South as objects of federal action, a distinction vital to any understanding of Seward's lurching moves. All along Seward had wanted to avoid conflict with the South; all along he had thought of some foreign adventure as a means of pressing together the sections of his country. It was thus no sudden reversal which took place in the last week of March: Seward's violence was born of his pacifism toward his fellow Americans.

Seward's astounding production, "Some Thoughts for the President's Consideration, April 1, 1861," was quietly buried by President Lincoln on April Fool's Day and lay quiet for almost a generation till Nicolay and Hay published it. The diplomatic corps were unaware of it, but they were well aware that Seward had long thought of a foreign war, and since Monday, 25 March, they knew his thought had become a policy to be advocated. Lyons, as we have seen, was alarmed. Mercier, less so, buried his comment in the middle of a long tract on a different topic:

> I know, in fact, that some party men consider a big foreign complication a means to reestablish the Union. In a meeting of the cabinet, one member . . . said that

[9] Nicolay and Hay, III, 429-33; Nevins, *The War for the Union*, I, 55-60; Randall and Donald, p. 173. At about this same time Seward also warned the diplomats that Civil War would mean a blockade (Stoeckl to Gorchakov, Washington, 28 March/9 April 1861, no. 20, Library of Congress, Washington, photostats, Papers of the Russian Ministry of Foreign Affairs, Dispatches of Édouard de Stoeckl, 1860-1864 [hereafter cited as Stoeckl Papers]).

the admission to French ports of ships flying the flag of the seceded states would be considered an act of recognition and that he would not hesitate to send me my passports.[10]

Although Seward's grand design for trouble with half the world never became federal policy, although Mercier was aware of it but dimly, it is still important to consider it for what it reveals of the secretary's attitude toward France and for the light it throws on his later decisions. "Some Thoughts" declares that Seward, taking, if necessary, the reins which Lincoln had allowed to go slack, would "seek" explanations from Great Britain and Russia and would "demand" explanations from Spain and France: "And, if satisfactory explanations are not received from Spain and France, Would convene Congress and declare war against them." Despite the secretary's agitated state of mind, it is perfectly clear that he chose his words carefully and set up a precise gradation of countries to be ruffled. Britain, indeed, had been rumored for a year to be in with Spain and France in some sort of Mexican intervention. And just before 1 April the papers were carrying stories about a coming Russian recognition of the South. But it was against Spain and France, which Seward mentioned twice in that order, that he would chiefly direct a united American attack.[11]

---

[10] Mercier to Thouvenel, Washington, 29 March 1861, AMAE, CP, E-U, 124: 121-29, no. 29.

[11] One of the best accounts of the whole episode is still that of Frederic Bancroft, *The Life of William H. Seward*, 2 vols. (New York: Harper & Brothers, 1900), II, 128-38. The text of "Some Thoughts" may be found in Nicolay and Hay, III, 445-47. It is also in Library of Congress, Washington, The Robert Todd Lincoln Collection of the Papers of Abraham Lincoln, fol. 8660-61, and in University of Rochester, Rochester, N.Y., Papers of William Henry Seward. Thus J. G. Randall's observation of 1945 that "Some Thoughts" is in neither of these collections is no longer valid, and

The immediate occasion to be seized upon was the re-imposition of Spanish rule upon Santo Domingo, where a pro-Spanish party had recently taken control and a Spanish force was in process of helping out. Seward well knew, as had Pierce and Buchanan before him, that of all foreign targets, Spain was the favorite of the slave states: Cuba could become an American territory for the expansion of slavery; moreover, if *Washington* took Cuba, slavery might well be abolished there should the South remain in secession. Cuba, for the South, was both a carrot and a stick.

France, while being relegated to a secondary position, also figured in the equation. If she aided Spain, her West Indian islands might also be seized. And there were several other factors which Seward may have considered. A French threat to Haiti concomitant with the Spanish return to Santo Domingo was one possibility. France, of course, was part of that old rumor of European intervention in Mexico, a rumor which had recently been revived by a dispatch from the United States minister in Mexico. And from Paris itself, more fuel: Faulkner had written on 4 March that a French naval force was being sent to the American coast. Faulk-

---

the authenticity of the document is beyond all question (J. G. Randall, *Lincoln the President*, 4 vols. [New York: Dodd, Mead and Co., 1945-1955], II, 30, n. 2). See also Case and Spencer, pp. 32-34.

The original of Lincoln's reply is in Lincoln Papers (fol. 8608-13) but not in Seward Papers. This suggests that the president never sent his written reply, perhaps contenting himself with a verbal reprimand. The copy of "Some Thoughts" in Lincoln Papers, i.e., the one presumably sent over from the State Department, is in Frederick Seward's handwriting. It has been emended, and it seems possible that this is merely a draft, shown to and left with Lincoln rather than officially presented. This interpretation would coincide well with the hypothesis that Lincoln wrote his reply only to file it away in his drawer (Case, *Revue d'histoire diplomatique*, LXXVII [1963], 304, n. 3; Patrick Sowle, "A Reappraisal of Seward's Memorandum of April 1, 1861, to Lincoln," *Journal of Southern History*, XXXIII [1967], 234-39).

ner's source was a good one: the Marquis de Montholon, consul-general in New York, who was home on a temporary leave. Seward may have been genuinely concerned about the possible threat to Mexico. On this same afternoon of 1 April, he sent to Lincoln a batch of orders which the president signed without reading. One of them would ostensibly have sent Captain Garrett J. Pendergast to Vera Cruz because of "important complications in our foreign relations." When Secretary of the Navy Welles brought the matter to Lincoln's attention, the order was countermanded, along with the more important mix-up as to where the *Powhattan* was to go—Sumter or Pickens. Finally, Seward may have intended his projected demands for explanations to be a rattle of the saber, a way of warning Europe against premature recognition of the Confederacy.[12]

President Lincoln's handling of Seward's suggestion managed to reject the "thoughts" out of hand without embarrassing Seward publicly or flattening him so thoroughly that he would have to resign. The dignity of Lincoln's reply saved the older man's career and enabled him to go on to eight years of highly effective work. "I remark that if this must be done, I must do it," wrote the president, and with that, the lines of authority were at last clearly established: Seward knew where he stood. The secretary himself deserves credit for the manly, unsulking way he accepted the new situation. Within hours he was writing politely to Mercier and filling him in on American objections

---

[12] On the threat to Haiti, see Harral E. Landry, "Slavery and the Slave Trade in Atlantic Diplomacy, 1850-1861," *Journal of Southern History*, xxvii (1961), 184-207. On the threat to Mexico, the French ships, and Lincoln's mistake, see Henry W. Temple, "William H. Seward," in Bemis, *American Secretaries of State*, vii, 30-31; Faulkner to Black, Paris, 4 March 1861, State Dept. Corres., France, Dispatches, xlix, no. 108; Nicolay and Hay, iii, 439-41. See also James Morton Callahan, *Evolution of Seward's Mexican Policy* (Morgantown: West Virginia University, 1909), p. 19, and Blumenthal, *Franco-American Relations*, pp. 122-23.

to the Spanish naval moves. He hoped that France would associate herself with the United States' position, a statement to which he probably expected no reply and which apparently received none beyond an equally polite acknowledgment.[13]

Henri Mercier saw no reason in the events of March to change his basic analysis of the American situation, an analysis he had favored all winter long: the sectional rupture was all but final; conciliatory efforts had some chance of success, but not much. The winds of war and peace were changing hourly. With Confederate commissioners on their way to Europe, Mercier had some advice to offer his government:

As long as the imperial government sees any chance for the reestablishment of the Union, I know it will not want to risk spoiling it by a premature recognition of the new confederation; but from the day when it becomes convinced that such a chance no longer exists, I ask myself what would be the preferable side to take, for us and for all European governments, as between the requests of the confederated Southern states, who will urge immediate recognition, and those of the Washington government, who will insist with equal vigor that such recognition in any case not be extended before she herself has acted first.

The state of the question, he continued, should be examined under four headings: law, expediency, diplomatic interest, and commercial interest.

[13] Lincoln to Seward, Washington, 1 April 1861, in Nicolay and Hay, III, 448-49; Case, *Revue d'histoire diplomatique*, LXXVII (1963), 305; Seward to Mercier, Washington, 2 April 1861, State Dept. Corres., Notes to the French Legation, VII, 55-56; Mercier to Thouvenel, Washington, 8 April 1861, AMAE, CP, E-U, 124: 148-58, no. 31.

So far as law went, he thought the United States had no case in opposing recognition. She herself had sent Ambrose Dudley Mann to Hungary in 1848 to look into the claims of the revolutionary government there. As for expediency and diplomatic interest, there surely was no bond of principle between the European monarchies and the American republic. In the North they were counting on the liberal governments' aversion to slavery. But considerations of self-interest were bound to matter more to governments than the antislavery principle. Diplomatic relations between Europe and America had always been determined by the traditional American policy of nonentanglement. In the present situation, therefore, European courts would mainly be concerned with the simple, negative problem of not poisoning those relations.

The final consideration, however, was the most important one—commerce. Europe's trade with America, he noted, was enormous and vital. Any cessation or even disturbance of this trade would severely affect Europe, and such disturbance would have to be faced if civil war broke out. The North would strike at Southern exports and provoke a servile war; the South would commission privateers to prey upon Northern merchantmen. If there were no recognition prior to such hostilities, European merchants would have either to submit to whatever measures Washington might take, or ask for recognition of the South, a step which in that future context would be taken as unfriendly by the North: "These reflections, Mr. Minister, seem to show that if [civil] war is inevitable, recognition must come before the outbreak of that war."

Mercier felt that the first conclusion to be drawn from the danger of Washington's anger was the need for close cooperation among the great powers, and especially between France and Great Britain. Such unanimity would even make it easier for the North to swallow the pill which

Europe would administer. Finally, recognition of the Confederacy should be held up so long as "this great republic" had a chance of surviving intact; that as soon as such survival became impossible, France should "seize the moment when she might ready the two groups for some peaceful accommodation," and that this should be done in concert with Britain.[14]

We may well ask, "What moment?" Mercier had set his government a nearly impossible task—to pick a precise point in time, a day or hour *before* the outbreak of war, when it would be clear that the Union could no longer be reunited. We know, of course, that even after months and years of fighting, even after stunning Northern defeats, that hour never did come. We know the inflexible will to national survival of the Lincoln administration and how it forbade the arrival of such an hour. Mercier, in three years of facing and probing that wall of determination, never did accept its impenetrability as an irreversible fact. Perhaps he was being less than frank with his government: perhaps he had already decided that the hour for recognition had arrived. It is important, however, to note that he did not say this. If he had such an opinion, he kept it within his own breast. Contrary to the statements of some observers, the plain, simple fact is that he did not recommend diplomatic recognition.[15]

[14] Mercier to Thouvenel, Washington, 29 March 1861, *ibid.*, fol. 121-29, no. 29, on which the preceding account of Mercier's thought is based except where otherwise noted.

[15] It is clear from Mercier's context that he was referring to diplomatic recognition of the independence of the Confederacy. The familiar distinction between diplomatic recognition and recognition of belligerency had yet to be refined in its application to the American conflict.

Glyndon Van Deusen, Henry Blumenthal, and T. K. Lothrop state flatly that Mercier recommended recognition of the Confederacy at this time (Glyndon G. Van Deusen, *William Henry Seward* [New York: Oxford University Press, 1967], p. 271; Blumenthal, p. 123;

If Mercier did feel that the moment for recognition had already arrived, then his capstone suggestion, made in this same dispatch of 29 March, was even more dangerous than it actually appeared to Thouvenel:

> The choice of this moment, I admit is quite hard to determine. In the best of circumstances an exchange of letters between Europe and America requires at least a month, and in one month events can go rather far.
>
> I see only one way to allow for this difficulty to any extent, namely that the European governments, after they have agreed to act simultaneously, grant their representatives the necessary authority to extend recognition, when those representatives judge it possible to do so in a way most consistent with identical instructions.[16]

In the next few days Mercier began to realize how little leeway there might be for diplomatic action before an outbreak. Washington began to bristle with expectation of a fight, and Mercier got wind of Lincoln's plan to ask for 75,000 volunteers and to call Congress into special session, a plan which the president kept in his desk until after the

---

Thornton Kirkland Lothrop, *William Henry Seward* [Boston: Houghton Mifflin Co., 1899], p. 320). C. F. Adams, Jr., says that "in the better informed circles it was whispered" that Mercier was "suggesting" formal recognition, an observation which is probably accurate (Charles F. Adams, Jr., *Charles Francis Adams* [Boston: Houghton Mifflin Co., 1900], p. 154). Korolewicz-Carlton says that Mercier favored recognition, which is accurate enough if we take "favored" carefully (Korolewicz-Carlton, p. 126). E. A. Adamov makes the most uninhibited comment, alleging that from the beginning of 1861, Lyons and Mercier urged the United States to accept British-French-Russian mediation (E. A. Adamov, "Russia and the United States at the Time of the Civil War," *Journal of Modern History*, II [1930], 589).

[16] Mercier to Thouvenel, Washington, 29 March 1861, AMAE, CP, E-U, 124: 121-29, no. 29.

South had begun the war. The French minister was able to cite Lyons in support of the view that some sort of recognition should precede hostilities. Lyons, however, declined to join Mercier in asking for decision-making authority.[17]

THE BEGINNING OF THE WAR

During the week after Mercier's first report of warlike goings-on, the most fateful episode in America's life exploded into world history. On the afternoon of April 11, General Beauregard's surrender demand was presented to Major Anderson at Fort Sumter. Later that day the secretary of state was seated in General Scott's lodgings on Pennsylvania Avenue, enjoying a quiet dinner. Silently he read the telegram which was brought in to Scott; he then suggested it be thrown into the fire, before which some bottles of claret were mellowing. The slouching, cigar-smoking New York politician is not everyone's picture of a swashbuckling hero, but in the months ahead his flamboyant duelling matches with Palmerston, Russell, and Lyons, with Napoleon III, Thouvenel, and Mercier, came to deserve some sort of baroque comparison. During the night, Beauregard's guns began, and a little after that, Seward drew his sword for the first time.[18]

Mercier was already suffering a slight recurrence of his allergy to the United States, as well as real physical trouble with his eyes. The harrowing events of April must have alarmed and disgusted Cécile-Élisabeth, and the need to

[17] Mercier to Thouvenel, Washington, 8 April 1861, *ibid.*, fol. 148-58, no. 31; Mercier to Thouvenel, Washington, 15 April 1861, *ibid.*, fol. 154-60, no. 32. Mercier also informed the Russian minister of his opinions and his conversation with Lyons. Stoeckl thought that Russia could let Britain and France take the lead in recognition, then follow along without seeming to be in concert with them (Stoeckl to Gorchakov, Washington, 2/14 April 1861, Stoeckl Papers).

[18] Randall and Donald, pp. 174-77; Charles Winslow Elliott, *Winfield Scott, the Soldier and the Man* (New York: Macmillan Co., 1937), pp. 708-09.

respect her feelings and to protect her and the two children seriously complicated her husband's feelings about his work. Mercier, in fact, expected the South to strike for the capital within two weeks. "Furthermore," he wrote, "without actually being afraid, I am beginning to find that my wife and babies are a bit too much baggage, and I wonder whether I should keep them with me or send them to a safe place."[19]

At the beginning of the Civil War, the federal government had only ninety fighting vessels and only forty-two in commission, most of which were on foreign station. Only three steam-propelled ships were immediately available for active service. In these circumstances to declare a blockade of the Confederate ports was a notable act of confidence. It was bound to raise sticky issues with maritime powers whose self-respect, concern for their merchants' rights, and worry about economic dislocation would guarantee a lively diplomatic exchange. On 19 April, nevertheless, President Lincoln proclaimed a blockade of South Carolina, Georgia, Alabama, Florida, Mississippi, Louisiana, and Texas; North Carolina and Virginia were added a week later as newcomers to the Confederacy. As the war went on, Secretary Welles was able to bring about a progressive increase in naval strength, and consequently the blockade came ever closer to being "effective." But the year 1861 was partly the year of the paper blockade, and Seward faced a great many inquiries.[20]

One point raised by the proclamation of a blockade was the view it implied of the Confederacy as an existent, belligerent polity. The call for volunteers had spoken of crush-

[19] Mercier to Thouvenel, Washington, 25 April 1861, AMAE, MD, Papiers Thouvenel, XIII, 359-61.

[20] Frank Lawrence Owsley, "America and the Freedom of the Seas, 1861-65," in *Essays in Honor of William E. Dodd*, ed. Avery Craven (Chicago: University of Chicago Press, 1935), pp. 196-99; Randall and Donald, pp. 275 and 440; Case and Spencer, pp. 126-48.

ing a rebellion, and even the blockade proclamation listed the states individually rather than countenance their confederation. Inevitably, however, the blockade gave a handle to all those who insisted that the United States was actually at war. London, Paris, and the others could scarcely be expected to submit their merchants to search and seizure by Union cruisers and at the same time be refused the status of neutral powers. But neutral status, of course, would imply the existence of two functioning states at war with each other, a view which Washington found intolerable. Thus by proclaiming a blockade, the federal government did much to undermine its own somewhat unrealistic claim that the Confederacy was merely a rebellion.[21]

If the North was embarrassed for ships at the start of the war, the South was destitute. As Mercier had foreseen, the South turned to what had been the classic American move in similar conditions, the commissioning of privateers. Though the first Confederate letter of marque was not issued until 18 May, and though privateers turned out to be ineffectual weapons, the matter was of serious diplomatic import in the first year of the war.

Europe viewed both the blockade and the matter of privateers in the light of the four-point declaration made at the Congress of Paris in 1856. The United States had not yet adhered to this liberal statement, but the inevitable object of French and British diplomacy was to achieve the condition envisioned in the four points:

1. Privateering is and remains abolished.

2. The neutral flag covers enemy's goods, with the exception of contraband of war.

[21] See, e.g., Philip Van Doren Stern, *When the Guns Roared: World Aspects of the American Civil War* (New York: Doubleday & Co., 1965), p. 63; Foster Rhea Dulles, *Prelude to World Power: American Diplomatic History, 1860-1900* (New York: Macmillan Co., 1965), p. 5; Lyons to Russell, Washington, 15 April 1861, Newton, I, 36-37.

3. Neutral goods, with the exception of contraband of war, are not liable to capture under an enemy's flag.

4. Blockades, in order to be binding, must be effective; that is to say, maintained by forces strong enough to prevent access to the coast of the enemy.[22]

That same historical reliance on privateering as a weapon in reserve had made President Franklin Pierce hesitate when the United States was first invited to adhere to the Declaration of Paris. Through William L. Marcy, his secretary of state, he counterproposed what came to be called the Marcy amendment: that all privately owned property, even the property of persons whose country was at war, be exempted from capture by armed vessels. The opposition of Great Britain and the fact that no amendment could be made without the unanimous consent of all the Paris signatories forestalled American adherence all through the Buchanan administration. There the matter remained when the Republicans took office in 1861.

Seward soon saw the possibilities of the situation. The South had not yet declared officially that it would issue letters of marque. If he could adhere quickly to the Declaration of Paris, Britain and France might ·be angled into the position of having to help Washington against Confederate corsairs. "Privateering is and remains abolished" is a relatively unequivocal statement; the matter of "effective" as applied to "blockade" could always be discussed, if necessary, to the end of the war. The secretary, therefore, notified Charles Francis Adams and William L. Dayton, the new ministers to London and Paris, that they should begin conversations, but he failed to emphasize for Dayton's bene-

[22] Stern, pp. 50-51 and 65; William Morrison Robinson, Jr., *The Confederate Privateers* (New Haven: Yale University Press, 1928), p. 343.

fit that the Marcy amendment was a dead issue. We shall follow this thread later.[23]

Mercier transmitted Seward's blockade notice on 27 April. He assured Thouvenel that in acknowledging its receipt, he had made it clear to Seward that France did not regard it as "a real notification, the date of which would mark the beginning of blockade rights."[24] He indirectly let his chief know that he was cognizant of the need for a blockade to be effective, and he noted with satisfaction Seward's wish to adhere to the 1856 declaration. (So far, at least, the old New York professional was one step ahead of his French colleague on those implications.) As for privateers, Mercier asked for instructions and correctly anticipated the whole thrust of Anglo-French diplomacy on the question of neutral rights. "It seems to me all the federal government can demand of us . . . is a strict neutrality between the belligerent parties." That neutrality could be and was maintained without recognition of Southern independence, viz., by recognition of Southern belligerency.

Thouvenel expressed his reaction to all this in a dispatch written in the last week of the month. By that time he had read everything of Mercier's to 8 April; he knew, that is, that fighting was about to begin and that Lincoln would probably call for volunteers and a special session of Congress. In addition, his conversations with American representatives enabled him to make preliminary soundings about the likely course of events. Faulkner, though a Virginian and ultimately a Confederate supporter, doggedly

[23] Temple, pp. 39 and 42-45; Seward to Dayton, Washington, 24 April 1861, State Dept. Corres., France, Instructions, xv, 522-26, no. 4.

[24] Thouvenel was unworried about "real notification." He took the stance that a blockade began when the first merchantman was stopped by a naval vessel.

performed his duties as Washington minister to the very last, staying some time beyond the point which the new new administration thought proper.[25] His predictions of how things would develop were colored by the Buchanan philosophy of limitations on federal power. As he wrote to Seward, "I cannot suppose that any Administration can be so mad and reckless as to attempt the exercise of force against the seceding states."[26]

Later in April Thouvenel spoke with Henry S. Sanford, United States minister to Belgium, who spent much of April and May in Paris; Seward could patently not work through Faulkner, and Dayton had not yet arrived. Mercier's own insistence on the importance of commerce appears to have impressed Thouvenel. The foreign minister stressed to Sanford that commercial considerations were France's chief worry vis-à-vis the American troubles, but that, far from doing anything to add to those troubles, France would profoundly regret the separation of the states.[27]

Thouvenel, in his instruction of 25 April, used this conversation with Sanford as the framework for describing French policy. He agreed with Mercier that the most important thing to know was the right moment, if any, for recognizing the Confederacy. Taking up some of the phrases Mercier had used, he told Sanford that "from the moment

[25] Sanford to Seward, London, 27 April 1861, State Dept. Corres., Belgium, Dispatches, v, unnumbered.

[26] Faulkner to Seward, Paris, 5 April 1861, State Dept. Corres., France, Dispatches, XLIX, no. 117.

[27] Sanford had arrived in Paris on 15 April. For over a week he was stymied by Thouvenel's insistence that he operate through the American legation, where Faulkner was stubbornly clinging to the helm. Thouvenel finally did see Sanford privately on 24 April (Sanford to Seward, Paris, 19 and 25 April 1861, State Dept. Corres., Belgium, Dispatches, v, unnumbered). See also Case and Spencer, pp. 28-31.

when it could be proven that a *fait accompli* had become irreversible, we would of course have to consider our own interests." Despite the foreign minister's insistence that France regretted American disunity, the overall effect of this conversation was not entirely to Washington's taste. In answer to particular inquiries, Thouvenel made it clear that he must put the rights of French merchants first in any question about Washington's authority over trade, and that American ships would be allowed into French ports without any close scrutiny of what flag they were flying. Realizing what impression this would make on Seward, he asked Mercier to see the secretary soon and make it clear that France wanted nothing else save peace and an undivided American Union.[28]

There was as yet no immediate question of European mediation or other intervention, though Seward did use the word in one of his early salvos: "Foreign intervention would oblige us to treat those who should yield it [*sic*] as allies of the insurrectionary party; and to carry on the war against them as enemies."[29] This attitude, however, did not prevent Seward from approving a visit to Richmond by Rudolf Schleiden, minister from Bremen. Schleiden, apparently, was expected to make armistice soundings, but nothing much came of it.[30] In that same week some of the residents of Washington went to Baron von Gerolt, the Prussian minister, and suggested that the diplomatic corps try to effect an armistice. Gerolt thought that Seward might be receptive,

[28] Thouvenel to Mercier, Paris, 25 April 1861, AMAE, CP, E-U, 124: 161-63, no. 6. See also Case, *Revue d'histoire diplomatique*, LXXVII (1963), 298-301.

[29] Seward to Dayton, Washington, 22 April 1861, State Dept. Corres., France, Instructions, XV, 506-21, no. 3, which is also in *For. Rel. U.S.*, 1861, pp. 195-200.

[30] Lutz, *Annual Report of the American Historical Association, 1915*, pp. 207-22; E. D. Adams, I, 121-23.

but Lyons saw no good in the notion, and neither did Mercier.[31]

Though Seward could hardly have expected Faulkner to mirror a Republican view of things, he was annoyed when he read the Southerner's report of his talk with Thouvenel. In a letter to his wife, Seward pictured himself as a sort of Horatio, defending the Union against Anglo-French threats to break the blockade. In fact he spent much of May in a sort of blustering frenzy, designed, probably, to keep Europe off balance. For Thouvenel's edification he primed Dayton with solid, nationalist declamations, most notably in his celebrated dispatch of 4 May: "You cannot be too decided or too explicit in making known to the French government that there is not now, nor has there been, nor will there be, any the least idea existing in this government of suffering a dissolution of this Union to take place in any way whatever."[32]

Seward was the secretary of state who began annual publication of selected diplomatic documents in *Foreign Relations of the United States*. Publication, in fact, was a diplomatic tool which he began to use almost immediately upon taking office. Wishing to coalesce Union emotion while clarifying the government's adamant nationalism, he gave the Faulkner note and his own clarion reply to the press.

Mercier, far from advocating an effort to break the blockade, told Thouvenel that he did not see "by what right we could stop the Americans from doing to their own ports

[31] Lyons to Russell, Washington, 27 April 1861, in C. F. Adams, Jr., *Massachusetts Historical Society Proceedings*, XLVIII (1915), 227.

[32] Seward to Mrs. Seward [Washington], 2 May 1861, in Burton J. Hendrick, *Lincoln's War Cabinet* (Boston: Little, Brown and Co., 1946), pp. 192-93; Seward to Dayton, Washington, 4 May 1861, State Dept. Corres., France, Instructions, xv, 530-33, no. 7, also in *For. Rel. U.S.*, 1861, pp. 206-07.

what we would not dream of stopping them from doing to foreign ports." This was scarcely a penetrating analysis since the whole point was whether or not Charleston and New Orleans *were* Washington's "own ports." Somewhat inconsistently Mercier agreed that the blockade was ineffective but stated that "from the moment when they speak of establishing an effective blockade, we have nothing more we can rightfully ask of them." What could be and was asked, of course, was precisely the question of real effectiveness as opposed to what Washington might speak about. By 1863, Jefferson Davis was positively apoplectic over Europe's failure to break what he still claimed was an ineffective blockade.

Mercier did think that the United States should be put on notice that if the blockade lasted through autumn, and the French economy began to slump, France might have to act in self-preservation. By that time, he thought, the Civil War would at least be suspended, and he hoped that he himself would be in Paris, talking it all over with his old friend: "All that I ask is for you to recall me to Europe and send me to some post where I can do better work, and I ask this more for my family's sake than my own. But pardon me, my dear friend, for bothering you so often with my complaints."[33]

[33] Mercier to Thouvenel, Washington, 6 May 1861, AMAE, MD, Papiers Thouvenel, XIII, 362-65. See also Lyons to Russell, Washington, 6 May 1861, in C. F. Adams, *Massachusetts Historical Society Proceedings,* XLVIII (1915), 231.

Callahan is wrong in stating that Mercier advised blockade-breaking in early May (James Morton Callahan, "Diplomatic Relations of the Confederate States with England, 1861-1865," *Annual Report of the American Historical Association, 1898* [Washington: U.S. Government Printing Office, 1899], 265-83).

Mercier appended to his letter a bit of historical flotsam, a letter home from Count Louis Barbe Serrurier, the then French minister in Washington, dated 14 January 1813. Serrurier alluded to the an-

The two-week delivery time for messages from Europe continued to hamper diplomatic reaction throughout the war, but was perhaps most frustrating in these early, formative weeks. It was late May before Mercier was able to take Thouvenel's note of his interview with Sanford to Seward, by which time it was quite stale. Seward, with a politeness bordering on the sarcastic, wrote thank-you notes to both Mercier and Thouvenel for Sanford's cordial reception and for being allowed to read the subsequent French essay. His additional remarks show the kind of unreserved sass which was quickly becoming his trademark:

> France, we know, wishes us well and she of course, is careful for herself. Let her avoid giving any countenance to treason against this Government. Foreign intervention would ultimately drive the whole people of the United States to unanimity, but the sympathies which have so long existed between the U.S. and France would in that case perhaps forever cease.[34]

---

nulment of the marriage between Jerome Bonaparte and Elisabeth Patterson, and he added a thought which Mercier found very apt: "The United States, Sir, have become unbearable to me; I owe it to my health and well-being to be allowed to leave" (AMAE, MD, Papiers Thouvenel, XIII, 366-67).

[34] Seward to Mercier, Washington, 23 May 1861, State Dept. Corres., Notes to the French Legation, VII, 57-58; Seward to Thouvenel, Washington, 24 May 1861, *ibid.*, fol. 58-59. See also Case and Spencer, pp. 35-37.

Mercier acknowledged receipt of Thouvenel's note in his own return dispatch (Mercier to Thouvenel, Washington, 20 May 1861, AMAE, CP, E-U, 124: 219-24, no. 37), but he probably had received it before then. Knowing Seward's ire, he may have thought it best to delay presentation. Korolewicz-Carlton, pursuing his Mercier vs. Thouvenel thesis, seems unduly harsh on Mercier in this matter, and accuses him of missing the last chance to guarantee good relations with America. Mercier, that is, should have hurried downtown with Thouvenel's dovelike dispatch (Korolewicz-Carlton, pp. 26-27). It may be noted that this same dispatch contained news which Thou-

On 13 May, the British had issued their proclamation of neutrality and recognition of Confederate belligerency; France waited an additional four weeks till 10 June. Weaving through these complications, Seward zigzagged with bellicose speeches written up as diplomatic notes, efforts to widen the Anglo-French split, and his own Declaration of Paris maneuver. And in the month between the British announcement and that of his own government, Thouvenel laid down the French line for Mercier's guidance.

France, he said, wished well to an undivided America but must look to her own interests first and last. Nor could France take a position on the constitutional questions involved in secession. But there, in fact, was the South, a vast region governed by a functioning authority which looked for all the world like a government. France must therefore regard the Americans as "two belligerents, using against each other the force at their disposal, in accordance with the principles of international law." In the face of Union blockade and Confederate privateers, France must protect her people.

More than that, the emperor's government stood ready to offer "words of peace and conciliation in line with the friendliness and loyalty of our . . . relations with Washington." But the emperor would intrude only if asked by Washington and only to help preserve the Union. This wan hope of friendly mediation may help explain that four-week gap between the British and French proclamations of neutrality, but it should not be overstressed: Thouvenel made it clear that North and South would be treated as "two belligerents."[35]

---

venel himself feared would exasperate Seward. In fine, it was the combination of American nationalism and French neutrality which strained relations, not Henri Mercier.

[35] Thouvenel to Mercier, Paris, 11 and 16 May 1861, AMAE, CP, E-U, 124: 194-201, 202-06, 216-17, nos. 7, 7 *bis*, and 8. See also Sanford

The queen's neutrality proclamation of 13 May was the worst thing the British had done since the days of Charles II, according to Senator Sumner of Massachusetts. On that same day, Charles Francis Adams landed at Liverpool, too late to argue against the deed. The achievement of a *fait accompli* was surely one reason for the British haste, a haste which would be an issue for ten more years, all during the war and the negotiations over the *Alabama* claims.[36]

This haste, moreover, threatened to some degree that closely concerted entente which both London and Paris prized and which Lyons and Mercier dutifully sought to effect in Washington. One point of difference concerned Seward's effort to adhere to the 1856 declaration. Lord John Russell was of the opinion that such an act could usefully bind the North in the matter of the first clause, the abolition of privateering. Thouvenel, however, had suspected Seward's ulterior motive; he felt that if Britain and France let Washington join them in outlawing privateers, they would be seriously embarrassed if later requested to enforce this agreement against those "American" privateers commissioned by Jefferson Davis. For his part, therefore, Thouvenel stressed only the second and third clauses in his letter to Mercier of 11 May. By the eighteenth, Russell had come partly around to the French view, but even so, his note asked Lyons to encourage Washington's acceptance of the first clause; Lyons should specify that this would not be applied against Southern privateers. Thouvenel alerted Mercier to this slight crack in the Anglo-French

---

to Seward, Paris, 12 May 1861, State Dept. Corres., Belgium, Dispatches, v, unnumbered; Dayton to Seward, Paris, 22 May 1861, State Dept. Corres., France, Dispatches, L, no. 5. For a full treatment of the whole recognition issue, see Case and Spencer, pp. 45-76.

[36] C. F. Adams, Jr., *Charles Francis Adams*, pp. 171-72; Stern, *When the Guns Roared*, p. 44.

front. He stressed the absolute need for close agreement with Lyons in approaching Seward.[37]

For their part, Mercier and Lyons seemed at this point to be in closer harmony than their governments. They realized more clearly than Russell that Seward should not be approached with any antiprivateering proposal. Should Lyons seek to except Southern privateering from Britain's responsibility, as Russell suggested, this would enrage the American secretary. With the British declaration of neutrality imminent and the French delayed, Lyons's worries were notably increased. Seward, confused as to whether there really was anything much in the Anglo-French split, wavered between attacks on the entente as an unfriendly combination and efforts to break it up by speaking softly to France. He penned his famous bellicose letter to Adams, the one which Lincoln had to tone down in the interests of peace. If Britain should recognize the South as a belligerent, Seward had written, "the law of nations afford an adequate and proper remedy and we shall avail ourselves of it." The president wisely took out that last clause.[38]

Nothing is more certain about the diplomatic history of the Civil War than the close, harmonious working of the

[37] Thouvenel to Mercier, Paris, 11 May 1861, AMAE, CP, E-U, 124: 194-201, no. 7; Russell to Lyons, London, 18 May 1861, *Sessional Papers*, LXII (1862), 542, no. 8; E. D. Adams, I, 157-63; Case and Spencer, pp. 83-85.

[38] Seward to Adams, Washington, 21 May 1861, *Abraham Lincoln, Collected Works*, ed. Roy P. Basler (New Brunswick, N.J.: Rutgers University Press, 1953-1955), IV, 376-80; E. D. Adams, I, 162-63; Van Deusen, *William Henry Seward*, pp. 296-98.

Lyons was so fearful of war with the United States that he warned Sir Edmund Head, Governor-General of Canada, to take proper defensive measures. Seward had said in 1860 that the United States might compensate herself for losing the South by annexing Canada, and his mood in May 1861 presaged a literal implementation of this policy (Lyons to Head, Washington, 22 May 1861, Newton, I, 39-40).

long-established Anglo-French entente. In a private letter probably written in the last week of the month, Mercier let himself range widely over the field of possibilities, including those bearing upon this understanding.[39] He began by underlining Seward's agitated state of mind:

> Mr. Seward is definitely beside himself; there is no longer any way to talk sense to him. Lord Lyons, who is surely the least provoking of men, no longer knows how to approach him. At heart, Seward is nothing but one of those demagogues who can sail only on the sea of popular emotion and who always try to stir up passion in order to exploit it.

The arguments for close cooperation between France and Britain, Mercier continued, were obvious. If America had to be offended, better to share the responsibility. Even more, mutual trouble with the United States would help draw the two European nations closer together, if such were the object of French diplomacy. But what of tomorrow? A place to buy cotton and a place to sell products—this was America's chief commercial meaning for France, a meaning which would continue only if there were peace. Peace was the main object; perhaps a foreign intervention would be indicated some time in the future, but certainly not at the moment. "Already many eyes are turning to Europe—in

---

[39] Mercier to Thouvenel, Washington, "22 January" [1861], AMAE, MD, Papiers Thouvenel, XIII, 345-49.

The date "*22 janvier*" is on this document, and the letter has accordingly been filed before all other letters from Mercier to Thouvenel of 1861. Internal evidence, however, rules out both 22 January 1861 and possibly 22 January 1862. It is clear, for example, that Seward was already secretary of state when this dispatch was written, and that he himself was writing dispatches to Dayton based on information he had received from Sanford (fol. 345). Also, Mercier asks Thouvenel that financial help be given the French-language New York newspaper *Courrier des États-Unis*, which had lost its Southern subscribers "since the crisis" (fol. 349).

the North with anxiety, in the South with hope, and circumstances might develop so that Europe could be asked to solve the question."

One thing was certain in Mercier's view: it was in the North and West, not in the South, that the sources of American vitality were located, and it was in the French interest that these forces be organized into a great and powerful state. Even without the South, the United States would be an enormously strong polity; it would continue to have, like England, "a huge merchant marine, iron like hers, coal and cotton, the same aptitudes, the same greed, the same bumptious roughness, . . . it will be her real rival in the world, and since its field of action will not be Europe, by the same token it will be our ally." Mercier continued that France could do nothing to bring any of this about, but should nevertheless keep it in mind: "But if Britain wants to act in her own way, it seems to me that, if possible, it would be well to let her become involved in the contest and to stay in the North's favor as much as possible without renouncing the South."

Fort Sumter had been taken, and though as yet there had been no pitched battles, the Civil War had begun. The moment had passed—in fact it had never come—for recognizing the South prior to the outbreak of fighting. From this time on, Mercier was consistent about two basic and interrelated points. First, he considered American territorial integrity, the Union of all thirty-four states, a difficult nationalist dream; all-out war to preserve such a dream would be an abomination. Second, he felt that the industrial future of a united North and West dictated the need for good relations between Paris and Washington.

INTERVIEWS WITH SEWARD

By 1 June, much of the diplomatic air in Washington had been cleared. Mercier had his instructions. He knew that he should continue cooperating as closely as possible with Lord Lyons, that France would soon recognize the South as a belligerent power and would maintain her own self-interest as a neutral in the Civil War. The whole problem of privateering was not such an obstacle, since Lyons agreed with the French about the uselessness of trying to beat Seward at his game. It was now a matter of formally notifying the secretary of state, of letting him know quietly but firmly what kind of limits Europe had set to the aims of Union diplomacy.

Mercier's first reaction to this assignment was a crashing understatement: "The circumstances require a great deal of circumspection and tact."[40] In fact he went to the state department on Thursday, 6 June, for a tactful talk with Seward. He read to the secretary Thouvenel's account of his second conversation with Sanford, the one in which Napoleon III's availability as mediator was strongly suggested. This brought up a point which Seward already knew from Dayton and which perhaps had seemed another chance to pry France loose from Britain: the emperor's preference for an American settlement based on a reunited Union. Lyons, in fact, was much troubled about these reports; Seward for his part was aware that the basic thrust of French policy was neutrality in concert with Britain. He therefore politely declined the proffered good offices. But he was still intrigued with Napoleon's alleged interest in preserving the Union, and he asked Mercier to leave him Thouvenel's dispatch of his interview with Sanford. He also gave Mercier a little lecture on the weakness of the South, its imminent demise, and so on.

[40] Mercier to Thouvenel, Washington, 2 June 1861, *ibid.*, fol. 371-72. Seward's ire was also caused by the reported reception of Southern commissioners in London and Paris (Case and Spencer, pp. 64-67).

76

Mercier's rejoinder was equally predictable. France loved the United States and wanted her strong but must protect the interests of her own merchants. The main thing was for everything to be discussed *calmly*. And if French policy accorded with British, "it is entirely natural that we should concert our diplomatic moves; for example, I can tell you that one of these days Lord Lyons and I will have a communication to make to you on the subject of neutral rights." Mercier then invited Seward to read the legal-historical defense of French neutrality which Thouvenel had sent him, and he left both this and the dispatch of the Sanford interview in Seward's hands.[41]

When Seward failed to return Mercier's documents promptly, Lyons again feared that Washington expected some sort of help from France. Mercier too was curious about the delay, and after talking it over with Lyons, went back to the state department on Thursday, 13 June. Seward urged him to refrain from any official démarche since the United States would readily concede full maritime rights to Britain and France, viz., the safety of enemy goods under a friendly flag and of neutral goods under an enemy flag. This, of course, was not to be taken as an admission of a state of war; in Seward's view it was still a matter of suppressing a rebellion. Mercier went right to the British legation to talk this over with Lyons and then wrote immediately to Paris.

He added his opinion that it was the uplift to Southern morale which Seward found most galling in the Anglo-French position; and he apologized for being so tender and hesitant with Seward and for abusing the latitude Thouvenel had granted concerning the manner of approach-

[41] Mercier to Thouvenel, Washington, 10 June 1861, AMAE, CP, E-U, 124: 301-10, no. 41; Lyons to Russell, Washington, 10 June 1861, Newton, I, 43-46. See also Case and Spencer, pp. 67-69.

ing him.[42] So far, in fact, no official notice had been tendered of French neutrality. Mercier need not have worried. The French proclamation had been held up until 10 June; and before being filed away for history, his dispatch was given a marginal notation of approval.

One point which came up in this meeting of 13 June concerned that confusion over the first clause, the abolition of privateering. Seward suggested that France use her navy to protect her shipping from Southern privateers; Mercier answered that France had no wish to do anything unfitting for a neutral power. This confusion about neutral responsibilities and rights seems to have impressed Lyons with the need to stop beating about the bush and make an official representation at the state department. Despite Seward's strong, express opposition to this, Mercier felt too that it was time for a formal move. On Saturday, 15 June, he and Lyons went to see Seward. Rarely if ever had an American secretary of state been so sharply brought up against the Anglo-French entente.[43]

Lyons and Mercier may have arrived at the department separately that morning, but they were together by the time a messenger brought word to Seward in his office. The secretary directed that they be asked to wait in the office of his son, Acting Secretary Frederick W. Seward, who greeted them politely and showed them to a sofa. As Frederick told it some years afterward:

A few minutes later, as the two Ministers were seated, side by side, on the sofa, the door opened, and Seward entered. Smiling and shaking his head, he said:

---

[42] Seward, in fact, was much irritated, or at least seemed so to the diplomats. His irritation, of course, may have been bluster intended to keep Europe off balance (see Stoeckl to Gorchakov, Washington, 29 May/10 June 1861, no. 41, Stoeckl Papers).

[43] Mercier to Thouvenel, Washington, 14 June 1861, AMAE, CP, E-U, 124: 311-18, no. 42; Korolewicz-Carlton, p. 53; E. D. Adams, I, 164.

"No,—no,—no. This will never do. I cannot see you in that way."

In Frederick's version, Seward, who had "instinctively guessed" why they were there, refused to let them state their business. Instead, he asked Lyons to stay and talk, and he invited Mercier to have dinner with him that evening.[44]

Frederick's colorful account, of which the above is the introduction, may not be entirely reliable. It seems more likely that Mercier and Lyons, while not "officially received" that morning any more than they had been on other occasions in the last ten days, did stay there and talk with Seward for several minutes at least. There is no independent record that Mercier left while Lyons stayed, nor that Mercier dined with Seward that evening. The fact that Frederick's account has his father "instinctively guessing" why Lyons and Mercier had come perhaps indicates its imperfect understanding. In fact, as we have seen, Mercier and Seward had talked about such a visit, and its objective, for several days. It is possible, however, that Seward did speak separately with the ministers, a development which is compatible with the short, unofficial joint conversation hypothesized here.[45]

[44] F. W. Seward, *Seward at Washington*, I, 581-82. Frederick wrote a slightly different version of the incident in *Reminiscences of a War-time Statesman*, pp. 178-79. For an excellent recent account of the interview, see Case and Spencer, pp. 70-73.

[45] The following account of the interview is based principally on two letters: Mercier to Thouvenel, Washington 18 June 1861, AMAE, CP, E-U, 124: 338-45, no. 43; Lyons to Russell, Washington, 17 June 1861, *Sessional Papers*, LXII (1862), 545-46, no. 14. See also Seward to Dayton, Washington, 17 June 1861, State Dept. Corres., France, Instructions, XVI, 1-12, no. 19, also in *For. Rel. U.S.*, 1861, pp. 224-28. Seward's version implies that the interview had been previously arranged and that he was not surprised. Stoeckl reported simply that Seward refused to discuss this matter in Washington and told Lyons and Mercier that he preferred to negotiate in Europe (Stoeckl to Gorchakov, Washington, 5/17 June 1861, no. 42, Stoeckl Papers).

Lyons began the official part of the meeting, saying that Seward must know why they had come, since Mercier had discussed it with him already. He courteously asked Seward how he would like the diplomatic communication to be made. Seward said that he had already read the French legal-historical exposition, and Mercier pointed out how it both conformed to the British position and indicated the direction of French policy. Seward then said he could not possibly receive officially any communication based on treating the Confederacy as a belligerent. In another fending, stalling maneuver, he asked that any further discussion be carried on in Europe through Adams and Dayton. Mercier wanted to make sure he had understood:

> "That is to say," I replied, "that you prefer to handle the question in Paris and London rather than through us?"
>
> "Just so," he answered. He added that in addition he would keep us informed about everything he wrote to Paris and London and that he would be very much obliged if we, for our part, could give him exact information on the views of our governments by letting him have the instructions we had received, in confidence and only for his personal use. We hastened to do so by leaving with him the dispatches we had been authorized to read him.

So at last Thouvenel's note of 11 May was presented to the United States government; but not really, for Seward emphasized the legal point that this was not an official notification of neutrality.

The secretary's note to Dayton leaves the impression that the interview terminated at this point. Mercier and Lyons, as noted, recount a short informal conversation which followed. The French and English ministers worked together so closely on their dispatches that each reads like a paraphrase of the other; in fact they may have conspired to give their governments a distorted picture, one which had them succeeding in their purpose of making a joint representation. But there is still good reason to credit the Anglo-French version over the Sewards' accounts, in view of the unreliability of Frederick's memory, the fact that William Seward's remarks were shortly published and probably intended for publication from the start, and especially the distinction between the official confrontation, now concluded, and the informal nonconversation which succeeded it.

Seward's part in this exchange can be rendered approximately as follows:[46]

> I have not been able to remain indifferent to the joint character your governments have given to your démarche. I have nothing to complain of in the conduct of France, but the queen's proclamation was a very sore point. For the rest, I realize the demands to which the British government is exposed, both from public opinion and from Parliament, and I shall ignore all words and acts which are not directly brought to my attention.

Mercier and Lyons both tried to convince him that concerted action was a normal thing in diplomacy and should not cause offense, and that Britain and France surely bore no ill will toward the United States. The interview ended on a relatively friendly note.

[46] This version is not found verbatim in any of the sources. Here the original indirect discourse has been changed to approximate the words of the principals. Such changes involve, for example, verb mood and the person of pronouns. In no case has anything been added, nor have statements been omitted except where indicated in the customary fashion. Such treatment will subsequently be signaled in a footnote as "reconstructed language."

The above reconstruction of Seward's remarks is from Mercier to Thouvenel, Washington, 18 June 1861, AMAE, CP, E-U, 124: 338-45, no. 43.

Ten years later Seward made a brief reflection of his own on the events of 15 June 1861. He was visiting France, where Mercier was living in retirement and Lyons was ambassador. In rehearsing the old days with Lyons, he made what must be the most venturesome historical comparison in all the syllables of recorded time. The three most impudent men in history, he said jokingly, were Hernando Cortés, Lyons, and Mercier: Cortés for the way he treated Montezuma, Mercier and Lyons for the fifteenth of June, 1861.[47]

One matter which Lyons and Mercier eventually had to drop was that same privateering issue which had been fouling the entente gears since mid-May. Seward kept at it even after the 15 June interview, but in fact there never was any chance of his binding Britain and France to act against Southern privateers. Neither European state could be maneuvered into acting contrary to its own interests, and though they might be embarrassed, as Thouvenel had early noted, they would still have refused to move even had the United States adhered to the 1856 declaration.[48]

As Thouvenel told Mercier, he was a bit worried when Seward's view of the Marcy amendment finally penetrated Dayton's consciousness. A simple American adherence with no reservations could still embarrass France and Britain. But with Lyons, Cowley (the British ambassador to

---

[47] F. W. Seward, *Reminiscences of a Wartime Statesman*, p. 425. The fact that Seward carried this memory into retirement shows, of course, that he always regarded his blocking of any official joint interview as a significant diplomatic triumph.

In June Mercier also presented Seward with Thouvenel's reasons for receiving the Southern commissioner Pierre A. Rost, albeit unofficially. Seward reacted in a comparatively calm manner (Case and Spencer, pp. 74-75).

[48] Quite simply, Seward's effort was "ingenious but ineffective" (Van Deusen, *William Henry Seward*, p. 302). One Seward's thinking, see Case and Spencer, pp. 79, 84.

France), and Palmerston all suggesting it, Russell finally decided not to accept Washington's adherence unless Seward included a recognition that Europe would not become involved against Southern privateers. That did it, of course. Seward huffily dropped the whole project, and Thouvenel breathed easier.[49]

Mercier obviously remained on the fringes of this particular negotiation, but his short comment on it is an adequate summary of its significance:

> Undoubtedly when Mr. Seward first conceived the idea of adhering to the declaration of the Congress of Paris relating to neutral rights, he wanted to draw Europe into denying the Confederacy the right to arm privateers. That was one of the many mistakes which resulted from his initial inexperience. But if he is still not completely over it, he has been sufficiently warned. . . .[50]

With an eye on the approaching special session of Congress, Mercier had warned as early as 14 June about the fourth major item of the neutral-rights problem—the fourth clause of the Declaration of Paris—that a blockade must be effective to be legal. Lincoln had already proclaimed a blockade; supposedly, therefore, effectiveness would be the

[49] Thouvenel to Mercier, Paris, 8 August 1861, AMAE, CP, E-U, 125: 15-16, no. 22; Thouvenel to Mercier, Paris, 19 August 1861, *ibid.*, fol. 23-25, no. 23; Thouvenel to Mercier, Paris, 29 August 1861, *ibid.*, fol. 49-50, no. 24; Dayton to Seward, Paris, 22 August 1861, State Dept. Corres., France, Dispatches, L, no. 35; E. D. Adams, I, 166-68; Cowley to Russell, Paris, 24 Sept. 1861, *Sessional Papers*, LXII (1862), 564, no. 41; Seward to Dayton, Washington, 10 Sept. 1861, State Dept. Corres., France, Instructions, XVI, 49-55, no. 56; Geofroy to Thouvenel, Washington, 13 Sept. 1861, AMAE, CP, E-U 125: 81-82, no. 56; Thouvenel to Mercier, Paris, 30 Oct. 1861, *ibid.*, fol. 181-83, no. 29; Case and Spencer, pp. 83-109.

[50] Mercier to Thouvenel, Niagara [Canada], 9 Sept. 1861, AMAE, MD, Papiers Thouvenel, XIII, 385-92.

nub of the argument. But as Mercier foresaw, there was another possibility, a logical corollary of the government's theory that the war was only a civil rebellion: "Lord Lyons also thinks that the Washington government has not entirely given up the idea of proposing to Congress . . . to close the ports to commerce by a law, a measure which would surely be more economical than an effective blockade."[51]

When Thouvenel got this and Mercier's further report on the interview of 15 June, he warmly approved of the delicate way Seward had been approached and the fact that the United States seemed reasonable about neutral rights. Such reasonableness, he thought, would preclude any effort to close the ports by a law, and in any case, France would respect only an effective blockade. Thouvenel and Russell were both very anxious that the strictest Anglo-French cooperation mark every step of any conversation with the United States on this dangerous subject.[52]

When Mercier saw Seward about this, the secretary listened calmly, said nothing definite, but gave the impression that he too opposed issuing a port-closing decree. He asked Mercier to send him an extract from Thouvenel's instructions for his guidance.

Before doing so Mercier consulted Lyons, and the two agreed upon which paragraph of Thouvenel's dispatch should form the extract. This paragraph stated simply that the same reasons which forced France to treat the South as a belligerent also would force her to refuse to countenance any measure short of an effective blockade. As he expected, Lyons himself was summoned to the state department on

[51] Mercier to Thouvenel, Washington, 14 June 1861, AMAE, CP, E-U, 124: 311-18, no. 42. For another treatment of the matter of the blockade-ports bill, see Case and Spencer, pp. 126-57.
[52] Thouvenel to Mercier, Paris, 4 July 1861, *ibid.*, fol. 368-69, no. 18; Cowley to Russell, Paris, 4 July 1861, *Sessional Papers*, LXII (1862), 55, no. 58.

20 July and there gave full support to the French position. Finally, Mercier returned to see Seward, also on the twentieth. Seward assured him that there would be no trouble, that in fact the Union would rely on an effective blockade. He even apologized a little for the past:

> Mr. Seward added that if at the beginning of the crisis he had found it necessary to submit foreign governments to rather energetic language in order to reflect the feelings of the American people, he would nonetheless use every effort to keep peaceful and friendly relations with those governments.

Both Seward and the entente could take satisfaction from the way the blockade issue had been left. The United States had admitted that a legal blockade must be effective. That principle having been established, Europe was willing to debate for months about whether the blockade was in fact effective. All the while, Europe treated the blockade as binding, thus giving Washington the benefit of the doubt. Of all the principals, therefore, Seward had the most right to feel satisfied.[53]

Mercier had said that he wanted to be recalled to Europe "as soon as there are no longer any serious complications to fear."[54] By that standard he would have a long time to wait—past *Trent* and Richmond, past intervention efforts, emancipation, and the Gettysburg Address. But at least the terms of debate had been defined, and thereby the Civil

[53] Mercier to Thouvenel, Washington, 21 July 1861, AMAE, CP, E-U, 124: 453-59, no. 48; Lyons to Russell, Washington, 20 July 1861, *Sessional Papers*, LXII (1862), 67-68, no. 68; E. D. Adams, I, 249-50. See also Thouvenel's approval of Mercier's course in Thouvenel to Mercier, Paris, 8 August 1861, AMAE, CP, E-U, 125: 15-16, no. 22, and Thouvenel to Mercier, Paris, 19 August 1861 *ibid.*, fol. 23-25, no. 23.

[54] Mercier to Thouvenel, Washington, 17 July 1861, AMAE, MD, Papiers Thouvenel, XIII, 377-80.

War delimited, kept from becoming a world war. In the winter and spring American events had been riding off in all directions, and everyone had predicted things which later would seem absurd. Seward wanted to abandon Sumter and fight Europe. Lyons was seriously worried about Canada. And Mercier's own thoughts shifted back and forth.

While he had much information and many suggestions to offer, Mercier never said, "We should positively do thus and so now." Policy was made in Paris—and in London. This policy had taken note of Seward's threats but had not panicked. In his turn Seward had been bellicose enough but not intransigent. The result was that by summer everyone knew where everyone else stood, and everyone stood for peace between Europe and America. The South had been recognized, but only as a belligerent; neutral rights were assured, but only as an informal concession. Privateering would be no problem. As for the blockade, it would all depend. Would Britain and France go on with the *modus vivendi*, would they tolerate even an effective blockade if the lack of cotton began to affect their vital interests? That question would be put off till later.

Meanwhile, on 21 July the Union army was defeated at Bull Run in Virginia. Whatever other avenues to peace might still be open, the way of quick Northern victory had been closed.

THE TRAVELS OF MERCIER AND PRINCE NAPOLEON

On Saturday, 27 July, Mercier was in New York to greet Prince Napoleon, cousin to Napoleon III and most distinguished visitor to the United States in the war's first year. Mercier had intended some tour immediately upon his own arrival a year earlier but had gone instead to Newport. Now as the prince's constant companion he would see the country east and west together with an entourage including the prince's aide, Colonel Ferri-Pisani, and Maurice Sand, son of the famous novelist. Clotilde of Savoy had accompanied her husband as far as New York but spent most of her American trip in that city.[55]

Prince Napoleon was known to Americans as a liberal sometime critic of his cousin's regime and as a Northern sympathizer in the Civil War. The North was therefore ready to acclaim him, and he received more than his share of journalistic praise and crowd enthusiasm throughout his itinerary. The appearance of the minister at yachtside in New York drew from the prince an unenthusiastic comment: he found Mercier "intelligent, friendly, maybe a bit flighty."[56] Ferri-Pisani was more generous and expansive:

Baron Mercier is one of our youngest plenipotentiaries, and the position he occupies now is one of the most important and most difficult which the French government can entrust to a diplomat. An ardent patriotism, combined with a general benevolence for foreigners and an uncommon ability to understand their view and mores; a typically French sociability; much intelligence, wit, and gaiety: such is the character of Baron Mercier. In addition, he is especially gifted in all physical exercises, fencing, equitation, swimming; he has a strong constitution; he has an endless good humor, courage to face anything, and a passion to see, to know, and learn everything. Thus, you have the portrait of the man who, as minister of France and as friend, will not leave the Prince during his stay in the United States.[57]

[55] For the first part of the trip, to Washington and back to New York, see Camille Ferri-Pisani, *Prince Napoleon in America, 1861* (Bloomington: Indiana University Press, 1959), pp. 41-92; "Voyage du Prince Napoléon aux États-Unis, 1861," ed. Ernest d'Hauterive, *Revue de Paris*, XL (15 Sept. and 1 Oct. 1933), 243. Hereafter cited as Prince Napoleon's diary.

[56] Prince Napoleon's diary, p. 243.

[57] Ferri-Pisani, pp. 41-42.

From New York the party entrained to the capital via Philadelphia. Declining an invitation to stay at the White House, the prince put up at Mercier's Georgetown house where the cuisine was French and the summer heat more bearable. A visit to Abraham Lincoln on 3 August proved almost disastrous as the war-distracted president with little small talk got his Bonapartes confused, or at least seemed to mix up the prince's father with one or two other brothers of Napoleon I. No wonder, then, that even the well-disposed prince found the president too humble for comfort. Seward went down in the diary as "very intelligent, very acute, quite ill-mannered, conceited and vain."[58]

Perhaps the most striking segment of the trip occurred when Seward gave the prince permission to visit Confederate headquarters in northern Virginia. He, Mercier, and the rest left Washington early on Thursday, 8 August. After toasting "the American people" with the Confederate escort which met them south of Alexandria, they went on through Fairfax to Manassas Junction and dined that night with Joseph Johnston and P.G.T. Beauregard. A tour of the Bull Run battlefield the next day produced the expected reflections about Confederate determination. What conclusion could one draw save the obvious, that the North, bearing the burden of offensive warfare, would not win quickly? By night they were back in Georgetown with many questions still to be answered.

From there it was back to New York for a short reunion with Clotilde and then the beginning of a western tour of some importance to Mercier's education.[59] Such tours are always detailed and particular, always rapid, and hence an impressionistic montage. There were, for example, that temperance hotel in Altoona, Pennsylvania, where the manage-

[58] Prince Napoleon's diary, p. 256.
[59] For the western tour see Prince Napoleon's diary, pp. 267-72 and 549-87; Sand, pp. 227-358; Ferri-Pisani, pp. 145-308.

ment perversely refused to serve anything worth drinking at dinner; the German-spa atmosphere of Cleveland; the ubiquitous and unappreciated shakers of hands en route; and the lake steamer *North Star*, which set out from Cleveland via Sault Ste. Marie to the wilds and mines of northern Michigan and Wisconsin.

After a week of this, an unfortunate whim of the prince's took the *North Star* off route to Mackinac Island where the party spent an uncomfortable few days in the rain, waiting for a ship to Milwaukee. From there it was across Wisconsin by train to Prairie du Chien, then a decision not to try for St. Louis by primitive river transport and a return across state to Chicago, where the incipient industrial might of the Midwest made its due impression. In St. Louis at the headquarters of General John C. Fremont the party ran right into the general's fight with the president over emancipation of slaves held by rebels. Jessie Benton Fremont, in fact, left immediately after the prince's departure for her famous confrontation in the White House.[60]

That was in the first week of September, and it was then that a gracious William H. Osborn, president of the Illinois Central Railroad, permitted both the prince and Mercier to name town sites within his gift. In this way Savoy and Lostant, Illinois were given names in honor of the gentlemen's young wives. (It does not appear how "Lostende" came to be so grandly misspelled, but in French pronunciation, at least, the mistake is understandable.)[61]

[60] Jessie Benton Fremont and Lt. Francis B. Fremont, "Great Events during the Life of Major General John C. Fremont," Bancroft Library, University of California, MSS, pp. 258-59, 268-69.

[61] The author is much indebted to Mrs. Henry J. Spitzer of Lostant, Illinois, for a generously detailed account of the town's origins. Thanks are due to officials of the Illinois State Historical Library for further information. See William K. Ackerman, *Early Illinois Railroads* (Chicago: Fergus Printing Co., 1884), p. 144, and William D. Barge and Norman W. Caldwell, "Illinois Place-Names," *Journal of the Illinois State Historical Society*, xxix (1936), 247, 283.

From St. Louis the troupe headed back across the country through Indianapolis to northern New York and Niagara Falls. A brief tour of French Canada followed, and the prince and his party embarked on 20 September from New York after a pleasant trip down the Hudson which included a visit to West Point. Mercier had time to catch his breath and bring himself up to date on diplomatic developments.

DIPLOMATIC BUSINESS

When in mid-August they had first returned to New York from Washington, and Mercier decided to accompany Prince Napoleon on his trip through the West, he was at pains to assure Thouvenel that his absence would in no way hamper official duty, for all recently touchy business had been settled. Four weeks later, as he was about to leave for the Canadian trip, Mercier again alluded to his absence from Washington. In fact Mercier did not return to the capital until 30 September; his seven weeks' absence, while not of great diplomatic import, caused a twinge or two of inconvenience.[62]

During these weeks such weighty matters as the blockade and the possibility of intervention continued to need discussion, as they would throughout the next two years, but they reach no point of resolution. Other matters came to a definite head. For example, Lord John Russell was still concerned lest Washington issue a port-closing decree. He ordered Lyons to take this up with Seward, then changed his mind and left it to Lyons to decide, after consultation with Mercier. Before receiving this note, Lyons had already agreed with Mercier on what course they should follow in the latter's absence, and with this in mind Lyons went to

[62] Mercier to Thouvenel, New York, 13 August 1861, AMAE, MD, Papiers Thouvenel, XIII, 398-401; Mercier to Thouvenel, Niagara [New York], 9 Sept. 1861, *ibid.*, fol. 393-94. (The folio numbers are correct; the letters have been filed out of chronological order.)

see Seward in mid-August. Both France and Britain had now made it clear that a statutory port-closing would be disregarded and an effective blockade insisted upon. In fact, as we have seen, the Union never stopped striving for this effectiveness. The solidity of the entente helped keep this principle inviolate, and this solidity was well evidenced by Lyons's actions in Mercier's absence; he even had his note to Russell read to Geofroy so that Mercier could be kept informed.[63]

Perhaps the most important matter which came to a boil during Mercier's absence was the representation to the Confederacy about neutral rights. From the beginning, that is from the middle of May when Thouvenel wrote his fundamental dispatches on French recognition of Southern belligerency, he and Mercier had worried about how to contact Jefferson Davis and elicit some guarantees for French merchants and other citizens. Thouvenel's first thought was to have Count Méjan, consul in New Orleans, go to Montgomery with the appropriate message.[64]

The general reluctance which Mercier and Lyons felt about approaching Seward had been especially acute on this point of contacting the Confederate government. They knew what they were about, for as it developed, Seward was indeed upset when he read the dispatch which Mercier left in his hands during the famous interview of 15 June, but he apparently agreed that some sort of contact between European and Confederate authorities would have to be

[63] Russell to Lyons, 8 August 1861, *Sessional Papers*, LXII (1862), 69-70, no. 70; Russell to Lyons, London, 9 August 1861, *ibid.*, p. 70, no. 71; Lyons to Russell, Washington, 12 August 1861, *ibid.*, p. 80, no. 81; Geofroy to Thouvenel, Washington, 13 August 1861, AMAE, CP, E-U, 125: 17-19, no. 49.

[64] Thouvenel to Mercier, Paris, 16 May 1861, *ibid.*, 124: 218, no. 9; E. D. Adams, I, 163, n. 1; Milledge L. Bonham, Jr., *The British Consuls in the Confederacy* (New York: Columbia University Press, 1911), p. 30. On the whole issue of French contacts with the Confederacy in 1861, see Case and Spencer, pp. 109-21.

tolerated. In choosing the method, however, Mercier and Lyons would have to step warily.[65]

The great difficulty was that any direct overture from the ministers in Washington to Jefferson Davis would be construed by the latter as *de facto* recognition of the Confederacy. Even a consul's making such an approach could be so interpreted and might enrage Seward all over again. But the consuls had received their exequaturs from the federal government and were incontestably legal in Washington's eyes; similarly, the governors of Southern states, even though "rebels," were in far better legal position from the Washington viewpoint than were the leaders of the Confederacy. Mercier now proposed, and Lyons went along, that Europe take advantage of this constitutional situation by having consuls approach the governor of a Southern state.

The Confederate government had decided on 21 May to move their capital from Montgomery to Richmond. This suggests that if consuls were to act, they would be the consuls in Richmond, but Lyons preferred working through Consul Robert Bunch in Charleston, and Mercier therefore thought he could entrust the French mission to Belligny, the French consul there. Mercier then wrote to Belligny, ordering him to concert with Bunch and either go to Richmond or, better yet, get Governor Francis W. Pickens of South Carolina to obtain assurance of neutral commercial rights from President Davis. When Thouvenel received

[65] Mercier to Thouvenel, Washington, 14 June 1861, AMAE, CP, E-U, 124: 311-18, no. 42; Lyons to Russell, Washington, 4 June 1861, *Sessional Papers*, LXII (1862), 544, no. 12; Lyons to Russell, Washington, 17 June 1861, *ibid.*, pp. 545-46, no. 14; Lyons to Russell, Washington, 4 June 1861, Newton, I, 42; Seward to Dayton, Washington, 17 June 1861, State Dept. Corres., France, Instructions, XVI, 1-12, no. 19, also in *For. Rel. U.S.*, 1861, pp. 224-28. The idea of having a Southern-stationed consul make the approach was Thouvenel's (Case and Spencer, p. 110).

Mercier's note, he quickly sent approval of the new *modus operandi*, an approval which Mercier had presumed and already acted upon.[66]

Bunch and Belligny, unable to see Governor Pickens of South Carolina who was at his estate in the interior, asked William Henry Trescot (Mercier's first official American contact in 1860) to take their case to Richmond. Trescot caught up with Jefferson Davis in late July and told the president of French and British concern; now it was the Confederacy's turn to be magnanimous about neutral rights in wartime.

The Confederate cabinet met immediately, agreed on a course and submitted it to the Confederate congress which on 13 August adhered to the second, third, *and fourth* articles of the 1856 declaration, that is, they threw in, for obvious reasons, acceptance of the principle that a blockade must be effective. Further, on the subject of their privateers, they made guarantees that the "law of nations" would be respected and that offended merchants would be able to present claims. Belligny added, in his report to Mercier, that the Richmond government was much hurt by the Europeans' refusal to allow Confederate privateers to bring prizes into their ports for condemnation. In fact this pro-

[66] Mercier to Thouvenel, Washington, 18 June 1861, AMAE, CP, E-U, 124: 338-45, no. 43; Thouvenel to Mercier, Paris, 4 July 1861, *ibid.*, fol. 368-69, no. 18; E. D. Adams, I, 165; Bonham, *British Consuls*, p. 28.

Mercier knew that Belligny was on the point of leaving his post and that Baron Durand de St. André was slated to succeed him, so he did not mention either by name in his salutation. As it turned out, however, Belligny stayed on in order to undertake this touchy assignment (Mercier to the French consul at Charleston, Washington, 5 July 1861, copy, AMAE, CP, E-U, 124: 390-91, enclosure no. 3 with Mercier to Thouvenel, Washington, 8 July 1861, *ibid.*, fol. 370-78, no. 46). See also Lyons to Russell, Washington, 8 July 1861, and Lyons to Bunch, Washington, 5 July 1861, *Sessional Papers*, LXII (1862), 549, no. 21 and enclosure; and Korolewicz-Carlton, p. 43.

hibition did render the whole privateering effort ineffective by the end of the year.[67]

Another somewhat embarrassing event during Mercier's absence was the arrival in Washington of the Orleans princes. The Prince of Joinville was the third son of Louis Philippe. He came to America with his sixteen-year-old son —the Duke of Penthièvre—and his two nephews, sons of the deceased Duke of Orleans, both in their early twenties— the Count of Paris and the Duke of Chartres. The Count of Paris was the Orleans pretender to the French throne.

Dayton has somewhat breathlessly signaled their trip to Seward. He noted that the Duke of Chartres would probably be willing to accept a commission in the Union army. As for possible affronts to the French government, "no ordinary attentions paid them would I think be misinterpreted or taken in ill part by the present Emperor of the French." Dayton's information was more than half correct. Although the princes may not have intended it before coming to Washington, both of them did wind up as McClellan's officers.[68]

As to taking "ordinary attentions . . . in ill part," the episode was a little annoying to French authorities but did not produce a diplomatic storm. Mercier found it hard to imagine what the princes thought they were doing. And if the Lincoln government expected to increase its prestige, he said, it was in for a disappointment; any lionizing of the princes would encourage the South to look more hopefully to Napoleon III. But the princes stayed on nonetheless, and

[67] Belligny to Mercier, Charleston, 19 August 1861, AMAE, CP, E-U, 125: 56-61, enclosure no. 2 with Geofroy to Thouvenel, Washington, 2 Sept. 1861, *ibid.*, fol. 51-55, no. 53; Bonham, *British Consuls*, pp. 27-29. See also Mercier to Thouvenel, New York, 13 August 1861, AMAE, MD, Papiers Thouvenel, XIII, 398-401.

[68] Dayton to Seward, Paris, 22 August 1861, State Dept. Corres., France, Dispatches, L, no. 36.

official Washington received them honorably and happily. Their pro-Northern attitude was a boost to Union morale. In October, Seward asked Mercier how Paris would take all this, and Mercier saw nothing to do but keep a cool reserve. His government, also in something of a quandary, approved this course.[69]

The Prince of Joinville wrote an account of the Virginia campaign of 1862, in which his nephews played an active role. Ruminating before Yorktown on the possible effects of a Union defeat, he was moved to say, "Upon yonder ramparts the blood of our soldiers had sealed an alliance unbroken down to our own times: an alliance to which the United States once owed their prosperity and their greatness."[70]

It was all very well for the prince to apostrophize the old Bourbon policy of alliance with America, but it was his father the citizen-king who broke diplomatic relations with Andrew Jackson's government. In fact both the Orleans monarchy and the Second Empire had been anxious to maintain a close rapport with Britain in everything affecting the Western Hemisphere, and had taken a cool view of France's role as America's "oldest ally." There is no need to question the prince's sincerity in his aversion to slavery

[69] Mercier to Thouvenel, New York, 29 Sept. 1861, AMAE, MD, Papiers Thouvenel, XIII, 406-09; Mercier to Thouvenel, Washington, 8 Oct. 1861, AMAE, CP, E-U, 125: 119-33, no. 63. See also Mercier to Thouvenel, Washington, 10 Oct. 1861, *ibid.*, fol. 137-43, no. 64; Salmon P. Chase to "Katie" [Chase], Washington, 25 Oct. 1861, Chase Papers, Historical Society of Pennsylvania; Blumenthal, *Franco-American Relations*, pp. 135-36.

It would probably be too much to say, as Beyens has, that Napoleon III's resentment over the warm acceptance of the Orleans princes had any substantive effect on his foreign policy aims (Baron Napoleon Beyens, *Le Second Empire vu par un diplomate belge*, 2 vols. [Paris: Plon-Nourrit & cie., n.d.], I, 304-05.

[70] Prince de Joinville, *The Army of the Potomac: its Organization, its Commander, and its Campaign* (New York: Anson D. F. Randolph, 1862), p. 45.

and his hope for a Northern victory. But like all opposition groups, the Orleans princes could afford a policy-latitude not open to the government in power. Had the Count of Paris been king in 1861-1862, his uncle would surely have seen matters a bit differently. By the time he wrote the passage quoted above, the federal government's determination to preserve the United States was seriously threatening the French economy and the daily lives of thousands of French factory workers. Napoleon III, constricted by the bonds of responsibility, could not afford to be romantic about Yorktown, even had there been no Mexico.

Mercier came back to Washington at the end of September 1861. It was autumn now, and he had said for a long time that if the war were not settled by autumn, France might have to make some dramatic or threatening move. Moreover, the possibility of some unpleasant and dangerous incident was, as always in wartime, a constant threat. Men were employing violence, were capturing, wounding, and killing one another. Whether or not diplomacy could keep this limited to one side of the Atlantic would depend to some extent on how the diplomats handled whatever incident might occur.

CHAPTER IV

The Trent *Affair*

THE ANGLO-FRENCH ENTENTE ON THE EVE
OF THE *TRENT* CRISIS

THE close working-relationship between Britain and France, an entente which, as we have seen, went back to such earlier events as the American annexation of Texas, was put to a number of severe strains by the Civil War. That it managed to survive these strains was owing primarily to the way in which it served the best interests of both countries. Even when France became thoroughly involved in Mexico, for example, she could see no advantage in a unilateral recognition of the Confederacy, a recognition which could have led to a Franco-American war in which the British fleet would stand aside and watch. Of secondary but nonetheless great importance was the Anglophile influence of key French individuals, most notably Thouvenel.

One of Mercier's first acts when he returned after his summer tour was to sound out Lord Lyons on the need for action in America. Mercier's own conclusion that the time for European intervention might be near was too venturesome for the prudent Englishman:

Lord Lyons tells me that nothing in his correspondence from his government foreshadows any change of attitude in the near future. When I asked him if they were not beginning to worry in London about the effects of the cotton famine, he said he had not gotten a single word on the subject.[1]

[1] Mercier to Thouvenel, Washington, 10 Oct. 1861, AMAE, CP, E-U,

Lyons's prudence, however admirable, was not a reliable guide to Russell's private thought. The foreign secretary, in fact, preferred Mercier's analysis to Lyons's, and said so in a letter of 17 October to Palmerston:

> There is much good sense in Mercier's observations. But we must wait. I am persuaded that if we do anything, it must be on a grand scale. It will not do for England and France to break a blockade for the sake of getting cotton.

Neither Mercier nor Russell, hawkish as they sounded, favored immediate action. In Russell's case it was Palmerston's caution as well as Lyons's which dampened his ardor at this time.[2]

Seward's preference for goading Britain rather than France was partly a response to Northern public opinion which regarded England as the most troublesome foreign state. Mercier assured Thouvenel that he would not try to capitalize upon this. "It goes without saying," he said, "that I am doing nothing to stir it up; on the contrary, I flaunt the close and harmonious accord which exists between myself and Lord Lyons."[3]

Mercier, then, while protesting his loyalty to the Anglo-French entente, could see some advantage in the relatively good light in which Americans tended to view France. If the Civil War should reach the point where both sides wished a conciliator, France should be ready to volunteer,

---

125: 137-43, no. 64. For Mercier's ideas about intervention, which will be treated in chapter v, see Mercier to Thouvenel, Quebec, 13 Sept. 1861, AMAE, MD, Papiers Thouvenel, XIII, 403-05.

[2] E. D. Adams, *Great Britain and the American Civil War*, I, 196-99, where the Russell letter may also be found. See also Spencer Walpole, *The Life of Lord John Russell*, 2 vols. (London: Longmans, Green & Co., 1889), II, 344; and Owsley, *King Cotton Diplomacy*, 2nd ed. (Chicago: University of Chicago Press, 1959), pp. 71-73.

[3] Mercier to Thouvenel, Washington, 7 Nov. 1861, AMAE, CP, E-U, 125: 186-97, no. 68.

even without Britain at her side. What Mercier did not foresee was an immediate, fearful crisis in Anglo-American relations, a crisis in which France would have to decide, quickly and unambiguously, how much the Anglo-French entente mattered.

The Crisis

In the Old Bahama Channel north of Cuba Captain Charles Wilkes of the Union navy made clear his responsibility for the long-planned business at hand:

> U.S. Steamer San Jacinto
> At Sea, Nov 8, 1861
>
> Sir—You will have the second and third cutters of this ship fully manned and armed, and be in all respects prepared to board the steamer Trent now hove-to under our guns.
>
> On boarding her you will demand the papers of the steamer, her clearance from Havana, with the list of passengers and crew.
>
> Should Mr. Mason, Mr. Slidell, Mr. Eustis and Mr. McFarland be on board you will make them prisoners.[4]

Thus did Captain Charles Wilkes make clear his sole responsibility for the afternoon's events. Minutes later Lieutenant D. M. Fairfax, executive officer of the *San Jacinto* and the addressee of the note, was on the *Trent*, facing Captain Moir. Above their heads flew the Union Jack, and in the distance the Stars and Stripes flapped over the staring field-glasses and cannon of a war steamer. It was quite a reversal of roles, taken in the full context of nineteenth-century history: the trained guns had normally been British and the offended captain some Yankee.

Recent reinvestigation of the *Trent* affair strongly indi-

---

[4] Wilkes to Fairfax, quoted in Thomas L. Harris, *The Trent Affair* (Indianapolis: Bowen-Merrill Co., 1896), pp. 101-02.

cates that the South was more the author than the victim of Wilkes's act, indeed that Jefferson Davis appeared to invite Union interference with British ships in order to provoke war between London and Washington. The long-delayed and much-heralded mission of the two ministers had already been permitted to excite speculation about what might happen should a Union warship intercept them. In Havana while they were waiting for the *Trent,* Mason and Slidell actually had the *San Jacinto* officers to lunch and told them they planned to cross the Atlantic in British ships. Attorney General Edward Bates even heard the Confederate envoys had arranged with Wilkes for the capture. However that may be, it is certain that Slidell later expressed to Napoleon III his regret over the Union's prudence in releasing him from prison, for it prevented the desired Anglo-American war.[5]

On the *Trent,* perhaps because he was waiting for it, John Slidell stepped forward promptly when he heard Fairfax's summons, but he and James Mason, envoy to England, insisted on a display of force in order to keep the legal-historical record straight. Indeed the deck and cabins of the *Trent* were a stage that afternoon, and those concerned showed every sign of awareness that their audience would be vast. Having been duly set upon with "violent" hands, the two Confederate envoys then went along quietly enough, and with them their secretaries, McFarland, and Slidell's friend Eustis. The ladies, including Louise Cor-

[5] See Case and Spencer, pp. 190-249. For the Case thesis that the South set up Mason and Slidell, inviting their capture and hence a Union break with Britain, see esp. pp. 190-94. On the beginnings of the crisis see also E. D. Adams, ii, 203-07; Mason to R.M.T. Hunter, Charleston, 5 Oct. 1861, *ORN,* 2nd ser., iii, 276-77; *New York Times,* 13 and 20 Dec. 1861; Edward Bates, *The Diary of Edward Bates, 1859-1866,* ed. Howard K. Beale, *Annual Report of the American Historical Association, 1930,* vol. iv (Washington: U.S. Government Printing Office, 1933), 213-14; Slidell Memorandum, Paris, 25 July 1862, *ORN,* 2nd ser., iii, 484.

coran Eustis, chose to stay on the *Trent* and continue to Europe. Whether or not the gentlemen would join them there was the world's most talked of question for the next seven weeks, for Charles Wilkes, acting on his own authority, had initiated the worst international crisis of the war.

Wilkes and his prisoners on the *San Jacinto* made for Fortress Monroe, Virginia, where they put in one week later on Friday, 15 November. News of the startling affair reached Washington the same evening. The next day was cold and raw, but Mercier, wrapped in a remarkable great cloak, lost no time in going downtown to see Lyons at the British legation. Mercier, then, was helping the entente to close ranks. Meanwhile, at the direction of a befuddled but generally elated government, the prisoners were transported to Fort Warren in Boston harbor.[6]

Mercier naturally wrote home about the affair that same weekend. As one would expect, he had some of his facts garbled in those first hours; for example, he thought the diplomats' and secretaries' families had been taken to Fort Warren, and he stated flatly that Wilkes had acted "in conformity with formal orders of the Washington government." He went on to recount the rumor that General McClellan, who might be the author of a new peace plan, was the most prominent antiseizure spokesman in Washington, that Jefferson Davis thought so little of Mason and Slidell he had sent them to Europe chiefly to be rid of them, and that Seward, who had revoked Bunch's exequatur at about the same time that Wilkes received his "orders," was looking for a pretext to break with Britain.

As for Lord Lyons: "He very much deplores an incident

---

[6] Randall, *Lincoln the President*, II, 37-39; Nicolay and Hay, *Abraham Lincoln*, v, 21-25; Stern, *When the Guns Roared*, pp. 90-91; William Howard Russell, *My Diary North and South*, 2 vols. (London: Longmans, Green & Co., 1925), II, 403; Evan John, *Atlantic Impact, 1861* (New York: G. P. Putnam's Sons, 1952), p. 172.

which puts his government in the position either of being involved without France—which it would like above all to avoid—or, should it give in, of seeing its prestige suffer a new and serious blow."[7] If it is true that Jefferson Davis was the real author of the *Trent* crisis, then Mercier had his facts reversed completely in ascribing it to Seward.

Communication between Europe and America was never so vital a factor of international relations as it was during these two months. Back and forth across the cold, unpredictable North Atlantic the ships toiled with their messages and rumors—the usual month's delay for receiving an answer lengthened by the weather. Lyons retreated behind a shell of reserve to wait out the word of peace or war; later he would say that had the Atlantic cable been in operation, had diplomacy been a quick exchange, war would have been inevitable.[8] Mercier knew along with everyone else that in these weeks his every choice and word mattered deeply. In slacker times he could afford to speculate about Franco-American rapprochement, he could play the game of choosing the moment, hypothetical and future, for stopping the Civil War. Hypotheses and leisurely discussion would have to be postponed now. Without word from Thouvenel he would nevertheless have to say things to Seward and to Lyons; somehow he would have to make knowledge, intelligence, instinct, and common sense do in place of dispatches from Paris.

[7] Mercier to Thouvenel, Washington, 17 Nov. 1861, AMAE, CP, E-U, 125: 204-12, no. 69. See also Lynn M. Case, "La France et l'affaire du 'Trent,'" *Revue historique*, CCXXVI (1961), 57-86, which is the indispensable account of the *Trent* affair as it relates to France. Stoeckl heard from "a reliable source" that Wilkes had acted on orders from Seward, orders given without Lincoln's knowledge—a version which Prince Gorchakov found "delightful" (Stoeckl to Gorchakov, Washington, 6/18 Nov. 1861, no. 68, Stoeckl Papers; see also Albert A. Woldman, *Lincoln and the Russians* [Cleveland: World Publishing Co., 1952], pp. 92-93).

[8] Newton, *Lord Lyons*, I, 77-78.

Mercier's own news and comments had little to do with the basic decision of Thouvenel and the emperor. They knew from other sources what Wilkes had done and what London thought, and they were quite prepared to decide the course of France. On 25 November, Mercier wrote Paris that American public opinion, at first alarmed about possible war, had relaxed a bit, and that Northern sentiment solidly approved Wilkes's act, which seemed perfectly in line with those sea liberties traditionally taken by British captains in time of war. Above all, Americans felt that the English would never risk a war in which France would stand aside.[9]

Like Mercier and Lyons, Seward too was notably quiet and statesmanlike—for him, at any rate—while the president did not so much as allude to the matter in his message to Congress of 3 December. In one sense the *Trent* affair was good material for Seward; he had long wanted something concrete with which to disrupt the entente, preferably something which put Britain in the wrong and left France free. But here, thanks to Captain Wilkes, it was Britain who stood forth as the aggrieved party. War with England, however thrilling he may have thought it in April when it seemed a way to reunite America, would be distasteful as well as potentially disastrous under November's conditions. Boston gave Wilkes a banquet; Secretary Welles wrote him congratulations; and the House of Representatives, as soon as it convened on 2 December, resolved that Wilkes's conduct was "brave, adroit, and patriotic." Seward and Lincoln listened and wondered, and the president was already uncomfortable about his country's questionable moral position:

> I fear the traitors will prove to be white elephants. We must stick to American principles concerning the rights

[9] Mercier to Thouvenel, Washington, 25 Nov. 1861, AMAE, CP, E-U, 125: 219-25, no. 70.

of neutrals. We fought Great Britain for insisting, by theory and practice, on the right to do precisely what Captain Wilkes has done.[10]

In so speaking, Abraham Lincoln had gone to the heart of the matter: the British flag had been violated. But in a country governed by lawyers, such a simple explanation could never be the only word. Lincoln the lawyer, Seward the lawyer, and everyone else the lawyer in Washington spent much of this autumn consulting their precedents. In this instance America's special relationship with the mother country was particularly plain, for English as well as American judges were cited. When word of the affair reached London on 27 November, the legal arguments went forward in a larger forum, and in Paris they came to the desk of Thouvenel the lawyer.[11]

In London it took only two days for Lord John Russell and the cabinet to digest the news, consult the crown lawyers, and prepare the first dispatch to Lord Lyons. Palmerston, as usual, consulted Queen Victoria. The ailing Prince Albert, in his last dramatic act on earth, ardently urged that the note be toned down, that America be given every possible escape route by being invited to disavow Wilkes and free the prisoners. Accordingly, Russell's note asked that the United States do this "of its own accord," and pointedly held out the hope of peace. Without leaning too hard on the neutral-rights argument, it stressed the point that the flag had been insulted and that Wilkes had acted wrongly in not taking the *Trent* to a prize court. In an ac-

[10] Quoted in Nicolay and Hay, v, 25-26. For this second stage of the crisis, from the announcement of the capture to the writing of notes by Russell and Thouvenel, see *ibid.*, pp. 24-26; Case, *Revue historique*, ccxxvi (1961), 65-67; Harris, pp. 90-135.

[11] In addition to the briefs to be discussed, see the dazzling display of legal citation in the speech of Senator Charles Sumner, *Congressional Globe*, 37 Cong., 2nd sess., pp. 241-45 (9 Jan. 1862).

companying note Russell told Lyons he had some latitude about when to present the demand, but that he should start home if the Washington cabinet delayed its answer beyond one week.[12]

Thouvenel came back from a sickbed on Monday the twenty-fifth.[13] On Wednesday, having just returned from a visit to the emperor at Compiègne, he found word of the *Trent* affair on his desk at the Quai d'Orsay. France now joined the United States and Great Britain in assessing what Wilkes had done. As Mercier had, Thouvenel and the emperor quickly moved to support the British in their difficulty. From a council meeting at Compiègne the following day, the entente emerged stronger than ever. The government of the United States would again have to face a united Anglo-French diplomatic front, France's need for English support in Mexico being an added reason at this particular juncture. Thouvenel sent the consoling word to London before the day was out.[14]

[12] Russell to Lyons, London, 30 Nov. 1861, *Sessional Papers*, LXII (1862), 614-15, no. 2; Russell to Lyons, London, 30 Nov. 1861, *ibid.*, p. 615, no. 4; E. D. Adams, I, 213; Case, *Revue historique*, CCXXVI (1961), 61-62; Harris, pp. 163-73; Nicolay and Hay, V, 26-30; Randall, *Lincoln the President*, II, 39-41; Newton, I, 62-63.

[13] Mercier, when he heard about the illness, gave Thouvenel some homely advice: he should walk for at least an hour a day in order to keep fit; Lord Palmerston leaned to trips in the country, Mercier went on, but that would probably bore Thouvenel (Mercier to Thouvenel, Washington, 18 Dec. 1861, AMAE, MD, Papiers Thouvenel, XIII, 416-18).

[14] Case, *Revue historique*, CCXXVI (1961), 59-61. Dayton got a rumor that France was on the verge of recognizing the Confederacy. In a disarming outburst of bluntness, he told Seward he could probably get more information from Mercier than from himself: "The news of the Government may however be got, I should think, as well & perhaps better from Mr. Mercier, (with whom I understand your relations are intimate) than from me. The communications between him and his Government are very constant and I doubt not, from what I have seen and heard, very full" (Dayton to Seward, Paris, 30 Nov. 1861, State Dept. Corres., France, Dispatches, LI, no. 87).

French policy, however, was far from being identical with British. It is true that maintaining the entente and earning diplomatic capital for deposit in London were probably the chief factors in the French decision. But the French government had no intention of going to war in support of England; that was a matter which might have to be faced separately and later. Moreover, the French position on neutral rights was considerably more liberal than that of the mistress of the seas. Now that Britain had been taught by America what it felt like to have a ship stopped and searched, with passengers taken from her cabins, she might appreciate better the traditional neutral's position. And the United States, with her long-standing devotion to that position, must be made to realize that unless Wilkes's act were disavowed, France would see the American government in the same bullying role for which that government had so often castigated London.[15]

The precedent-conscious British wanted to achieve their diplomatic aim without planting any legal seeds about the right of visit, the definition of contraband, and so on. Thouvenel, whose note went out to Mercier on 3 December and to the world a bit later, shone by contrast, his dispatch pitched on the high plane of human rights, which would later become associated with Woodrow Wilson. What Wilkes had done, Thouvenel began, was so contrary to the ordinary canons of international law that the French people were loath to think he had acted under instructions. Her friendship for both Britain and the United States and her need to defend her own shipping demanded that France speak to the subject. Washington was as firm as Paris that a neutral flag covers everything—and everyone—beneath it, save actual combatants and contraband; by any reasonable standard, Mason and Slidell were neither. Furthermore, he said, the *Trent* had been going from one neutral

[15] Case, *Revue historique*, ccxxvi (1961), 62-65.

port to another, and a neutral flag makes of its ship a piece of neutral territory, territory which can be violated no more lightly than the soil of the country itself.[16]

Three days later, 6 December, Dayton hesitantly stepped into the picture by bringing up the subject with Thouvenel. In addition to the points he had made in the dispatch, Thouvenel told Dayton that should war break out, France would remain neutral, but benevolently neutral in favor of England.[17] In fact Thouvenel did not expect things to go that far. On the ocean the ship carrying Russell's note was well on its way; his own note had just left port. For the moment there was little for France to do but wait and bask in the gratitude of the English.[18]

A full three weeks elapsed from the time Thouvenel's note left his desk till the time it reached Mercier's. For the first two of those weeks, Mercier's task was relatively easy: it was easy to wait, to speculate, to talk generalities, to observe and report. After one conversation with Seward, Mercier saw a little sunlight:

> Some remarks of Mr. Seward's to me make me think he is ready to make as much reparation as public opinion may support. But will he go so far as to release the prisoners? This will doubtless be the question, and such a great sacrifice of self-esteem will seem very difficult to American pride especially after so many demonstrations.[19]

[16] Thouvenel to Mercier, Paris, 3 Dec. 1861, AMAE, CP, E-U, 125: 241-45, no. 32. This dispatch, one of the two or three most important which Thouvenel ever wrote to Mercier, was published that same month and is found in a number of printed sources, e.g., *LJ*, II (1861), 99-101, and in English translation, *ORN*, 1st ser., I, 164-65.

[17] Dayton to Seward, Paris, 6 Dec. 1861, State Dept. Corres., France Dispatches, LI, no. 91, also in *For. Rel. U.S.*, 1862, p. 307.

[18] Thouvenel to Flahault, Paris, 12 Dec. 1861, Thouvenel, *Secret*, II, 205-08.

[19] Mercier to Thouvenel, Washington, 3 Dec. 1861, AMAE, CP, E-U, 125: 246-52, no. 72.

Mercier was probably right about Seward's thinking. At a cotillon two weeks later, the secretary took the line that an Anglo-American war would be terrible and would affect many countries: "We will wrap the whole world in flames! No power so remote that she will not feel the fire of our battle and be burned by our conflagration."[20] A few days later Seward again spoke of avoiding war, this time less dramatically, directly to Mercier:

> Mr. Seward . . . will surely use all his talent to avoid a break, and he seems to be sure that he will succeed. Speaking to me just now, he used this language: "We shall not have a war; great nations like England and the United States do not make war from emotion."

Asked by Mercier, Seward then gave permission to be quoted in a dispatch.[21]

Mercier's own Anglophilia was never so strong as in this tense month; Lyons had good reason to be happy. As excitement mounted with each day in anticipation of the notes from Europe, Mercier freely painted pictures of a beautiful future for the entente. Should the English go in alone, he thought, they would beat the Americans and emerge more proud and intractable. But if a joint Anglo-French demonstration were made, a big war might be avoided and the groundwork laid for a later intervention to stop the Civil War. In fact, the entente should be the keystone of a whole new balance of power: "For my part, I think that

[20] Quoted in W. H. Russell, II, 421-22. Senator Orville H. Browning, Lincoln's friend from Illinois, recorded that on 10 December, "President told me had heard thro the French Minister that the law officers of England had decided that we were justifiable by the law of Nations in the arrest of Mason & Slidell, and that there would probly [sic] be no trouble about it" (Orville H. Browning, *The Diary of Orville Hickman Browning*, 2 vols. [Chicago: Blakely Printing Co., 1927 and 1933], I, 513-14).

[21] Mercier to Thouvenel, Washington, 19 Dec. 1861, AMAE, CP, E-U, 125: 288-95, no. 75.

this equilibrium . . . is the one which best conforms to the order of things on which the power of our dynasty depends."[22] In the course of a whole career-full of written dispatches, a diplomat will say a great many things, some of which may later seem more clever than they were. There is no evidence nor even probability that Mercier had Prussia in mind when he wrote that. In the light of the next decade's shifts in the "equilibrium," however, of what they did to the Bonaparte dynasty, and of the crucial part played by withdrawal of British support, Mercier's thoughts appear, if not brilliant, at least correct.

At 11:00 P.M. on the night of 18 December, Russell's dispatches reached the British legation in Washington, having been brought the final forty miles via specially commandeered train. The following day Lyons saw Seward twice, once at the secretary's office, where he let him read the note, and later at the legation, where Seward came to make further inquiries. The conversations were quiet, measured, serious; Prince Albert, among others, had done his work well, and Seward remained courteous and even thankful. Pressed by Seward, Lyons stated that he would have to leave in seven days if he had not received a satisfactory reply. As yet Lyons had not officially presented the note, and Seward got him to postpone that, first until Saturday and then until Monday the twenty-third. Lyons conceded that much, partly because he wanted to allow time for the French note to arrive. On Monday, however, that dispatch had still not come, and the clock began to tick on the seven-day vigil.[23]

From 19 December till Christmas, Mercier's role was difficult and crucial. The British position was now clear. Even

22 Mercier to Thouvenel, Washington, 18 Dec. 1861, AMAE, MD, Papiers Thouvenel, XIII, 416-18.

23 Lyons to Russell, Washington, 19 Dec. 1861, Newton, I, 65-67; Case, *Revue historique*, CCXXVI (1961), 67-68; E. D. Adams, I, 230.

more, the French position was known to Mercier, for Lyons had this from Russell, which he quickly relayed to Mercier: "M. Thouvenel promises to send off a despatch on Thursday next giving our cause moral support, so that you may as well keep the despatch itself a day or two before you produce it, provided you ask at once for an interview with Seward."[24] Mercier thus knew that his course so far had been absolutely correct; in helping the entente stand indivisible in Washington he had rightly anticipated his government's decision. Mercier was undoubtedly encouraged by this, and he and Lyons discussed what he might now do to make sure that Seward understood the French position. France, after all, as the leading power with some claim to impartiality, was now a sort of moral arbitrator in the dispute. With the American cabinet and president about to choose, it was important that the voice of such an important third party be heard. In a further display of the decisiveness he had shown all along, Mercier went to see Seward on 21 December, despite the fact that Thouvenel's note had not yet arrived.[25]

Mercier found the secretary predictably still trying to split the entente and even to extract some help from France. "Do you think," Seward asked, "that Lyons' leaving would necessarily mean war?" Mercier said yes, adding that the United States would wait in vain for any French support in such a case. On the other hand, France would help make the pill easier to swallow should Seward succeed in talking the president into yielding. Mercier even offered to talk with senators and others in favor of such a course. He admitted that he as yet had no note from Paris but said he expected it momentarily.[26]

Seward declined Mercier's offer to lobby for peace and

[24] Russell to Lyons, Pembroke Lodge, 1 Dec. 1861, Newton, I, 62.
[25] *Ibid.*, p. 63; Case, *Revue historique*, CCXXVI (1961), 68-69.
[26] Mercier to Thouvenel, Washington, 23 Dec. 1861, AMAE, CP, E-U, 125: 308-17, no. 76.

said he would rather wait to see Thouvenel's note. In the ensuing two days, Mercier twice saw Lyons and gave him a detailed account of what he and Seward had said to each other. Lyons, as noted, had reason to be very grateful:

> M. Mercier went of his own accord to Mr. Seward the day before yesterday and expressed strongly his own conviction that the choice lay only between a compliance with the demands of England and war. He begged Mr. Seward to dismiss all idea of assistance from France and not to be led away by the vulgar notion that the Emperor would gladly see England embroiled with the United States in order to pursue his own plans in Europe without opposition.
>
> . . . . .
>
> M. Mercier reports the conversation today to his government. . . . I am disposed to speak in very high terms of the moral support given to my demands by M. Mercier.
>
> . . . . .
>
> P.S. I have kept M. Mercier *au courant* of all my communications, confidential as well as official, with Mr. Seward, but I have given no information as to either to any one else.[27]

Great Britain and France were clearly inseparable in this crisis, and thanks to Mercier, the American government knew it before making its own decision. That decision, of course, was ultimately the decision of Abraham Lincoln, and the French stance had much to do with changing the president's mind on a very crucial point—the possibility of arbitrating the dispute. It is possible that Lincoln had been considering arbitration for as much as two weeks, or he

[27] Lyons to Russell, Washington, 23 Dec. 1861, Newton, I, 67-70. See also Lyons to Russell, Washington, 27 Dec. 1861, *Sessional Papers*, LXII (1862), 630, no. 23.

may have been brought to it later by suggestions from several quarters, including Thurlow Weed in France and John Bright in England. He expressed his own idea in a draft dispatch which, if delivered, would surely have sent Lord Lyons on his way since it contained no promise to release the four prisoners immediately:

> Upon a submission, containing the foregoing facts, ... together with all other facts which either party may deem material, I am instructed to say the government of the United States will, if agreed to by Her Majesty's government, go to such friendly arbitration as is usual among nations, and will abide the award.[28]

On Christmas day, in the first year of the Civil War, the leaders of the United States met in the White House. They put into one side of the scale their pride and sensitivity as representatives of a proud and sensitive young nation; into the other side went the probability of war with England, with its attendant probability of failure in reuniting America under one flag. As of 10:00 A.M., when they sat down, there were perhaps but two who had already determined that the prisoners must be released— Seward and the postmaster general, Montgomery Blair. For four hours they weighed and weighed. Specific pieces of evidence included letters from Bright and Richard Cobden, presented by Senator Sumner in person, which showed how British opinion had waxed bitter; a dispatch from C. F. Adams to the same effect; letters from Thurlow Weed and John Bigelow, consul in Paris, which rightly showed that

[28] "Draft of a Dispatch in Reply to Lord John Russell Concerning the *Trent* Affair [December 10?], 1861," *Lincoln Works*, ed. Basler, v, 62-64; Case, *Revue historique*, ccxxvi (1961) 74-76. Nicolay and Hay also give the draft dispatch, implying it was written about 23 December. The editors of *Lincoln Works*, as noted, date it two weeks earlier, with a question mark (Nicolay and Hay, v, 32-34). For suggestions from several quarters that France arbitrate, see Case and Spencer, pp. 209-13, 225-26.

France stood with England, though Bigelow thought the emperor might like to arbitrate the dispute or even see England kept busy in an American war; and finally that letter from Dayton, stating that France would be benevolent toward Britain if war should ensue.[29]

There was one piece of evidence which Seward, now the leading peacemaker, needed to buttress the argument in favor of releasing the prisoners. So long as it was Mercier's interpretation versus Bigelow's, those who favored delay might continue to hope for something from France. What was desperately needed then, for clarification and for peace, was Thouvenel's dispatch. Sometime after 10:00 A.M. Mercier appeared at the state department with the document in his hand; its arrival could hardly have been more dramatic. Frederick Seward told the undoubtedly breathless diplomat that his father was already at the cabinet session. In response to Mercier's request, he took the note to the White House and into the meeting, where it joined the other evidence on the table. There is every reason to think that it weighed heavily with those present. Thus, Attorney General Edward Bates:

> The French government fully agrees with England that the seisure of S[lidell] and M.[ason], *as made* (i.e. without bringing in the Trent, for adjudication) was a breech [*sic*] of the laws of nations. And this appears by the instructions sent to Mr. Mercier, the minister here, who has furnished Mr. Seward with a copy.

[29] Case, *Revue historique*, ccxxvi (1961) 71-74; Dayton to Seward, Paris, 6 Dec. 1861 (rcd. 25 Dec. 1861), State Dept. Corres., France Dispatches, li, no. 91, also in *For. Rel. U.S.*, 1862, p. 307. For other treatments of the Christmas meeting, see Randall, *Lincoln the President*, ii, 48-49; E. D. Adams, i, 232; Harris, pp. 190-91; Nicolay and Hay, v, 34-38; Bates, *Diary*, pp. 212-17; Marvin R. Cain, *Lincoln's Attorney General: Edward Bates of Missouri* (Columbia, Mo.: University of Missouri Press, 1965), p. 244; Korolewicz-Carlton, pp. 69-72.

The meeting ended with the cabinet divided evenly on whether to release the prisoners, i.e., whether to approve Seward's draft dispatch acceding, albeit bumptiously, to the Russell demands.[30]

President Lincoln's draft dispatch on arbitration was not discussed at the meeting, but afterwards he told Seward he was going to prepare a brief in favor of retaining the prisoners, while Seward, he urged, should go on polishing his own contrary statement. Of all the evidence and arguments presented at the cabinet session, it is quite obvious that the newest were the letters from Dayton and Thouvenel spelling out the French condemnation of the *Trent* affair. What the president had to mull over, then, and try to integrate with his thinking was precisely the French position. That he was doing just that appears from his remarks that Christmas night to Senator Browning, namely that Thouvenel's note showed that Europe was against the United States on the question of neutral rights. For the rest we can only speculate about his trend of thought, but one thing is clear: if the leading potential arbitrator had already decided that the prisoners must be released, what was the sense of arbitration? Far better to take the Russell–Prince Albert hint and let the prisoners go of one's "own accord." Further, whatever the advantage of an arbitration award in smoothing American public opinion, this could be gained more quickly by simply publishing Thouvenel's dispatch. It would then be apparent that the United States had yielded, not merely to British power, but also to the moral force of third-party judgment—judgment based upon tra-

[30] Bates, *Diary*, p. 215. "The dramatic arrival of the French dispatch advising the release of Mason and Slidell at the very moment when the cabinet was discussing the subject is a matter of history. The Austrian and Prussian notes, which were of the same tenor, arrived too late to have any influence on the decision" (Lutz, *Annual Report of the American Historical Association for the Year 1915*, p. 215).

ditional American views of neutral rights. It could all be put quite nobly, and embarrassment might be kept to a minimum.[31]

Whatever Abraham Lincoln's logical process was, the fact is that the cabinet meeting was resumed the following day, that all including the president approved of Seward's dispatch, and that in consequence the Civil War remained a limited war. The Christmas of 1861 was a time of peace after all.[32]

Seward sent his note on 27 December. Through tortuous legal pathways, with much ado about high-minded American principles and British insensitivity, it came out at the point which Russell had sternly indicated: the prisoners could leave Fort Warren and go to England and France. There was no apology, though Wilkes's act was of course disavowed. As with so many of the secretary's major pronouncements, it was obviously intended as much for Republican ultras and American readers as it was for the British foreign office. There was a great deal in it to quarrel over through diplomatic channels, but there was nothing in it to justify war, and that was the only thing which mattered.[33]

It was also on the twenty-seventh that Seward informed Lyons and Mercier, his guests at dinner, of the great dénouement. The following day, at the end of a long week, several of the key documents appeared in the press, including Thouvenel's note of 3 December.[34]

In a notably less than frank statement, Seward told Mer-

[31] Case, *Revue historique,* ccxxvi (1961), 76-78; Case and Spencer, pp. 223-30; Browning, *Diary,* I, 518-19.

[32] Lincoln told Seward after the meeting that in trying to write his brief in favor of keeping the prisoners, he had become convinced that they must be released (F. W. Seward, *Seward at Washington,* II, 26).

[33] Seward to Lyons, Washington, 26 Dec. 1861, State Dept. Corres., Notes to the British Legation, IX, 72-94.

[34] *National Intelligencer* (Washington), 28 Dec. 1861.

cier that Thouvenel's note was interesting and helpful but
not really important:

> Before receiving the paper, however, the President
> had decided upon the disposition to be made of the
> subject which has caused so much anxiety in Europe.
> That disposition of the subject, as I think, renders un-
> necessary any discussion of it, in reply to the comments
> of Mr. Thouvenel.[35]

Even from a purely technical viewpoint, this language is
incomplete, that is, even if the word "receiving" means
more than hearing the dispatch read. As noted, the president
left the meeting of 25 December still ready to argue for
keeping the prisoners. Among the thoughts of the next
hours which may have changed his mind, those in the
French note were among the newest and most germane;
just as obviously, they tended to make arbitration imprac-
ticable. But even apart from this, thanks to Mercier the
American government knew the gist of the French position
as early as 21 December. It is certain that the firm opinion
of the world's leading "neutral" nation, on a point of international law such as the *Trent* affair posed, must have had
considerable weight with the American president and cabinet. The only statement to the contrary is the one quoted
above from Seward, and he patently had an axe to grind,
namely, to keep the entente from appearing to be the
arbiter of American fortunes.[36]

[35] Seward to Mercier, Washington, 27 Dec. 1861, State Dept.
Corres., Notes to the French Legation, vii, 77-78.

[36] F. W. Seward supports his father's statement (*Seward at Washington*, ii, 34-35). For a complete argument against the Seward
thesis, and a review of the authors who have followed it, see Case,
Revue historique, ccxxvi (1961), 58, n. 1, and 82-86: "Although
the false disavowal of the secretary has misled historians into dis-
regarding the French note, it fooled neither statesmen nor political
observers in Europe. In a word, after a new examination of the documents, we see that before its delivery the English and the French

Year's end was a suitable time for reflection and summing up; in this mood Mercier set himself to some new political philosophizing about America. Americans, he said, were not sticky about honor, but they were proud, and they had just taken a stiff blow to that pride. They were used to thinking of themselves as the best people on earth, with the best institutions. Their material strength, the growth of their population, their past successes—all had accustomed them to this self-esteem. But now they must realize that their institutions could prevent neither civil war nor corollary reverses. What the future might hold was anyone's guess, perhaps even a dismal fragmentation followed by a new beginning.

In the immediate picture, he continued, Seward was sure to be the butt of chauvinist criticism. Maybe the secretary had judged things wrongly in the first days of the crisis, and maybe he knew more about Wilkes's action than he let on. But once he saw the danger of war, he acted resolutely and effectively. Seward, thought Mercier, deserved credit for helping to keep the peace, and in this regard, his quick publication of Thouvenel's dispatch showed how greatly France had helped him.[37]

---

expected it to have a great influence, and that Seward both needed it and used it effectively to influence the president, the Cabinet, Congress, and the public to yield to the demands of England" (p. 86).

Lyons certainly had no reservations about the effect of Thouvenel's note, and he so told Mercier. It is interesting to compare Mercier's original report of this with the version which Thouvenel had printed: "Lord Lyons attributes this success, which to him seemed less and less likely, to Your Excellency's dispatch" (Mercier to Thouvenel, Washington, 27 Dec. 1861, AMAE, CP, E-U, 125: 322-25, no. 77); vis-à-vis "The honorable minister of England attributes the success of these initiatives in large part to Your Excellency's dispatch" (LJ, II [1861], 103). Thouvenel, perhaps, was afraid of getting Lyons into trouble, since the original version states flatly that the French note turned probable English failure into success.

[37] Mercier to Thouvenel, Washington, 30 Dec. 1861, AMAE, MD, Papiers Thouvenel, XIII, 420-21.

In the constitutional nature of things, one could not claim that Henri Mercier was anything but a secondary figure in the *Trent* crisis. Peace depended upon and was kept by Lincoln and Seward, by Russell and Prince Albert, by Napoleon III and Thouvenel. But on that secondary plane, Mercier's performance was creditable indeed. He refused to be confused about the central issues. Specifically noting that "many people in France will be glad to contemplate the Americans and the English at odds with each other," he sternly added, "I think they are wrong."[38]

When Russell's dispatch arrived and the clock began to tick on the British ultimatum, Mercier was faced with a vital decision. Had he kept silent until Christmas, when Thouvenel's dispatch arrived, the pacific influence of France would have been greatly reduced. Instead, he went quickly to see Seward, acting on the strength of Russell's statement as to the basic French position, on Lyons's need for support, and on his own judgment of what the situation demanded. In doing so, he strengthened Seward's hand in the cabinet as the secretary tried to effect the prisoners' release. Lord Lyons was almost effusive in his gratitude to Mercier, and altogether the cause of international peace was well served. Only the Confederacy had reason to grumble, for despite Wilkes's brashness, Britain withheld her hand. In helping to bring this about, Henri Mercier played his part well.

[38] Mercier to Thouvenel, Washington, 18 Dec. 1861, *ibid.,* fol. 416-18.

CHAPTER V

The Blockade and Diplomacy

THE POSING OF THE PROBLEM

Iɴ the normal course of events, if there had been no Civil War, most of Mercier's time in Washington would have been spent on commercial concerns. As it turned out, such things as market opportunities and the tariff were subsumed into the larger question; but for France and Britain that question remained one of trade, of cotton mostly, and therefore of something like life and death for those thousands whose livelihood was affected. To France, America sent cotton and tobacco, along with such foreign-derived produce as sugar, coffee, and cocoa; from France she bought silk goods, wine, and other luxuries. Nothing approached the importance of cotton, which accounted for something like eighty percent of all United States exports to France. The war's effect upon this can be judged from two statistics: between 1855 and 1859 almost a billion pounds of cotton left America for France; the corresponding figure for 1860-1864 is about one-third that amount. The worst point of the famine was reached in 1862 as the joint effect of the Union blockade and the Southern embargo overcame the stored bumper crops which had been shipped before the outbreak of the Civil War. France received 311,000 bales in 1862 as contrasted with 621,000 in 1860 and 578,000 in 1861. By 1863, as we shall see, the situation had eased, owing partly to better techniques of blockade-running and partly to imports from Egypt and other areas.[1]

[1] Owsley, *King Cotton Diplomacy*, p. 138; see also pp. 134-37.

In considering the war's disruption of trade, we must also mention the North's tariffs, second in importance only to the blockade itself. For years prior to Mercier's arrival, America and France had been negotiating a liberalization of tariff duties. John Y. Mason had begun the talks which occupied so much of Faulkner's time in Paris; the chief French negotiator was Eugène Rouher, minister of agriculture and commerce. Reciprocal reductions had been subjected to long, drawn-out scrutiny by the time that France, as part of her overall shift to a liberal trade policy in early 1860, repealed her duties on raw cotton. The talks had continued throughout 1860, but the Americans then favored a treaty which would affect only navigation rights, while Thouvenel continued to press for tariff revision. Thus on the eve of the Civil War there was still no treaty, and America was about to opt for economic nationalism.[2]

In February 1861, Lord Lyons had made the astute observation that a combination of Republican victory and civil war could cut off trade with Europe—in the North by higher tariffs and in the South by a federal blockade. Mercier relayed this prediction to Thouvenel; for summary neatness it could scarcely be improved upon.[3] There was reason to fear Republican protectionism. The platform of 1860, in a successful effort to win votes from iron-mongering Pennsylvania, had promised duties which would "en-

---

For a complete picture of how the blockade-embargo affected French manufacturers and workers in 1861, see Case and Spencer, *U.S. and France*, pp. 158-71.

[2] Blumenthal, *Franco-American Relations*, pp. 93-99; Faulkner to Cass, Paris, 20 Nov. 1860, State Dept. Corres., France, Dispatches, XLVIII, no. 66; Faulkner to Cass, Paris, 8 Dec. 1860, *ibid.*, no. 76; Faulkner to Black, Paris, 1 March 1861, State Dept. Corres., France, Dispatches, XLIX, no. 106.

[3] Mercier to Thouvenel, Washington, 11 Feb. 1861, AMAE, CP, E-U, 124: 53-60, no. 23.

courage the development of the industrial interests of the whole country."[4]

The first implementation of this policy came quickly enough. The Morrill tariff bill, defeated in 1860 by Southern senators, was passed on 20 February 1861 after the Southerners had left. Its rates, moderate when compared with the future, were nevertheless resented in Europe as a reversal of the nineteenth century's "free trade" trend.[5] Salmon P. Chase, secretary of the treasury, was paradoxically an economic liberal himself. Yet it fell to him to recommend even higher rates to the special session of Congress which met on 4 July. The simple fact was that to prosecute a war, the federal government needed more money.

Mercier at this time had the benefit of special expert advice from Ernest Baroche, son of the prominent minister Jules Baroche, and long a leading French promoter of expanding international trade, as well as the government's director of foreign commerce. He had been implicated in a financial scandal and consequently had been sent to America on a speaking and observation tour. In the spring and summer of 1861 he spent some time with Mercier in Washington.[6] Baroche helped Mercier prepare a memo-

[4] Quoted in Randall and Donald, *Civil War and Reconstruction*, p. 287.

[5] Ida M. Tarbell, *The Tariff in our Times* (New York: Macmillan Co., 1912), pp. 7-8.

[6] For an appreciation of Ernest Baroche, see Arthur L. Dunham, "The Development of the Cotton Industry in France and Anglo-French Treaty of Commerce of 1860," *Economic History Review*, I (1928), 281-307. Baroche, among others, was accused of taking a bribe from the financier Jules Mirès. His trip to America and Canada lasted till October of 1861. The emperor quietly dropped him from the post of director of foreign commerce, but he was not put on trial (Jean Maurain, *Un bourgeois au XIXe siècle: Baroche, ministre de Napoléon III après ses papiers inédits* [Paris: Librairie Félix Alcan, 1936], pp. 256-75). Baroche, who visited the South as well as the North, became convinced that the Union was completely dissolved

randum on the tariff which buttressed the envoy's arguments before Chase and various legislators. But the need of the North for war money was too much for even this special effort. The tariff of 5 August, while clearly revenue-producing and not of protectionist parentage, managed to exceed the Morrill restrictions. Silk goods remained at thirty percent, and the rate on wine was higher yet.[7] Mercier's reaction was grimly philosophical:

> We have been decisively beaten on the tariff question, . . . but I am doing as the Americans do who have such a sturdy spirit that they always see a good side to their defeats. . . . The more ridiculous the tariff is, the more one can blame it for the deficit which the customs duties will inevitably show.[8]

---

and that the South had the resources to maintain its independence (Mercier to Thouvenel, Washington, 6 May 1861, AMAE, MD, Papiers Thouvenel, XIII, 362-65; A. Belmont to James de Rothschild, New York, 25 June 1861, August Belmont, *Letters, Speeches, and Addresses of August Belmont* [New York: privately printed, 1890], pp. 74-75. See also Reinhard H. Luthin, "Abraham Lincoln and the Tariff," *American Historical Review*, XLIX (1944), 609-29.

[7] Mercier to Thouvenel, Washington, 15 July 1861, AMAE, CP, E-U, 124: 393-401, no. 47; Mercier to Thouvenel, Washington, 21 July 1861, *ibid.*, fol. 453-59, no. 48; Mercier to Thouvenel, Washington, 17 July 1861, AMAE, MD, Papiers Thouvenel, XIII, 377-80. See also F. W. Taussig, *The Tariff History of the United States* (New York: G. P. Putnam's Sons, 1905), p. 413; and Bray Hammond, "The North's Empty Purse, 1861-1862," *American Historical Review*, LXVII (1961), 1-18.

Mercier stressed the traditional liberal argument that increased rates would cut imports and hence revenue. For an interesting counterargument—that the American rates were no more protectionist than the French under the Cobden–Chevalier treaty, and that "free trade" and slavery worked together to keep America a producer of primary products—see Henry C. Carey, *The French and American Tariffs Compared, in a Series of Letters Addressed to Mons. Michel Chevalier* (Philadelphia: Collins, 1861), p. 28.

[8] Mercier to Thouvenel, Washington, 5 August 1861, AMAE, MD, Papiers Thouvenel, XIII, 395-97.

It was not the higher price of silk and wine that strangled trade, however. The federal cruisers outside Charleston, New Orleans, and the other Southern ports were a far more tangible and immediate choking force. Thanks to a long coast and the skill of her blockade-runners, the Confederacy continued to breathe irregular gasps. But Secretary Welles applied enough pressure of increasing strength to keep his victim weak throughout the war. By the end of 1861, seventy-nine steam-propelled and as many sailing warships were in action, and by the end of the war this number had grown to six hundred naval vessels of all sorts. Despite this, Confederate blockade-running showed a slight increase in effectiveness in 1863. The overall picture, as we have seen, shows that the worst crisis of the cotton famine came in the fall of 1862. This helps to explain the frenzied diplomacy of intervention which accompanied that phase of the war.[9]

Where cotton was concerned, Southern theory in 1861 was a firm ally of the Union navy. The notion that King Cotton could issue decrees to Washington had been current for years in the South and had played some part in the very decision to secede. Europe's necessity would be Dixie's opportunity. The problem, though, was to find some effective way for the king to wield his scepter. One school of thought believed an embargo on cotton would be the best way to prod Europe into action. Such theorists failed to get legislation from the Confederate congress, but state laws and private agitation did result in a sharp reduction of exports and new planting. In places, existing cotton was burned. The year 1862 would show the effect of blockade and embargo.[10]

[9] Owsley, *King Cotton Diplomacy*, p. 137; see also Owsley, *Essays in Honor of Dodd*, ed. Craven, pp. 197-98. Lincoln, in fact, declared only the Southern *ports* blockaded, not the entire coast (See Case and Spencer, pp. 134 and 139).

[10] Mercier to Thouvenel, Washington, 14 Oct. 1861, AMAE, CP, E-U,

The full effect of the cotton famine would thus not be felt immediately in France. As noted, abnormally large stocks of raw cotton were on hand because of the bumper crops of 1859 and 1860. But cotton fabric was also in over-supply, partly from French production, partly too from the Cobden–Chevalier treaty: in October of 1861, British yarn and cloth began pouring across the lowered tariff-barrier. The shape of the future was complicated and bleak for French cotton producers and their operatives, for the cost of the raw material was bound to rise, and the price of the finished product to fall.[11]

For Thouvenel, Mercier, and the other French authorities, reckoning with the future as well as the present, the diplomatic problem was already there in the last quarter of 1861. The blockade and the reduced Northern consumption of luxuries were spreading misery far beyond the cotton industry. Silk, lace, hats, china were names of things which, when translated, meant less food, poorer clothes, fewer savings, and eventually even the threat of starvation to Frenchmen for whom Napoleon III and his advisers felt an acute responsibility. French public opinion remained friendly to the antislavery North and anxious that France not get involved in the American War. But Frenchmen from the emperor down hoped mightily that the bloody affair, with all its dreadful implications for France, would soon end.[12]

125: 145-50, no. 65, in which Mercier signals the coming crisis in cotton.

[11] Dunham, *Economic History Review*, i (1928), 291-92; Blumenthal, *Franco-American Relations*, pp. 154-55.

[12] Lynn M. Case, *French Opinion on the United States and Mexico, 1860-1867, Extracts from the Reports of the Procureurs Généraux* (New York: D. Appleton-Century Co., 1936), p. 244; Blumenthal, p. 156.

See, for example, the report of the advocate general of the Lyons district, 8 Oct. 1861: "I have already made known to Your Excellency the nature of the business crisis which currently affects the

THOUVENEL, MERCIER, AND THE BLOCKADE

Mercier, during a lull in his odyssey of summer 1861, neatly drew the factors together, calling for "a settlement which would end this disastrous war and reopen the American market to us, or at the very least would head off the losses which the lack of cotton would mean to our industry." Mercier, however, saw little chance of success for any immediate French move; for one thing, the North was determined to revenge Bull Run. The only thing to do was to wait—and stand ready. France and Britain, he thought, should take a firm enough line with the United States so that their commercial rights and interests would be respected. To this end, he again urged that Lyons and he be given more liberty of action to prepare for recognition of the Confederacy. He also suggested that Thouvenel send him a dispatch detailing the economic harm which the war would inflict on France.[13]

In Mercier's mind the twin matters of intervention against the blockade and diplomatic recognition of the South were somewhat illogically joined. He seems to have felt that if Britain and France were to break the blockade they should first recognize the Confederacy since otherwise they would be open to the charge of shooting their way into United States ports. The moment for such recognition-intervention would of course have to be decided in Paris, he said, and

---

city of Lyons. The hope . . . of an upswing in the silk industry has been completely disappointed. The political difficulties in the United States of America are certainly the cause of this trouble, and it will last . . . as long as peace is not reestablished" (quoted in Case, *French Opinion on U.S. and Mexico*, pp. 20-21). See also Jordan and Pratt, *Europe and the American Civil War*, p. 208.

[13] Mercier to Thouvenel, Niagara [New York], 9 Sept. 1861, AMAE, MD, Papiers Thouvenel, XIII, 385-92. This letter is a private one only because Mercier was away from his desk; in form and substance it was patently intended as an official dispatch. Its consequent vagueness was cleared up in the following private letter, 13 Sept. 1861.

now was not the right time. But circumstances would change, and "liberty of action" would enable him to sound out Northern opinion and get its thinking about the probable effect of European recognition of the Confederacy. The alternative course of intervening to help the North would be chasing a shadow, for the Union could not be reestablished. Mercier had difficulty at this point in conceiving of the North's actually subjugating the South by main force, constraining a vast population against its will to remain in the Union. And it is apparent that by the end of the war's first summer, Mercier had given up the faint hopes of spring that the South could be lured back. Sumter, the call for 75,000 volunteers, and first Bull Run had effectively seen to that.[14]

One debilitating factor from Mercier's point of view was British foot-dragging on the intervention issue and Lyons's relative calm about the whole deteriorating situation. Mercier was in complete agreement with the Quai d'Orsay about the need for joint movement with Britain. France might take the lead to the extent of setting things in motion, but unless England came along, nothing else could be done. So long as Russell thought the economic burden tolerable, so long as Lyons kept his reserve and failed to prod Russell, European intervention would fail. "When you go in tandem," he said, "you are rarely guilty of taking too many chances; and especially with England, you don't often get there on time."[15]

By the third week of October, Mercier had received Thouvenel's instructions. They clearly showed that the foreign minister was just as concerned as Mercier about the war's effect on the French economy. In fact, they were an apt response to Mercier's suggestion of 9 September that

[14] Mercier to Thouvenel, Quebec, 13 Sept. 1861, *ibid.*, fol. 403-05.
[15] Mercier to Thouvenel, Washington, *ibid.*, fol. 410-13. See also Mercier to Thouvenel, Washington, 10 Oct. 1861, AMAE, CP, E-U, 125: 137-43, no. 64.

he be furnished a full description of the difficulty caused by the blockade and the general disruption. Even were cotton the only problem, said Thouvenel, that problem would be serious enough:

> Today it has completely taken the place of other products both in consumption and in manufacture that there is no longer anything which can replace it if the supply dwindles. You know what the needs of France are in this regard, with a textile production of seven hundred million francs. . . . Therefore I ask myself if things have not already reached the point where it is the merest prudence to anticipate certain developments, so that we will not suddenly find ourselves facing needs which might leave no one his full liberty of judgment and action.

Having thus set the stage for a dramatic announcement, Thouvenel then produced something of an anticlimax. France, he said, would appreciate a special understanding with the United States, an arrangement whereby the blockade could be somehow relaxed so that cotton would be forthcoming.[16]

The clear implication, however, was that intervention might follow should France not get the cotton. Given Mercier's wish to say something strong in Washington, this dispatch was permission enough. His immediate reaction

16 Thouvenel to Mercier, Paris, 3 Oct. 1861, *ibid.*, fol. 108-13, no. 27. Korolewicz-Carlton sees this dispatch as a sharp departure from Thouvenel's previously pro-Northern tone. He postulates an interview between Thouvenel and the emperor at which the latter broached his interest in pacifying Mexico (Korolewicz-Carlton, pp. 115-19). This is, of course, completely conjectural. Thouvenel later made it clear that the exception he sought to the blockade was meant for the benefit of all nations and was not an effort to obtain some advantage over Great Britain (Dayton to Seward, Paris, 6 Dec. 1861, State Dept. Corres., France, Dispatches, LI, no. 91, also in *For. Rel. U.S.*, 1862, p. 307).

was to discourage Thouvenel from the blockade-exception idea. The North would never do it, he said, for they were counting on the blockade to help them win, and a relaxation would encourage the South to fight on. And even should the North cooperate, the South would demand recognition before allowing the cotton to move.

Should the South be recognized immediately? Mercier thought no, not yet: "I think, therefore, that recognizing the South at this time could not be done without risking a conflict which could be very short, but which it is nevertheless desirable to avoid. Will the maritime powers succeed better by relying on the course of events? I think so." Nevertheless, Mercier thought the Americans should be warned of what they might have to face and be prepared "to accept with resignation the sacrifices which events require."[17]

Mercier began his overture by sending Seward a copy of Thouvenel's dispatch; two days later they faced each other. The American's style had changed since the spring: he was less the swashbuckler now and used the broadsword less often, but his rapier was quick to parry and to thrust. Why should France bring up such subjects when it was clear that Franco-American relations were so much more amicable than Anglo-American? Of course war caused suffering through trade disruption, but America was learning to live without buying so much from Europe. And in any case, the entire situation might have been avoided had Britain and France not encouraged the South by recognizing her belligerency. America might expect such things from England. But not from France! No matter what, the United States would fight on and on, would never consent to its own dissolution; and if Europe wished to come in, America would respond as France had done in 1792 and 1793. Recent moves

[17] Mercier to Thouvenel, Washington, 22 Oct. 1861, AMAE, CP, E-U, 125: 151-63, no. 66.

by the American navy for coastal protection should be taken as a solemn warning to Europe. Seward had achieved an interesting mixture of subtlety and steel—undermining the entente, hinting about economic nationalism, taking the high ground of patriotic self-sacrifice, sadly threatening war. Mercier had need of patience.

There is of course no stenographic record of Mercier's reply, but he quoted himself directly in his report and thus left us an interesting example of his method:

Mercier: We have always wished the Union well and have expressed these wishes to you on many occasions. . . . Whatever stance we take, our political and commercial interests are both bound up with the strength and health of the United States. . . . In this crisis you and we have the same objective so far as the United States are concerned—that they emerge as strong and powerful as possible. But you know from your own experience that a government cannot always do as it wishes. . . . At this moment the sufferings which affect and which threaten our commerce, our industry, our working population are such that they constitute a need for which we absolutely must find a quick solution. . . . I am not unaware of the energy and superior resources of all kinds which the North commands in the fight, and I admit that in the long run, it could end by beating the South. But what I also see no less clearly is that each blow it delivers against the physical force opposing it means a moral obstacle to reestablishing the Union.

France could not simply fold her arms, he added. There must be an end to the war, an end which would leave the North powerful.

Seward, with Thouvenel's dispatch in his hands, could feel the difference of emphasis between what Paris had sent and what Mercier had said; indeed, Mercier repeated that his observations were his own. When Mercier brought the conversation back to the dispatch, Seward asked what Thouvenel might have in mind about an understanding with America leading to a relaxation of the blockade. "We ask nothing of you save moral support," said Seward. "Have confidence in the reestablishment of the Union, and let this be well enough known, so that the South is convinced of it, and for our part we shall find a way to supply your industry with cotton." As Mercier reported it, he was unable to get Seward to be more precise. It would seem clear, however, that the secretary was hinting at withdrawal of the recognition of Southern belligerency. Mercier was quite rightly of the opinion that any promise about cotton might be hard to fulfill. The Union's seizure of one or two Southern ports would not solve the problem so long as the Civil War continued, for the South would do everything it could to prevent her planters from selling their cotton, and patriotic planters would readily cooperate.[18]

Seward was actually little interested in granting France any blockade concessions in return for her "moral help." He would not insult France, he said, by supposing she intended to use force if not satisfied. Europe, after all, had introduced slavery to America, and America could not permit any intervention geared to defend such an institution. "We do not expect any proceeding on the part of France."[19]

[18] The above conversation is from Mercier to Thouvenel, Washington, 28 Oct. 1861, AMAE, CP, E-U, 125: 167-80, no. 67. See also Owsley, *King Cotton Diplomacy*, pp. 69-71; Burton J. Hendrick, pp. 211-12.

[19] Seward to Dayton, Washington, 30 Oct. 1861, State Dept. Corres., France, Instructions, XVI, 66-80, no. 75. See also E. D. Adams, *Great Britain and the American Civil War*, I, 200; Bancroft, *Life of William H. Seward*, II, 215-19. In a conversation with Mercier, Edward Everett, the Constitutional candidate and friend of Corcoran, elaborated an interesting parallel to Seward's arguments. He told Mercier frankly that French blockade-breaking would mean

Maybe not, but Mercier continued to press the opinion that since reestablishment of the Union seemed so unlikely, some "arrangement" should be the long-range aim of French policy. This arrangement should specifically be one which would minimize the question of where to draw boundaries and facilitate continued intimacy of communication and trade: in other words, it should include a common market.

When Seward spoke of a strong Union emerging from the war, he spoke as an American nationalist for whom political unity was beyond discussion. But one man's national patriotism may be another's most boring topic. Mercier quite understandably found American national tenacity an annoying phenomenon, one which was costing lives in the New World and threatening tragedy in the Old. To him it seemed the merest common sense that if the economic advantages of the old boundaries could be preserved in a common market, the question of new political frontiers should not be allowed to go on killing people. It seems apparent that Seward, who felt so strongly about the inseparability of South Carolina and Texas from Washington, would have been more relaxed about, say, the separation of Alsace and Lorraine from Paris.

When Mercier spoke of a strong state emerging from the

---

war and that he thought Mercier was bluffing (C. F. Adams, Jr., "The Trent Affair," *Massachusetts Historical Society Proceedings,* XLV [1911], 35-148).

Seward entrusted his dispatch of 30 October to "a special messenger." In early November his old political friend Thurlow Weed and Archbishop John Hughes, whom Seward had come to know well when he was governor of New York, went to France as special ambassadors to plead the Union cause. By the time they arrived, their diplomatic dispatch was out of date; Thouvenel already had the news from Mercier, and the *Trent* affair had preempted the stage (Seward to Dayton, Washington, 26 Oct. 1861, State Dept. Corres., France, Instructions, XVI, 64-65, unnumbered; Seward to Dayton, Washington, 2 Nov. 1861, *ibid.,* p. 80, unnumbered; Dayton to Seward, Paris, 25 Nov. 1861, State Dept. Corres., France, Dispatches, LI, no. 86).

war, he spoke as a detached observer. It was manifestly inaccurate for him to allege, as he had in his conversation with Seward, that France and the United States hoped for the same result from the war. For him, the common market plan, approved by no less an American patriot than Stephen Douglas, had hopeful possibilities. "The fact is that a number of arguments can be marshalled in its favor, and that if it were adopted, the question of boundaries and even other questions would be considerably simplified."[20]

The discussions of autumn, then, left the situation at stalemate. Thouvenel was obviously nervous about the Civil War and its potential effect on the French economy. Seward, while less pugnacious than he had been in April, amply and clearly expressed the intransigence of his government on the key point, namely, that the war could end in only one way, with the South acknowledging federal sovereignty. Mercier, going beyond Thouvenel's notes, broached the possibility of Southern political independence. He was not surprised by Seward's adamant stand, and congratulated himself for having laid the groundwork for future European intervention. Mercier, in other words, refused to take the stated word of the Lincoln government as the *final* word. He persisted in that refusal when the discussion resumed after the *Trent* episode.

THE BLOCKADE AFTER *Trent*

The international war which seemed so close in December might well have ended the Union blockade of Southern ports—a possibility which was clear to all the *Trent* debaters. Nevertheless, the immediate issues of international law, of neutral rights in wartime, preempted the main line of the *Trent* discussion and shunted the blockade debate to a siding. In January, however, Paris, London, Washing-

[20] Mercier to Thouvenel, Washington, 7 Nov. 1861, AMAE, CP, E-U, 125: 186-97, no. 68.

ton, and Richmond were again buzzing with cotton statistics, rumors, military prognostications, constitutional
formulations, and patriotic declamations—all designed to
end the blockade and the Civil War, in one way or another.
Mercier, on Thouvenel's precise insistence, assured
Seward that France was not leading any attack on the
Union, nor even on the blockade.[21] But it was the publicly
stated word of the French government itself which allayed
apprehensions in Washington, at least temporarily. On
12 February the American press carried word of Napoleon
III's brief reference to America in his speech to the legislature, a reference which offered nothing to the South save
cool neutrality. A month later it was the orator Adolphe
Billault, minister without portfolio and official spokesman
for the government, whose Senate speech on benevolent
neutrality reassured Northern supporters.[22] Mercier himself
found an opportunity to please Senator Sumner, who said
he expected an Anglo-French "admonition" any day. Replied Mercier, "How can you, sir, have such notions? You
are too great a nation to be treated in this way. Such letters would do for Greece, etc., but not for you."[23]

On the level of rumor and public proclamation, then, the
game was still at stalemate. But the economic crisis was
deepening in France, and professional diplomacy had to
keep pace with its complications. Seward wanted Mercier
to understand that he really did appreciate the rights of
neutrals in the war and the blockade.[24] His dogged effort

[21] Mercier to Thouvenel, Washington, 11 Feb. 1862, *ibid.*, 126:
128-42, no. 84.

[22] *New York Times*, 12 Feb. 1862; Dayton to Seward, Paris, 27
Jan. 1862, State Dept. Corres., France, Dispatches, LI, no. 109; Dayton to Seward, Paris, 27 Feb. 1862, *ibid.*, no. 120. These two dispatches are also in *For. Rel. U.S.*, 1862, pp. 310-12, 318. See also
Case and Spencer, pp. 262-64.

[23] Quoted in Gurowski, *Diary*, I, 176.

[24] Mercier to Thouvenel, Washington, 11 Feb. 1862, AMAE, CP, E-U,
126: 128-42; see also *LJ*, III (1862), 111.

to stave off European action came increasingly to rely upon Union military victories, victories which would open Southern ports and get the cotton moving in that way. In western Tennessee, Forts Henry and Donelson fell to the Union Generals Halleck and Grant in early February; seven weeks later the Union victory at Shiloh paved the way to the opening of the Mississippi. In Virginia the epochal victory on 9 March of the Union ironclad *Monitor* over the South's formidable *Merrimac* made possible McClellan's "oversea" campaign against Richmond. Later, the Union victory at New Orleans would provide a spectacular climax to this season of Northern advance.

Thouvenel asked Mercier, when the extent of the Union victory in Tennessee became known, whether the North's self-esteem had now been restored enough to allow the Lincoln administration to consider a compromise and end the war. France must certainly do her part, for the sake of Europe, and direct America's attention to this point.[25] And in case such a hint were well received in Washington, Thouvenel thought it might be useful to have John Slidell in Paris, where French good offices could be put to use. Dayton, he continued, had said something vague to the emperor about getting cotton, and Mercier should inquire whether this was anything definite, like special export licenses, or just wishful thinking about military victory.[26]

Peripheral to the main debate on blockade intervention there were a number of other matters which either increased the tension of early 1862 or, by their friendly resolution, helped to relax it. One was the affair of the "stone fleet" in Charleston harbor: as part of the blockade, the federal navy in late autumn of 1861 had sunk some old ships

[25] Thouvenel to Mercier, Paris, 6 March 1862, AMAE, CP, E-U, 126: 211-12, no. 7; see also *LJ*, III (1862), 116-17; Case and Spencer, pp. 275-76.

[26] Thouvenel to Mercier, Paris, 13 March 1862, Thouvenel, *Secret*, II, 247-49.

filled with stone and partially blocked the approaches to the South Carolina port. Lord John Russell made a great storm and alleged that the act was a barbarous, permanent act of destruction. Thouvenel, feeling perhaps that the British were overreacting, protested too, but specified to Mercier that he should merely talk things over with Seward and not make a démarche. Mercier and Seward had that talk on 17 February. As it turned out, the United States could calmly point out that the "stone fleet" was a temporary war measure and was intended to clog up the harbor neither permanently nor completely.[27]

Seward Reacts

William Seward showed every sign of friendliness in the early months of 1862, and this cordiality is not hard to understand. So long as rumors of foreign intervention proved to lack substance, the *status quo* was eminently tolerable from the Union viewpoint: European abstention and Northern military advance. In addition, European credit was needed to help set the government's finances aright, for the *Trent* crisis had touched off a financial panic, and New York banks suspended specie payments on 30 December. On 25 February, Congress approved Secretary Chase's bond schemes as well as the first issue of federal greenbacks. Seward's gentleness, therefore, may partly have

[27] Thouvenel to Mercier, Paris, 23 Jan. 1862, AMAE, CP, E-U, 126: 61-62, no. 4, a translation of which is in State Dept. Corres., Notes from the French Legation, vol. xviii, and in *For. Rel. U.S.*, 1862, p. 409; Mercier to Thouvenel, Washington, 25 Feb. 1862, AMAE, CP, E-U, 126: 173-83, no. 87; Seward to Mercier, Washington, 20 Feb. 1862, State Dept. Corres., Notes to the French Legation, vii, 88-90, also in *For. Rel. U.S.*, 1862, pp. 411-12; Thouvenel to Mercier, Paris, 20 March 1862, AMAE, CP, E-U, 126: 263-64, no. 9. See also Stern, *When the Guns Roared*, p. 113; and E. D. Adams, i, 253-58, which blames the diplomatic flare-up on Russell's fear that the Union blockade might really become effective; Case and Spencer, pp. 251-58.

been a reflection of this overall financial picture, though its main purpose was to keep Europe neutral.[28]

To Thouvenel and Mercier the great business of February, March, and April was to press the Lincoln government on the blockade and to elicit, if possible, something more tangible than friendly words and gestures. Union victories gave the French foreign minister hope that Washington might actually do something to assuage French suffering, might even settle with the South and end the war.

By the time that Thouvenel made this hopeful statement, i.e., in early March, Seward had already made a move of his own, the net effect of which was to negate the French suggestion. Union victories, he said, would soon be opening more coastal ports. What was needed to expedite the resumption of trade in cotton was clearly the withdrawal by Europe of her recognition of Southern belligerency. If the war was long and the cotton famine harsh, Europe should look within herself for the reason: the encouragement given the South by the quasi-recognition.[29]

If Europe would withdraw her recognition of belligerency, she could begin some trading through the ports already captured and could look forward to an end of the war by early May. Mercier told the secretary that the

---

[28] Newton (*Lyons*, I, 81-82) suggests the double motive for Seward's gentle tone. This reasonableness extended also to those problems of ship damage which enforcement of the blockade inevitably entailed. For example, an American cruiser injured the French gunboat *Milan* as the latter was trying to reach New Orleans to effect the repatriation of certain French nationals. About the same time, the brig *Jules et Marie* was damaged by the famous *San Jacinto* in an accidental collision. In both cases the federal cabinet offered quick amends (Mercier to Thouvenel, Washington, 3 Feb. 1862, AMAE, CP, E-U, 126: 111-23, no. 83; Seward to Mercier, Washington, 7 March 1862, State Dept. Corres., Notes to the French Legation, VII, 91).

[29] Thouvenel to Mercier, Paris, 6 March 1862, AMAE, CP, E-U, 126: 211-12, no. 7; Seward to Dayton, Washington, 28 Feb. 1862, State Dept. Corres., France, Instructions, XVI, 117-18, no. 120.

French neutral stance was based on principles of international law and that he did not foresee a change in his government's policy. That, in fact, was Thouvenel's reaction when he received word of Seward's proposal.[30]

Under the circumstances, Mercier rightly concluded that Thouvenel's note of 6 March—the one which looked for peace now that the Tennessee forts were taken—was rather out of date by the time it reached Georgetown. He exercised again that independent judgment expected of diplomats in this period before the Atlantic cable:

Having thought it over, I decided to content myself for the moment with emphasizing to the Washington government the seriousness of our griefs and the duties they impose upon us, but certainly not to insist as yet on the course it should take to end this situation. In fine, it is beyond question that any effort of mine to deflect the government from its aims would in the present circumstances be fruitless.

The North's current offensives, he continued, militated against a negotiated peace; and even more, the debates in the London and Paris legislatures (Billault's speech) and the way in which the Union's *Monitor* stopped the terrifying *Merrimac* both gave Washington confidence in her ability to resist pressure from European maritime powers. "In these circumstances," Mercier advised, "any hint of urgency would likely not be well received and could lead to con-

[30] Mercier to Thouvenel, Washington, 28 Feb. 1862, AMAE, MD, Papiers Thouvenel, XIII, 437-39; Mercier to Thouvenel, Washington, 3 March 1862, AMAE, CP, E-U, 126: 192-207, no. 88; Thouvenel to Mercier, Paris, 27 March 1862, *ibid.*, fol. 295-96, no. 10. See also E. D. Adams, I, 274-275; and Seward to Dayton, Washington, 26 March 1862, State Dept. Corres., France, Instructions, XVI, 130-35, no. 133, also in *For. Rel. U.S.*, 1862, pp. 325-26, in which Seward, commenting on a conversation between Dayton and Napoleon III, elaborates his thesis about Union victory and the likelihood of getting cotton.

versations which would be useless at best; but with a little patience we can hope that the trend of events will create conditions favorable for positive diplomatic moves."[31]

In this tentative mood Mercier went to see Seward. The secretary, having heard all the rumors of intervention and read their contradiction in Billault's speech, was naturally anxious to know what the official word was, but Mercier frankly told him he thought it was the wrong time to reveal Thouvenel's latest note. Seward then made his standard comeback and asked for an unofficial reading of the dispatch.

A quick glance convinced him that this was basically the same complaint about cotton, with implications for blockade-exception and intervention, which had been broached these several months. He thereupon showed Mercier two dispatches, one from Dayton recounting a conversation in which Napoleon III had bemoaned the manufacturing crisis, the other his own reply to Dayton and the emperor.[32] That reply, while it stated the usual line about cotton being available through continued Union victories, was a bit swaggering—an indication, perhaps, that Seward meant to publish it. "In regard to this strife I have been sanguine of only one," the secretary asserted, "and that the cardinal point, namely that the national forces would prevail, and the Union be thus maintained." Rather inaccurately, he implied he had never promised cotton-through-victory, but then he reversed himself in the same dispatch and told Dayton to sooth the emperor about the destruction of cotton by Southerners: "Upon this point you may safely assure him that all apprehensions are, in our view,

[31] Mercier to Thouvenel, Washington, 31 March 1862, AMAE, CP, E-U, 126: 297-318, no. 93.

[32] Dayton to Seward, Paris, 4 March 1862, State Dept. Corres., France, Dispatches, LI, no. 124; Seward to Dayton, Washington, 26 March 1862, State Dept. Corres., France Instructions, XVI, 130-35, no. 133, also in *For. Rel. U.S.*, 1862, pp. 325-26.

groundless. The American people in the Southern as well as in the Northern states, are a civilized . . . people."

Mercier thought this dispatch friendly, but professed to be "astonished" that Seward repeated the business about European recognition of Confederate belligerency being the chief obstacle to peace. The entire conversation served only to strengthen Mercier's original conviction that now was not the time to approach Washington with talk of peace and compromise.

In this connection the talk came round to a recent remark of Lord John Russell's. Seeking, as Mercier saw it, to mollify British interventionists, the foreign secretary had foretold the definite breakup of the American Union within three months. Mercier, in his report to Paris, noted that Lord Lyons was most surprised by this apparent shift in the English line. As Mercier quoted him, Lyons felt that "in the North not one voice would today speak out with any proposal other than the reestablishment of the Union." The two diplomats were of one mind in this: it simply was not the right time to be talking compromise in Washington.[33]

It was Mercier now who had to assure Thouvenel that he was not being too soft with the Washington cabinet:

You can well imagine how dearly I want to help you find a way to relieve the terrible conditions of our population. In this respect you should fear the excess of my zeal more than my indifference, and if I am reduced for now to saying I see nothing that can be done,

[33] The above account of this Mercier–Seward interview is from Mercier to Thouvenel, Washington, 31 March 1862, AMAE, CP, E-U, 126: 297-318, no. 93. See also Owsley, *King Cotton Diplomacy*, pp. 271-72; Owsley reads into Thouvenel's dispatches of 27 February and 6 March "a growing intention on the part of the Emperor to intervene in some form or other," and even connects this supposed intention with Mercier's trip to Richmond. This last is pure speculation and almost certainly incorrect.

please realize that this is not from any taste for passive resignation.

The end of the Union's spring offensive, he thought, might find the North dissatisfied and ready to speak of peace; in that, Russell was probably right. Whatever the military outcome, "we can think of extending our good offices, either to convince the South that further resistance is useless, or to help the North find a peaceful compromise."[34] As ever, diplomacy, and indeed the very national life of the United States, would depend upon the young men who were shooting at one another in Virginia and in the West.[35]

For Mercier, as for many European officials, the Civil War was largely a matter of blockade and cotton. This was not necessarily a coldly economic position: a significant drop in cotton imports could and did mean severe physical and moral anguish for thousands of French citizens. In the spring of 1861 Mercier had already seen what was coming, and he warned that if the war went on into autumn, intervention might then become necessary. By September he was speaking of a need to break the blockade, and he tended to think that diplomatic recognition would have to be extended to Richmond, since otherwise the Confederate government would forbid cotton shipments. But at

[34] Mercier to Thouvenel, Washington, 31 March 1862, AMAE, MD. Papiers Thouvenel, XIII, 443-45.

[35] The classic battle involving the Confederate ironclad *Merrimac* and John Ericsson's little *Monitor* occurred on 8 and 9 March. Captain Gautier of the French warship *Gassendi* was a professionally interested observer. Mercier passed on Captain Gautier's valuable reports, the only eyewitness accounts by a foreigner, together with his own recommendation that a special officer—in effect a naval attaché—be sent out to gather available information of this sort (Mercier to Thouvenel, Washington, 11 March 1862, AMAE, CP, E-U, 126: 215-30, no. 89; Gautier to Mercier, Hampton Roads, 9 March 1862, *ibid.*, fol. 213-14; Mercier to Thouvenel, Washington, 14 March 1862, *ibid.*, fol. 241-47, no. 90; Gautier to Mercier, Hampton Roads, 11 March 1862, *ibid.*, fol. 248-49).

no time did Mercier call for immediate intervention, immediate recognition. First, he thought, the North must get used to the idea of a peace based on separation. To that end, he exceeded Thouvenel's dispatch of 3 October. The foreign minister had spoken of some special relaxation of the blockade in favor of French needs. Mercier, while careful to make it clear where his government's words ended and his own began, spoke openly to Seward about a broken Union and about French survival, a survival, he implied, which might come to depend on intervention in the Civil War.

In early 1862, with the *Trent* crisis over but the cotton crisis deepening, France and America returned to the great debate with no more decisive outcome. Thouvenel kept pressing for an exception to the blockade; Seward countered with a request that France rescind her recognition of Southern belligerency. With the capture of New Orleans seemingly imminent, Seward began to hold out the hope that cotton would be shipped through Union-held ports in the South. Mercier showed clearly in his handling of Thouvenel's notes and in his own reports that he expected little from either the blockade-exception idea or from Union seizure of Southern ports.

The Northern spring offensive was something else again. Mercier felt that at the end of it the North might be so exhausted that she would willingly settle for less than an integral Union; should the offensive succeed, he said, then the South might be ready to submit. Other issues were inseparably intertwined. The evolution of the French adventure in Mexico was beginning to complicate Franco-American diplomacy, and its ultimate effects could as yet only be guessed. Whatever was cloudy, it was at least clear that much depended on how firmly the Confederate government would insist upon independence. While there was still time, an arrangement was thinkable. But if the North did anything serious about emancipation of the slaves, political compromise would be almost impossible. Mercier strongly wished that he could talk to someone who knew what was really going on in Richmond.

CHAPTER VI

The Trip to Richmond

THE GEORGETOWN HOUSE DESTROYED

THE grandest Washington social event of the entire war took place in the White House on Wednesday, 5 February, 1862, a vast entertainment which found a thousand guests promenading to the music of the Marine Corps band, imbibing champagne-rum punch, and picking at a ton of turkeys, duck, venison, pheasants, partridges, and hams. The President and Mrs. Lincoln surely meant no frivolity by this display: they spent a good bit of the evening at the bedside of their son Willie, who died some days later. Mercier may have attended the funeral as the body was laid to rest in Oak Hill Cemetery, in Georgetown, across the street from the legation.[1]

The biggest public event of the 1862 season was the celebration of Washington's birthday on 22 February. For obvious historical and ideological reasons, the Union government wanted to do right by this event. The world would be reminded that the capital had been named for a Virginian, that the South had sent her sons into it as presidents, and that those other children who on this same day in Richmond were inaugurating the "permanent" government of the Confederacy were not of royal lineage. There was a solemn reading of the Farewell Address in the house, marred somewhat by the absence of the mourning president. There were salvos and bells throughout the day and

---

[1] Leech, *Reveille in Washington*, pp. 295-97; *National Intelligencer* (Washington), and *Evening Star* (Washington), 25 Feb. 1862.

an illumination at night. Mercier was there and reported it all home.[2]

The social life of the French minister, then, was a full one. It went on busily till Shrove Tuesday, 4 March, when Mercier and his wife were the guests of Secretary of the Navy Welles.

They returned home toward midnight. Before going to sleep, Madame Mercier thought she smelled smoke; her husband sent two of his servants to check the furnace in the basement, but they found nothing wrong. The Merciers then retired for the night. A week later Mercier had recovered enough from the succeeding events to write two long accounts. The more personal of the two reads like a polished short story. "My dear friend," he began to Thouvenel, "I am going to tell you the story of a very sad accident."[3]

> Toward two o'clock, while we were sleeping soundly, we were awakened with a start by cries of "Fire!" coming from the street level. I jumped to my feet and opened the door of the bedroom, which was instantly filled with a thick cloud of smoke. I realized there was no time to lose. I put a cloak over my wife's shoulders. I wrapped up my children in their blankets, and through the already very dense smoke, I led the escape of this dear center of my world; they went to find refuge in the stable some distance away.

[2] Mercier to Thouvenel, Washington, 25 Feb. 1862, AMAE, CP, E-U, 126: 173-83, no. 87. See also *Evening Star* (Washington), 22 Feb. 1862, and *National Intelligencer* (Washington), 24 Feb. 1862.

[3] Mercier to Thouvenel, Washington, 11 March 1862, AMAE, MD, Papiers Thouvenel, XIII, 440-42; and Mercier to Thouvenel, Washington, 11 March 1862, AMAE, CP, E-U, 126: 215-30, no. 89. (The private letter in the Papiers Thouvenel employs the "past definite" verb formation, a sign that its author was trying to match his language to the importance and narrative character of the event.) The following account is based on these two documents except where otherwise noted.

Going back to the house, Mercier risked being choked in order to save what he could. He was able to make only one trip and managed to take a chest with his wife's jewelry and more expensive clothes. Almost everything else was lost—books, documents, scrapbooks, pictures, clothes, furniture. Meanwhile, those of his servants "who had not been celebrating Mardi Gras or who had not entirely lost their heads" had gone for help, and the fire company arrived, complete with pumping apparatus. By that time there was little left, for the fire had begun when a spark from a defective flue ignited some beams which had been dried by years of warmth from the same source. The firemen knocked out windows and doors and saved a few things of value: two boxes of silver service, some furniture, and part of Mercier's wardrobe. From the window of Mercier's dressing room they threw out the contents, most of which were stolen by the crowd in the street. Even more, "a raid was made into the wine cellars by the soldiers, firemen, and citizens, who thought it was better to drink the juice of the grape than have it destroyed, and the very choicest brands washed the smoke from throats not often made the channels for such expensive fluids."[4] By 4:00 A.M. only the four walls remained, but Cécile-Élisabeth, Madeleine, and little Maurice-Henri were safely lodged with a kindly neighbor.

As with most such occurrences, the accident left its vic-

[4] *Evening Star* (Washington), 6 March 1862. The press garbled the story almost humorously. For instance, ". . . most of the valuables . . . were saved" (*National Intelligencer* and *Evening Star* [Washington], 5 March 1862); "All the papers were saved." (*Courrier des États-Unis* [New York], 6 March 1862); "The wife of Count Mercier (an American lady) . . ." (*Evening Star* [Washington], 6 March 1862). The *Courrier des États-Unis*, however, showed the superiority of its contacts with the French minister in its issue of 10 March 1862, in which it reported the loss of the documents and went on as follows: "Madame Mercier is in very delicate health following the shock of this terrible night when she thought for a moment that her children were in danger."

tims with much to regret but something to appreciate. The destruction, of course, was irremediable and left Mercier in a financial hole. Psychologically Mercier seems to have snapped back well, though the same cannot be said for his wife. The actions of the crowd and the fire company's work left an embarrassing memory. But on the other hand there was that generous neighbor, and this was only the beginning of the kindnesses shown. Seward immediately offered his house to Mercier, but the minister had already accepted a like offer from Elisha Riggs, Jr., half brother of Corcoran's old partner George Riggs. This house stood on the northeast corner of Seventeenth and "I" Streets, currently the site of the Army-Navy Club. Though it remained the minister's residence for half a year, he was relatively seldom in it.[5]

THE GENESIS OF THE RICHMOND IDEA

Mercier's personal trouble may well have influenced his course in the next major development of his relations with the secretary of state. In the second week of April, when the news of Shiloh reached Washington, Seward again talked with Mercier and brought him round to the topic of Northern military success. It meant, said the secretary, the early reestablishment of the Union. "While we were talking," as Mercier described it, "I made some objections, and I dropped a remark, almost accidentally, that I very much regretted not being able to go and see for myself the way things were in Richmond." Seward, as quoted by Mercier, shot back this: "Well go ahead. . . . Have one of your warships come and take you to Norfolk, and I'll give you a pass. Your visit, at just this time, could have a very good effect and render us a valuable service." Mercier,

---

[5] The author is indebted to Mr. John Beverley Riggs for information about the Riggs house.

taken aback by this quickness, and perhaps wondering if he had overbid, asked for time to reflect.[6]

In this way there began the strangest, best-known, and certainly most controversial incident of Henri Mercier's American career. Mercier's version of how it began is pre-eminently our best source, but is obviously subject to the same interrogations as any other such report; it was meant for Thouvenel's eyes, and it may have been phrased in anticipation of raised eyebrows. At the time of Mercier's visit, again in February of 1863, and ever since in secondary accounts, it has been questioned, amended, and discussed. Even apart from ulterior motives, two antithetical questions pose themselves at the outset: Did Mercier scheme to achieve permission for the visit? Did Seward maneuver him into it?

Mercier surely had wished to visit Richmond for some time and had been mulling over the possibility.[7] It would be far more remarkable, for him or any other foreign observer, had he never had such a thought. It was a year now since Rudolph Schleiden, the Bremen representative, had gone to Virginia as unofficial spokesman for the Washington cabinet.[8] What was the South's real view of the mounting and successful Union attack? How capable were they of deflecting it? Any diplomat worth his salt would want to know. Mercier certainly did.[9]

On 24 March the press reported that "a French gentle-

[6] Mercier to Thouvenel, Washington, 13 April 1862 (recd. 3 May 1862), AMAE, CP, E-U, 127: 35-47, no. 96; a completely rewritten and hence inadequate version of it is in LJ, III (1862), 120-22. See Case and Spencer, 275-85.

[7] As he told Lyons on 10 April (E. D. Adams, I, 281).

[8] See Lutz, Annual Report of the American Historical Association for the Year 1915, pp. 207-22; and E. D. Adams, I, 121-23.

[9] See, for example, Mercier to Prince Napoleon, Washington, 24 Feb. 1862, AMAE, MD, Papiers Thouvenel, XIII, 431-36, on fol. 431.

man of distinction," previously a Southern sympathizer, had recently returned from Richmond to report a feeling of "utter depression" in that city.[10] Even if Mercier only read about this in the papers, it must have rekindled his wish to see and judge for himself the possibilities of peace. At this time, following the loss of Roanoke Island under his aegis as secretary of war, Judah P. Benjamin was removed from the Confederate war department and made secretary of state. Mercier and Benjamin had come to know each other in Washington in quieter days when Benjamin represented Louisiana in the United States Senate. What might personal diplomacy accomplish now?

In his own version of it, written to Dayton at the time, Seward said that Mercier "proposed" visiting Richmond and that once "the President" was satisfied that the minister would not compromise Franco-American relations, he granted the permission. Seward continued:

> It is impossible not to see now that the insurrection is sinking and shrivelling into very narrow dimensions. I hope that Mr. Mercier may come back prepared with some plea to alleviate the inconveniences of his countrymen in the South, who are not acting against this Government, and, in that way, against the peace and harmony of the two countries.[11]

Reading between these cryptic lines, it would seem that Seward had something like this in mind: Mercier, having seen the desolation of the South, would second him in his own pet plan for knocking out the Confederacy's supports—

[10] *National Intelligencer* (Washington), 24 March 1862.
[11] Seward to Dayton, Washington, 22 April 1862, State Dept. Corres., France, Instructions, xvi, 147-48, no. 141, also quoted in *The Works of William H. Seward*, ed. George E. Baker, 5 vols. (Boston: Houghton Mifflin & Co., 1884), v, 56, and in F. W. Seward, *Seward at Washington*, ii, 82-83.

withdrawal of European recognition of belligerency in return for the use of captured Southern ports.

Mercier, then, remains the only source for saying that Seward gave his permission in the first interview, immediately upon hearing the "proposal," which in Mercier's version was not a proposal at all but a remark dropped "almost accidentally."[12] Indeed Mercier specified that he would undertake the trip "with the agreement of the secretary of state, and even to some extent upon his request."[13] Seward probably did give a quick verbal permission; he would naturally have checked this later with Lincoln and obtained official approval.

Nothing very new had developed on this when in February of 1863 publication of some of the documents precipitated a debate in the United States press and congress. Seward was then at pains to show—and he may have stretched things a bit—that Mercier had not gone as an informal diplomatic agent, as Schleiden had the year previously. But the *National Intelligencer*, a paper close to the secretary, thought that "it appears that [Mercier] undertook [the trip] at the suggestion of Mr. Seward himself, who then believed in the speedy re-establishment of the Union."[14] The most important point, which no one has ever questioned, is that both men wanted the trip to take place.

Now as to ulterior motives. At various times throughout

[12] Or did he mean "as if accidentally"? The French is "comme par hasard."

[13] Mercier to Thouvenel, Washington, 13 April 1862, AMAE, CP, E-U, 127: 35-47, no. 96, on fol. 36. In the printed version (*LJ*, III [1862], 120-22), this is changed to read "with the very explicit approval of the secretary of state, and almost, it even seemed, following his wish." It is difficult to see just which man, Seward or Mercier, was being spared any embarrassment by this tampering with the record.

[14] *National Intelligencer* (Washington), 7 Feb. 1863. See also *ibid.*, 11 Feb. 1863; *Evening Star* (Washington), 12 Feb. 1863; *Courrier des États-Unis* (New York), 13 Feb. 1863.

the war, from 1861 and Seward's contacts through Stoeckl to the 1865 summit conference at Hampton Roads, the Union government tried to sound out Richmond on terms. In the beginning the only reservation was that the Union must be preserved. When Seward said, therefore, that Mercier's trip to Richmond, hard upon major Union victories, could "render us a valuable service," it was something like this which he had in mind—as his later remarks showed. There is another possibility, purely hypothetical, but quite compatible with this first motive. Seward had been laboring for some months to pry apart the Anglo-French entente. It was still a little early to discern the excellent wedge which the Mexican venture would become. But if the French minister went off to the Southern capital and left Lyons behind, what might that produce? Seward's alacrity, his "Go ahead," may have stemmed from his ever-present desire, amply illustrated already, to separate the entente partners.

As for Mercier, he described himself as thinking over Seward's proffered permission and realizing that some peace move through French good offices might result from the trip. There is no question, therefore, that his aims extended beyond mere fact-gathering, and we must conclude that this had crossed his mind *before* his talk with Seward. Furthermore, while he was in Richmond he developed the common-market idea for the consideration of Confederate Secretary of State Benjamin, and we must further conclude that this too had probably crossed his mind earlier. In fact he was going to Richmond to talk peace, with the full blessing of the United States secretary of state. Seward, of course, was no part of the common-market idea and spoke only of restoring the Union. Undoubtedly he would have rejected such a plan had Benjamin shown any interest in it. But Seward was nobody's fool, and he must have known that Mercier's remarks in Richmond were not going to echo what he himself would say. Nevertheless, he practically urged Mercier to go ahead.

Finally, what effect might Mercier's personal problems have had on all this? The destruction of the Georgetown house heightened his persistent desire to go home. Did any of this help to make him reckless? Another man, or Mercier himself at another time, might have taken a month out and asked his foreign minister's permission. On the other hand, there was a chance to do something, perhaps even to help end the Civil War. And if it all blew up, if he were re-assigned to one of the smaller German states, Cécile-Élisabeth, at least, would be happy.

After leaving Seward, Mercier went to the Russian legation to tell Stoeckl what had developed. As Stoeckl reported it: "Mercier suggested to me that we make the trip together in the hope, if not of beginning negotiations, at least of looking over the situation and seeing if we could open some avenue of reconciliation." Stoeckl declined, saying that he saw no hope for any solid diplomatic achievement. Two days later, with Mercier on his way, Stoeckl saw Seward. The secretary said that France's role in the American crisis was not such as to inspire great confidence and that if mediation should even be indicated, Russia would be a preferable mediator.[15] It would appear from this that the favor France had earned in the North for her role in the *Trent* affair was more than offset by the fact that she was a maritime power vitally interested in cotton.

Knowing what a high value Thouvenel put upon the Anglo-French entente, Mercier went to see Lyons before giving Seward his decision. The British minister's reaction was a predictable chagrin. Mercier, whose contempt for his

[15] Stoeckl to Gorchakov, Washington, 23 April/5 May 1862, no. 34, Stoeckl Papers; see also Woldman, *Lincoln and the Russians*, pp. 94-95.

151

colleague's caution was already on the record, held his ground:

> *Lyons*: Frankly I do not like to see you take an initiative that will certainly draw attention to itself and with which I cannot be associated, because I fear that important men will conclude that France and England are taking divergent paths.
>
> *Mercier*: Since I do not have to contend with such touchy feelings as you, it would be stressing prudence to an absurd degree not to take advantage of this chance to draw closer to our common goal, and . . . I shall be careful to tell Mr. Seward . . . that I did not make up my mind till I had come to an understanding with you.

Mercier then told Lyons that he had thought of asking Stoeckl to go along with him. As Mercier had it, Lyons, "again fearful of how things would be interpreted and talked about," said he would rather Stoeckl stay home, and Mercier "did not hesitate to make that concession to him." Whether it was Stoeckl, Mercier, or both who decided against a Franco-Russian trip, the decision was a good one from Thouvenel's viewpoint. The foreign minister would become upset enough about Mercier's going alone. If he had had to explain to Russell about France and Russia's acting together in such an enterprise, his friendship for Mercier would have been strained indeed.[16]

When he returned to see Seward, Mercier discussed the line he would take with the Confederate officials. As a "cover" for the trip, he would give it out that he wanted to talk with his consuls, to judge the Southern situation for

[16] The Lyons–Mercier exchange is reconstructed language. The above account of the conversation is from Mercier to Thouvenel, Washington, 13 April 1862, AMAE, CP, E-U, 127: 35-47, no. 96, on fol. 38-39.

himself, and to look into the interests of the *Régie*, the French government corporation which handled the state tobacco monopoly and had some tobacco stored in Richmond. In the city Mercier would say that the war was hurting French interests; that he wanted to see what the chances were for its early termination; that in his position he could speak only of the reestablishment of the Union as a means to that end; that French traditions and interests made her regret the separation; that diplomatic recognition of the South would not help France because the North would continue the blockade; that France had just as much need of Northern customers as she had of Southern cotton; that in consequence peace alone would help her, and she stood ready to do everything possible to facilitate a peace acceptable to North and South. Mercier would then offer to report back to Seward whatever the Confederate authorities might authorize him to say. According to Mercier, Seward seemed satisfied with this proposed line of talk: "Mr. Seward told me I could add, when I found the chance, that he was convinced the North was not inspired by any vengeful feeling, and that for his part, he would gladly serve again in the Senate alongside whomever the South might wish to send there." That last, of course, was meant for ex-Senator Benjamin, ex-Senator Jefferson Davis, or any number of other Confederate officials.[17]

As will shortly be seen, Mercier's actual statements to Secretary Benjamin followed this line rather closely, though they went beyond it in the matter of the common-market proposal. With Lyons, however, whom he saw again before leaving, Mercier left a different impression about what

[17] According to Stoeckl, however, Seward was against any diplomatic effort on Mercier's part: "Mr. Seward . . . took the offer of the minister of France in bad part and refused to authorize him to make any proposals to the Confederates" (Stoeckl to Gorchakov, Washington, 23 April/5 May 1862, no. 34, Stoeckl Papers; Woldman, p. 94).

he would say in Richmond. As the English minister got it, Mercier would tell the South bluntly that their cause was all but lost, and in this way he might even deliver the Confederacy a knockout blow.[18] It is quite possible that some such line was discussed by Mercier with Seward and with Lyons, perhaps in a hypothetical way: "If I say this, then maybe that," and so on. It is also possible, however, that Mercier had deliberately left both Seward and Lyons with a more stiffly Unionist notion of what he would say than his actual intention would warrant. Again it is well to remember that Seward and Lyons knew Mercier's views quite fully and that whatever Mercier told them, either craftily or in innocent, rambling exuberance, they had a fairly good idea of the range of things he might or might not say in Richmond. It is also possible that Mercier began by thinking of knockout blows, but that on finding the South so inflexible, he decided that this would be a fruitless line to take.

As his parting thought for Thouvenel, Mercier tried to show that his view of possible success was realistic:

> I am . . . thoroughly convinced beforehand that my words will not bring the men of the Richmond government to accept the reestablishment of the Union, any more than they would bring Mr. Seward to accept separation. Each side is too much committed to be able to draw back. But if I could discover the secret of the need which must end by imposing itself as law, I would think I had done a real service for Your Excellency, for then we would know where to concentrate our efforts.[19]

Depending upon what he found in Richmond, then, Mercier hoped to clarify French policy: either to help the

---

[18] E. D. Adams, I, 281-82.

[19] Mercier to Thouvenel, Washington, 13 April 1862, AMAE, CP, E-U, 127: 35-47, no. 96, on fol. 45-46.

North subdue the South or to help the South achieve recognized political independence.

A telegram brought the *Gassendi* to fetch Mercier. On the morning of 15 April, accompanied by Louis de Geofroy, he arrived at Fortress Monroe and received a hospitable thirteen-gun salute from the Union commander, General Wool. Within a few hours the *Gassendi* had contacted the Union fleet at Hampton Roads. Captain Gautier and his passengers went briefly aboard the *Minnesota* to explain themselves to Commodore Goldsborough. Mercier unsettled Goldsborough by failing to discuss his visit, "although he was on board and in conversation with me for some time."[20] They arrived at Norfolk under cover of night, and Mercier was greeted by the Confederate officer in charge of the sector, General Benjamin Huger. Huger telegraphed to the capital, and permission to come ahead having been obtained, the minister of France went forward to Richmond.[21]

DIPLOMACY IN RICHMOND

It was a pinched, deprived, and hurting city which received Mercier that Wednesday, 16 April; war and the blockade had reduced it, and Mercier was struck as Seward had intended. "Confederate affairs are in a blue way," wrote Mrs. Chesnut, and losses like Donelson, Shiloh, and Roanoke Island were harder to accept with butter at fifty cents a pound and wood eight dollars a cord.[22] The French minister, renowned giver of gourmet dinners, was most impressed by the lack of anything worth drinking. ". . . Mercier did not taste tea, coffee, wine or Brandy while in

[20] Goldsborough to Welles, Hampton Roads, 16 April 1862, *ORN*, 1st ser., VII, 239-40. See also Wool to Stanton, Fort Monroe, 15 April 1862, *ORA*, 1st ser., LI, 574.

[21] Mercier to Thouvenel, Washington, 28 April 1862, AMAE, CP, E-U, 127: 50-79, no. 97.

[22] Stern, p. 123.

Dixie," wrote Sam Ward, the Washington lobbyist and epicure. "All Richmond could not furnish him a cup of coffee or a bottle of claret. The courage, confidence, and serenity evinced by *bons vivants* under such *trying* circumstances had a great moral effect upon him."[23] Ward had it right. In his report home, Mercier showed that he understood not only the desperate gustatory situation but also the pluck of the Richmond people. The government, in order to check inebriation both in the army and among civilians, had just forbidden the manufacture of fermented drink; yet the South would fight on.[24]

It had been a bitter season altogether in Richmond, despite such brave efforts as a presentation of *The Rivals* by "the great of the city," with Mrs. Clay as Mrs. Malaprop. The death of ex-President John Tyler on 18 January had punctuated the solemn winter with a fittingly somber note. And then there came the war setbacks. For months near Manassas, General Johnston's men in gray had waited as McClellan's massive force rose to three times the Confederate army. Many from Richmond had subsequently gone down to Norfolk to watch the *Monitor-Merrimac* duel of 9 March; now that was over, and McClellan's army, moving south by water, had disembarked in the peninsula and brought Yorktown under its guns. In the north, across from Fredericksburg, McDowell sat ready to advance, sixty miles from the Southern capital.[25]

The worst disaster yet had occurred when Roanoke Island fell in February. Ambrose Burnside had gathered in

[23] Ward to S.L.M. Barlow, Wilmington, 27 April 1862. The author is indebted to Mr. Lately Thomas for this letter.

[24] Mercier to Thouvenel, Washington, 28 April 1862, AMAE, CP, E-U, 127: 50-79, no. 97, on fol. 71-72.

[25] Clay-Clopton, *Belle of the Fifties*, p. 175; John B. Jones, *A Rebel War Clerk's Diary* (New York: Sagamore Press, 1958), pp. 72-73; Alfred Hoyt Bill, *The Beleaguered City, Richmond, 1861-1865* (New York: Alfred A. Knopf, 1946), p. 100.

the historic site most easily, thanks to Benjamin's failure to reinforce the army of Richmonders under Henry A. Wise. The latter's brilliant son, Jennings Wise, had been killed, and when the Union yielded up his body, it was met in Richmond with solemn, public dirge. And then that inauguration on Washington's birthday—a dismal, rainy day and a colorless, damp speech from Jefferson Davis. En route to the morning's ceremony, Mrs. Davis had noted four Negroes dressed in black, with solemn faces and shiny white gloves, accompanying her carriage. "In answer to her impatient question her coachman had told her: 'This, ma'am, is the way we always does in Richmond at funerals and sichlike.' "[26]

Mercier's contacts during his six days' stay form a *Who's Who* of Confederate notables, though he and President Davis, by mutual, tacit consent, did not meet. There were R.M.T. Hunter, former senator from Virginia and till recently, though Mercier failed to note it, Confederate secretary of state; James L. Orr of South Carolina, once speaker of the federal house of representatives and now chairman of the Confederate senate's committee on foreign affairs; L. T. Wigfall of Texas, whose loyalty Stephen Douglas had challenged in one of the last Senate debates before Sumter; Clement C. Clay of Alabama, husband of the famous diarist and amateur actress; Bishop John McGill, the Catholic bishop of Richmond; General Robert E. Lee, and others.[27] William Cabell Rives of Virginia had more than a passing interest in the French visit. Approaching seventy, he had been United States minister to France both at the time of Louis Philippe's accession in 1830 and again when the president of the Second Republic became Napoleon III.

[26] Bill, pp. 99-102; see also Nevins, *The War for the Union*, II, 90-91.

[27] Mercier to Thouvenel, Washington, 28 April 1862, AMAE, CP, E-U, 127: 50-79, no. 97, on fol. 67-68.

157

He had opposed secession, and like Tyler he had been a
member of the Washington peace convention of February
1861. At the moment he was at Castle-Hill, his estate in
the interior, where he noted the minister's presence:

> I should have been very glad to have the opportunity
> of conversing with him in regard to the *true* policy of
> his government with regard to American affairs. I am
> quite curious to know what brought him to Richmond.
> . . . I can hardly suppose that so paltry an object as
> the tobacco they bought in Richmond constituted the
> sole or chief object of his visit.[28]

All told, the trip to Richmond was quite a reunion for
Mercier; he was socializing with Americans he had met in
Washington, men who had run the United States before
the strangers came in 1861. One and all they impressed the
minister with their determination to run the Confederate
States of America, to defend it vigorously and make it
work. Of all these eminent political and social figures, none
was more interesting than Matthew Fontaine Maury, pio-
neer nautical scientist, former head of the naval observa-
tory and hydrographical office in Washington, and now the
South's director of coastal defense. He was an old friend
of Corcoran, and Mercier had known him in Washington,
and had waxed enthusiastic about his scientific ideas which
notably included an international expedition to the Antarc-
tic. When Virginia seceded, Maury turned down an offer
from Russia to pursue his researches abroad, and he rejected a similar offer now from Mercier. Indeed, he and
the French minister had a long conversation which touched
on the *Trent* affair, the *Monitor–Merrimac* engagement,
and foreign affairs, in which respect Maury elaborated his
plan for a Franco-Confederate alliance which would reap

[28] W. C. Rives to [his son] A. L. Rives, Castle-Hill, 20 April 1862,
University of Virginia Library, Charlottesville, Rives Papers.

important commercial and economic rewards for the Second Empire. Mercier, in reporting the conversation to Thouvenel, wrote strongly against the Maury plan. France, he said, could not take advantage of a Confederate offer of free trade, if only because the French merchant fleet was not large enough and the North's great merchant marine would of course be unavailable. What France needed was neither an alliance with the Confederacy nor a war against the Union. She needed peace in America and trade with the North. A strong, albeit truncated, United States, he felt, was definitely in the best interests of France.[29]

The only important Unionist whom Mercier noted in Richmond was John Minor Botts, but Botts was in jail for complicity with the United States, and Mercier was not permitted to see him. He spoke, however, with a businessman friend of Botts who tried to convince him that a reign of terror was in progress and that no one was telling him the truth about the overwhelming reunionist feeling in the city. Mercier was reserved:

> I must say that everything he said to me on that subject seemed to be in flat contradiction with the facts I was able to weigh, and with the admission he himself made that the slave states, once conquered, could be governed only after being reduced to territorial status.

[29] On Maury in Washington, see Francis Leigh Williams, *Matthew Fontaine Maury, Scientist of the Sea* (New Brunswick, N.J.: Rutgers University Press, 1963), p. 360. On the Russian and French offers, see *ibid.*, pp. 384-90, and Diana Fontaine Maury Corbin, *A Life of Matthew Fontaine Maury, U.S.N. and C.S.N.* (London: Sampson Low, Marston, Searle, & Rivington, 1888), pp. 191-93. On Maury's conversation with Mercier, see Williams, p. 390, and Mercier to Thouvenel, Washington, 6 May 1862, AMAE, CP, E-U, 127: 85-105, no. 98, on fol. 97-98. See also Patricia Jahns, *Matthew Fontaine Maury and Joseph Henry: Scientists of the Civil War* (New York: Hastings House, 1961), pp. 190-98.

Mercier concluded that, although there might be some constraint in the town, it was no worse than the summer and fall of 1861 had been in Washington, and that in any case, such intimidation could not make Americans feign their sentiments.[30]

The heart of Mercier's Richmond trip was obviously his conversation with Judah P. Benjamin, whom he saw soon after arriving on the sixteenth. As we have noted, Mercier and the Confederate secretary of state had known each other in Washington in another era—much longer gone than the calendar's sixteen months—when Senators Slidell and Benjamin had been Louisiana's pair in the senate. They talked now of what had happened in the time between and of where they stood at present.

Mercier: The only object of my trip is to find out for myself the way things really are, and I have come to ask your help in this.

Benjamin: I shall give it with great pleasure, and I'll be delighted when you know the truth, which from everything that reaches me from the North, seems to be quite unknown there.[31]

Benjamin then admitted he had been wrong a year and a half earlier when he told Mercier the South could secede without a major war. Nor had King Cotton been very helpful. But much more would be endured if necessary to secure victory. The federal government was clearly richer in resources than the South, and it had control of the sea; it

[30] Mercier to Thouvenel, Washington, 28 April 1862, AMAE, CP, E-U, 127: 50-79, no. 97, on fol. 69-71. See also Ella Lonn, *Foreigners in the Confederacy* (Chapel Hill: University of North Carolina Press, 1940), p. 355.

[31] This introduction is reconstructed language. Mercier to Thouvenel, Washington, 28 April 1862 (rcd. 14 May 1862), AMAE, CP, E-U, 127: 50-79, no. 97, a small extract of which is in *LJ*, III (1862), 122-24.

might even end by taking all of the South's ports. No matter.

> *Benjamin*: . . . when they take our cities, they will find only women, old men, and children. All the people who can bear arms will withdraw into the hinterland. . . . In the face of such resistance, the North must decide to yield.[32]

The secretary went on to rehearse the familiar parallel with the American War of Independence. Like the Northern aggressors, he said, the British at one time held almost all the seacoast towns. They had lost, and so would the North. "Like the English, the Yankees are fighting today to keep their power and their riches, and we, like the Americans, are fighting to win our independence."

> *Mercier*: But suppose that before things come to such an extreme pass, the North, as I think it might, should offer you substantial guarantees, more than you have ever asked for, would you refuse to engage in a compromise?
>
> *Benjamin*: It's too late for that kind of patching up. . . . In fact we are two distinct peoples and should each have a separate life. Our population today hates the Yankees as much as the French have ever hated the English. Look at the women. They are the first to push their husbands, sons, and fathers to take up arms. They single out those who don't and pursue them with sarcasm. Things have come to the point that the North must make up its mind either to exterminate us or to accept our separation.
>
> *Mercier*: With numbers, money, and the sea against you, it is a very unequal fight.
>
> *Benjamin*: Not so much as you think.

[32] This and the quotations below are as reconstructed by Mercier.

The secretary went on to admit the military performance had not always been up to Confederate hopes; as secretary of war he had good reason to know, especially after Roanoke. But Southern men were more fit to fight than Northerners, and man for man could beat them readily. Look at the way Beauregard's outnumbered force had accounted for itself at Corinth.

The secretary painted the military situation as he wanted Mercier to see it: The Confederacy had to let the North advance at some points in order to concentrate its forces in more strategic places. The logic of the war would force the Union to do battle in those places; they would be beaten and would withdraw, especially where the absence of rivers prevented the use of the gunboats-with-armies technique which had so far proved so successful. At Corinth and on the Virginia peninsula were two great Confederate armies ready for the fight. New Orleans' defenses were holding up well, he added, and two new ironclads should save the city in the end. But even should McClellan come ahead, even should Richmond and Virginia itself have to be evacuated, the South would yet fight on.

Mercier turned to cotton and tobacco. Would the South really destroy them? Could they keep the planters from selling their crops once the North had opened the ports to commerce? Benjamin assured him that they could and would; patriotic local action would see to it.

The secretary then circumspectly brought up the question of diplomatic recognition. Mercier replied that the South had not considered this question in its true light; that, for example, France had sincerely regretted the breakup of the Union and that, so long as this dissolution had not proved to be final, France could do nothing along the lines of encouraging it; that a premature recognition would have no effect other than to create trouble with the federal government which France would dearly like to avoid, for it would surely not bring about the lifting of the blockade; in a word, that France must keep recognition as a reserve measure, a weapon of peace which would work only if used appropriately.[33]

> *Benjamin*: I understand all that. Also, we do not complain precisely about not yet being recognized. But what surprises us is the readiness you have shown in accepting the blockade as effective. . . . I can show you more than twenty ports before which a warship has never been stationed.

Mercier, who a year earlier had thought it legal for the United States to close its own (Southern) ports by passing a law, now found himself unable to answer what he considered a cogent argument. He lamely answered that in this matter France had to move in step with the other maritime powers. Benjamin, however, was overstating his case. Had he been so disposed, Mercier might have answered, with Lord John Russell, that the blockade, though not foolproof, was effective because it was "sufficient to create an evident danger" to ships coming in.[34]

Four days before Mercier's arrival, Benjamin had written to Slidell and asked him to sound out the French on the following proposal. France would shoot her way into Southern ports and thus end the blockade; in return, she could sell her products within the Confederate States free of tariff. As a bribe—technically as a reimbursement for the losses this might occasion—the South would ship, say a hundred thousand bales of cotton, which could be sold

[33] This passage has been given in indirect discourse here because that is the way Mercier wrote it; i.e., he went out of his way not to quote himself directly on this sensitive issue, though the rest of his account is within quotation marks.

[34] Quoted in Randall and Donald, *Civil War and Reconstruction*, pp. 502-03.

for over twelve million dollars.[35] Mercier heard of a plan to exchange blockade-breaking for free trade, notably from Matthew Fontaine Maury, but he did not specify that Benjamin had raised the point. The secretary may have preferred that the matter be handled by Slidell, though with the trouble he had in sending and receiving messages, he would have done well to put it in Mercier's relatively rapid pouch. (In this connection it is important to note that Louis de Geofroy was going home on leave. Undoubtedly there is much about this Richmond trip which Mercier never put on paper and which was given to Thouvenel verbally by Geofroy.) Mercier, as we have seen, thoroughly disliked this Confederate offer.[36]

Mercier referred to his interview with Benjamin as "this first conversation," and later mentioned a last interview. Benjamin himself, writing three months later, gave a short summary of his talk with Mercier, essentially compatible with the one just recounted, and then said, "I saw nothing further of him except in social parties at dinner and in a farewell visit I made him of a few moments on the eve of his departure."[37] This slight discrepancy may not be important, for Benjamin also alluded to the further topic about to be presented. It may be, however, that Mercier felt it would be enough of a shock for Thouvenel to learn that he had gone to Richmond and said as much as this. He saved the last part—the common-market discussion— for a later dispatch. Whether there were two discussions or one, there seems no other explanation for why Mercier left the common-market conversation out of his first dis-

[35] Benjamin to Slidell, Richmond, 12 April 1862, Richardson, II, 227-33, no. 3.

[36] Mercier to Thouvenel, Washington, 6 May 1862 (rcd. 19 May 1862), AMAE, CP, E-U, 127: 85-105, no. 98.

[37] Benjamin to Slidell, Richmond, 19 July 1862, Richardson, II, 260-68, no. 5, also in ORN, 2nd ser., III, 461-67. Mercier's references are respectively in nos. 97 and 98, cited above.

patch, except that he was loath to admit that in Richmond he had spoken for American political separation.

As Mercier told it, then,[38] Benjamin stated that peace would not be in sight till the North was facing financial bankruptcy. Mercier asked him what kind of arrangement would follow such a peace. "Complete separation of all the slave states" was the pugnacious reply.

Before he left Washington, Mercier had told Lyons that he might deliver a "knockout blow" against the South by telling the Confederate officials he considered their cause all but lost. After his first conversation with Benjamin, Mercier knew that such an attempted strike could knock out nothing save French influence and the chance for French good offices to help end the war. Instead, therefore, Mercier steered the talk toward his favorite project. He told Benjamin that even should things go as the South hoped, they would one day have to negotiate over boundaries, a common frontier with the United States. Shouldn't they be thinking about that now? "Maybe you would succeed if you agreed to maintain commercial union throughout the former territory of the United States."

Benjamin fobbed off the suggestion by reminding Mercier of the long-standing North–South disagreement over tariffs. Mercier, however, thought the North would be willing to give up protectionism after the war; twenty to twenty-five percent overall rate would do her nicely, especially with Southern markets open to her products. In grasping at the figure of twenty-five percent, Mercier was apparently trying to prove that a free-trade South and a protectionist North could negotiate some sort of tariff compromise. Benjamin, however, would speak of nothing but independence, and he discouraged Mercier from discussing such tariff details. In concluding, Mercier tried to show

[38] Mercier to Thouvenel, Washington, 6 May 1862 (rcd. 19 May 1862), AMAE, CP, E-U, 127: 85-105, no. 98.

how patly his plan for a *Zollverein* fitted into Benjamin's rosy future. If the North did go under financially, "maybe then the chance to see the economic ties reestablished to which she owed her prosperity would decide her to compromise." Benjamin, as Mercier read him, "seemed struck by this idea." R.M.T. Hunter, to whom Mercier also confided his plan, was also struck. One would imagine that any Confederate statesman would be rendered somewhat pensive by this phenomenon—the minister of the emperor in Richmond with a "solution" based on political independence for the South.

To note the obvious, Mercier's suggestion, like all his other recommendations for American peace, was firmly planted in the future, not the present. With him it was always "if this, then that." No check to McClellan and McDowell, then no Confederate independence and no common market. One is also impressed again with the minister's calm assurance that Americans cared that much about financial prosperity. It was a pardonable error, coming from the representative of the Western world's oldest nation-state and the mother of red-hot nationalism, coming from a European who thought he knew the crassness of the wide-open, materialist, new democracy. How could he be expected to equate Lincolnian American patriotism with the exalted sentiments of Napoleonic France? The United States was so young and had been such a tentative thing from the start, its bits and pieces threatening with regularity to go chipping and flying off. For half a year in 1860, he had listened to distinguished Americans like Benjamin and Slidell, to Northerners even, like Jesse Bright and Stephen Douglas, and they had seen nothing so very unthinkable in the kind of "solution" he was proposing. If he was exceeding the terms of Seward's pass, was not the end of all this killing worth it? At base, then, Henri Mercier was something less than an American patriot and something more than an obedient career diplomat. His view of the Civil War came to be resented by many in the North, but no one could fault his good will. And he thought he had said nothing improper in Richmond: "In taking a chance and suggesting this plan to Mr. Benjamin, I do not think, Mr. Minister, that I have stopped being true to the friendly attitude toward the North which I was determined to maintain during my entire time in Richmond."[39]

Mercier arrived back in Washington on Thursday, 24 April. Seward had sent him off hoping he would be convinced that the North was winning the war, could end it soon if Europe would stop recognizing the South as a belligerent state. The secretary was about to learn how Richmond had actually impressed the minister of France.

AFTERMATH IN WASHINGTON

The *Gassendi* steamed up the Potomac that Thursday morning, grounding herself several times in the unaccustomed channel, but happy to receive the salutes and hospitality of the American navy.[40] That hospitality was a sign of how her distinguished passenger would be received after his week behind enemy lines, for Seward bustled about and fussed over Mercier with great ostentation. He was out to demonstrate that the French minister's trip to Richmond was somehow a Union success, or at least not subversive of her indivisible future. Within hours that future would seem brighter than ever, for Admiral Farragut was even then passing Forts Jackson and St. Philip, and the way to New Orleans was open at last.

That same afternoon Mercier went to see Seward and report on his trip; no Southern senators, however, were

[39] *Ibid.*, fol. 96.
[40] *Evening Star* (Washington), 24 April 1862; *New York Times*, 25 April 1862; Seward to Mercier, Washington, 25 April 1862, State Dept. Corres., Notes to the French Legation, vii, 103.

about to return to their desks in Washington. Understandably enough, Seward seemed disappointed with the minister's report; as Mercier sized him up, the secretary was still hoping for an easy reconciliation with his former colleagues now in Richmond, something on the order of a post-election political reunification. Mercier, who had heard the bitter Southern words, knew that this was beyond possibility. In his mind the South was now like Spain in 1808: if need be, she would fight on in the hills against the invader. Seward, still thinking of appearances, also took Mercier to see the president, who listened carefully but said nothing at all. Bravely, to Lyons, the secretary claimed that Mercier's visit had brought precious information to light about the South's weakness; talk about guerrilla warfare, he thought, was idle whistling.[41]

Mercier had appearances of his own to worry about, and he had already been to see Lyons, directly after his visit with Seward. His remarks to his British colleague were factual as far as they went: the South would fight on and on; he had found no chance for knockout blows; tobacco might be burned, but the French store would probably be spared; the Confederate government had abandoned the idea of requiring foreign consuls to apply to them for exequaturs; Richmond would like the blockade broken long enough to buy arms, but did not rely on diplomatic recognition. In assuring Lyons that France had not been offered any special commercial advantages, Mercier was probably being truthful: the Maury plan was an unofficial thing; Benjamin, though he had broached a similar plan with Slidell, may not have mentioned it to Mercier; and anyhow,

[41] Mercier to Thouvenel, Washington, 28 April 1862, AMAE, MD, Papiers Thouvenel, XIII, 446-47; Mercier to Thouvenel, Washington, 28 April 1862, AMAE, CP, E-U, 127: 50-79, no. 97; Lyons to Russell, Washington, 25 April 1862, Newton, I, 82-85. See also E. D. Adams, I, 286-87.

the free-trade privilege was predicated on the wild condition that France break the Union blockade. Finally, Lyons agreed completely with Mercier that the time was still not right for any European initiative.[42]

The big display of friendship between the federal government and Mercier went on into the weekend. On Friday night there was a party for the *Gassendi* crew, probably at Seward's:

> My dear President
> I called at your House on my way from the Department, to say that perhaps it would have no bad effect if you should drop in about 9 o'clock and be seen at your ease by the French Sailors. Welles, Fox and Dahlgren will be here.
>
> Faithfully yours
William H. Seward[43]

It would appear, however, that Lincoln had a headache and spent the evening reading poetry with Senator Browning of Illinois.[44]

Then on Saturday they all went down to the navy yard for a courtesy visit to the French frigate: President and Mrs. Lincoln, Seward, F. W. Seward and his wife, Mercier, and others. Record-minded journals reported that the *Gassendi* was the first French warship to visit Washington and that Lincoln was the first American president to be hon-

---

[42] E. D. Adams, I, 284-86. See also *ibid.*, II, 24, n. 2; and C. F. Adams, Jr., *Massachusetts Historical Society Proceedings*, XLVII (1914), 376-77, 381.

[43] Seward to Lincoln, Washington, 25 April 1862, Lincoln Papers, 1st ser., fol. 15692. Gustavus Vasa Fox was assistant secretary of the navy; Captain Dahlgren was commander of the Washington navy yard.

[44] See *Lincoln Day by Day: A Chronology, 1809-1865*, ed. Earl Schenck Miers, 3 vols. (Washington: U.S. Government Printing Office, 1960), III, 108; Browning, *Diary*, I, 542.

ored as guest of a French warship; if it was not exactly Washington and Lafayette all over again, it would nevertheless do. The party was received at the yard by Captain (later Admiral) John A. Dahlgren. As a band played the "Star-Spangled Banner," they got into a barge and were rowed out to the ship, where Admiral Reynaud, who had just come in that day, joined Captain Gautier in welcoming them. The two nations' flags flew side by side, the guns shot off their twenty-one rounds, the crew huzzahed the president.[45]

What happened after that was recorded by F. W. Seward:

Champagne and a brief conversation in the captain's cabin came next; then a walk up and down her decks to look at her armament and equipment. Though the surroundings were all new to Mr. Lincoln, he bore himself with his usual quiet, homely, unpretentious dignity on such occasions, and chatted affably with some of the officers who spoke English. The visit over, we were escorted to the side ladder, and re-embarked in our barge.

As Mr. Lincoln took his seat in the stern he said: "Suppose we row around her bows. I should like to look at her build and rig from that direction." Captain Dahlgren of course shifted his helm accordingly. The French officers doubtless had not heard or understood the President's remark, and supposed we were pulling off astern in the ordinary way.

We had reached her bow, when, on looking up, I saw the officer of the deck passing the bridge, watch in hand and counting off the seconds, *"Un, deux, trois,"* and then immediately followed the flash and deafening roar of a cannon, apparently just over our heads.

[45] *New York Times*, 27 April 1862; *Evening Star* (Washington), 28 April 1862; *National Intelligencer* (Washington), 28 April 1862.

170

The guns were not shotted, of course, but flying bits of wadding were a distinct danger, and in fact the President of the United States might have been injured or killed by the guns of a French warship. Thouvenel was lucky to have nothing more to worry about than Mercier's visit to Richmond! The president gave no sign that he realized the danger, and he did not refer to it afterwards.[46]

For a month now, General McClellan's Army of the Potomac had been sitting down before Yorktown on the Virginia peninsula. The government leaders in Richmond had spoken openly to Mercier about the possibility of having to go somewhere else; since then, they and General Joe Johnston had reason to wonder at the Union's course, for they knew how weak the Yorktown line really was, and they further could not understand why McDowell's army, still lying near Fredericksburg so as to cover the federal capital, was not yet upon them. On 4 May, Johnston finally decided that the bluff had lasted long enough, and he marched his army out of Yorktown and up toward Richmond. McClellan's incipient charge on the town became a scraggly pursuit, but at least, thought his Radical critics, he was moving. Mercier was there at the beginning to see for himself.

On Monday, the fifth of May, Mercier had set out with a party of senators and other guests on board the *Mt. Washington* to view the scene of battle. About noon the next day they landed at Yorktown, just hours then in Union hands, and stayed there as guests of Union General James Van Alen. On Wednesday they left for Fortress Monroe, whence they rowed out to inspect the *Monitor* and met President Lincoln and Secretaries Stanton and Chase who had come down separately to see the war. Mercier's group returned

[46] F. W. Seward, *Reminiscences of a Wartime Statesman*, pp. 173-75; see also Stern, pp. 133-34. The press did not report the incident.

to Washington the next day, having first watched the naval shelling of Sewell's Point. The president and the secretaries stayed on for three more days and were there when Norfolk was taken.[47]

Mercier was impressed. He knew now, better than before, that the North was as intent on its task as the Confederacy:

> On both sides the same confidence and determination, but in opposite directions, and no ability to say the word "compromise." . . . Yorktown was evacuated; in my whole life I have never seen a more desolate scene. Not a single inhabitant; all the houses abandoned or destroyed. The Confederates, who had to retire quickly, had left behind . . . almost all their large cannon, a great store of munitions, tents, tools, etc.

The minister had the general picture straight: the North was powerful and the South was retreating; but he misread the scene at Yorktown as a probable sign of Southern moral breakdown. It was clear in any event that the United States of America was well on its way to becoming a world power of significance. "So let us be very careful," Mercier concluded, "not to fall out with them; without ignoring the present, let us think about the future. . . . I think it is good policy to cultivate [their] anti-English disposition."[48]

Mercier was on firm ground there, for despite the trip to Richmond, Seward was still disposed to favor France, even to the point of being overly nice. "We acknowledge that France has faithfully practiced the neutrality she proclaimed," the secretary avowed, "and that in the whole progress of the domestic strife she has not only spoken the

[47] *National Intelligencer* (Washington), 12 May 1862; *Lincoln Day by Day*, III, 109-11.

[48] Mercier to Thouvenel, Washington, 8? May 1862, AMAE, MD, Papiers Thouvenel, XIII, 448-51.

language, but acted in the character of a well-wisher and friend."[49]

As McClellan ground on, Mercier continued to think that the North was bringing on a dénouement, though he could not shake the memory of Richmond and all those threats about fighting on from the interior. And what about slavery? Would the North allow it to go on as the moderates wished, or would the growing abolitionism prevail? Mercier could be quite decisive in such peripheral matters as the trip to Richmond. When it came to recommending French intervention, however, he was usually loath to conclude that the time had arrived for action. Northern victory *seemed* imminent, but the Southern threat to fight on even should Richmond fall kept Mercier from making a definite conclusion. As he put it to Thouvenel: "I think we are finally reaching the decisive moment of the crisis. The Federals will shortly be in Richmond; there is no longer a shadow of a doubt about that. Then we shall see whether the Southerners are capable of persevering. . . . For myself, I would not yet dare to say anything positive."

The Confederates had burned the *Merrimac*, since it was too large to be taken upstream, and this struck Mercier forcibly as an act of desperation. The moment for Europe to do something seemed close, but it was still not easy to say what:

> But listen to what I say: whatever we do, let us be tactful with the North. I have a great deal of respect for them since I have seen what they can do. . . . It is truly astounding what their navy has achieved in the last year through its resources and the valor of its men. We

[49] Seward to Dayton, Washington, 7 May 1862, State Dept. Corres., France, Instructions, xvi, 156-58, no. 151, also in *For. Rel. U.S.*, 1862, p. 338.

must be friends with this people, all the more because they very much want that and because we do not know where their bellicose mood might push them.[50]

Mercier seems to have kept in the forefront of things throughout the spring. On 23 May, he, President Lincoln, Secretary Stanton, Captain Dahlgren, and an unnamed aide of Mercier's all showed up at General Irvin McDowell's headquarters near Fredericksburg, having come by boat to Aquia and from there by baggage-car. In Fredericksburg, Mercier looked about; the president and Stanton had things to talk over with McDowell, including, no doubt, Confederate General Thomas Jonathan Jackson. The visitors shared McDowell's first reaction to one of the war's most crucial events. Then back in Washington by dawn on the twenty-fourth, they watched this event apprehensively: near Front Royal, Virginia, Stonewall Jackson was striking his most telling blow to date in his Shenandoah Valley campaign, defeating General Banks and threatening to cross the Potomac. That was the end so far as McDowell's going on to Richmond was concerned; it was Washington now which seemed to be in danger.[51] Mercier reflected the fear in the Northern newspapers: "You know the confidence which reigned here some days ago; I myself ended by

[50] Mercier to Thouvenel, Washington, 12 May 1862, AMAE, MD, Papiers Thouvenel, XIII, 452-53. See also Mercier to Thouvenel, Washington, 12 May 1862, AMAE, CP, E-U, 127: 123-29, no. 99, an altered version of which is in *LJ*, III (1862), 129-30. To Lyons, Mercier still sounded as if he favored European intervention in order to stop a long and drawn-out war—intervention, that is, on the basis of Southern independence (E. D. Adams, I, 297-99; Newton, I, 85-86). We can assume, however, that his private letters to Thouvenel are a better index of his thinking: in effect, Mercier did not know what to think.

[51] *ORA*, 1st ser., LI, 75; *Lincoln Day by Day*, III, 114-15; Lincoln to McClellan, Washington, 25 May 1862, in Nicolay and Hay, *Abraham Lincoln*, V, 402-03.

giving in to it; today it has given way to a real panic. Washington is thought to be threatened."

It took a while, and a great many more lives, for the situation to become perfectly clear, but its broad outlines were visible already. Richmond was safe; that being so, the war crisis had passed; that being so, the intervention crisis would begin.

REACTIONS IN PARIS AND LONDON[52]

While Mercier was hustling here and there along the line of battle, the time bomb he had shipped to France had exploded resoundingly and was rocking the chancelleries of Europe. The detonation began on 29 April when Thouvenel heard, first from news telegraphs and then from Lord John Russell (citing Lyons), that Mercier had gone south. Thouvenel's annoyance can well be imagined; he, more than anyone, realized the importance of the entente, and his minister in Washington had now thrown it into danger. The business about Stoeckl, also recounted in Lyons's report, was the crowning imprudence. After first doing his best to clear things up in London, Thouvenel administered his friend Mercier a restrained but firm rebuke:

Having found nothing in your dispatches which could warn me of such a decision, I was first ready to question the accuracy of the information, but the honorable ambassador of England relayed information received by his government which confirms it exactly. Lord Lyons writes . . . that having first intended to visit Richmond with the minister of Russia, you then decided to go alone, and that the goal of your move was to support with the Government of the Confederate

---

[52] In this section the author is especially grateful for being allowed to consult the preliminary draft of Dr. Case's account of the European reaction; he has liberally drawn upon this account.

States all the reasons which ought to induce it to rejoin the Union and to give up a resistance which the
recent military developments should prove was useless.[53]

Uninformed opinion, then and since, has leapt to the
conclusion that Napoleon III sent Mercier to Richmond
himself, probably to see what the South might be willing
to offer, both in cotton and in toleration for France's Mexican venture. Not only is there no single shred of evidence
for this assertion, there is good documentary reason for
rejecting it. The day after he wrote to Mercier, Thouvenel
again addressed his minister in London, Count Flahault:
"The emperor seemed to me very much annoyed at Mr.
Mercier's initiative, and I am again sure that His Majesty
intends to do nothing in the United States which is not in
total accord with England."[54]

Thanks to Thouvenel's quick and intense reassurances,
the British government, after its initial shock, seems to have
taken Mercier's trip in stride, and Paris breathed a little
easier. On 3 May Thouvenel at last received Mercier's dispatch of 13 April, which the minister had written some
three days after his first interview with Seward. Mercier
sent this dispatch via the same courier who carried Lyons's
note. The time required to convey the French note through
Liverpool and London to Paris, including a possible delay
within the French embassy in London, may explain the fact
that Thouvenel did not receive Mercier's news until four
days after Russell had received Lyons's. Thouvenel now

[53] Thouvenel to Mercier, Paris, 1 May 1862, AMAE, CP, E-U, 127:
83-84, no. 12. Thouvenel's letter shows a number of interesting
things, e.g., that he was most relieved that Stoeckl had stayed in
Washington and that in following the tale as told by Lyons, he had
thought Mercier was playing the Union part in Richmond.

[54] Thouvenel to Flahault, Paris, 2 May 1862, Thouvenel, Secret,
II, 298-300.

knew that Mercier had gone not to speak for Seward but rather to gather "precious information" and if possible "to prepare the way for recourse to our good offices."[55] Till now, Thouvenel had worried that Mercier was undermining relations with England; he could now begin worrying about France's relations with the United States. By 14 May Thouvenel knew from Mercier's dispatch of 28 April the bulk of what had passed between the minister and Secretary Benjamin.

Along with everyone else, John Slidell had been speculating about Mercier. He thought there were two real possibilities: either Washington wanted the emperor's mediation, or the emperor had sent Mercier south without telling Thouvenel.[56] Slidell went to see Thouvenel on 14 May. The foreign minister was gracious, but he questioned Slidell pointedly about the fall of New Orleans and what that might mean to Southern hopes. He withheld some things from Slidell, saying that he had heard nothing from Mercier, when in fact he "knew" that Mercier had gone to Richmond to speak for reunion of the states. Thouvenel did say, however, that he had heard from Russell (citing Lyons) that Mercier had been most impressed by the Southern will to go on fighting, so impressed that he had felt it futile to present Seward's conciliatory suggestions. Finally, Thouvenel offered to inform Slidell fully when he received Mercier's dispatch.[57] Within a few hours the dispatch had arrived, and Thouvenel now knew what had passed be-

[55] Mercier to Thouvenel, Washington, 13 April 1862 (rcd. 3 May 1862), AMAE, CP, E-U, 127: 35-47, no. 96.

[56] Slidell to Benjamin, Paris, 9 May 1862, Richardson, II, 244-45, no. 7, also in ORN, 2nd ser., III, 414-15.

[57] Slidell to Benjamin, Paris, 15 May 1862, Richardson, II, 245-48, no. 8, also in ORN, 2nd ser., III, 419-20. Interestingly enough, Slidell at this time, in urging French recognition of the Confederacy before any offer of mediation, said that a six-months' armistice could probably be arranged. This is similar to the French proposal of autumn 1862.

tween Mercier and Benjamin—everything except that part about the common market and Maury's plan to exchange blockade-breaking for free trade.[58]

Thouvenel was still angry at being kept in the dark. "I have just received the dispatch," he began; then he changed it to "Not until yesterday did I receive the dispatch." He went on to caution Mercier about the delays in his correspondence—delays which, he said, were "sometimes" experienced; then he changed that to "habitually." That bit of knuckle-rapping out of the way, Thouvenel settled into a familiar word of warning against premature action, and since Mercier's letter itself had counseled a waiting policy, there was here a congenial meeting of minds. Thouvenel, in effect, told Mercier to continue watching and waiting; it was still too early to say whether a Union victory was imminent or whether the South, as it claimed so insistently, would fight on, no matter what.[59]

On 19 May Thouvenel received Mercier's additional details on the Richmond trip, especially the account of his common-market conversation with Benjamin.[60] Preferring not to go into that, Thouvenel in his reply of 21 May instead described a conversation he had just had with Dayton. Seward, trying hard to capitalize on the North's favorable military situation, and especially on the capture of New Orleans and other ports, was pressing Europe to withdraw her recognition of Southern belligerency. A neutral stance, he felt, was encouraging the South to fight on, prolonging the war unnecessarily. Dayton brought all this up with Thouvenel. The latter, however, had been thoroughly informed by Mercier—and briefed by Geofroy, who was

[58] Mercier to Thouvenel, Washington, 28 April 1862 (rcd. 14 May 1862), AMAE, CP, E-U, 127: 50-79, no. 97.

[59] Thouvenel to Mercier, Paris, 15 May 1862, *ibid.*, fol. 151-52, no. 13.

[60] Mercier to Thouvenel, Washington, 6 May 1862 (rcd. 19 May 1862), *ibid.*, fol. 85-105, no. 98.

now in Paris—about the real determination of the South to go on fighting. As Dayton related it: "Putting his finger upon a map and pointing to the central parts of the Southern Cotton States, he said that when beaten they would retire there: that it was a vast country and consequently very difficult to foresee the future."[61]

It was a fencing-match kind of debate between Thouvenel on the one hand and Dayton and Seward on the other. The Frenchman took up Seward's claim that the South was losing all her ports and turned it around: if so, then it did not matter so much whether Europe withdrew her quasi-recognition. A certain "delicacy of feeling" he said, prevented France from doing to the South in her extremity what she would not do in earlier days, especially without the consent of Britain.[62]

The delayed reaction caused by the Atlantic Ocean also affected the timing of Mercier's responses. By the time he had received Thouvenel's rebukes, the matter was dying down in Europe. He was "very disagreeably surprised," he told his superior, to learn that Lyons's had been the first word of his Richmond trip to reach Paris. Lyons, he continued, appreciated the good results of his voyage and knew that he wished to maintain the most perfect accord "in appearance and in reality" with the British legation.

EVALUATIONS OF THE TRIP

So Mercier had come and gone, and though his voyage had unsettled affairs a little, though things could hardly

[61] Dayton to Seward, Paris, 22 May 1862, State Dept. Corres., France, Dispatches, LI, no. 149, also in *For. Rel. U.S.*, 1862, pp. 341-42. See also Seward to Dayton, Washington, 2 May 1862, State Dept. Corres., France, Instructions, XVI, 154-55, no. 149; Seward to Dayton, Washington, 1 May 1862, *ibid.*, pp. 152-53, no. 148, also in *For. Rel. U.S.*, 1862, p. 336.

[62] Thouvenel to Mercier, Paris, 21 May 1862, AMAE, CP, E-U, 127: 176-81, no. 14, an altered version of which is in *LJ*, III (1862), 127-29.

be quite the same again between himself and Lyons, there were other factors of ultimately greater significance for the entente—the Mexican venture and Napoleon III's conversations with British members of parliament.

Persons particularly concerned to prove that they could not be fooled assumed that there was more to the trip than met the eye. In going beyond the "cover," of course, they were right, though it was truly one of Mercier's chief purposes to see and listen to Richmond for himself. But the only real ulterior motives were Seward's and Mercier's—in the former case to let Mercier see the South's poor condition, to get information about Confederate conditions and intentions, and to find out if the South would consider peace with reunion. Mercier's reasons were almost the same, but with a different twist: to see how dearly his Southern acquaintances held their political independence; to find out if they would consider peace, either with or without reunion, on any terms which the North might ever be willing to consider; and in doing this to lay the groundwork for French mediation. Seward and Mercier, then, had axes to grind, but they were honorable axes and were directed against the war. No other official, not even Napoleon III, was part of the project. There is no part of the written record which points at the emperor, and we have seen his explicit denial to Thouvenel. Even on the hypotheses that the denial was false and the instructions to Mercier so secret they were lost, the charge against the emperor falls of its own weight. For if he had wanted an agreement with the South, he could have had one by breaking the blockade. As subsequent events showed, however, he was not willing even to extend diplomatic recognition without the concurrence of Britain. He would hardly, therefore, have risked breaking up the entente in April by ordering Mercier to go south.

One very palpable result of the trip was its effect upon Mercier, and through him upon France and even England. The facts he gathered were quite important after all. First, he discovered that the South meant to fight on no matter what, and he knew, therefore, that mediation was pointless since the South said nothing but "independence" and the North nothing but "Union." Nationalist Americans would criticize this conclusion as if Mercier had somehow created the conditions which he found in Richmond. The key point, however, is the correctness of the information. No other diplomat in Washington, and perhaps no other person, was so sure about this point until Mercier went and found out for himself. (Even afterward, of course, they would not be sure unless they had confidence in Mercier's ability to tell sincere determination from bluff.) If we grant that one of a diplomat's prime duties is to gather information, then no other chancellery was so well served as the Quai d'Orsay; Thouvenel's debate with Dayton shows that. For the fact of the thing is that Mercier was right about this war. The South did fight on. The war *did* become a frightful slugging match. Political reunion *was* transcended as an objective, principally by emancipation. Thanks to Lee and Jackson, to McClellan's critics and McClellan himself, the real test of Mercier's information never came, for Richmond remained in Confederate hands. All the same it was important information, and however unfortunate, was accurate.

Second, Mercier's fact-gathering in Richmond should be seen as part of the overall story of his life in April and May of 1862. It was not only Richmond which he visited, but Yorktown and Fredericksburg too, and after that there was no one more respectful of United States strength than he. His ardent advice to Paris—it was almost a plea—was to steer clear of that muscular force, to avoid war with the Union no matter what. It is not easy to assess the effect of this information, again very accurate, upon decisions in Paris and London; but we know that his superiors listened to Mercier, and in doing so they were influenced away from violent intervention.

Writers who have dealt with Mercier's Richmond trip have generally not been very happy about it. Bancroft, Seward's biographer, finds Mercier "quite devoid of the balance and good judgment that characterized Lord Lyons," and criticizes Seward for "quite unnecessarily" authorizing a trip which he should have foreseen would turn out badly for the Union.[63] Newton, Lyons's biographer, is more concrete along the same lines, saying that Mercier, like other Second Empire diplomats, was striving to bring off a coup. Lyons was wise not to go with him, for Mercier's trip ended by giving rise to "all sorts of comments."[64] And C. F. Adams, Jr., telescoping a great deal of French history into a small section of his article on British policy, sees Mercier and John Slidell as birds of a feather, linking up the Richmond trip with Mercier's earlier request for discretionary authority to recognize the South. In his view Mercier was a particular friend of Judah Benjamin, "Creole Senator from Louisiana," and the trip to Richmond against Lyons's ever-sage advice was "an officious act, characteristic of the man and of the imperial diplomatic service."[65]

There is a common denominator to these earlier evaluations. They exhibit a sort of Anglo-Saxon reserve about France and especially the Second Empire; in the cases of Adams and Bancroft, they are biased in favor of the Union cause. Lyons the prudent and Mercier the threatrical become counterparts of Queen Victoria and Napoleon III; having avoided "all sorts of comments," Lyons has made a good

[63] Bancroft, *Life of William H. Seward*, II, 298-99; also 370-72.
[64] Newton, I, 82.
[65] C. F. Adams, Jr., *Massachusetts Historical Society Proceedings*, XLVII (1914), 376-77.

show, while Mercier has frivolously undermined the Union cause. Another common factor is lack of reference to the French documents, a gap for which the French government (Third Republic) was to blame, and was indeed blamed severely by C. F. Adams, Jr.

E. D. Adams presents a comparatively full and balanced account of the trip written from the British sources.[66] A mood of mild disapproval pervades his story, and he correctly lays the blame on Mercier, not his government. Frank Owsley, on the other hand, ventures to put two and two together and comes up with six. He notes that Mercier's trip and the emperor's contacts with British political figures occurred simultaneously and "seem part of the same plan." The "probabilities are strong" that the trip was "the second diplomatic move of Napoleon," and its "real purpose . . . was to obtain, as the basis of the intervention which was now on foot, a first-hand estimate of the ability and determination of the South to win her independence."[67] The Owsley account is full enough, with an especially valuable summary of the Mercier–Benjamin talk, but the author's willingness to draw conclusions beyond the historical record leaves the reader with some misapprehensions.

Henry Blumenthal's recent study, covering almost half a century of Franco-American relations, touches briefly on the Richmond trip. Blumenthal rejects the idea that Napoleon III initiated the démarche and says that Mercier's version about origins—his remark dropped almost accidentally—is at least plausible. He takes up the common-market proposal at some length, concluding incorrectly that Mercier violated French neutrality in making it. Finally, he is on marshy ground in this generalization: "Thouvenel studied Mercier's despatches, but did not follow the envoy's often unrealistic and inconsistent recommendations. It was the

---

[66] E. D. Adams, I, 279-300.
[67] Owsley, *King Cotton Diplomacy*, pp. 268, 273, 282-91.

Emperor who found them suggestive enough to play with them."[68]

Henri Mercier went to Richmond to help his country by obtaining information and to stop the war. In doing so he seriously embarrassed his friend and superior at the Quai d'Orsay, risked diplomatic complications for his country, and probably betrayed Seward's mandate, if such it was. As it turned out, the friendship survived, the diplomatic complications were not catastrophic, and Seward seemed relatively content. The information which Mercier picked up was valuable, but it is questionable whether it was fully worth the trip and the excitement caused by it.

One of Judah Benjamin's predictions of Southern success was disproved the very day that Mercier arrived back from his Richmond trip. Despite the Confederate ironclads, New Orleans fell to the Union navy. With that event a whole new series of diplomatic problems began to arrive at the French legation in Washington, and Louisiana occupied a great deal of Mercier's time throughout the rest of 1862.

[68] Blumenthal, *Franco-American Relations*, pp. 141-42. Korolewicz-Carlton's doctoral dissertation elaborates many variations on the theme of Thouvenel the just versus the emperor and Mercier. For the Richmond trip see Korolewicz-Carlton, pp. 154-57.

CHAPTER VII

Renewed Pressure for Peace

MAY TO AUGUST 1862

NEW ORLEANS

BEFORE ten o'clock on the morning of 24 April 1862, news reached New Orleans that David Farragut was at hand, breakfasting seven miles downstream before coming on to lay the town beneath his guns. Stores closed, bells rang, troops and steamboats headed north, and the cloudy skies were alight with burning tobacco and cotton. During the next several days, as the warships and the city sat looking at each other, the French consul, Count Méjan, had some dealings with Farragut; he and other consuls tried to soften the admiral's threat to fire on the town should anyone stop the Stars and Stripes from being hoisted.[1] Then on Thursday, 1 May, the new military commander of the district arrived to inaugurate his tenure. Shortly thereafter he met Méjan, and shortly after that, Mercier's time and correspondence began to fill to overflowing with the career of Major General Benjamin Franklin Butler, U.S.A.[2]

General Butler later admitted that in New Orleans he had hoped to distinguish himself "in one thing, if no more, and

[1] Nevins, *The War for the Union*, II, 100-01; Milledge L. Bonham, "The French Consuls in the Confederate States," *Studies in Southern History and Politics Inscribed to William Archibald Dunning* (New York: Columbia University Press, 1914), p. 99.

[2] For problems of New Orleans French nationals wanting to go home, see Bonham, "French Consuls in the Confederacy," *Studies in Southern History and Politics*, pp. 92-93.

that is that I did not carry on war with rose-water."[3] His stringency against the consular corps became a regular duel as the weeks wore by. The general seems to have derived a particular pleasure from writing all those sarcastic notes; no history of American humor should pass them up. For their part the consuls, with Méjan leading, made it their business to unsettle him at every turn. It got so bad that the New Orleans *Delta* complained out loud: "If Gen. Butler rides up street, the consuls are sure to come in a body, and protest that he did not ride down. If he smokes a pipe in the morning, a deputation calls upon him in the evening to know why he did not smoke a cigar."[4]

Most of Butler's actions concerned France directly. Shortly after taking command of the town, Butler had a run-in with the Dutch consul about some Mexican silver he was keeping in the consulate on the plea that it belonged to an Amsterdam firm. The dispute found its way to Washington, where Lyons and Mercier both supported their Netherlands colleague, Roest van Limburg. On 31 May, Mercier discussed this and other Butler acts with Seward, specifying that this was an informal conversation, not an official protest. Seward was eager to please and told Mercier that he had already gotten Stanton to warn Butler, that Butler would be detached from the civil administration of his sector, and that Reverdy Johnson of Maryland would be sent to inquire about what was going on in New Orleans. General George F. Shepley was quickly appointed "military governor of Louisiana," a post parallel to that of Andrew Johnson in Tennessee.[5]

[3] Benjamin F. Butler, *Autobiography and Personal Reminiscences of Major-General Benj. F. Butler: Butler's Book* (Boston: A. M. Thayer & Co., 1892), p. 421.

[4] Quoted in Robert S. Holzman, *Stormy Ben Butler* (New York: Macmillan Co., 1954), p. 83.

[5] Mercier to Thouvenel, Washington, 3 June 1862, AMAE, CP, E-U, 127: 194-203, no. 102; Memorandum of the Seward–Mercier con-

It would be tedious to rehearse all or even most of the varieties of cases engendered by this remarkable general in his unique surroundings. One whole set of problems concerned his brushes with French naval and commercial ships.[6] Another arose when Méjan objected vehemently to French merchants' being forced to pay a second tax for their licenses on the grounds that those issued by the rebel government of Louisiana were invalid.[7] But one of Butler's

---

versation, 31 May 1862, State Dept. Corres., Notes to the French Legation, vii, 106-08; Hans L. Trefousse, *Benjamin Butler, the South Called him Beast!* (New York: Twayne, 1957), pp. 125-26; Bonham, "French Consuls in the Confederacy," *Studies in Southern History and Politics*, p. 99.

[6] Part of this began about two weeks after Butler's taking charge, when the French warship *Catinat* entered the river waters near New Orleans. As Butler told it, the captain gave "a great jubilee" on the ship, and rebel songs were sung. Shortly afterward, Butler was sent some kind of verbal alert by Seward concerning the possibility of Anglo-French intervention—or at least so Butler remembered it in later years. Butler saw all this and the French action in Mexico as part of a French plan to attack New Orleans, giving as a reason for thinking so that "it was so characteristic of the French Emperor." To cap the climax, on 16 June the city government of New Orleans, headed by Major John T. Monroe, a Confederate sympathizer, passed a resolution welcoming a visit by units of the French navy in the Gulf area. Butler thought that the government, in seeking to extend this hospitality, was inviting itself "to the calaboose or the hospital," and he decreed the French navy a health hazard, offering to fire upon it if necessary as a sanitary precaution (*Butler's Book*, pp. 464-69; Trefousse, p. 113).

Simultaneously the *Harriet Ralli* of Marseilles came up to New Orleans with a cargo of wine and liqueur. Butler, who had of course had to authorize this, then seized ship and cargo, claiming that the ship had earlier violated the Union blockade. Again the same pathways: a protest through the legation in Washington got quick action from Seward and Chase, though the ship was later held up for a while in New York (Méjan to Mercier, New Orleans, 17 June 1862, translation, State Dept. Corres., Notes from the French Legation, xviii; Treilhard to Seward, Washington, 29 July and 6 and 10 Aug. 1862, *ibid.*).

[7] Mercier gave the license problem his close personal attention, telling Thouvenel it hardly seemed right for French café and restaurant

imaginative decrees deserves some explanation: general order no. 55. Before 24 April, many New Orleans persons and firms had bought defense bonds for the protection of the city against Union attack. Now Butler was there, and on 4 August he proclaimed that all such subscribers should pay a special tax amounting to one-fourth the total of their defense-bond holdings. Then there were the cotton brokers who, in October of 1861, had taken an advertisement in the papers urging planters as a patriotic measure not to send down their cotton. Order no. 55 provided that they too pay a special penalty, the money to be used for the poor of the city. All told, the defense-fund subscribers were supposed to pay $312,716.25, and the ninety-six cotton brokers a total of $29,200.00 at one to five hundred dollars a firm.[8]

This time the normal channels became clogged, perhaps because Seward genuinely felt that Butler had a point or because he feared Radical criticism of an overly soft policy. With Mercier away on vacation, Jules Treilhard relayed the inevitable complaint: two firms—Rochereau & Co. and Jeannet Questier & Co.—and a proprietor, Mr. Levois, had filed against the bondholders' penalty. In his note Treilhard alleged that his countrymen had bought the securities as an investment, never thinking that this would one day be regarded as an act of hostility against the federal government. Seward let it ride until November and then notified Mercier that he thought the complainants had forfeited their immunity by their overt act in support of New Orleans' defense. Mercier replied without anticipating his government's view of that argument, contenting himself with a general condemnation of Butler's regime. Seward later tried to

owners to have to pay their $150.00 twice over (Mercier to Thouvenel, Washington, 27 June 1862, AMAE, CP, E-U, 127: 272-76, no. 106).

[8] Jefferson Davis Bragg, *Louisiana in the Confederacy* (Baton Rouge: Louisiana State University Press, 1941), pp. 120-21.

smooth things over by telling Mercier confidentially that a judge would soon go to New Orleans to hear such cases. Finally, in early December, the other fine, the one on the cotton brokers, was sustained in Washington, but before Butler could actually collect any cash, he was transferred; its collection apparently remained a dead letter.[9]

Far the most important matter in New Orleans to engage Mercier's attention involved the large amount of money belonging to French residents which Méjan brought into the consulate as Farragut was ascending the river. When Butler subsequently began his scavenger hunt for specie, claiming it for the government on the least suspicion of rebel ownership, Méjan's move seemed wise indeed and was supported as such by Mercier. Butler, however, had other cards to play, and with the usual caution demanded by his narratives we may recall the game as he described it. Méjan, accosted by Butler, denied that the consulate contained any Confederate contraband and insisted that the sanctity of the building as French soil be respected:

> "But," I said, "Count, there need not be any emotion about this. How much of the territory of Louisiana do you think the French flag flying on your consulate will protect from United States occupation?" .
>
> "My house and courtelige," was the answer. . . .
>
> "Well, then, Count, agreeing with you that the line

[9] Treilhard to Seward, Washington, 29 Aug. 1862, State Dept. Corres., Notes from the French Legation, xviii; *Butler's Book*, pp. 430-36; Benjamin F. Butler, *Private and Official Correspondence of Gen. Benjamin F. Butler, during the Period of the Civil War*, 5 vols. (Norwood, Mass.: Plimpton Press, 1917), ii, 361-68; Seward to Mercier [Washington], 14 Nov. 1862, State Dept. Corres., Notes to the French Legation, xix; Drouyn de Lhuys to Mercier, Paris, 24 Dec. 1862, AMAE, CP, E-U, 128: 304-07, no. 35; Mercier to Seward, Washington, 17 Jan. 1863, State Dept. Corres., Notes from the French Legation, xix. For the Mercier-Seward correspondence, see also *For. Rel. U.S.*, 1863, pt. 2, pp. 819-26.

of French territory is as you claim, I will set no foot on French territory . . . as I have a grateful record for France, I will content myself with putting a guard on United States territory . . . so that nothing shall come out of French territory onto American territory without my leave."[10]

Suspicion and sarcasm marked a long summer of maneuvering by the general and the count. On 30 June Butler asked again for an account of the money, those "large amounts of specie placed under your charge, just previous to the coming up of the Fleet of the United States," and presumed that "a press of business" had prevented Méjan's attending to this little detail.[11] The largest piece of the bullion, some $716,196.00, was credited to the firm of Dupasseur & Co., and this became the main subject of the correspondence between New Orleans and Washington and between Washington and Paris. Mercier was annoyed by the matter from the start, feeling that some of the hoarded coin must be the property of American citizens and hence a potential embarrassment, but believing also that Méjan was basically right and had even conceded too much in promising Butler not to release the funds from the consulate.[12]

The good offices of Reverdy Johnson were engaged in this matter above all others. Johnson was in New Orleans in July, heard the case, and told Édouard Dupasseur that he would report favorably when he got back to Washing-

[10] *Butler's Book*, pp. 523-25. For brief accounts of the affair, see also Trefousse, pp. 117 and 126-28; and John D. Winters, *The Civil War in Louisiana* (Baton Rouge: Louisiana State University Press, 1963), p. 129.

[11] Butler to Méjan, New Orleans, 30 June 1862, Butler, *Private and Official Correspondence*, II, 25-26.

[12] Mercier to Thouvenel, New London, 29 July 1862, AMAE, MD, Papiers Thouvenel, XIII, 479-83.

ton.[13] Or as Butler put it, "Seward sent that secession spy and agent, Reverdy Johnson, to New Orleans . . . ," and "instructed [him] to decide, as he did in every case, in favor of the foreigner."[14] Johnson returned to Washington in the first part of August, and Mercier hoped that everything would be all right. A week later Treilhard was able to report just that: Méjan would be allowed to pay money to whoever had it coming.[15]

In September the whole friendly structure began to come unhinged. First, Seward got word that some Confederate agents in Europe were waiting for money with which to buy cloth ultimately destined for the backs of Lee's and Beauregard's boys. The money, it turned out, had been in Méjan's vaults all the while. By this time Méjan had left the city at Mercier's suggestion to come north and deliver a verbal report on his various concerns. Méjan may have withheld some vital information from that report, for Mercier seemed unaware of the complication over the blankets. He was happy that the Dupasseur fortune had been freed to its owners and that the other deposits had likewise been removed out of the consulate. At his suggestion Thouvenel granted Méjan a leave; it was best to keep him and Butler apart if at all possible.[16]

[13] Méjan to Mercier, New Orleans, 24 July 1862; Édouard Dupasseur to Méjan, New Orleans, 24 July 1862; and the unsigned memorandum dated 31 July 1862—all in State Dept. Corres., Notes from the French Legation, XVIII. See also Bernard C. Steiner, *Life of Reverdy Johnson* (Baltimore: Norman, Remington Co., 1914), pp. 58-59.

[14] *Butler's Book*, pp. 522 and 525.

[15] Mercier to Thouvenel, New London, 12 Aug. 1862, AMAE, MD, Papiers Thouvenel, XIII, 484-85; Seward to Treilhard, Washington, 20 Aug. 1862, State Dept. Corres., Notes to the French Legation, VII, 118, also in *For. Rel. U.S.*, 1862, p. 430.

[16] Bonham, "French Consuls in the Confederacy," *Studies in Southern History and Politics*, pp. 101-02; Mercier to Thouvenel, New York, 2 Sept. 1862 (rcd. 16 Sept. 1862), AMAE, CP, E-U, 128:

Meanwhile the investigation into the case of the blankets was going forward; Butler having been ordered to join the hunt, did so, in his own words, *con amore.* In November he found that some of Méjan's holdings had indeed been earmarked for the benefit of the Confederate army with Méjan's approval. Bullion had recently left New Orleans to that end, and a shipment of cloth was simultaneously waiting somewhere in the Gulf area for shipment into Texas. Butler was removed from his New Orleans post in December; his general talent for being obnoxious had finally borne results. But as he saw it, the move was inspired by Seward and craven:

> I learned afterwards that Napoleon required that I be recalled from New Orleans. It was done. Under the cowardly administration of the State Department, the officer ordered to catch the thief, and who did catch him and convict him, was punished to a very much greater extent than the thief himself.[17]

All this, of course, was pure imagination on Butler's part. He was removed probably because Seward and Lincoln had had enough of the unnecessary abrasions which Butler's conduct was causing in the Union's relations with European states, most notably France.

Méjan, of course, was "the thief," and though no one but Butler was calling him that, he was in great trouble. Seward handled the thing delicately enough, and he and Mercier both put as little into writing as was possible. The secretary told Mercier, in effect, that it was his move. Mercier moved. "I will immediately draw my government's attention to the

---

67-72, no. 112; Thouvenel to Mercier, Paris, 18 Sept. 1862, *ibid.*, fol. 93-95, no. 24.

[17] *Butler's Book,* pp. 525-26.

complaints which Your Excellency made to me . . . ," he told Seward, "and while awaiting the decision it thinks best, I am inviting Mr. Méjan to return to France to make his explanations there."[18]

So it was over. On 17 December Butler had been replaced by General Nathaniel P. Banks, the same whom Stonewall Jackson had chased about northern Virginia in the spring; Banks was a former speaker of the house of representatives, a favorite of Seward's, and a moderate man. General Butler came to the capital from New Orleans and was being serenaded at the National Hotel on 5 January, about the time Seward was telling Mercier that Méjan should leave the country. The squalls stirred up by general and count had little specific impact of any dimension. Had England been willing to intervene in the Civil War, had she and France then wished to fight, matters like the case of the blankets might have been brought forward as vital grievances. Had the Civil War not been so draining, had the United States been looking for a *casus belli* in order to get France out of Mexico, then Méjan's intrigue with the Confederate quartermaster would have done very nicely. But to say that is to beg the question, for if the Civil War had not been what it was, Mercier and most other Europeans would never have known Benjamin Franklin Butler. To Mercier he must have seemed a tragically typical prod-

[18] Mercier to Seward, Washington, 4 Jan. 1863, State Dept. Corres., Notes from the French Legation, XIX; Mercier to Drouyn de Lhuys, Washington, 6 Jan. 1863, AMAE, CP, E-U, 129: 7-11, no. 134, annexed to which is the Mercier–Seward exchange of notes (fol. 13-14). See also Seward to Mercier, Washington, 3 and 6 Jan. 1863, State Dept. Corres., Notes to the French Legation, VII, 170-71; Seward to Dayton, Washington, 14 Jan. 1863, State Dept. Corres., France, Instructions, XVI, 323-24, also in *For. Rel. U.S.*, 1863, pt. 2, p. 710; Drouyn de Lhuys to Mercier, Paris, 23 Jan. 1863, AMAE, CP, E-U, 129: 41-42, no. 2; Mercier to Drouyn de Lhuys, Washington, 23 Jan. 1863, *ibid.*, fol. 26-28, private.

uct of the country and the war, a harbinger of the future if the North should win. It was a grim enough prospect.[19]

FLUCTUATIONS ON THE BATTLEFIELD
AND IN MERCIER'S MIND

The Shenandoah Valley campaign of Stonewall Jackson, which threw Washington into a panic in late May of 1862, appears in retrospect to have been crucial indeed, but not in the precise way that Mercier and others initially conceived. Washington was not really in that much danger, but it was enough to induce President Lincoln to cancel Mc-Dowell's descent upon Richmond. With McDowell's force retained near the federal capital, the cautious McClellan was even more loath to launch his long-expected frontal assault on the Confederate capital, and three more months of indecisive campaigning could only exasperate Europe the more and bring intervention closer.

Mercier and his contemporaries, however, had to watch all this day by painful day, and at several points it seemed to everyone from Lincoln and McClellan down that the summer might see the end of it. On 31 May at Fair Oaks, Joseph

---

[19] "Beast" Butler was also known in unfriendly quarters as "Spoons" Butler. One source of the latter title was the case of A. Villeneuve, whose spoons were in the bag of a Mrs. Ferguson as she traveled north out of New Orleans on 9 August 1862. She was arrested at the frontier by Union guards, and the "contraband" spoons taken from her. Mercier became involved when, in 1863, Villeneuve filed a claim. Butler denied having the booty, and in fact the whole thing seems to have been a mistake caused by the complicated ownership-trail of the famous spoons; as Butler claimed, they were most likely still "on Banks' table to-day." Butler, however, was unsympathetic both to Mrs. Ferguson ("a strong-minded, high-cheek-boned, and rather brazen-faced Scotch woman") and Mr. Villeneuve (with no more real claim to French protection than "Lafitte the pirate") (William Dana Orcutt, "Ben Butler and the 'Stolen Spoons,'" *North American Review*, ccvii [1918], 66-80; Trefousse, p. 124; Mercier to Seward, Washington, 18 Nov. 1863, State Dept. Corres., Notes from the French Legation, xxi).

E. Johnston struck hard at McClellan's force astride the Chickahominy with dubious military result beyond the one vital fact of his own wounding. Robert E. Lee was at hand, and for a long while it seemed as if that would make all the difference. Mercier, who had met Lee in Richmond, could not foresee any of that. His chief reaction to Fair Oaks was to note how it pulled the rug from under William Seward: if Southern defeat were no longer imminent, then Washington could scarcely expect Europe to withdraw recognition of Southern belligerency, though it must be made clear that there was nothing personal in that, just the usual national self-interest: "I will do my best to make him understand . . . that this reserve should in no way be attributed to the least shade of an unfriendly disposition on our side."[20]

Meanwhile diplomacy-watchers had something rather big to gossip about:

> Lord Lyons leaves for London in a week. Happy mortal! From what he has told me, I think he has been called by Lord John Russell, who wants to question him. He is, as you know, a rather timid man but very prudent and honest; his advice, I am sure, will be essentially moderate.[21]

"How happy I should be if I could help you hurry the end of [this crisis]!" That was what Mercier wrote to Thouvenel on 1 July, and by then the Army of the Potomac, still going on to Richmond, had been through Mechanicsville and Gaines's Mill. Tuesday, 1 July, in fact, was the day of Malvern Hill, when Lee tried to end it all in one great charge, and five thousand Southerners were killed or wounded in the effort. Tuesday, 1 July—the day that Mc-

[20] Mercier to Thouvenel, Washington, 9 June 1862, AMAE, CP, E-U, 127: 215-25, no. 103; see also LJ, III (1862), 134.

[21] Mercier to Thouvenel, Washington, 9 June 1862, AMAE, MD, Papiers Thouvenel, XIII, 457-58. See also Newton, I, 86-89.

Clellan for the hundredth time let caution be his guide, caution which was publicly called "cowardice or treason" by one of his own generals. With Richmond still the Confederate capital, what else could Seward do but play for time? Mercier understood that, but he hoped the agony could somehow be ended. "I do not want to give up the hope that summer will not go by without giving us a chance to contribute to the reestablishment of peace," he wrote. "If it presents itself, be assured I will not let it escape."[22]

Mercier was in New York in early July; he went back to Washington for about two weeks and then took his family to New London. In Washington he found that the growing discouragement which he had predicted was already well advanced, "more even than I had supposed. . . ." Seward, except for his opposition to foreign mediation, was being very conciliatory, and "if the wind should change, it would change with him. . . ."

> Things being so, the only basis on which we could operate is popular feeling. If we should wait for it to come and ask for our good offices through its regular organs, we might wait too long a time; but if [this sentiment] should come to want [our help], then we could easily give it a slight push. Will autumn bring us this situation? . . . This people is too much itself, if I can put it that way, not to be disposed to react in some way against any decision which would seem to be forced on it; I think, therefore, that we ought to avoid carefully letting it think that we want to force it in this or that direction, but simply that we want to facilitate what it chooses for itself.[23]

[22] Mercier to Thouvenel, Washington, 1 July [1862], AMAE, MD, Papiers Thouvenel, XIII, 463-64.

[23] Mercier to Thouvenel [Washington], 15 July 1862, *ibid.*, fol. 471-72. See also Mercier to Thouvenel, Washington, 15 July 1862, AMAE, CP, E-U, 128: 26-34, no. 109.

When Mercier wrote that assessment, the check to the Union armies was already causing considerable talk in the North about a negotiated settlement. From this point on until March of 1863, the trend of public opinion had a notable effect on Mercier's judgment of the possibilities for peace, and we shall trace that line of development in the account which follows. In July and August of 1862, however, Mercier was content to stand by expectantly, listening to Northerners talk of peace, hoping that the fall elections would dramatize the new psychological climate.

Mercier was perfectly willing, when he thought trends were sure enough, to hint, suggest, indicate, and discuss policy—word after word after word. But he was not the emperor nor the minister of foreign affairs, and he saw no reason to prod those officers more than a little. His supposed wish to end the Civil War via European intervention was always a hypothesis; at no time did he trumpet a now-or-never call to the colors. The only thing he urged France to do "now" was to wait, to respect Northern power, to consider the "all sorts of complications" which intervention might mean. Had he been an executive officer of the Second Empire, perhaps he would have been more decisive. As a diplomat, he was somewhat detached, and in his writings, discursive. But he was clear enough in recommending that France wait, watch, and refrain from premature intervention. "We will lose nothing by waiting," he advised, "and I think that, barring the unforeseen, the moment of the elections will be the nearest point when we can hope to be able to act with any safety."[24]

Mercier's thought, then, in the period after McClellan's failure, had not moved to the point of recommending French action. Any offer of mediation would be rejected, and any such offer accompanied by threat of force would

[24] Mercier to Thouvenel, New London, 26 Aug. 1862, Mercier Family Papers, also in AMAE, MD, Papiers Thouvenel, XIII, 490-92.

simply inspire one of Seward's bellicose blusters and might end by provoking international war. Americans set great store by their political unity. "Up until now they thought of themselves as the first people in the world, the model people par excellence; they had the most limitless confidence in their strength and in their future; but their unity was the foundation of all these dreams."[25]

What was needed, Mercier thought, was an increase of economic self-interest, enough so that the old nationalism would be superseded. In effect, the minister of France was unhappy that Americans were as yet not materialist enough:

As yet this has not happened, but the trend is in that direction, and events are pushing that way more and more. I see only military successes so great that they could stop it, or an untimely foreign interference which could renew and excite national pride.

As to military success, he continued, this seemed to be eluding the North for fair. Moreover, the price of gold was rising, and a new issue of greenbacks would be a financial disaster. The reluctance of volunteers to come forward, the reluctance of the border states to accept President Lincoln's gradual emancipation—these too showed that the North was up against it. Wait; that was the best policy at present. Wait till the picture cleared. Then, perhaps, the common-market suggestion would be a good way to open the discussion.

[25] Mercier to Thouvenel, New York, 22 July 1862, AMAE, MD, Papiers Thouvenel, XIII, 473-78. This letter is also in the Mercier Family Papers. The author has concluded that the documents in Mercier Family Papers are probably earlier drafts of copies actually sent. (Similar drafts of earlier Mercier correspondence were undoubtedly destroyed in the Georgetown fire.) Where there are significant or interesting differences between the two, they will be mentioned in footnotes. To some extent, as one would expect, it is a matter of touching up.

But on the other hand, Mercier went on, the British seemed altogether *too* patient, at least so he gathered from Lyons's recent letter to his chargé d'affaires, Stuart:

> That is pushing philosophy rather far. When I think of all the difficulties inevitably connected with the indefinite waging of this war, it seems to me that it is well worth the trouble to take some risk in order to prevent them, to the extent that occasions might arise where the risk would not be too great. However that may be, if the English government has definitely decided upon abstention, and public opinion should not force them to give it up, our role becomes peculiarly difficult. Everything I have . . . said to you is based on the hypothesis that we would act together with England.

France should be cautious, but not too cautious; should be ready to do something, but not too much, not yet, and definitely not alone. In New London, some time in the second or third week of August, Mercier received word that Paris, too, thought the Union gone and the war an intolerable burden:

> We are following with an interest more painful every day the development of a situation the duration of which belies the hopes . . . expressed in Washington. . . . It is impossible to hide the fact that no government could remain deaf indefinitely to pleas which are made to it, when they echo the general feeling of the country. Thus it is easy to see that the necessity for a solution of the American conflict appears to be clearer every day and . . . that there is not a statesman who thinks the Union can possibly be reestablished as it was before. . . . And it is because we think that a truce[26] . . . would

[26] Thouvenel used the impersonal: "Et c'est parcequ'on croit

permit the search for terms of a new balance . . . that we aim at the possibility of friendly interposition between the belligerents. . . . Therefore, Sir, encourage such tendencies.[27]

Thouvenel published a slightly variant form of this letter, and to some degree it may have been meant to satisfy French workers and manufacturers, and even the impatient Napoleon III. But there is nothing in it which would make one say it was not a real reflection of Thouvenel's own thought.

If Mercier had this dispatch by 12 August, i.e., almost three weeks after it was written, he could not see any particular use to make of it. "I have just had news from Mr. Seward," he reported. "His attitude toward Europe is not changed, and his only concern with mediation is to try to avert it."

But how long could that go on? In Virginia, McClellan's army, still unbeaten and still not victorious, had been ordered north to join General Pope nearer Washington. Everybody could see it now—all the Europeans and everyone else: Richmond was safe, and the war would drag on, unless. . . . McClellan, under fire as nothing less than a traitor, had written to Stanton: "If I save this army now, I tell you plainly that I owe no thanks to you or to any other persons in Washington." At Harrison's Landing the general had urged a Buchananesque war to President Lincoln: no emancipation, no confiscation, just gentlemanly combat and a return to 1860 when day was done. It was the sort of program that Mercier, among many others in America and Europe, would have applauded.[28]

---

qu'une trêve, . . . qu'on aspire à la possibilité d'une interposition amicale. . . ."

[27] Thouvenel to Mercier, Paris, 23 July 1862, AMAE, CP, E-U, 128: 53-55, no. 19; see also LJ, III (1862), 136-37.

[28] McClellan to Stanton, Savage's Station, 28 June 1862, Nicolay

In this atmosphere of recrimination and charges of treason, it is not too amazing to find one of McClellan's officers opening up to the French minister in New London:

> Like almost all who have been able to judge the enemy close up, he is quite convinced of the necessity of separation; but he told me—and I give his opinion to you as not being without value—that he thought it would be only an appropriate foreign pressure which could bring about peace. This idea, as you know, is one of those on which I keep my attention fixed, but it can be realized to advantage only when the government is in over its head; and at the rate the waves are rising, this could come soon.[29]

With a quantity of thunderous pronouncement, John Pope, the Radicals' pet, was preparing to move south, and the sulking McClellan was ordered to come back to the Potomac and join him. In Mercier's view, "This time it is by numbers that they seek to crush the enemy." Despite Thouvenel's dispatch, he sensibly concluded that just as it had been wrong in April to launch a diplomatic offensive while the North was en route, it would be equally wrong to do so now: ". . . I am quite convinced that we would make a great mistake in trying to put ourselves in the way of the supreme effort which the North is now making."[30]

To the intervention-minded in Paris, Mercier's repeated calls for restraint and delay must have been painful, but he was on the spot, after all, and it would be hard to fault his judgment. There was no hope for peaceful mediation, and

---

and Hay, v, 441-42. See also *ibid.*, pp. 447-49, and Nevins, *The War for the Union*, II, 156-62.

[29] Mercier to Thouvenel, New London, 12 Aug. 1862, AMAE, MD, Papiers Thouvenel, XIII, 484-85.

[30] Mercier to Thouvenel, New London, 17 Aug. 1862, *ibid.*, fol. 486-89, also in Mercier Family Papers.

forcible intervention carried more risks than opportunities, as everyone eventually agreed. On 26 August, as the armies in Virginia groped toward each other, Mercier stretched his call for a two months' delay:

> It is becoming more and more probable that between now and the month of November events will occur which will bring pressure for peace, and since the general elections will be over during that period, we can hope that the struggle which they will occasion will be a chance to judge the true dispositions of the country. However, in saying this, I would not want to raise too much hope. In time of war and revolution, shifts of the wind are always hard to predict.[31]

As early as the seventeenth, Mercier had spoken of going down to New York to meet with Seward, but he apparently did not do so until the twenty-seventh or twenty-eighth.[32] Whether or not he saw the secretary then, he seems to have gone on to Washington in an effort to introduce him to Count Méjan, who was just up from New Orleans; finding that Seward was not in the city, Mercier then returned to New York. When the two men did meet again, what seemed to be the final act of the drama had begun. For Lee had

---

[31] Mercier to Thouvenel, New London, 26 Aug. 1862, *ibid.*, fol. 490-92, also in Mercier Family Papers.

[32] Mercier to Thouvenel, New London, 17 Aug. 1862, *ibid.*, fol. 486-89. The *New York Times* of 29 Aug. 1862 states that Seward had arrived in town from his home in Auburn, New York, on Wednesday (27 August), and had left the following day; the same source puts Mercier in New York on 29 August. See also Mercier to Thouvenel, New York, 2 Sept. 1862, AMAE, CP, E-U, 128: 67-72, no. 112, and Seward's statement from Washington on 8 September: Mercier "came to this city to converse with me last week while I was absent for a very few days" (Seward to Dayton, Washington, 8 Sept. 1862, State Dept. Corres., France, Instructions, XVI, 240-47, no. 207).

detached Stonewall Jackson's force and sent it through Thoroughfare Gap to attack Pope from the rear. With McClellan dragging his feet at Alexandria, the superior generalship of Lee and Jackson was closing in near Bull Run, closing in quickly on General Pope, as befuddled now as he had been fierce, and closing in on the national life of the United States. As Mercier had said, the waves were rising, and Europe's time might well be at hand.

DEVELOPMENTS IN EUROPE

Europe in this summer of 1862 had been moving through its own channel toward some sort of intervention, a journey whose progress, of course, was deeply affected by cross-ocean winds like Mercier's views, Seward's diplomacy, and above all the fights of soldiers, but one which also had its own momentum. One figure central to this part of the story was the British shipowner William S. Lindsay, member of parliament and leading interventionist. On 9 April he crossed to France in a maneuver meant to flank the Palmerston cabinet. Through the British ambassador, Lord Cowley, and then through Thouvenel, he quickly got what he had come for, and in the Tuileries at 1:00 P.M. on 11 April, he spoke with Napoleon III.

The emperor was as heartsick as anyone in France over the sufferings his people had to endure as a result of the American war, and over the consequent political weakening of his own regime. He was willing to talk of such things with Lindsay, but after a second conversation on 13 April, he also told the Englishman that he had better talk with Russell and Palmerston if matters were to go any further. Russell, however, was chagrined at this informal new initiative and refused to see Lindsay. Finally, Lindsay returned to France and again saw the emperor on 18 April. Napoleon was annoyed at Russell's attitude, but he rejected Lindsay's suggestion that France take the lead in recognizing the South.[33]

Lindsay subsequently drew up a motion calling for European mediation of the American struggle, which he intended to introduce in the House of Commons on 18 June. But the continuing conservatism of Palmerston and Russell, especially after Donelson and Shiloh but even when news began to come in of Stonewall Jackson's victories in the Shenandoah Valley, induced him to postpone his move. Count Persigny, as noted, was favorable to the Confederate cause, but he was also known for his Anglophilia, and his trip to London in mid-June resulted in little more definite than increased knowledge of British attitudes. Nevertheless, the Shenandoah Valley campaign, with its resultant check to McClellan's drive on Richmond, did create a new interventionist flurry. It was now, for example, that Thouvenel wrote his 12 June dispatch to Mercier, gently reminding him that French good offices were still available to Americans.[34]

Thouvenel and Palmerston continued to urge caution as a fog of rumor and counterrumor enveloped western Europe. Many wondered whether the time had not come to intervene. Thouvenel's visit to London to represent France at the international exposition set off a round of gossip about an imminent Anglo-French move. "Ask the English government if it does not think that the moment has come to recognize the South": this from the emperor himself to the foreign minister. But the imperial inquiry did not catch

[33] The present account of European developments is merely a sketch needed to understand Mercier's role. For a fuller treatment, see, for example, Owsley, *King Cotton Diplomacy*, pp. 268-329, and especially Case and Spencer, 258-64, 269-75, 299-315.

[34] Thouvenel to Mercier, Paris, 12 June 1862, AMAE, CP, E-U, 127: 228-29, also in *LJ*, III (1862), 130; Owsley, *King Cotton Diplomacy*, pp. 305-06; Dayton to Seward, Paris, 12 June 1862, State Dept. Corres., France, Dispatches, LI, no. 160, also in *For. Rel. U.S.*, 1862, p. 349; C. F. Adams, Jr., *Charles Francis Adams*, p. 249.

up to Thouvenel until after his return home, and continuing British reluctance foreclosed any immediate European action. Thouvenel's reaction to his sovereign's question, contained in a later note to Flahault, showed the real state of things. Had the moment come to recognize the South?

It may be, but if I go by a letter of Mr. Mercier,[35] written after the recent events, then before coming to that point, France and England would first have to risk war with the United States. The opinion of our minister in Washington is . . . firm [and] . . . categorical in this respect. . . . On the other hand, he does not despair that the Federals, left to themselves for two or three more months, might not realize the need to give up the dream of reestablishing the Union.[36]

Thouvenel also took time to let Mercier know what was going on. He agreed with his minister that the Union was gone in view of the South's intransigent stance, but he also agreed that intervention now would be dangerous. That surely was the British view of it, but there were voices in France pushing for some sort of action.[37]

Napoleon III was less disposed than Thouvenel to resist such pressure. At Vichy on 16 July, he granted an interview to John Slidell. The Confederate minister had now received that dispatch from Benjamin suggesting that in return for breaking the Union blockade, France could have 100,000 bales of cotton and free trade with the South. On his own initiative Slidell threw in the idea that Richmond would

35 Mercier to Thouvenel, New York, 6 July [1862], AMAE, MD, Papiers Thouvenel, XIII, 465-70.
36 Thouvenel to Flahault, Paris, 26 July 1862, Thouvenel, *Secret*, II, 351-56.
37 Thouvenel to Mercier, Paris, 24 July 1862, *ibid.*, pp. 348-50. On Thouvenel's trip to London see also Owsley, *King Cotton Diplomacy*, p. 310; E. D. Adams, II, 19-20; Clapp, p. 175; Émile Olivier, *L'Empire libéral*, 17 vols. (Paris: Garnier Frères, 1895-1915), V, 456-57.

smile favorably on French progress in Mexico. The emperor certainly did not commit his country to anything, but Slidell got the impression that if things went right, France might end by taking the lead in recognition, and he concluded that the time was right to ask for it formally.[38] On the same day in Westminster a report on Lancashire revealed to Parliament that Britain's cotton supply was down from over a million bales the year previous to a mere 200,000 bales. Two days later Lindsay finally introduced his mediation resolution.

That motion finally had to be withdrawn for lack of support. Principally it was this continuing British opposition which denied success to the Southerners. For his part, the French emperor was not going to become involved alone with the Yankees, especially not with the Mexican affair unresolved. And then there was Italy, again the main foreign preoccupation of the French, where things were not going smoothly at all. Garibaldi was assembling his army in Sicily. Receiving at first no opposition from the Italian government, he assumed he would be allowed to march on Rome. The French were still defending the Patrimony, and whichever way the emperor moved, he was apt to lose favor within France. Under French pressure the Italian army finally stopped Garibaldi on 30 August at Aspromonte.

No sooner had the immediate intervention crisis seemed to pass, than Palmerston and Russell began to have second thoughts. According to William E. Gladstone, at that time chancellor of the exchequer, the prime minister "has come

---

[38] Owsley, *King Cotton Diplomacy*, pp. 308-12; Louis Martin Sears, *John Slidell* (Durham, N.C.: Duke University Press, 1925), pp. 198-99; Beckles Willson, *John Slidell and the Confederates in Paris, 1862-65* (New York: Minton, Balch & Co., 1932), pp. 78-89; Clement Eaton, *A History of the Southern Confederacy* (New York: Macmillan Co., 1958), p. 77; E. D. Adams, II, 21-23; Case and Spencer, pp. 300-05.

exactly to my mind about some early representations of a friendly kind to America, if we can get France *and* Russia to join."[39] And Russell, about to leave for a vacation on the Continent, told Palmerston that "Mercier's notion that we should make some move in October agrees very well with yours."[40] Thouvenel too was off on a trip to Germany with his wife, who was ill, and the emperor transferred his own vacation from Vichy to Biarritz. Slidell and Dayton, Americans in Paris, had time for stocktaking now. Dayton, uneasy about all the rumors of intervention, wondered what information Mercier might be giving Seward to make the secretary so confident.[41] For his part, Slidell knew part of that story:

> Still, from what fell from Mr. Baroche, whom I saw this morning, I am very much inclined to think that the waiting policy of England is to be followed here. The idea is that the isolated action of France would not be attended with any favorable results; but that, on the contrary, it would stimulate the North, give a fresh impetus to enlistments, and have an [untoward] . . . influence on the approaching Congressional elections. Such is the opinion expressed by Mr. Mercier, and which naturally has great weight here.[42]

As always when people are killing one another, responsible leaders devoted time to plans of reconciliation. Mercier was still hopeful about the common-market approach. Despite his preoccupation with Italy, Thouvenel too was formulating alternatives to death:

[39] Quoted in Herbert C. F. Bell, *Lord Palmerston*, 2 vols. (London: Longmans, Green & Co., 1936), p. 327.

[40] Quoted in E. D. Adams, II, 32.

[41] See, for example, Dayton to Seward, Paris, 3 Sept. 1862, State Dept. Corres., France, Dispatches, LII, no. 189.

[42] Slidell to Benjamin, Paris, 12 Aug. 1862, Richardson, II, 309-10. See also Korolewicz-Carlton, pp. 178-79.

What I would like, if I were the master of desires and dreams, would be the formation of two *federated confederations*, if you will forgive the barbarism. North and South would each make their own laws; and if they could not guarantee them, they would at least agree to mutual respect for each other's institutions. . . . They would have the same representation abroad and the same economic regime. The question of a possible joint Senate would have to be examined. . . . I am giving you my ideas as my pen writes on, ideas which might be silly, but if they have any value whatever, I rely on you for the labor of developing them, and I also give you the absolute right to criticize and modify them. In any case, if the hour for real mediation or official action should ever ring, it would be useful to have a rough draft of a plan in our pocket.[43]

It was reasonable indeed to propose such an *Ausgleich* for America. The relatives and friends of boys who fell at Antietam and Fredericksburg might well have appreciated such a New World Austria-Hungary. Another fact which shines from this letter is the untarnished friendship between Thouvenel and Mercier. At least until September, the foreign minister and his man in Washington spoke with one voice in the counsels of the Second Empire.

What the entire diplomatic question depended upon—and the cotton, the hungry workers, the blockade, the recognition, the danger of international war, and all the rest of it—was the battlefield. In August of 1862 that battlefield was neither metaphor nor generalization. It was a specific piece of ground lying about twenty-five miles west of Washington, D.C., in the state of Virginia. Upon this ground were trees and streams, towns and other sites with names

[43] Thouvenel to Mercier, Paris, 20 Aug. 1862, Thouvenel, *Secret*, II, 364-65.

like Centreville and Manassas. For the sake of convenience, it was called Bull Run. Upon it men now set themselves once more, as they had a year before, to "have it out," to smash one another with bayonets and shot, in a basic confrontation which they thought inevitable. To move one piece of matter forcefully against another—one child's hand against another's face, one army's shot against the bodies of the other—this was the course the world had taken before and would take again when someone had to have something and someone else had to keep it: a piece of candy, a piece of ground, a national identity welded to a social ideal. Now it was happening again.

CHAPTER VIII

The Three-Power Proposal

MERCIER AT THE BRINK

BY evening on 30 August, it was at last clear to General Pope that, unlike Robert E. Lee, he had not really known what was happening over the last forty-eight hours. Second Bull Run was a clear Confederate victory. To the Union soldiers who had fought now as they would again under inept leadership, it was a shattering and demoralizing blow (but the impact was softened and even turned to advantage by the reappointment of the popular McClellan). By every historical precedent, every tendency of human nature, every logical deduction, the federal government should now have had its eyes wide open to "reality" and been willing to seek an "arrangement" with the Confederacy. That the iron-willed national patriotism of the Lincoln government might survive this blow was as unlikely as the military victory which Seward never ceased to predict. To leading Unionist Americans the hour for making peace seemed to be close, and leading neutral Europeans might have been excused the same thought. When McClellan assembled on the peninsula, Mercier went to see if Richmond might surrender; when he saw Yorktown, he thought the North might be on the way to victory; now with the sick and bloody survivors of Union disaster beginning to fill the streets of Washington, he thought the time might be close for Europe to act.

Even now Mercier interjected his usual adverbs.[1]

[1] Mercier to Thouvenel, New York, 2 Sept. 1862, AMAE, MD, Papiers Thouvenel, XIII, 493-96, from which the following account of Mer-

The South is working wonders; she must be admired and perhaps recognized. . . .

In my last letter I told you that it would be advisable for us, apart from the unforeseen, to put off any decision until the election-crisis could bring new light to bear on the true disposition of the country. The unforeseen is here; . . . it could be that before long [events] will give us the occasion to act.[2]

That would depend, he thought, on whether popular discontent in the North rose to a high enough pitch, for the Northern government was not yet willing to listen. The coming elections might end by bringing enough pressure on Washington "to reduce it to impotence." Mercier, then, was not sure whether the "unforeseen" had obviated the need to wait for the elections.

He now reverted to the idea he had had the year previously, a way to overcome the Atlantic Ocean as an obstacle to choosing the right moment, a way also to find larger scope for his own talents: discretionary authority for himself and Lyons to recognize the South. It might be well to hurry, he had said:

You would empower me with a very categorical note, but one in which you would display all the art which you have of coating the pill. Lord Lyons, who has set 11 October as the date of his departure, would leave immediately with a similar note, and having put ourselves in accord, . . . we would present these notes or

cier's thought is taken. An earlier draft of this document—dated, however, 3 Sept. 1862—is in Mercier Family Papers.

[2] Mercier's original draft reads that events may ". . . nous inviter à prendre un parti sur le champ," which could be translated more than one way, e.g., ". . . invite us to choose sides immediately." Perhaps the metaphor "champ" (field) seemed too bellicose on reconsideration. Whatever the reason, Mercier's final wording is softer and more abstract than his original thought.

keep them in our pockets until a better time, according to our judgment.

That was written in New York. Mercier ordered up the French warship *Gassendi* for his return to Washington; someone had told him that the Union defeat might have severed rail connections with the capital.[3] At some point during his vacation, Mercier had conversed with his friend William W. Corcoran. Corcoran had been staying with the Riggs family in Newport. From there he had gone to New London, possibly to see Mercier, and then to the New York Hotel, where he and Mercier were both guests. His friend and agent Anthony Hyde had sent Corcoran dramatic news of a specific casualty in the battle of Bull Run. Stanton wanted the Corcoran house for a soldiers' hospital. As one of Washington's most prominent Southern sympathizers, Corcoran had been increasingly uncomfortable in the last year, and this apparently was the last straw. He therefore agreed to rent the house to Mercier. By hoisting the French flag over it, Mercier would keep it away from Stanton and would acquire a gracious set of rooms for himself and his family. Corcoran then got ready to leave for France where he would join his daughter and son-in-law, the George Eustises.[4]

Shortly after the *Gassendi* got him to Washington, then, Mercier had moved one block from the Riggs house to his new residence at "H" Street and Connecticut Avenue, very much a part of the city's nucleus, i.e., close by Lafayette

[3] Mercier to Thouvenel, on the *Gassendi*, 3 Sept. 1862, AMAE, MD, Papiers Thouvenel, XIII, 497.

[4] Hyde to Corcoran, Washington, 1 Sept. 1862, Corcoran Papers; Laurason Riggs to Corcoran, Newport, 1 Sept. 1862, *ibid.*; Hyde to Anne Fletcher [Corcoran's housekeeper], [Washington], 4 Sept. 1862, *ibid.*; Hyde to Corcoran, Washington, 8 Sept. 1862, *ibid.* See also Gideon Welles, *Diary of Gideon Welles, Secretary of the Navy under Lincoln and Johnson*, ed. Howard K. Beale, 3 vols. (New York: Norton & Co., 1960), I, 99.

Square, the White House, the State Department, the British legation, and so on. Mercier had been anxious to see Seward as soon as possible after Bull Run's last shot, and after the previous week's failure, he feared the secretary might be deliberately dodging the diplomats. As it turned out, though, there was no problem, and on Sunday, 7 September, within hours of Mercier's return, the secretary and the minister of France held what each felt might be their weightiest talk.

In giving Dayton an account of this, Seward first set down his estimate of Mercier:

> Mr. Mercier is understood by us to enjoy the confidence of Mr. Thouvenel. He is also regarded by us as being governed by high sentiments of honor and fidelity in the discharge of his mission. We were aware indeed that his acquaintance and perhaps his social relations with some of the leaders of the insurrection befor [sic] the war began had caused him to be impressed more strongly than others of the diplomatic corps here with a belief not probably of the justice of their cause but of their strength and resolution. Without distinctly knowing the fact, I have believed that he has constantly desponded of the success of this Government in preserving the Union.[5]

Dayton's eyes must have opened wide as he read the next page, for Mercier's first question to Seward concerned the rumors he had heard of Dayton's imminent dismissal, partly for his supposed softness on the subject of French mediation. Second, Mercier wanted to know if the United

[5] Seward to Dayton, Washington, 8 Sept. 1862, State Dept. Corres., France, Instructions, xvi, 240-47, no. 207. The account which follows is from this dispatch, including the direct quotations of Mercier and Seward, which are given as Seward recorded them except where noted. See also Bancroft, ii, 299-301, and Case and Spencer, p. 340.

States was satisfied to date with Thouvenel's fairness. Seward spread reassurance all round on both counts. That out of the way, the conferees got down to cases:

Mercier: I will now tell you what is our opinion, the opinion of our Government exactly and fairly. . . . I think now that the Union is no longer possible; We, therefore, think, my Government thinks, that what is best is that which will be nearest to what has been before, what is most like to what the Union has been. So that if there must be two confederacies, then that they should be confederated confederacies.

Seward: Mr. Mercier, you can do this country and your own no greater service than by telling your Government at once that this Government neither has the thought, nor can entertain it by whomsoever it may be suggested, that there are or can ever be two confederacies here or any other government than this Union just as it constitutionally exists and has always been. . . . Chaos, even, if it must result from our efforts to save the Union could not be worse than the best substitution that could be offered or found for it, if it were to be overthrown. . . . We shall prosecute this war to its end. . . .

Mercier: Yes: but we have our interests also in the matter which must be looked to.

Seward: Certainly, but the sovereignty of a State is our interest—which in its own councils must be held paramount in its importance to any incidental or foreign question. . . . Your Government can see with what moderation and prudence we are conducting our affairs. We think France has trouble enough in Mexico, and she is likely to have some trouble in Italy. But we have draw [sic] back our hands and sealed our lips in regard to those concerns. We forbear at all points, with all parties, on all sides.

214

Seward again expressed the hope that Thouvenel would stay in office and that Mercier would remain in Washington, "so long as circumstances should permit us to be represented at Paris." He told Dayton that he did not think it expedient to ask Mercier how much of what he said was his own and how much Thouvenel's. He gave Dayton permission to discuss Mercier's remarks with the foreign minister and to elicit Thouvenel's frank comments "concerning the purposes and policy of the French Government, if they have one. . . ."

Mercier at this juncture engaged in a sort of debate with Thouvenel about the question of "federated confederacies" which the foreign minister had broached in his private letter of 20 August. Mercier had decided views about that:

> Now as to the terms of an accommodation. . . . I think . . . that we should take as a starting point that . . . we should depart as little as possible from the principles of the old Union. This starting point leads directly to the preservation of the economic unity which I consider the chief point to introduce. . . . I am persuaded that the South will insist on a separate representation abroad, and for my part I would not see any great harm in that if solidarity of interests could be had in another way.[6]

It is clear from this that Mercier made free use of Thouvenel's polite invitation to modify and criticize his tentative plan for an American Austria-Hungary, *federated* confederacies with a joint foreign office and possibly a joint senate. Mercier, having sounded Richmond opinion a short time before, felt sure that after second Bull Run the South would never settle for a nonsovereign role in such a federation. In

---

[6] Mercier to Thouvenel, Washington, 9 Sept. 1862, AMAE, MD, Papiers Thouvenel, XIII, 498-500. See also Thouvenel to Mercier, Paris, 20 Aug. 1862, Thouvenel, *Secret*, II, 364-65.

his conversation with Seward, therefore, he spoke of *con-federated* confederacies, i.e., his old common-market solution whereby each state would remain sovereign and would conduct its own foreign relations. The nineteenth century saw a great deal of this sort of discussion, most notably in central Europe, where debates over German unification were going forward intensely and debates over Italian unification were of special interest to France. It was Mercier's lot now to be at the very center of his century's chief political question. As for the notion that Delaware, Maryland, Kentucky, Tennessee, and Missouri should join the South as part of a peaceful arrangement, one can only conclude that Mercier had learned little indeed from his talk with Seward (and that perhaps he had given too little thought to locating the United States capital). Mercier correctly sensed that slavery was an increasingly key issue in the war. Where he failed was in thinking that peace and economic well-being would one day, one day soon, mean more in the North than the cause of national unity.

Meanwhile, to the accompaniment of emotional cheers from soldiers stung by defeat, George B. McClellan had resumed command of the Union armies, and at the same time, Robert E. Lee was leading his tired and ragged victors onto Union ground, hoping vainly to arouse Maryland support. Again the armies were tracking each other, closing in for another "decisive" fight.

Antietam and Europe

In an idyllic section of the Maryland countryside near the little town of Sharpsburg, the seventeenth of September began quietly and mistily. Revealed as they had been thousands of times before were a cornfield, some woods, a small church, farm buildings, and an undistinguished little stream called the Antietam. There were also men present, more than the spot had ever seen before or ever would again. Here the armies had gathered for reasons sublime and almost ridiculous, from high national purpose to a set of Confederate instructions wrapped around three cigars and left lying in a field some days before. As the trees and the buildings gradually became visible in the mist, the men began to kill one another, sporadically at first, and then in bloody alignments which have left the name "Antietam" awful in Western history. Of all that day's most pregnant scenes, Union sympathizers would remember their own General Joseph K. Mansfield, hat in hand, white hair astream, riding down the line as his men moved up to the fight: "That's right, boys, cheer—we're going to whip them today!" It was far from a whipping. But when it was done, the Confederate army did walk back into Virginia. Federal politicians and officers—and, one hopes, the soldiers too— were aware of the day's most pressing need: to tell Europe something about Northern purpose and capability. In a sense the battle of Antietam was a sanguinary show with an audience of Englishmen and Frenchmen. By the time the sun went down, Mansfield's boys and all the rest had done their work. Though few realized it then, the Confederate cause, founded of necessity on the hope of Europe's strength, was all but done.

The news of Lee's retreat reached Europe at the end of September. For three weeks previously it had all been second Bull Run, and intervention had seemed close. One obstacle to it was Édouard Thouvenel, beset with Italy and Mexico, convinced that Mercier's idea of waiting for the fall elections was in the circumstances sound. Before the Bull Run news had gelled, he was sure France should wait,[7] and even after he received Mercier's excited news of 2 September about Pope's defeat, he was still not ready to move, though he hoped the North would now listen to reason.[8]

[7] Thouvenel to Mercier, Paris, 11 Sept. 1862, *ibid.*, pp. 387-88.
[8] Thouvenel to Mercier, Paris, 18 Sept. 1862, AMAE, CP, E-U, 128: 93-95, no. 24, also in *LJ*, III (1862) 138-39.

To Dayton, Thouvenel also spoke of compromise and federation; the new American joint government would guarantee unity of action in "certain military arrangements and in matters relating to foreign affairs, diplomacy &c, in fact, something of the nature of the German confederation."[9] As it turned out, that comparison was grossly infelicitous, for on that very day, the day of Antietam, Dayton's Prussian colleague Otto von Bismarck received a telegram from Berlin: "There is danger in delay. Hurry up." The new chancellor would view the German Confederation about as dimly as Lincoln and Seward viewed Thouvenel's grand design for America.

Thouvenel's reluctance to intervene lost some of its weight because of the open secret—the emperor's divergent view. It was Lord John Russell, in fact, who was pushing hardest for action, and at the moment he was carrying Palmerston along. But nothing had solidified as yet; Napoleon III was still at Biarritz; and the American military news, even when the first word of Antietam came in, was scrambled enough and did not at first halt the intervention-fever in Europe. As late as 2 October, Palmerston was still for recognizing the South: if it were done simultaneously by England, France, and other powers, America would probably not seek a quarrel with Britain alone, and would not like one against a European coalition.[10] And Thouvenel's view of Mercier's proposals was appreciative enough, though slightly reserved:

> I want Lord Lyons to rejoin you with elastic instructions, of the kind you indicated to me, but we are very close to the American elections, and I ask myself if

[9] Dayton to Seward, Paris, 17 Sept. 1862, State Dept. Corres., France, Dispatches, LII, unnumbered.

[10] Palmerston to Russell, n.p., 2 Oct. 1862, Lord John Russell, *The Later Correspondence of Lord John Russell, 1840-1878*, ed. G. P. Gooch, 2 vols. (London: Longmans, Green & Co., 1925), II, 326-27.

before deciding we should not wait for the further data they will furnish us. If the recognition of the South in your reasoned opinion would lead to peace, I would no longer hesitate to advise it; but if this resolution . . . should set off the powder in the North and force us to fight, . . . I admit that I would think it over well. Mexico, the American question, and above all the course of affairs in Rome—it is really too much at once![11]

On 7 October, Chancellor of the Exchequer Gladstone delivered himself of his famous speech signaling that the South had "made a nation"—an extracurricular sentiment which far too largely anticipated his government's policy. And in France too, there was confusion, for the public career of Édouard Thouvenel had only days to run.[12]

EMANCIPATION

It had been obvious to Henri Mercier, as to all other thoughtful observers, that the fight in America was not a war to free the slaves. Repeated insistence upon this point by every responsible officer from Abraham Lincoln down had made that point clear. Outright abolitionists had never controlled the Republican party, and even the "Radical" Republicans, a hard-to-define group who stood in general for harsher means against the South, could not claim Lincoln and Seward among their number. In the fall of 1862,

---

[11] Thouvenel to Mercier, Paris, 2 Oct. 1862, Thouvenel, *Secret*, II, 414-16.

[12] For secondary accounts of Europe in these weeks, see Case and Spencer, pp. 333-46; E. D. Adams, II, 38-43; Owsley, *King Cotton Diplomacy*, pp. 330-31; Walpole, *Lord John Russell*, II, 349; Korolewicz-Carlton, pp. 181-84; Bigelow, *Retrospections*, I, 550; Norman Graebner, "Northern Diplomacy and European Neutrality," *Why the North Won the Civil War*, ed. David Donald (Baton Rouge: Louisiana State University Press, 1960), pp. 49-75; Stern, *When the Guns Roared*, pp. 153-58; C. F. Adams, Jr., *Massachusetts Historical Society Proceedings*, XLVII (1914), 372-424; Nevins, *The War for the Union*, II, 267-70.

in fact, the Radicals' chief target was still the supreme field commander of Union forces, General McClellan—Pope, the Radicals' favorite, having failed completely at his task.

Still in all, the times were changing as week followed week, and no one was more sensitive to the change than Mercier. His dispatches were peppered with warnings of servile insurrection which might attend any tampering with America's "peculiar institution." In a long-range sort of way, Mercier probably favored compensated, gradual emancipation. There are two ways of assessing that datum: on the one hand, Southern moderates might go that far, so Mercier deserves little credit for such a stand; on the other hand, however, Lincoln himself did not go far beyond it until the summer of 1862. Like Lincoln, and unlike most Southerners, Mercier regarded slavery as one of America's worst institutions. (The other, in his view, was democracy.) But as the "danger" of emancipation came closer, Mercier spoke far more often in fear of freedom than in contempt of slavery. It was not only servile insurrection he foresaw. Emancipation, he thought, would separate Negroes from their fields in some permanent sort of way, and the consequent ruination of cotton cultivation would seriously harm his fellow Frenchmen who wove, spun, and otherwise depended on cotton for a living.

Finally, with Mercier as with most Americans, it was not so much slavery which was under discussion, but *Negro* slavery. Mercier could see no better than most how the two races could ever live together happily on terms of equality. And here again—though it defends neither man to note it— Mercier was no more retarded than President Lincoln, whose various plans for encouraging Negroes to emigrate bespeak his own fears for the future. The aggressive charity of a Thaddeus Stevens would have chilled Mercier as it did Lincoln, a circumstance made all the more interesting by the fact that morally Stevens was right.

Distant, rolling thunder had announced the future as early as 1861, when Fremont tried to free the Missouri slaves and Ben Butler gave work to "contrabands." On 6 August of that year, Congress passed the first confiscation act, including emancipation of slaves engaged in helping the Confederate armed forces. Then in March of 1862, the storm seemed imminent as Congress decreed against the return of "contrabands," and the president began pressing his plans for gradual, compensated emancipation. Mercier's contacts told him, correctly as it turned out, that the president would have rough sledding:

> . . . today it would be impossible to get the Border States to do with the help of the federal government what most of the free States did of their own accord in another era. The reason would not be the number of slaves, but the number of free men of color. If it were only considerations of interest which were under discussion, the slave-owners would easily be sacrificed for the mass of the population, but beyond interest there is racial antagonism which everywhere is more violent and weighty as there are more free colored men.

Mercier's anonymous informant then told him that Lincoln was doing this in an effort to interest Europe, and especially Britain, in the Northern cause by trying to identify it with human freedom.[13]

Mercier's judgment was sometimes faulty, but he knew the subtle ins and outs of this delicate business, even to the fact that poor whites feared emancipation more than did the American nobility:

> It would seem beyond argument that it would be infinitely more easy to deal with the slave-owners than

[13] Mercier to Thouvenel, Washington, 11 March 1862, AMAE, CP, E-U, 126: 215-30, no. 89.

221

with the lower class of whites, a class which, wherever there is a free colored population, would not for any cause submit itself to the principle of racial equality.

In concentrating on the racial aspect of American slavery, Mercier anticipated some of the best professional studies of a century later.[14]

On 16 April 1862 Congress finally ended slavery in the District of Columbia. A month later Jackson had broken through in the Shenandoah Valley, and Mercier thought he could see the shape of the future:

> As I have told you several times, the question is tending more and more to be put as a choice between separation and a war of emancipation. . . . A war of emancipation would necessarily involve tremendous horrors, would ruin both countries for a long time, and would deprive us of cotton, not only for the present, but also the future.[15]

On 20 May notifications were exchanged of the Anglo-American treaty for the suppression of the slave trade. Civil War and an Anglophobe administration, which only one half year before had almost stumbled into war with England, had done what no earlier American government could bring itself to do. Even more, the second confiscation

[14] Mercier to Thouvenel, Washington, 17 March 1862, *ibid.*, fol. 250-61, no. 91. On slavery and race, see e.g., Allan Nevins: "Had it not been for the difference in race, the slavery issue would have presented no great difficulties. . . . Those historians who write that if slavery had simply been left alone it would have withered overlook this heavy impediment. The South as a whole in 1846-61 was not moving toward emancipation, but away from it. . . . Why was it going from bad to worse? Because Southern leaders refused to nerve their people to pay the heavy price of race-adjustment" (*The Emergence of Lincoln*, 2 vols. [Charles Scribner's Sons, 1950], II, 468).

[15] Mercier to Thouvenel, Washington, 26 May 1862, AMAE, MD, Papiers Thouvenel, XIII, 454-56.

act of 17 July 1862 went almost as far, at least on paper, as would the Emancipation Proclamation, "freeing" the slaves of actively rebel owners. And since the Union slave states failed to help the president with his gradual plan, Lincoln by midsummer had about decided upon emancipation as a war measure, to be applied against the Confederate States under his mandate as American commander-in-chief.

It was Seward who threw up a cautionary hand at this point. He feared that Europe, reacting as Mercier already had, might see cotton threatened for all time and thus be moved to intervene. More, he knew the mind of Europe fairly well by now, and he could see that were emancipation declared in the military malaise caused by McClellan's failure before Richmond, it would seem the desperate act of a last-ditch stand, "the government stretching forth her hands to Ethiopia, instead of Ethiopia stretching forth her hands to the government."[16] There is every reason to think that Mercier's views were a fair reflection of much European sentiment on all these points; that being so, Seward was right.

Then there was Antietam. That battle did a great deal to human history, for it was not alone the military lift it gave the North which accounts for its diplomatic effects. By providing Lincoln with the victory he needed to receive the outstretched hands of "Ethiopia," it put the war on the high international plane of human advance and gave some real bite to the United States' claim that it showed forth man's future. On 22 September, in the hard, legal wording from which the English-speaking world had learned to expect so much, the President of the United States sent out his decree.

[16] Quoted from Seward, as repeated by the president, in Bancroft, II, 334. See also Nicolay and Hay, VI, 121-30, and Welles, *Diary*, I, 70-71.

Mercier's reaction was apoplectic:

> This measure, of which I have received the first news
> this very moment, is nothing less than the emancipation
> of the slaves, decreed as of 1 January in all the sepa-
> ratist States which have not returned to the Union. It
> seems to me so inconceivable and so serious that I do
> not yet dare to broach with Your Excellency the con-
> jectures which my first impression is engendering.[17]

But sometime later in the day, Mercier got back his breath
and began to express himself:

> I have been so struck by the proclamation of the
> president . . . that it is all I can do to retain enough
> mental clarity to write you. At first glance it seems
> that this is an act of desperation, atrocious in the in-
> tent it reveals and the consequences it might entail, but
> one which might also clear up the situation and bring
> on its solution.

Mercier's apprehension of what had happened near
Sharpsburg was still cloudy: he thought the situation back
where it had been before Lee entered Maryland. In that
context he saw the Emancipation Proclamation as a desperate incitement to slave insurrection, the very conclusion
which Seward had hoped to prevent. In his anger and excitement, Mercier came closer than ever to recommending
intervention. The decree, he felt, was all the more reason
to do so:

> I think, then, that we should not hesitate to get our-
> selves ready to make our announcement as soon as pos-
> sible if we have not already done so. But my advice
> today would be that we should not make it in the form

[17] Mercier to Thouvenel, Washington, 23 Sept. 1862 (rcd. 8 Oct.
1862), AMAE, CP, E-U, 128: 98-103, no. 116. See also Case and
Spencer, pp. 316-28.

I had first suggested. I am always afraid of the effect of the word *separation* [and of] the advantage which those who want a war to the end might draw from it, and I want us to avoid saying it as well as [the word] *recognition* which is connected to it; [we should] say even, if need be, the word *union* and limit ourselves for the moment to a call for an *armistice* which could be used to attempt a reconciliation. . . . I think that a declaration of this sort, coming in the middle of the political struggles and the trouble which the president's proclamation cannot avoid stirring up, could bring about an armistice; and once we had an armistice I am convinced that we would be very close to peace.

This call for armistice, he added, should naturally be accompanied by an offer of mediation.[18]

In this whole question of what Europe might or should do about America, the generic term was "intervention." Most often when Mercier used that word, he had in mind either diplomatic recognition of the South or an offer of European mediation, the latter on the assumption that some sort of sovereignty would ultimately be accorded to the Richmond government. In a sense, then, recognition would give to the Confederacy the very prize which would be the principal subject of any mediation. It is conceivable, however, in this wholly hypothetical discussion, that the South, having been granted diplomatic recognition, might then be nudged back into some kind of Austro-Hungarian arrangement as a result of mediation. Behind both recognition and mediation was the threat of force, the application

---

[18] Mercier to Thouvenel, 23 Sept. 1862, AMAE, MD, Papiers Thouvenel, XIII, 502-09. This document is also in Mercier Family Papers, where it is not in Mercier's handwriting and agrees word for word with the copy sent to Thouvenel. In this case it would seem that Mercier had a secretary make a copy for his own files, a fact which indicates the great importance he assigned to it.

of which might include breaking the Union blockade or even attacks on Northern territory, principally from the sea. In the case of mediation, the unspoken threat was that force might be applied against the party which either refused mediation outright or refused the final decision of the mediators. It was expected that this might be the North.

The object of all this was patently to end the war and more precisely to get the cotton moving again. Each European state and each statesman within each state had one or more further motives, all the way from a charitable desire to stop the killing to harder-eyed aims such as success in Mexico. The desire for an American peace was mighty in Europe, but so was the desire to avoid war with the United States, and so long as the Lincoln government took the adamant stance that American nationality was indivisible, there would be no solution of that dilemma. And even more, there would be other unpleasant aspects of an Anglo-American or Franco-American war beyond the obvious one of casualties. For example, the Emancipation Proclamation, limited as it was and cynical as it seemed, would still mean that whoever fought Washington would be fighting to protect slavery. In France and especially in England, the strong abolitionist sentiment of larger segments of the population would thereby be offended.[19] Then too, each country had other problems to settle which made the thought of war against Washington exceedingly grim. In the case of France, Thouvenel had named two of them explicitly to Mercier: Mexico and especially Italy. If the North had really been on her last legs, shattered in the field and undermined by overwhelming peace sentiment at home, then a quick, painless tap might have been thinkable as a way of ending the Civil War.

[19] On abolitionist sentiment in France see Gavronsky, *The French Liberal Opposition*, pp. 40-44, 70-79, 181-200.

Mercier reported the rising strength of the "peace" party and the seeming inability of Northern arms to crush the South. But in contradiction he had insistently begged his government not to challenge the power he saw at Yorktown and Fredericksburg, and he faithfully reported the popular determination in the North not to accept separation, a determination which persisted even after second Bull Run. One other factor worth noting was the time of the congressional elections, fixed in the eighteenth century when states were thought to run best like clocks set to a rigid, classical pattern. In 1862 these elections were just far enough off to give men like Thouvenel a cogent argument for delaying intervention.

There was another possibility of "intervention" which might avoid the dilemma by accepting and respecting both the power of the North and her determination to resist European force—a call for an armistice. Mercier now turned to this expedient, and his frustration can be gauged by that, for it was precisely now, after the Emancipation Proclamation, that he came most furiously to resent the Civil War. There is an almost foot-stamping quality to this new development in the face of circumstances which were intolerable but at the same time more tolerable than war against the North.

MERCIER AND NEW YORK POLITICS

Mercier was back in New York now, with a sudden interest in Horatio Seymour and in "others" who wanted peace but were "too much involved in another direction" to do any more than "let things happen while hoping for a success to which they do not dare contribute in a more active way."[20] The following suggests the explanation: "In recent

[20] Mercier to Thouvenel, New York, 30 Sept. 1862 (rcd. 14 Oct. 1862), AMAE, CP, E-U, 128: 107-13, no. 117.

days I have had a very long and I think very important conversation with Mr. Thurlow Weed who, as you know, is not only the confidant but often the inspirer of Mr. Seward." Seward was being very quiet and was refusing to talk about the Emancipation Proclamation, but with Weed it was different:

> With Mr. Thurlow Weed it is possible to speak more freely, and I have taken advantage of that. I did not hide from him any of the fears which the present state of things is causing me, and I expressed to him the opinion that a peace which would preserve economic unity while giving up something of political unity would be the happiest solution for the North in the present circumstances.

Weed told Mercier that he was disturbed too and that he would not be far from Mercier's views if he saw a chance for their success. Mercier was equally hopeful:

> I then told him that I thought I could give him the assurance that the emperor would ask for nothing better than to find an opportunity to render such a service to the United States and to use his influence to lead this crisis to a result which would affect as little as possible the foundations on which the Union rested.[21]

The New York campaign was an especially complicated one. Briefly, the Democrats and a splinter group of former Whigs nominated Horatio Seymour, who, while remaining loyal to "the Union as it was and the Constitution as it is," assailed such measures as emancipation and arbitrary arrests of suspected Confederate sympathizers. The moderate Republican faction, including Seward and Weed, lost out

[21] Mercier to Thouvenel, New York, 30 Sept. 1862, AMAE, MD, Papiers Thouvenel, XIII, 510-13.

in their convention, which nominated Radical General James S. Wadsworth. The campaign developed into a moderate versus Radical contest, with Weed and Seward remaining cool to Wadsworth.[22]

Mercier returned to New York later in October and again met prominent moderate politicians. At the same time he received that private letter from Thouvenel, dated 2 October, in which the foreign minister suggested kindly that "Mexico, the American question, and above all the course of affairs in Rome—it is really too much at once!" That letter ended with another polite and subtle suggestion that Mercier was maybe a little too excited. "Good-by, my dear friend," Thouvenel concluded. "I will write you officially as soon as I have agreed on something with the emperor. Till then, help me, as you know how to do, with your calm and impartial dispatches."[23]

Mercier's touchy rejoinder seems out of proportion to the slap on the wrist which Thouvenel had administered:

I see by your letter of 2 October that you feared for a moment that zeal was carrying me away and that I wanted to hurry you into overstepping the bounds which prudence has set for you. My recent correspondence, official and private, will bring you, I hope, a little reassurance in this respect. You know very well that I am not a charlatan, and my ambition has always been to avoid any embarrassment to you. Up until now, thank God, I have been quite successful in this, and I shall spare nothing in order to keep on succeeding until the end. In any hypothesis, I would regard a fight

[22] Nevins, *The War for the Union*, II, 302-05. On Weed see also Glyndon G. Van Deusen, *Thurlow Weed, Wizard of the Lobby* (Boston: Little, Brown & Co., 1947), pp. 273-75, 299-302.

[23] Thouvenel to Mercier, Paris, 2 Oct. 1862, Thouvenel, *Secret*, II, 414-16.

with this country as a great misfortune, and all the more so since we already have such weighty concerns in hand.

It would be well in such a stormy sea to be ready to act quickly, but "now I shall acknowledge to you that if today I had in my hands the powers I have asked you for, I would not hurry to make use of them." His idea, he said, had been to consider using that authority to "tip the balance to the right side" in the elections. But the elections were turning out very well without such encouragement, and if Seymour became governor of New York, "this would decidedly be a door open to peace."[24]

Mercier also spoke with another moderate, William Evarts. As Weed noted it to Seward:

> I must talk with you about things, for it is evident that there is to be action over the water. Evarts, in a conversation with the French Minister, was told that Europe would soon intervene, but with designs looking to some sort of re-Union.[25]

Mercier, in fact, spoke with Judge Edwards Pierrepont as well as with Evarts and he gave them his usual discourse about regret for the Union and the advantages of a new quasi-union.

There were rumors this autumn that Weed might be sent

[24] Mercier to Thouvenel, New York, 21 Oct. 1862, Mercier Family Papers. This document is found neither in Thouvenel, *Secret*, nor in the *Papiers Thouvenel*.

[25] Weed to Seward, New York, 25 Oct. 1862, University of Rochester, Rochester, N.Y., Papers of William Henry Seward. It is evident from Weed's phrasing that he was not all that close to Mercier. He did not use Mercier's name, and his second-hand remark to Seward about "some sort of re-Union" suggests that Mercier's proposal had been less than a constant topic of conversation between Weed and Seward. On his side Mercier always called Weed "Mr. Thurlow-Weed," as if it were all a family name.

back to Europe on a diplomatic errand, though ultimately the trip had to be canceled because of unfriendly criticism of the project. Mercier thought that the object of the trip would be to forestall intervention and give the North time for a new military success; he felt, too, that in any case Weed would be less adamant than Seward.[26]

Mercier indulged in a certain amount of straw-clutching in October, though in fact there was a strong current for peace, and it was bound to impress him. He probably underestimated the devotion of men like Seymour and Weed to the American Union. After all, the old proposal for an unamendable constitutional amendment to guarantee slavery had itself been a suggestion that the United States surrender some of its sovereignty. Mercier was apparently vague enough with Weed so that the New Yorker could listen in good conscience without being untrue to his national patriotism. Mercier's description of Seymour—that he would use his authority as governor to block the drastic measures which alone were making the war possible—came close to implying a strain of treason in the governor-elect.

In the long summer during which he had elaborated his thoughts on intervention, Mercier had given considerable thought to Russia's role. It was axiomatic, of course, that nothing could be done without England. Though Mercier felt that Russia deserved no such veto-power, he referred to the obvious benefit of her participation. If the old Crimean allies were to prod the United States, it would be best to have Russia at their side, not free to capitalize on the ensuing commotion. Stoeckl was wary, however. His country had no such vital interest in an American peace as Britain and France, and the czar's government saw nothing wrong with the high regard its pro-Northern policy had earned it in Washington.

<hr/>

26 Mercier to Thouvenel, Washington, 25 Oct. [1862], Mercier Family Papers.

In August and September, then, Stoeckl remained as calm as Mercier was excited, and the French minister saw little to hope for in that direction.[27] As the intervention fever mounted, Stoeckl did intrude himself into the discussion, however, and in late October Mercier expressed some annoyance:

> I must now tell you that I found out that my Russian colleague was bestirring himself a great deal to the end that if there were a mediation, France and Russia should be addressed to the exclusion of England. Feeling against England is very strong, it is true . . . ; but it is quite evident that his aim is nothing else except to throw a stumbling block between Paris and London.

At this point, so far as Paris knew, Mercier was still recommending a joint call for an American armistice, a call issued by England and France with the participation of Russia and other countries if that were possible. But the reluctance of Stoeckl and especially of Lyons, waiting for the quail to fall into his mouth already cooked, would not be absolutely prohibitive factors in Mercier's view. What follows did not affect the French initiative of October–November, but it is indicative of the trend diplomacy would take in early 1863. Mercier continued to discuss the supposed Russian maneuver:

> I need not tell you that you do not have to fear that I will fall into such a trap; but taking the question from a purely American point of view, here are the observations which come to my mind.
>
> There is no doubt that it would be much better if Russia could advance together with France and Eng-

[27] Mercier to Thouvenel, Washington, 23 Sept. 1862, AMAE, MD, Papiers Thouvenel, XIII, 502-09.

land, but in my opinion the Americans, although they would be very much disposed in that direction, would be completely wrong to prefer the combined action of Russia and France to that of England and France.

If Americans were prejudiced against Britain, he continued, their best course would not be to offend her and allow her an independent role, but rather to associate her "with us who should inspire them with every confidence." But what if American distaste for England were seen to be the only obstacle to a successful initiative?

I confess to you that I would prefer that we convey the word alone if we could be assured in advance that in case we were brought to recognize the South, England would immediately do as much on her side. I am not even sure that this line of conduct would not be the one with the better chance of success, for it could have the twin advantage of keeping the same measure of intimidation resulting from the prospect of recognition and at the same time not giving a pretext for initially inciting the anti-English passions which exist in the country.[28]

With Mercier it was at least thinkable, now, that an initial démarche be made by France alone, one which would still require British participation in the second stage. But first there would be an effort to present a united European front. Mercier, Weed and Seymour, Russell and the French leaders, were all caught up in the same dilemma: how to

[28] Mercier to Thouvenel, New York, 21 Oct. 1862, Mercier Family Papers. See above, n. 24. See also Newton, I, 90-91. British participation may have been a significant reason for Russia's rejection of the eventual French proposal. After it was all over, Mercier heard that should France renew her initiative, Russia might come along (Mercier to Drouyn de Lhuys, Washington, 8 Dec. 1862, AMAE, CP, E-U, 128: 275-88, no. 129).

end the war without outraging or being untrue to American Union patriotism. For European peace-seekers this was translated into a parallel dilemma: how to bring the North to its senses without getting into a war. In fact it could not be done. The combination of Northern strength and Union nationalism was too much for Richmond, too much for peace-minded Northerners, and, in the absence of a willingness to shoot, too much for Europe.

Decision in Europe

In the first week of October, the European trend was roughly as follows. Lord John Russell and Napoleon III hoped greatly that some sort of effort toward mediation and recognition might be successfully made before the month was out. Palmerston was momentarily persuaded that something should be done, but he was more uneasy than his foreign secretary and hedged his position by saying that Europe should first make a suggestion to the American belligerents that they get together by themselves.[29] Thouvenel wanted the American war to end as much as anyone else, but he was convinced that for France the probable bad effects outweighed the good. Since the emperor's role was passive at the moment, it was England which was leading the move toward intervention, and within England, Russell.

Yet even Russell was open to argument, and after reading the anti-interventionist brief of one cabinet colleague, he frankly told Palmerston of his hesitation:

This American question must be well sifted. I send you a letter of G. Lewis who is against moving. . . .

My only doubt is whether we and France should

[29] Palmerston to Russell, 2 Oct. 1862, Russell, *Later Correspondence*, II, 326-27.

stir if Russia holds back. Her separation from our move would ensure the rejection of our proposals.[30]

Russia was not the only problem. In the second and third weeks of October, the French government underwent a severe crisis only tangentially bound to the American question but sure to affect it seriously. On 9 October the emperor returned from Biarritz determined to reshape his cabinet to suit his policies and in particular his continuing defense of Rome against Italian designs. The "Italianissimes" among his counsellors were accordingly in danger of their positions, Thouvenel and Persigny among them. In fact Napoleon's first thought was to ask the entire cabinet to resign and then make Walewski, the symbol of a pro-papal stand, his new foreign minister. By 13 October, however, he was feeling pressure from the leading pro-Italians, Fould, Rouher, Baroche, Morny, and Flahault, who sought to save Thouvenel's career and policy by threatening to resign en masse. On 15 October the emperor settled upon a compromise: all the ministers would stay except Thouvenel, who would be replaced by the veteran diplomat Édouard Drouyn de Lhuys. The nation reacted apathetically, so Napoleon at least avoided any great outcry from left or right.[31]

It was and is well-known that Thouvenel's abstentionist American policy was in conflict with the emperor's interventionism, but the precise effect of this upon the foreign minister's forced resignation must remain conjectural. What

[30] Russell to Palmerston, 2 Oct. 1862, in E. D. Adams, II, 44-45. For a full discussion of the crucial October developments, see *ibid.*, pp. 33-74.

[31] Lynn M. Case, *French Opinion on War and Diplomacy during the Second Empire* (Philadelphia: University of Pennsylvania Press, 1954), pp. 152-53. Thouvenel himself told Mercier that Italian policy was the reason for his resignation (Thouvenel to Mercier, 1 Dec. 1862, Thouvenel, *Secret*, II, 448-49).

seems certain is that the Italian question was the chief cause of that resignation and that without it, Thouvenel would have remained in office. American policy, while it probably supplied Napoleon III with an added reason, was not the cause of his action. The question now, however, was what effect this would have on Europe's actions toward America.[32]

When compared with Thouvenel, Drouyn de Lhuys quite certainly was more conservative and was friendly to the Empress Eugénie and Count Walewski, a fact which seemed to augur well for French interventionism in Italy, Mexico,

[32] The chief contemporary observer to claim that American policy was Thouvenel's undoing was John Slidell, and, among recent historians, Richard Korolewicz-Carlton has strongly stressed this factor. Slidell, speculating that Thouvenel had not pushed hard enough for intervention to suit the emperor, said this: "I have had strong suspicion on this score for some time past, and am inclined to think that the feeling that Mr. Thouvenel did not fairly represent his views on this as well as on the Italian question may have had some influence on the decision of the Emperor to dispense with the services of Mr. Thouvenel as Minister of Foreign Affairs" (Slidell to Benjamin, Paris, 28 Oct. 1862, no. 19, Richardson, II, 341-44, also in ORN, 2nd ser., III, 572-74). Serge Gavronsky agrees with Korolewicz-Carlton that "until the time of his removal from office in October, 1862, Thouvenel was the one most responsible for keeping France out of any American entanglement" (Gavronsky, The French Liberal Opposition, p. 61).

Dayton gave Seward a just assessment of what it all meant, singling out the Italian question as the principal cause, but adding, "We lose a friend at an important point" (Dayton to Seward, Paris, 17 Oct. 1862, State Dept. Corres., France, Dispatches, LII, no. 211). See also Tyrner-Tyrnauer, Lincoln and the Emperors, pp. 59-62; Owen F. Aldis, "Louis Napoleon and the Southern Confederacy," North American Review, CXXIX (1879), 342-60; Elliot A. P. Evans, "Napoleon III and the American Civil War," doctoral dissertation, Stanford University, 1940, pp. 61-63 and 270-75.

The opinion of the emperor's American dentist and friend, Dr. Evans, that Napoleon III was more pro-Union and antislavery than either Thouvenel or Drouyn de Lhuys, is an exaggeration (Thomas W. Evans, Memoirs: The Second French Empire [New York: D. Appleton & Co., 1905], pp. 138-39).

and perhaps America. He had been foreign minister three times before, and as he again got the feel of the reins, he realized that Thouvenel's American policy had been best for France for the precise reasons which Thouvenel had assigned: the danger of an involvement when France was already tied down in Italy and Mexico. Increasingly the rise of Prussia under Bismarck also attracted his concern, and the net effect of all this was a continuity of policy between the old and the new courses. No one knew it yet, but the American Union had almost as little to fear from Drouyn de Lhuys as it had had from Thouvenel.[33]

The development in France should have helped Russell in his drive for intervention, but it was only one factor, and the combined, countervailing weight of emancipation, Antietam, and Russia was ultimately greater. As noted, the British foreign secretary was already slowing up as early as the first week of October. Like others before him, including Mercier, he now began to talk of armistice as a way of having his cake and eating it too—a "suspension of arms" for "weighing calmly the advantages of peace."[34] There always seemed to be something left out of this armistice idea, whether proffered by Slidell, Mercier, Russell, or Napoleon III, namely, the matter of what would happen during and after such an armistice. There was a basic, perhaps intentional, ambiguity there which those who considered the South's independence a certainty seemed willing to use in order to get the North to stop shooting. Mercier let Thurlow Weed and William Evarts think that some

---

[33] Spencer, *Revue d'histoire diplomatique*, LXXVII (1963), 314-41; Case and Spencer, pp. 347-53. See also Bernard D'Harcourt, *Diplomatie et diplomates: les quatre ministères de M. Drouyn de L'Huys* (Paris: E. Plon et cie., 1882), pp. 356-57. Blumenthal, on less evidence, reaches the same conclusion as Spencer: "The two French foreign ministers differed only in degree regarding the Civil War policy of France" (Blumenthal, *Franco-American Relations*, p. 139).

[34] Russell memorandum, 13 Oct. 1862, in E. D. Adams, II, 49.

kind of reunion might be the result of an armistice, and who knows but it might? At base, however, Mercier felt that the Union was dead. That kind of ambiguity was not lost on Seward, who consistently rejected the armistice idea, nor did it eventually escape Russell.

Palmerston, impressed by Antietam, was there before him. On 22 October, he laid down the line:

> All that we could possibly do without injury to our position would be to ask the two Parties not whether they would agree to an armistice but whether they might not turn their thoughts towards an arrangement between themselves. But the answer of each might be written by us beforehand. . . . I am therefore inclined to change the opinion on which I wrote to you when the Confederates seemed to be carrying all before them, and I am very much come back to our original view of the matter, that we must continue merely to be lookers-on till the war shall have taken a more decided turn.[35]

British policy—the crucial policy since France would as yet not act without Britain—remained steady on the armistice idea from this point on. But now it was the French who were going ahead; the idea which had been developed by Slidell in the spring, and more recently by Mercier, was about to become an initiative of the Second Empire, an officially made proposal that France, England, and Russia

[35] Palmerston to Russell, 22 Oct. 1862, in *ibid.*, pp. 54-55, also in Russell, *Later Correspondence*, II, 327-28. After Russell had notified the cabinet of the new direction in a somewhat grumpy paper, Clarendon, speaking of Russell, made a pungent, accurate summation of the diplomatic situation: "He had thought to make a great deal of his colt by Meddler out of Vanity, and you have shown his backers that the animal was not fit to start and would not run a yard if he did. He is therefore taken back to the country, where he must have a deal more training before he can appear in public again" (Clarendon to Lewis, 26 Oct. 1862, in E. D. Adams, II, 58).

tell the Americans they should stop the fighting and the blockade for six months. This was it, the climax of all the thinking, writing, and weighing by Mercier, Thouvenel, the emperor, and others, over a period of twenty months. All in all it was an unimpressive move, and officially it never left Europe.

Drouyn de Lhuys had not yet been affected by reading Mercier's thoughts about a French solo effort. As the three-power French proposal was maturing within the government, he let Mercier know that if anything were done, England and Russia would have to come along too.[36] On Monday, 27 October, Napoleon III discussed intervention with Lord Cowley, and the next day he spoke with Slidell. Each of the conversations followed the same pattern: the emperor began by speaking of three-power mediation and then came up with the alternative of a six-months' armistice proposal. As Slidell told it, Napoleon frankly stated "that his sympathies were entirely with the South . . . and intimated that if he acted alone England, instead of following his example, would endeavor to embroil [sic] with the United States, and that French commerce would be destroyed." The emperor then said:

> My own preference is for a proposition of an armistice of six months, with the Southern ports open to the commerce of the world. This would put a stop to the effusion of blood, and hostilities would probably never be resumed. We can urge it on the high grounds of humanity and the interest of the whole civilized world. If it be refused by the North, it will afford good reason for recognition, and perhaps for more active intervention.[37]

[36] Drouyn de Lhuys to Mercier, Paris, 23 Oct. 1862, AMAE, CP, E-U, 128: 142-43, no. 23.

[37] Slidell to Benjamin, Paris, 28 Oct. 1862, no. 19, Richardson, II, 341-44, also in ORN, 2nd ser., III, 572-74; E. D. Adams, II, 59. See also C. F. Adams, Jr., *Massachusetts Historical Society Proceedings*,

Drouyn de Lhuys now wrote Mercier and described the new initiative:

> The emperor has decided that there is an opportunity to ask Great Britain and Russia to unite with France in a joint effort to obtain an armistice of six months between the Federal government and the Southern Confederates. The offer which the three courts would make of their good offices with a view to this end . . . would have to be based firmly on its friendly character. . . . They would not prejudge anything as to the decisions which the United States could adopt later in perfect freedom to put a definite end to the conflict.[38]

For the moment there was nothing for Mercier to do, and in fact by the time he received this notice, the affair was all over.

Russia's reaction to the French overture was predictably negative, and this helped the Palmerston cabinet arrive at its decision, which it did in two meetings on 11 and 12 November. Russell had come to favor a positive answer, a sort of play to the galleries, supporting peace, some effort to continue the American Union, and compensated emancipation of the slaves. Even Palmerston had been willing to go along, principally as a gesture of sympathy for the unemployed in Lancashire. Despite this, the cabinet hacked the proposal apart.[39]

XLVII (1914), 384; Korolewicz-Carlton, pp. 189-92; Owsley, *King Cotton Diplomacy*, pp. 333-36.

[38] Drouyn de Lhuys to Mercier, Paris, 30 Oct. 1862, AMAE, CP, E-U, 128: 148-49, no. 27. On the three-power proposal see Case and Spencer, pp. 347-73.

[39] E. D. Adams, II, 60-65. On Russia see Woldman, p. 133. For brief comments on the French initiative, see also Max Beloff, "Historical Revision no. CXVIII: Great Britain and the American Civil War," *History*, XXXVII (1952), 40-48; Henri Hauser et al., *Du Libéralisme à l'impérialisme, 1860-1878*, 2nd ed. (Paris: Presses Univer-

On the day of the British rejection, 13 November, the French government published its offer in the *Moniteur*, and this may have been the chief aim all along. Just as Russell and Palmerston, knowing the effort would be rejected in Washington, still wanted to make their position clear in Lancashire and all Europe, so Napoleon III wanted his people to know that he was trying against all odds to obtain peace in America. Dayton could see that clearly enough:

> One of the purposes, at least, of this Dispatch has been, in my judgment, to satisfy the workmen and manufacturing interests of France that the Emperor has been, and is, anxious to do what he can to alleviate their distress. The French are not like the English people; they have little forbearance with their government.[40]

It remained only for Drouyn de Lhuys to notify Mercier of the failure. Mercier was to assure Seward that France meant well and stood ever ready to proffer good offices should they be wanted.[41]

MERCIER AND REACTION IN AMERICA

Because of the oceanic time-lag, it was beyond mid-November before Mercier knew of the French notes to Russia and Britain, and it was the end of the month before he knew of their rejection. Politics and war continued to make him think that the moment for doing something was near. As to the elections, Mercier interpreted the results as a victory

---

sitaires de France, 1952), pp. 120-21; Graebner, *Why the North Won the Civil War*, p. 69; C. F. Adams, Jr., *Charles Francis Adams*, p. 290.

[40] Dayton to Seward, Paris, 14 Nov. 1862, State Dept. Corres., France, Dispatches, LII, no. 226. For the British answer see Russell to Cowley, London, 13 Nov. 1862, *Sessional Papers*, LXII (1863), 3-4, unnumbered, a copy of which is in AMAE, CP, Angleterre, 722: 178-84.

[41] Drouyn de Lhuys to Mercier, Paris, 18 Nov. 1862, AMAE, CP, E-U, 128: 181, no. 30, also in *LJ*, III (1862), 145-46.

for peace,[42] but in fact the piebald pattern of moderate gains here, losses there, was not a clear-cut mandate for a peace of separation.[43]

With the war seemingly at stalemate and the Union army taking its time about re-invading Virginia, Mercier saw another ray of hope in the current hiatus. It was a sort of *de facto* truce:

> The essential thing, if one desires to intervene, would be to prevent the possibility of hostilities' being resumed in the spring. If at that time the radicals should begin a new campaign, it could be very difficult to stop the course of events and the consequences of it would surely be disastrous in every respect. A consideration which should have some weight is that the work of cotton cultivation begins in the month of March, and that if between now and then peace has not at least become probable, this cultivation would be abandoned and . . . never resumed.[44]

Since the three-power suggestion emanated directly from Paris and never officially got beyond London, Mercier was not directly concerned with its handling. This time there would be no breathless dash to the State Department, nor any cause to say anything there unless Seward should bring it up. When word of the effort reached America, Mercier could do little more than say that he liked it, that Lyons seemed to like it, and that the American newspapers were as yet noncommittal.[45]

[42] Mercier to Drouyn de Lhuys, Washington, 10 Nov. 1862, AMAE, CP, E-U, 128: 151-55, no. 124.

[43] Nevins, *The War for the Union*, II, 318-22.

[44] Mercier to Drouyn de Lhuys, Washington, 18 Nov. 1862, AMAE, CP, E-U, 128: 182-99, no. 125; see also *LJ*, III (1862), 148.

[45] Mercier to Drouyn de Lhuys, Washington, 24 Nov. 1862, AMAE, CP, E-U, 128: 210-16, no. 127.

Mercier and Seward had little to say to each other these days; for understandable reasons neither man was anxious for a confrontation. Through Lyons, the secretary let Mercier know that "it was thought one could be busy about our business without consulting us, and since no communication was made to us, we have neither an answer to give nor an opinion to express."[46] But Mercier was afraid, nevertheless, that his stock would decline now with Seward. That was inevitable, of course. Thanks to the Mexican affair and now to the armistice proposal, France was beginning to press as a hurtful thorn in the Union's side. This was the season of the *Alabama's* escape from Liverpool and her first attacks on Northern merchantmen;[47] but for that, France might have eclipsed Britain as a worry for Union diplomacy.

Among other comments on the affair, Mercier had one of most special interest to contemplate—Thouvenel's:

> I made it my business to communicate to Mr. Drouyn de Lhuys all your private letters since the month of August. I am afraid that he was moved a little too quickly by their contents, but knowing how difficult the art is, I refrain from any criticism, quite certain that you are a man to make the best of what is put between your hands. Courage, then, my dear friend, and if it is no longer my office to reward your successes, no one will applaud them with better feeling than I.[48]

Nothing could be more eloquent, both on and between the lines. If Mercier's overheated reports had been a factor in

[46] Mercier to Drouyn de Lhuys, Washington, 1 Dec. 1862, *ibid.*, fol. 218-35, no. 128. See also Lyons to Russell, Washington, 2 Dec. 1862, *Sessional Papers*, LXXII (1863), 56, no. 51.

[47] Seward hinted that France might help the United States with Britain in the *Alabama* matter (Seward to Dayton, Washington, 30 Nov. 1862, State Dept. Corres., France, Instructions, XVI, 296-97, no. 262, also in *For. Rel. U.S.*, 1863, II, 707).

[48] Thouvenel to Mercier, 1 Dec. 1862, Thouvenel, *Secret*, II, 448-49.

the November fiasco, Thouvenel seemed to be saying, at least his superior ability could help make the best of a bad job now.

Looking back on the year behind, Mercier must have found it hard to believe that the *Trent* affair was only twelve months into the past. The author of that French note was writing him letters from retirement now. Words which meant little then had become famous in the weeks between—"Antietam," for example, and, in Europe, "Bismarck." The Civil War was pounding the old American order into an unrecognizable new shape, and if Sartiges had cringed at Buchanan's country, Mercier feared what Lincoln's might become. Ineluctably, implacably, the war was becoming a social and political revolution, powerful in what it was doing for American industrial and military strength: Mercier saw this. And slaves would be legally free tomorrow; the day after that, the country would see that Negroes were somehow Americans too, that being an American no longer meant being a white man. Despite the recent elections, the day of the gentle compromiser was gone; Corcoran's withdrawal to France was among other things a richly symbolic act, for his Washington and his America, the America of Buchanan and Taney, was now a chapter of history.

George B. McClellan, a young man but mentally one of the old order, had had his days numbered for some time. The leisurely pace of his southward march after Antietam had again given substance to his critics' charges, and for military reasons his commander-in-chief was thoroughly dissatisfied with him too. On 5 November the notice of dismissal went out to McClellan in the field. With some reason, albeit small, the government feared that Young Napoleon might turn his men around and seize Washington, so Ambrose Burnside was given the Army of the Potomac the second McClellan lost it. Burnside, changing McClellan's strategy, then turned to the southeast, and in the second week of December the army found itself opposite the town of Fredericksburg, Virginia. On the west side of town, on Saturday, 13 December, 12,650 of Burnside's soldiers lost life or some part of life in another bloody Union defeat. Richmond was safer than ever, and another crisis was upon the American Union.

In these circumstances Mercier still found the French position sound. The American question was a matter of either subjugating the South to preserve territorial integrity or reaching some compromise as close as possible to the old Union:

> In effect, the essential point in the event of a negotiation being to obtain . . . conditions which would least affect the general principles . . . , it is clear that it is not by destroying towns, pushing Negroes to abominable excesses, humiliating the population to the point of degradation as in New Orleans . . . that these conditions would become easier to settle. As for slavery, it is doubtless necessary to detest it, but beside the principle there is the fact which policy cannot excuse itself from considering. What to do with these four million slaves?[49]

There was a question to which a great many people had been giving serious thought. Lincoln had begun his emancipation program with high hopes for colonization as a way

[49] Mercier to Drouyn de Lhuys, Washington, 16 Dec. 1862, AMAE, CP, E-U, 128: 299-301, private. Mercier's private, personal letters to Thouvenel are in the Papiers Thouvenel. His "private" letters to Drouyn de Lhuys, however, are of a noticeably less personal, more formal character, a fact which stems from the more formal character of their relationship. These "private" letters are in the "Correspondance Politique" section of the foreign ministry archives, along with the official correspondence, and are unnumbered and labeled "particulière." Here they will simply be noted as "private" in the place usually reserved for the document number.

to alleviate the problem of interracial relations: if enough free Negroes could be persuaded to leave America, there would be no interracial relations and hence no problem. Plans were forwarded for settlement of Negroes in places like the Chiriqui district of Panama. In addition, Seward was directed to sound out friendly foreign governments to see if they would like to recruit Negro immigrants for their countries or, in the case of the colonial powers, their tropical colonies. As yet the light had not shone on the federal government; it would be a little while before they realized that a man whose forbears had been in, say, South Carolina for five generations had at least as much claim on the word "American" as, say, the boys in Franz Sigel's corps who spoke German among themselves.[50]

Seward discharged his duty with a circular letter on 30 September. He had been cool all along to the emancipation idea, and his early association with abolitionists had convinced him that colonization was impractical. Nevertheless, he set himself manfully to work, composing a dispatch which showed great imagination in its detailed suggestions for a hypothetical colonization treaty. Many "free persons of African derivation" had been inquiring about emigration, he began, and some foreign countries had expressed interest in the idea, so here were some thoughts about implementing it. There followed a whole bagful of guarantees that would have to be secured, from freedom itself down to "sea-worthy vessels" and "an education of the children in the simple elements of knowledge." The only trouble with this scheme was that very few American Negroes and

[50] On matters relating to Negro colonization, see Walter L. Fleming, "Deportation and Colonization: an Attempted Solution of the Race Problem," *Studies in Southern History and Politics*, pp. 3-30; Nevins, *The War for the Union*, ii, 6-7; 115, n. 9; 241, n. 61; Nicolay and Hay, vi, 357-65.

almost no foreign countries were interested in it. Guatemala, Salvador, Nicaragua, and Costa Rica sent regrets. So did Lord John Russell.[51]

So did Drouyn de Lhuys. He thought that the matter might better be postponed, but meanwhile he had an idea for Mercier to mull over:

> While putting off for now a response to the overtures . . . it seemed to us, however, that the dispositions which they display could be put to use in another way and to a much more restrained degree. Because of our expedition in Mexico, we would be interested in recruiting a certain number of Negroes whom we would employ either as soldiers or as workers. Since the aim which the federal government has in view . . . is evidently to relieve its territory of a population which can create embarrassment for it, its aim would be attained as well by a recruitment like the one we are considering as by recruiting for the more particular destination of our colonies. . . . If it were possible, moreover, to enroll Negroes already trained in military discipline, the operation would entirely conform to the purpose we have in mind.[52]

It is equally difficult to detect any trace of conscious humor in this dispatch and to understand how the foreign minister could have written it seriously. Perhaps in its own way Drouyn de Lhuys's suggestion illustrates the wild improbability of the whole colonization idea: a silly question deserved and had gotten a silly answer, an answer which

---

[51] Seward to Dayton, Washington, 30 Sept. 1862, State Dept. Corres., France, Instructions, XVI, 262-65, no. 227; Bancroft, II, 345-48.

[52] Drouyn de Lhuys to Mercier, Paris, 4 Dec. 1862, AMAE, CP, E-U, 128: 265-66, no. 32. See also Dayton to Seward, Paris, 31 Oct. 1862, State Dept. Corres., France, Dispatches, LII, no. 218.

remained a diplomatic nullity.[53] As the first of the year approached, and with it the date of emancipation, Abraham Lincoln could see that the abolitionists had been right: Americans of African descent were not Africans and had no wish to become Panamanians or Mexicans. One abolitionist, Benjamin Rush Plumly of Philadelphia, wrote the president about the special New Year's Eve vigil which Negroes of that city had held in their churches, welcoming in the new year and the new America. They felt—rightly as it turned out, for Lincoln was not proposing involuntary emigration and was already souring on colonization—that God would not let their president send them from their native land.[54]

Henri Mercier's thinking on the subject of French intervention in 1862 divides rather sharply at the second battle of Bull Run; in wartime, diplomacy is determined by what soldiers do. At the beginning of the summer, Mercier was impressed by the firmness of Northern will; even after Stonewall Jackson's breakthrough in the Shenandoah Valley, even after McClellan's failure before Richmond, sentiment in the North seemed firmly committed to going on with the war. In New London Mercier heard the first rumblings of a growing peace sentiment, but he still felt that the only sane policy was to wait, at least until the fall

[53] Mercier gently and tactfully tried to alert Drouyn de Lhuys to the inanity of this suggestion (Mercier to Drouyn de Lhuys, Washington, 30 Dec. 1862, AMAE, CP, E-U, 128: 308-14, no. 132). In answer to the foreign minister's renewed request for information, he replied that the time did not seem right for cooperating in any colonization scheme. For one thing, Stanton had come to want Negroes for the Union army; for another, Mercier implied, the slave who left the plantation might not be the most useful sort of worker (Mercier to Drouyn de Lhuys, Washington, 17 May 1863, *ibid.*, 130: 77-80, no. 151).

[54] Bruce Catton, *Never Call Retreat* (New York: Doubleday & Co., 1965), pp. 113-14.

elections. Until September, therefore, Mercier's dispatches buttressed Thouvenel's arguments against any immediate intervention.

General Lee's smashing triumph at second Bull Run, however, spun Mercier around quite dramatically. As he had done before, Mercier now reacted sharply to a new military situation, and before September was a week old, he had penned a breathless letter to Thouvenel and accosted Seward verbally. The game was over, he said in effect; he and Lyons should be given authority to pick the moment when France and Britain should say "Stop, or else." But Thouvenel was not moved, and his earlier praise of Mercier's dispatches was now succeeded by some pointed if indirect complaints. Nor could Seward be budged from his position: European intervention, he clearly implied, would mean war against the United States.

Mercier later said that even had Paris granted him the discretionary authority he requested, he would not have used it before the fall elections. For one thing the Army of the Potomac and the Army of Northern Virginia were moving towards each other again. Their clash at Antietam did not appear so decisive to Mercier as it would to later analysts, but it was at least clear to him that the Northern leaders could and would go on with the war, and he stopped talking about intervention before the elections. When emancipation was announced on 22 September, Mercier reacted strongly against the move. The government, he felt, was desperately stretching forth its hand to Ethiopia. But what could Europe do about it, with the North so firm for the Union and the South so determined upon separation? Mercier's answer preceded the French three-power initiative and undoubtedly influenced its formation: let Europe call for an armistice, he said, without using the terms "Union" or "separation." The rest would take care of itself, especially if Europe threatened to intervene should the armistice talks fail. Mercier probably expected the net result of this to be Southern independence.

With Thouvenel gone, the French government made its move, a move decisively checked by Russia and Britain. Even before he knew this, Mercier was considering the chances for a French solo effort, an offer of mediation which might stand a better chance with Britain out of the picture in the initial stage. Should events then move on to the point of recognizing the South, however, Mercier felt that Britain must then be involved. Mercier seemed not to see that the same Union firmness which helped to stymie the three-power proposal would also stop any individual French effort. No common market, no picture of North and West going on to a glorious future without the bothersome South, could alter that rocklike Union position. It had stood in the path of one French initiative; it was about to break another.

From Mercier's viewpoint it was all an unsatisfactory jumble at year's end. The North would not quit and was too powerful to be taken by the ear. Social revolution was threatening racial chaos and hampering the liberties of white men. Mexico and now the armistice proposal were giving Americans some second thoughts about their "oldest ally," France. The great peace hopes of early September had gone aground on the monolithic determination of the Union government. Thouvenel was gone. There was nothing very exhilarating to contemplate.

CHAPTER IX

The French Proposal of 1863

MERCIER, HORACE GREELEY, AND PEACE PROSPECTS

THE first two months of the new year were in many ways the zenith of dissident peace sentiment in the North, and Mercier came to believe that there was material enough in that sentiment for a new European overture. Burnside's defeat at Fredericksburg had come on the heels of Democratic electoral victories, and this had produced a broad and deep peace movement. It had also produced a hardening of Radicalism, and one early result of that was the abortive effort to unseat the moderate Seward. "I believe he would prefer to see England and France intervene," Zach Chandler said, "rather than see the Rebellion crushed by force of arms." That was wrong, of course, but they were yeasty times that could cause a senator to write such a thing, even in a letter to his wife. Chandler was upset, as Mercier was heartened, by the chance that Northerners themselves might settle for something less than "territorial integrity."[1]

Many moderates could even agree with Congressman Clement Vallandigham in his speech on the House floor, 14 January 1863: "Stop fighting. Make an armistice. . . .

[1] See Nevins, *The War for the Union*, II, 350-62, for the story of how Lincoln stopped the Radical effort to force Seward to resign. For the whole picture of Northern dissent at this juncture, see *ibid.*, pp. 369-93. Writing on 19 December, the day of the special cabinet meeting, Mercier reported the "ministerial crisis" and guessed that Seward would be replaced (Mercier to Drouyn de Lhuys, Washington, 19 Dec. 1862, AMAE, CP, E-U, 128: 302, private).

Withdraw your army from the seceded states. . . . Declare absolute free trade between North and South. . . . Visit the South. Exchange newspapers. Migrate. Intermarry. Let slavery alone. . . . Let us choose a new President in sixty-four."[2] Such sentiment was especially high in the West, in Indiana and Illinois, where abolition, the new aim of Union arms, was an unappreciated good and high tariffs had underwritten the bitter dissatisfaction. Here governors were moving like minor versions of Charles I to prorogue and circumvent peace-minded legislatures.

Such conditions were bound to stimulate a great many individual peace efforts, one of which was the work of William C. "Colorado" Jewett. This flamboyant person was forty years old in 1863. A native of New York, he had gone west as a young man and become interested in the development of the Colorado Territory, emerging as a self-made representative from Pike's Peak. When the Civil War began, Jewett busied himself with disjointed, passionate letters to Lincoln and the cabinet, taking the general line that coercion was wrong and that the sections should clasp hands and forget about ending slavery. There is no evidence that any except perhaps the first such note met the president's eyes, and White House secretary John Hay heatedly took the trouble to tell Jewett so. Undaunted, Jewett made several trips to Europe during the war, trying to stir up mediation fever, especially that of Napoleon III. He seems to have felt that his letters to the world's great personages tended to make him one of them, and in this frame of mind he now launched another effort to stop the American bloodshed, an effort which came to center upon Henri Mercier.[3]

[2] Quoted in Catton, *Never Call Retreat*, p. 103.

[3] See the following letters from Jewett to Lincoln in Lincoln Papers, ser. 1 [Philadelphia], 20 March 1861, fol. 8251-52; Brooklyn, 25 March 1861, fol. 8338; Philadelphia, 11 April 1861, fol. 8968-69; Hay to Jewett, Washington, 6 Dec. 1863, *ibid.*, fol. 28465.

Jewett spent New Year's Eve in Washington, where he fired off another letter to the White House: "Should you . . . desire my views upon European matters—in connection with the American Nation—I will be pleased to give them."[4] He also contacted the French minister. The point about Jewett now was that he had enlisted the aid of Horace Greeley, and Greeley had access to everyone who counted, from the president down. Accordingly, Mercier thought that he should at least listen.[5]

Having listened, Mercier gave a completely bland answer about explaining his government's position to anyone who wanted it. With this and an implied invitation from Mercier, Jewett went back to Greeley in New York. Horace Greeley was a mercurial and unpredictable man. His published "Prayer of Twenty Millions," a strong plea for abolition, had energized that issue the previous August and provoked the president's famous moderate reply: "What I do about slavery, and the colored race, I do because I believe it helps to save the Union."[6] In reality Greeley was fairly consistent; he was both a Jeffersonian and an abolitionist: that is, if the South could prove that secession was genuinely popular, he was willing to tolerate secession, but he was not willing to permit slavery if that could be helped.[7] Jewett had a willing listener, therefore, but not one who already agreed with him on all points. For one thing, Greeley was not ready to admit the divisibility of the Union; for another, he was suspicious of France and was currently thinking of Switzerland, powerless and a republic, as the preferred mediator.[8]

[4] Jewett to Lincoln, Washington, 31 Dec. 1862, *ibid.*, fol. 20650.

[5] Mercier to Drouyn de Lhuys, Washington, 19 Jan. 1863, AMAE, CP, E-U, 129: 30-34, private.

[6] *New York Tribune*, 20 Aug. 1862; Randall and Donald, p. 376.

[7] Greeley to the editor, *New York Times*, 14 March 1863.

[8] Greeley to Jewett, New York, 2 Jan. 1863, in Harlan Hoyt Horner, *Lincoln and Greeley* (Urbana: University of Illinois Press, 1953),

Jewett was not the only force for peace being applied to Horace Greeley just then. On 12 January, the *Tribune* editor received a letter from Clement Vallandigham, who two days later delivered his antagonizing speech in the House of Representatives.[9] Greeley thought he had better go to Washington and see what was what, and in this way, toward the middle of January, he came to discuss things with Mercier.

The minister began the conversation by insisting that France was nothing for America to fear as a mediator. To prove it, he read Greeley a passage from Drouyn de Lhuys's post mortem on the three-power proposal, probably that part about the emperor's government always being happy to contribute to the pacification of a friendly people—a work of humanity and good policy.[10] According to Mercier, Greeley came away persuaded of French good intentions and even said that the earlier French proposal was of benefit in that it forced the question of peace to be discussed.

Having sounded out the French minister, Greeley went to see the president (17 January) and other of his fellow-Republican leaders, especially Senator Sumner, whose opinion both he and Jewett were especially anxious to sway. Mercier himself had a long talk with Sumner on the evening of the eighteenth. He found this intransigent Unionist quite ready to admit that the situation was grave and that unless there were a military success in the spring, the government might be reduced to impotence. But Sumner wisely warned Mercier that the United States must and would have that chance for a military success, and that if France

---

pp. 291-92. On the Greeley–Jewett affair see Case and Spencer, pp. 393-95.

[9] William Harlan Hale, *Horace Greeley, Voice of the People* (New York: Harper & Brothers, 1950), pp. 267-68.

[10] Drouyn de Lhuys to Mercier, Paris, 18 Nov. 1862, AMAE, CP, E-U, 128: 181, no. 30, also in *LJ*, III (1862), 145-46.

offered mediation now, it would be rejected. Mercier was impressed with the fact that even Sumner did not write off the possibility of a mediation at some future time.

All of this was heady for the French minister, but he wanted the foreign ministry to know that he was not being swept off his feet. He tabbed Jewett unstable, but he felt that if Jewett could bring Greeley along, that would be significant. Mercier also made sure to inform Lyons, that paragon of prudence. Lyons conceded that Mercier's predictions of the war's course seemed to be working out, but he thought that North and South should be left to solve their own problems, that is, to cook the quail without benefit of European chefs. Lyons was concerned about the new reason for Anglophobia which a mediation offer would produce. This brought Mercier back to two earlier themes in his report to Paris:

But if England for one reason or another should want to persist in abstention and give up any initiative, should we necessarily imitate her example? . . . It is clear that acting alone or even with Russia . . . we should have to proceed with greater prudence because our share of responsibility would become larger. It would then be necessary to be very sure in advance of the result of our démarche. And I do not think that this would be difficult if after having fixed the terms, you would wish to leave it to me to settle upon the date.[11]

[11] For Mercier's talks with Greeley, Sumner, and Lyons, and for Mercier's conclusions and recommendations, see Mercier to Drouyn de Lhuys, Washington, 19 Jan. 1863, AMAE, CP, E-U, 129: 30-34, private, also in Mercier Family Papers. For Jewett's reaction see also Jewett to Mercier, Washington, 16 Jan. 1863, ibid., fol. 32; and Mercier to Greeley, Washington, 20 Jan. 1863, Columbia University Libraries, New York, Papers of Sydney Howard Gay. (In the latter note, Mercier simply assured Greeley that his efforts would be bent as always toward peace. He wrote in French and implied an apology

Despite his continuing closeness to Lyons, then, Mercier had decided that a French or a Franco-Russian offer would soon be advisable and might even be preferable to a three-power approach. Yet another time he asked Paris for discretionary power to pick "the moment," and in the hypothesis of a solo French move, it would be he, Mercier, who might give the signal for the end of the Civil War.[12] But a number of improbable ingredients would first have to be found before the casserole could be heated. For one thing, though Greeley was not yet willing to concede it, Mercier was convinced that the South was and would remain independent. For another, Mercier's idea about being assured beforehand of Washington's willingness to accept mediation was an idle dream despite the dissidence in the North. Not Bull Run, not Fredericksburg, not Vallandigham nor even Greeley could bring the Union government to such a point. If Mercier really meant it when he laid down this prior condition, then "the moment" was no closer now than it had ever been.

Stoeckl did not entirely reject Mercier's thoughts in these excited weeks, but he insisted that Europe first be sure of a friendly reception in Washington for her offer, and he preferred that this offer speak merely of armistice. He felt that France, "basing herself on the favorite report of her

---

for his spoken English during his conversation with Greeley. Sumner, incidentally, spoke fluent French, and this helps account for the "long conversation" between him and Mercier.) On the Mercier–Lyons discussion, see also E. D. Adams, II, 75-76, and Newton, I, 96.

In January Mercier disappointedly gave up hoping that Governor Seymour would interpose New York against the war (Mercier to Drouyn de Lhuys, Washington, 13 Jan. 1863, AMAE, CP, E-U, 129: 19-24, no. 135).

[12] Mercier's strong desire to help end the war is the principal reason for this new request. His repeated desire to be recalled was evidently less strong than his wish to play a diplomatic role in the making of peace. Should such an effort be successful, of course, i.e., should the Civil War end, he might *then* expect to be recalled promptly.

representative in Washington, might make new overtures to the imperial [Russian] government" about trying to stop the American war. Mercier even asked Stoeckl to see Seward and try to find out how seriously Greeley should be taken. "Since your relations with the secretary of state," he told Stoeckl, "are of longer standing and greater informality than mine, you might be able to broach this subject in a friendly way with him." Stoeckl saw Seward immediately, but the secretary suggested he tell Mercier not to credit Greeley's influence too much.[13]

Greeley launched a formal proposal in the *Tribune* of 22 January, a ten-point program which featured a hard, abolition-centered drive against the South, followed, in the event of failure, by peace talks in three months. Point IX of this scheme looked forward to the possibility of European interposition in aid of such peace talks. Simultaneously in Virginia, Ambrose Burnside began a vast flanking drive out of Fredericksburg which would at last set the federal power on the road to Richmond. Rain and mud relieved General Lee of the need to do very much about this, as the Army of the Potomac literally sank to its knees in viscous Virginia soil. Such a setback naturally gave a little added impetus to the mediation project. Greeley himself was sanguine enough. "You'll see," he told Raymond of the *Times*, "that I'll drive Lincoln into it."[14]

MERCIER AND DROUYN DE LHUYS REACH
THE SAME CONCLUSION

By this time Mercier's fever was high indeed, and his recommendations must have brought on some head-scratch-

---

[13] Stoeckl to Gorchakov, Washington, 14/26 Jan. 1863, no. 2, Stoeckl Papers; Woldman, pp. 97-98.

[14] *New York Tribune*, 22 Jan. 1863; Henry J. Raymond, "Extracts from the Journal of Henry J. Raymond," *Scribner's Monthly*, XIX (1880), 703-10. For background on Greeley and mediation, see *New York Tribune*, 6, 9, 14, 19, and 31 Jan. 1863.

ing in Paris. Was he advocating the threat of force or not? Would it really be right for him to go off to Richmond again? Mercier would make it clear that France had no intention of intervening in American "domestic affairs." Should the United States refuse an initiative, "a refusal could even give you more freedom of action for the future."

> In the event circumstances might make that mode of action practical, perhaps you might also authorize me to go first to Richmond to make certain of the attitude of the government there. . . . This trip, which would not avoid arousing a great deal of attention, could give the signal for a movement of opinion which would carry along the Federal government.

Mercier assured Drouyn de Lhuys that he was asking such latitude only because of the time-lag caused by distance and the ocean, not from any desire to cut a great figure. He again set Lyons down as timid but claimed that Stoeckl was "more enterprising" as long as England was not in the party.[15]

The part about not intervening in domestic affairs would be very misleading if not read in conjunction with Mercier's overall view of the situation. "Here it is no longer a matter of domestic affairs," he had said. "The rebellion has not been put down; it is a matter of regulating relations between States."[16] That might be all very well in theory, but the crucial point was that the commander-in-chief of North-

[15] Mercier to Drouyn de Lhuys, Washington, 23 Jan. 1863, AMAE, CP, E-U, 129: 42-44, private.

[16] Mercier to Drouyn de Lhuys, Washington, 19 Jan. 1863, *ibid.*, fol. 30-34, private. Here Mercier used "États," capitalized, which probably means states of the (former) United States but could also mean sovereign states like France and Belgium; "entre," of course, can mean either "between" or "among." The key point remains clear: Mercier, like Gladstone, thought that Jefferson Davis had made a nation.

ern power did not and never would see it that way, and short of war there was nothing France could do about it— no matter how much "freedom of action for the future" might be developed.

A notable embarrassment gave Mercier some cause for concern at this juncture. On Monday, 26 January, Seward dined with his friend Henry Raymond of the *Times* and complained to him about Greeley's meddling.[17] Three days later Raymond aired the entire matter, and the French legation was caught up in something very like a scandal. According to Raymond, Napoleon III now knew that the United States wanted no foreign meddling:

> Does the French Minister at Washington understand this declaration and act upon it in the sense which its language implies? *Or is he engaged* either on his own responsibility, or under secret instructions from the Emperor, in *building up a party here in favor of European intervention in our affairs?* . . . The *Tribune* has avowed itself in favor of foreign mediation; and that circumstance perhaps gives color to the future statement that Mr. Greeley, its Editor has *entered into personal negotiations* with M. Mercier for the promotion of the same end.[18]

Greeley was in for it now, and Seward's other friend, Thurlow Weed, joined the attack in the Albany *Evening Journal* for 31 January. Greeley replied on 2 February to Weed's many-pronged attack, including the assertion that he had been interfering in foreign affairs:

> And now if any one on earth *can* imagine that the Emperor Napoleon is represented in this country by a person who enters into negotiations with private indi-

17 Raymond, *Scribner's Monthly*, xix (1880), 706.
18 *New York Times*, 29 Jan. 1863.

viduals respecting our National Affairs, and especially so delicate a matter as Intervention, I will not contradict him. . . . I once met M. Mercier, and, being kindly received by him, *did* venture to ask him some questions touching the *disposition* of the Emperor toward this country. . . . I knew before—for it was plainly avowed —that France desires to see our Civil War ended; but what the Emperor proposes to do in the premises I neither know nor have sought to learn from M. Mercier.[19]

In his report to the foreign minister, Mercier chalked the whole thing up to an intra-party Republican fight, an anti-Greeley thrust. But he indirectly noted that the *Times* belonged to the Seward faction and that this could be annoying to diplomacy. Sometime during the 30 January–2 February weekend, therefore, he went to see Seward and put things right.[20]

Seward held all the cards in this particular game, and under the circumstances he knew how to be magnanimous. His opening remarks put all the blame on Greeley and Jewett, and he suggested gently that if it ever happened again, Mercier should keep the State Department informed. Playing along gratefully and courteously, Mercier assured him that he would do so, that he had informed the secretary through a colleague (Stoeckl) about Greeley, and that his reticence in the present case was proper: all he had done was to clarify his government's position and listen to advice. On broader issues, Mercier found the secretary noncommittal; even were he in process of changing his

---

[19] *New York Tribune*, 2 Feb. 1963.

[20] This paragraph and the following account of the Mercier–Seward conversation are based on Mercier to Drouyn de Lhuys, Washington, 2 Feb. 1863, AMAE, CP, E-U, 129: 65-68, private, also in Mercier Family Papers.

mind, Mercier thought, Seward would be anxious not to reveal publicly any shift in the Union's uncompromising attitude toward the South, at least not before definite decisions had been taken.[21]

By 3 February, Mercier had even more reason to regret the publicity he had been receiving and the fact that the time was not quite right for intervention, for he was back in Seward's office, this time as bearer of an official French initiative. All during January this message had been en route, in various stages of composition, endorsement, and transportation. Totally unrelated to the Greeley storm as it was, the French dispatch nevertheless arrived in Washington just after the climax of that difficulty. It was anticlimactic in several senses. French seekers after peace had no special reason to acclaim this initiative: it was the only one of the entire war which ever made the whole trip from Paris to Washington; it was so mild that prudence seemed its only virtue; and it passed across the desks of men who were utterly unimpressed with its suggestions.

It is quite clear that the real objectives of the 9 January note were in France, not America. As with the November three-power proposal, so now: the emperor and his government were as interested in mollifying unemployed French workers as in shortening the American war, though that would be good too should it somehow eventuate. The French textile and exporting industries were in such a bad way that everything from fatherly instinct to good politics

[21] "So far as the public goes, it is clear that he is anxious to seem not to have given up on the reestablishment of the Union." This little hint that Seward might be considering compromise is not contained in the earlier draft in Mercier Family Papers. There Mercier alluded to his autumn talk with Thurlow Weed and wondered if Seward might now want to drop the reserve he had maintained in the last three months. "But he made me understand clearly that he does not yet dream of abandoning his attitude."

261

dictated another imperial attempt at ending the Civil War. This can be inferred from the 1862 reports on French public opinion submitted by the *procureurs généraux*:

> Thirteen of these reports urged immediate action by France, either alone or together with the other powers, while only five advised neutrality and nonintervention. These pleas for action must have been particularly influential because they were accompanied by an almost unanimous expression of sympathy for the South.[22]

What the French proposal suggested was merely that peace talks begin forthwith, with no foreign mediation, no interruption of the blockade, not even an armistice. Each side would send commissioners to some neutral spot, and there they would speak of peace and of terms. Drouyn de Lhuys was careful to coat even this placebo with a heavy layer of Franco-American sugar.

France, he began, was motivated in its peace efforts by friendship for the United States. He saw nothing demeaning to the federal government in the earlier French effort to bring about a three-power mediation, but he fully appreciated the national patriotism of the United States, its distaste for foreign interference, and its apparent desire to achieve its aims by force of arms. Very well, then. Let North and South talk without Europe's help and without an armistice:

> Mutual grievances would be examined in this conference. A debate about the interests which divide North and South would take the place of the accusations which they are exchanging today. They would seek to discover . . . whether these interests are definitely irreconcilable, whether separation is an inevita-

[22] Case, *French Opinion on U.S. and Mexico*, p. 257; Case and Spencer, pp. 386-93.

ble extremity, or whether the memories of a common life, the ties of every sort which have made of North and South one federal state and brought it to such a high degree of prosperity are not more powerful than the causes which have put arms into the hands of the two populations.[23]

Dayton could see very well that this would not work. He frankly told Drouyn de Lhuys that American statesmen needed no advice about when to begin talks, that the Mexican business had generated some anti-French feeling in America, and that further interference in the Civil War was apt to increase that feeling. In other words, the American people "would not like to see His Majesty's hand always in this business."[24] After Drouyn de Lhuys's note was published, Dayton also knew that "its first object was to operate at *home*, to satisfy the manufacturers and workmen of France."[25]

Mercier and the Aftermath of the French Note

In the circumstances Seward's reply to the French proposal was completely predictable. It came first in his note to

[23] Drouyn de Lhuys to Mercier, Paris, 9 Jan. 1863, AMAE, CP, E-U, 129: 15-18, no. 1, also in *LJ*, IV (1863), 109-10, and (original and English translation) in State Dept. Corres., Notes from the French Legation, XIX. According to Dayton this note, though dated 9 January, was not sent to the emperor for final approval until the ninth. It was received back on the fourteenth and sent sometime after the middle of the month. This explains the apparent discrepancy between the 9 January date and the fact that Mercier did not receive it until early February (Dayton to Seward, Paris, 15 Jan. 1863, State Dept. Corres., France, Dispatches, LII, no. 255).

[24] *Ibid.*

[25] Dayton to Seward, Paris, 30 Jan. 1863, *ibid.*, no. 263. There is no documentary support for the view of Slidell and A. Dudley Mann that should Washington reject the 9 January proposal, France would recognize the South (Slidell to Benjamin, Paris, 21 Jan. 1863, *ORN*, 2nd ser., III, 666-68; Mann to Benjamin, Brussels, 29 Jan. 1863, *ibid.*, pp. 670-71).

Dayton of 6 February, and it is a mark of the bad position Mercier was in that Seward withheld this reply from him until the tenth. Like Drouyn de Lhuys, Seward rang the changes of Franco-American friendship, calling the French "faultless sharers" of America's trouble. But his expression of the federal will to victory was as definite as ever, and he sought specifically to counteract the Northern peace sentiment which Paris had heard of from Mercier, among others: "Mr. Drouyn de L'Huys, I fear, has taken other light than the correspondence of this Government for his guidance in ascertaining its temper and firmness." The federal government, he continued, was not about to discuss with rebels the question of maintaining its authority. If a meeting place were required for talk, the Congress of the United States held seats in readiness for the returning representatives of the South.[26]

Mercier went twice to see Seward and get the American reaction, once on the fifth and again on the tenth. Both times he was told that the decision had not yet been taken. Finally, later in the day on 10 February, Seward sent word that his answer, a refusal, was en route to Dayton. Mercier remained optimistic, telling his chief that his move was an excellent one and would encourage peace talk in America.[27]

Lyons was disquieted a little when the new French effort became known. Lord John Russell, indeed, was tired of all the mediation talk and thought it useless until North and South were exhausted enough to want it. "When that time comes Mercier will probably have a hint; let him have all the honor and glory of being first."[28] Mercier did in fact

---

[26] Seward to Dayton, Washington, 6 Feb. 1863, State Dept. Corres., France, Instructions, xvi, 328-37, no. 297. See also F. W. Seward, *Seward at Washington*, ii, 154-55, and Case and Spencer, pp. 395-97.

[27] Mercier to Drouyn de Lhuys, Washington, 10 Feb. 1863, AMAE, CP, E-U, 129: 88-90, no. 137, also in Mercier Family Papers.

[28] Russell to Lyons, 14 Feb. 1863, in *ibid.*, p. 155. See also Newton, i, 98-99.

keep at it. From this time on, however, his ruminations on separation and common market, on peace sentiment in America, on what the next Union defeat might bring, on Southern determination to win—all have a hollow sound which differentiates them from most of his earlier observations. He seems to have sensed that "the moment" was farther off than ever.

Seward's rejection of the French peace-talk initiative was only one reason for the cooling of Mercier's ardor. As we shall see, Mercier and France came into some disrepute in the North in the early part of 1863. Newspaper discussion of Greeley–Jewett talks, the French involvement with Mexico, and part of Mercier's 1862 correspondence made it less likely than ever that France could play the role of acclaimed mediator. With the coming of spring there was an abatement of Northern peace sentiment, and the Union's preparations for battle—this time Chancellorsville—were themselves a reason against any talk of immediate negotiation, as Sumner had warned Mercier. The Union victories in July at Gettysburg and Vicksburg were the final blow to the hope that 1863 would be the year for French mediation. Mercier then began to talk wistfully of what might happen after the presidential election of 1864. It is thus the American events themselves, and especially the military events, which account for Mercier's changed tone after February of 1863.

There would be no point in rehearsing Mercier's thought too closely. The essays which his superiors perused week after week make repetitious reading when taken all at once. It is noteworthy, though, that his first reaction to Seward's rejection of the French note was to revert to a harder line, a line which again underscored the need for British participation. He had learned a lesson in early February which Seward had not intended—that suggestions made to Washington were vain unless backed by a threat. It would be no favor to America, he said, for Europe to help the North in crushing the South. That being so, separation was the proper starting point, and to bring Washington to see this, some pressure would be needed:

> I think that the three maritime powers, by a joint action, could do it easily enough, that France and England . . . would no longer encounter much difficulty, but that France alone could hardly do it. . . . It goes without saying that in the revolutions ahead we would not dream of a direct intervention. They should be the result of a spontaneous reaction; but as the doctors say, maybe we can help nature a little.[29]

On 2 March, in a last-minute rush of unfinished Senate business, Charles Sumner introduced resolutions which were meant as a rebuke to Greeley, Jewett, and Mercier, and a warning to Seward. In view of his own conversation with Mercier, Sumner may have been a little embarrassed by this, and he claimed to Mercier that his committee's resolutions were such as to head off even stronger rebukes. The resolutions stated that "Congress cannot hesitate to regard every proposition of foreign interference in the present contest as so far unreasonable and inadmissible that its only explanation will be found in a misunderstanding of the true state of the question, and of the real character of the war in which the Republic is engaged."[30] Despite the fact that the resolutions sailed through both houses by large majorities, Mercier saw nothing there to worry about. With the end of American slavery now dependent on a full Union victory, Mercier felt that Sumner was playing upon antislavery sentiment in Europe, encouraging it to oppose any European initiative which could result in

[29] Mercier to Drouyn de Lhuys, Washington, 2 March 1863, AMAE, CP, E-U, 129: 157-63, private, also in Mercier Family Papers.
[30] *Congressional Globe*, 37 Cong., 3rd sess., p. 1360 (28 Feb. 1863).

the retention of the peculiar institution. In any case, Mercier felt, any future European intervention would have to presume an overwhelming desire for peace on the part of the North, a desire so large that the resolutions of 2 March would readily be overlooked. He therefore discounted the importance of their passage at this time.[31] Seward told Dayton to assure France that the resolution signaled no change in American policy.[32]

Drouyn de Lhuys, as he had after his first setback in November, reacted to Seward's rebuff with calm and pleasant dignity, a stance made easier by the fact that the rebuff was fully expected. On 24 February he had received Mercier's first word of it, a short postscript to the note of the tenth. He showed no particular disappointment, then, when Dayton brought him Seward's dispatch two days later.[33] Seward followed up with one of those speech-dispatches of his, the real aims of which went far beyond the ostensible addressee. He noted the congressional uneasiness about mediation. "Notwithstanding these debates," he continued, "this country will remain friendly henceforth and forever, if its rights and honor continue to be respected, as they have hitherto been by every Government of France, which has existed during the last half century."[34] Between the lines the secretary of state seems to have been hinting that the Second Empire might not be the last government of France, and that people in glass houses should not throw stones at the "territorial integrity" of others.

[31] Mercier to Drouyn de Lhuys, Washington, 6 March 1863, AMAE, CP, E-U, 129: 168-69, private.

[32] Seward to Dayton, Washington, 9 March 1863, State Dept. Corres., France, Instructions, XVI, 344-45, "circular."

[33] Dayton to Seward, Paris, 26 Feb. 1863, State Dept. Corres., France, Dispatches, LII, no. 277, also in *For. Rel. U.S.*, II (1863), 714.

[34] Seward to Dayton, Washington, 2 March 1863, State Dept. Corres., France, Instructions, XVI, 343-44, no. 309, also in *For. Rel. U.S.*, II (1863), 716.

Caught between the upper and nether millstones of Congress and France, Seward did well in these weeks to avoid being ground. He was relieved and gladdened when he received Drouyn de Lhuys's temperate reaction and said so to Mercier.[35]

Prescinding a moment from the domestic aims of the 9 January démarche, one can see that its diplomatic character reflected the same basic dilemma which underlay all the diplomacy of the American Civil War. An American government whose basic position was its own authority and territorial integrity, a government for which second Bull Run and Fredericksburg were not fatal, could not be talked, hinted, or nudged into reconsidering that basic position by a mere diplomatic note. So long as separation was on the agenda, the Lincoln administration wanted no part of the conference table. Apart from that, the Union showed every willingness to talk, but two more years of war would be needed before the South would give up *its* basic position, independence. That being so, there would be no conference unless the European powers should try to arrange one at the point of a gun.

There were many reasons in each case why the two major European powers did not want to risk war, but perhaps the most fundamental was the fact that their grievances were mainly economic; on the evidence of this limited history, economic factors seem the least likely to produce war. Finally, there was the peculiar constitutional situation in America. A president, once elected, has power for four years; no shift in public opinion nor even in Congress can change that, short of impeachment. Mercier may have overestimated the strength of antiwar feeling in the North, but it was strong. Even had it been as strong as Mercier thought, however, its capacity to influence the federal government was severely limited: Seymour might be elected governor

[35] Mercier to Drouyn de Lhuys, Washington, 16 March 1863, AMAE, CP, E-U, 129: 237-46, private.

of New York, but only Abraham Lincoln could make him secretary of war, and that, of course, was out of the question. In a sense, then, the constitution, with its rigid pattern of quadrennial presidential elections, helped mightily to defend the "more perfect union" which had given it birth.

MERCIER AND FRANCE UNDER ATTACK

The months of January and February of 1863 were a bad time for France so far as American popular attitudes were concerned; for Mercier personally they were at their nadir. The publicity given to his conversations with Jewett and Greeley was one reason for this. But that is not the entire explanation: a number of other factors and incidents converged this winter to sour America's feelings toward France and toward the minister of France. The controversy surrounding Count Méjan's dismissal has already been touched upon, but there was more, even, than that.

At the end of January, American newspapers began to pick up, translate, and republish the Yellow-Book correspondence which had appeared in the *Moniteur* for 16 December 1862. Without going into the whole question of diplomacy and public opinion, it may at least be noted that publishing recent documents is bound to be a tricky and dangerous business for all concerned. Foreign ministers withhold vital dispatches and vital paragraphs from those published—that is obvious and understandable. The very institution of such publication means that ministers may write with the public more in mind than the recipient, as is especially clear in the case of some of Seward's dispatches. Dayton for one had complained when Seward published one of his dispatches, and Lyons too had reason to want more privacy.[36] It was not only democratic republics and

---

[36] "I am in trouble altogether, for the good will to me personally, which had miraculously survived so long, seems at last to have sunk altogether under the stroke of the last Blue Book" (Lyons to Russell, Washington, 13 April 1863, Newton, I, 101).

parliamentary regimes which had to wrestle with this problem. Napoleon III depended upon popular support in as real a sense as Palmerston and Lincoln, and since 1861 his foreign ministry regularly published a selection from its files. Now it was Mercier's turn to worry.

By the end of the first week of February, the week in which Mercier presented the suggestion of January 9, the American public had read all about the diplomatic troubles of 1862: how Thouvenel thought the United States should negotiate a settlement (March); how Mercier wondered if the time for mediation were not at hand (July); how Thouvenel asked Mercier to gather information bearing upon mediation (September); how Mercier interpreted the election results to mean that the time was right for "conciliatory steps" (November); and how Mercier thought the "essential point" was that any armistice should last long enough to protect the 1863 cotton crop (November).[37]

Harper's Weekly had the best time with this. Under the heading "M. Mercier *vs.* the United States," they sallied forth to attack the "French yellow-covered literature" and, in particular, Mercier's post-election comments of 10 November 1862:

> The sympathies of M. Mercier have been well known from the beginning of the war. . . . He writes . . . "But if it (the war) should be restrained within the limits and principles and rights recognized by the Constitution, it would not completely attain its aim."
>
> This is a doctrine which M. Mercier learned from his friends the rebels. It is the doctrine which was held by Mr. Buchanan and his friends. Mr. Buchanan said in his message that people had no right to destroy the Government, but if they tried, the Government had no right to help itself. "None at all," said Mr. Mason cheer-

[37] *National Intelligencer* (Washington), 7 Feb. 1863. See also *Evening Star* (Washington), 31 Jan. 1863.

fully, and Mr. Hunter, and Mr. Slidell, and Mr. Benjamin, at those charming soirees and dinners of which his Excellency the French Minister was an ornament.[38]

In this context, and after so many rumors of French intervention projects, the actual French démarche of 9 January produced something like a feeling of relief in America. Not only did Greeley's *Tribune* give it a friendly hearing, but Raymond's *Times* found Napoleon III's new idea "a better, more practicable and more just device than his last."[39] Greeley went further in his comment on Seward's reply, stating that the United States could really have gone to the suggested North–South conference without necessarily admitting the South's right to independence.[40] The *National Intelligencer*, after printing five columns of relevant correspondence which the State Department had made public, went on to praise the French move: "It is impossible to overlook the frank and friendly spirit which breathes in these respectful representations."[41] Mercier sent home clippings illustrating press reaction to the démarche, and Seward had a word for Dayton about recently printed documents. "Some little excitement," he wrote, "has followed the publication of recent correspondence with the French Government. But the effect seems to be not unwholesome. You will give no credit to rumors of alienation between Mr. Mercier and this Government."[42]

That observation probably related to the most controverted segment of the French published correspondence, that describing Mercier's trip to Richmond ten months earlier. Once again Mercier was caught in the middle as

---

[38] *Harper's Weekly*, 28 Feb. 1863.

[39] *New York Times*, 10 Feb. 1863.

[40] *New York Tribune*, 14 Feb. 1863.

[41] *National Intelligencer* (Washington), 14 Feb. 1863.

[42] Seward to Dayton, Washington, 24 Feb. 1863, State Dept. Corres., France, Instructions, xvi, 342, no. 307. Mercier's report is in Mercier to Drouyn de Lhuys, Washington, 20 Feb. 1863, AMAE, CP, E-U, 129: 138-39, no. 139.

Seward's congressional critics tried to get the secretary in their sights for having "sent" Mercier to invite secessionist leaders back to their seats in Washington. It all began, of course, when the Yellow-Book dispatches were published in the American press. Among them was an altered version of Mercier's dispatch of 13 April 1862, which showed Mercier undertaking his trip "with the very explicit approval of the secretary of state, and almost, it even seemed, following his wish."[43] On 9 February, Senator James W. Grimes of Iowa offered a "resolution of inquiry" into

> . . . the character of the suggestions made by the Secretary of State . . . to M. Mercier . . . which induced M. Mercier to undertake his mission to Richmond . . . and what representations, if any, he was authorized to make from this Government, or from the Secretary of State, to the confederate authorities.[44]

Lincoln sent up the correspondence,[45] and Seward's note accompanying the documents picked up the language of the resolutions resoundingly:

> That no suggestions were made to M. Mercier by the Secretary of State that induced, or were designed or calculated to induce him to undertake a mission to Richmond. . . . He was not . . . authorized by this Government, or by the Secretary of State, to make any representations of any kind on any subject to the . . . so-called authorities at Richmond.[46]

---

[43] *National Intelligencer* (Washington), 7 Feb. 1863. See also Mercier to Thouvenel, Washington, 13 April 1862, AMAE, CP, E-U, 127: 35-47, no. 96, the altered version of which is published in *LJ*, III (1862), 120-22.

[44] *Congressional Globe*, 37 Cong., 3rd sess., p. 817 (10 Feb. 1863).

[45] *Lincoln Works*, ed. Basler, VI, 99.

[46] Seward to Lincoln, Washington, 9 Feb. 1863, *Evening Star* (Washington), 12 Feb. 1863.

Press reaction ran true to factional form. Papers friendly to Seward, like the *National Intelligencer*, rightly stressed that Mercier had himself stated in his note that the idea for the trip originated with him, that Northern fortunes had been high the previous spring, and that the message Seward sent to Richmond spoke, in effect, of a Southern surrender, i.e., the return of Southern legislators to their Washington seats.[47] In an effort to dilute the effect of the criticism, comparisons were made with Schleiden's visit and with the trip of Prince Napoleon to Bull Run.[48] The *Courrier des États-Unis* sought to support Mercier by pointing out that Seward really had given him something to say in Richmond and that the secretary should be proud rather than ashamed of it.[49]

Observers unfriendly to Seward had rather a different slant on things. To Count Gurowski, Seward had "proffered to the traitors a hearty welcome." *Harper's Weekly* chose to highlight the fact that Mercier told the Southerners —as if they needed his advice!—that it was important to defend Richmond, whereupon they did so and thus defeated McClellan's peninsular campaign:

> Should this extraordinary statement—which is intrinsically of the utmost probability—prove to be true, it is not a pleasing revelation. It is not Louis Napoleon's fault that his Minister at Washington was a boon companion of traitors. But it will certainly be the fault of our Government if a confidential adviser of the rebels is tolerated in an official position at the capital.[50]

[47] *National Intelligencer* (Washington), 11 Feb. 1863.

[48] *Evening Star* (Washington), 12 Feb. 1863. See also Ralph Lutz, *Die Beziehungen zwischen Deutschland und den Vereinigten Staaten während des Sezessionkrieges* (Heidelberg: Carl Winter's Universitätsbuchhandlung, 1911), pp. 38-39.

[49] *Courrier des États-Unis* (New York), 13 Feb. 1863.

[50] Gurowski, *Diary*, II, 127; *Harper's Weekly*, 7 Feb. 1863.

A growing American Francophobia, then, was the unfortunate background of the emperor's peace suggestion in early 1863. The publication of Mercier's contacts with Greeley and Jewett and of the 1862 correspondence—all of it together plus a general fear of French intervention—added up to a wreckage of trust and good relations. Whatever chance might have existed for French good offices was gone, despite Fredericksburg, Seymour, Western legislators, Greeley, and all the rest.

At the base the same three factors which had controlled events from the beginning were still controlling them: the federal will to preserve the United States, the French unwillingness to use force without Britain, and the British decision to abstain. Even had Washington wanted mediation, Greeley's first thought was probably accurate—it would have been some powerless ideological friend like Switzerland, not the great monarchies, which would have been asked. But the same quality which made Switzerland acceptable is the very one which kept her from coming forward: she had no private axe to grind as had Great Britain and France.

American feeling against France was notably exacerbated in 1863 by the growing French involvements in Mexico. From the beginning, i.e., since 1861, Mercier had feared that any strong attempt by the Second Empire to shape Mexican events would bring on a confrontation between France and the United States. We must now go back and pick up this sorry thread, one in which Franco-American relations became almost disastrously enmeshed.

CHAPTER X

Mexico

THE TRIPARTITE CONVENTION OF LONDON

ONE of the first diplomatic problems which Henri Mercier had to address shortly after his arrival in Washington in 1860 was the question of European intervention in the Mexican revolution. Throughout the next three and a half years, this problem continually accosted Mercier, and as the extent of French involvement increased, so did the dimensions of the difficulty. Long after his return to Paris in 1864, Mercier was still concerned about Mexico, and as late as 1867 he was writing to Seward about it.

Toward the close of 1860, the long-running Mexican war had reached a decisive point: General González Ortega had taken Mexico City for the liberal revolutionary party of Benito Juárez. By July, however, the new government's shaky financial situation moved it to slap a two-year suspension of interest payments on its foreign debts, obligations which totaled some eighty million dollars. Such summary action by a weak Latin American state almost inevitably led to plans for intervention. Great Britain, Spain, and France were seriously concerned; so, of course, was the United States of America.

Henri Mercier was never so directly involved in the Mexican business as he was in the matter of ending the Civil War, and the whole Franco-Mexican affair did not become acute in 1861. But the subject came up that early; its intrusion was startling enough to preclude being ignored; and

275

Mercier had ideas about it which throw considerable light upon his career in Washington.

The one most patent fact about the entire situation was not often talked about openly in the course of direct negotiations, namely the inability of the United States, preoccupied with internal upheaval, to shape events. America's weakness, however, was recognized from the beginning as a helpful precondition for European intervention in Mexico. Obligingly, in recognition of the historical American preponderance in North America, the European states planned to invite Washington to join the endeavor. But Thouvenel was not prepared to accord veto-power to the United States. Writing in September to Count Flahault, his ambassador in London, he outlined the facts and showed how the Mexican matter and the Civil War could easily become intertwined with France's policy toward Britain:

> I am entirely in agreement with you on the unfavorable reception our proposal would probably receive in the United States; thus, in my view, it would merely be a matter of putting ourselves in order with respect to [Washington], without waiting for their agreement. They have at the moment other fish to fry than the Mexicans, and it seems to me almost impossible that the cotton question will not within three months make it necessary for England and France to consider above all an interest vital for the prosperity and peace of their industrial cities.[1]

Before hearing from his chief what had been decided in Europe, Mercier alluded to what he had heard from other sources. He seems a bit pained that he was not being kept informed. "For myself, Mr. Minister, I do not think I should broach this question until Your Excellency makes me

[1] Thouvenel to Flahault, Paris, 19 Sept. 1861, Thouvenel, *Secret*, ɪɪ, 167-70.

acquainted with his views, especially since I now have no other information than what my colleagues have given me."[2] By that time, mid-October 1861, Lyons and Tassara had already heard from their governments and been to see Seward. They found the secretary relatively calm but anxious to stave off the intervention by agreeing to lend Mexico money with which she could meet her financial obligations. Parenthetically we can note that neither at this time nor at any other point did Seward use the term "Monroe Doctrine," though others, including Mercier, did.[3]

The following week Mercier received a dispatch from Thouvenel on this new and tricky subject. France would in no case accept the American plan for interest-payment on the Mexican debts. Moreover, this plan said nothing about indemnity to French citizens for damages resulting from the war, nor did it guarantee the future safety of French nationals in Mexico. Intervention, in other words, would proceed on schedule. In a later note Thouvenel again brought his minister up to date, but it was now apparent to Mercier that he would be left on the sidelines of this particular negotiation. Seward too seemed disposed to deal through Dayton.[4]

Despite this, Mercier meant to be heard in Paris:

I must state to Your Excellency that I cannot help regretting that the maritime powers find it necessary, in order to safeguard their interests and dignity, to return at this juncture to coercive measures against Mexico. The American people will not be so analytical in

[2] Mercier to Thouvenel, Washington, 14 Oct. 1861, AMAE, CP, E-U, 125: 145-50, no. 65.

[3] See, e.g., Mercier to Thouvenel, Washington, 10 Oct. 1861, AMAE, MD, Papiers Thouvenel, XIII, 410-13.

[4] Thouvenel to Mercier, Paris, 3 Oct. 1861, AMAE, CP, E-U, 125: 105-07, no. 26; Thouvenel to Mercier, Paris, 30 Oct. 1861, *ibid.*, fol. 181-83, no. 29; Mercier to Thouvenel, Washington, 22 Oct. 1861, *ibid.*, fol. 151-63, no. 66.

considering it, and they will be made to see in this resolution an eagerness to take advantage of their difficulty which will be very irritating to them. The deep regret with which they see themselves deposed from the position they have gained in the world is a feeling which in itself is worthy of respect, and one which I think that we have a very special reason not to hurt, so that we can avoid its being turned against us.[5]

Here, at least, the American nationalist could wish heartily that the emperor listen to his minister in Washington.

At the end of October, the three maritime powers concluded the Tripartite Convention of London, covering their objectives and methods in the coming Mexican intervention. Washington, of course, was the best place for all three states to get together with Seward, and Mercier was at last given a small role to play. Supplied with a copy of the convention and full power to accept American adherence, he proceeded with Lyons and Tassara to the futile business of inviting United States' approval of European intervention in the Western Hemisphere. The matter was formally laid before Seward in the first week of December.[6]

Official American reaction was predictable and swift: Seward rejected participation. Mercier was unimpressed with his obiter dicta about George Washington, nonentanglement, and the United States' tender regard for Mexico's friendship. The proposed American loan he saw as an

[5] *Ibid.*, fol. 159.

[6] For the negotiation of the convention and the text, see Carl H. Bock, *Prelude to Tragedy: the Negotiation and Breakdown of the Tripartite Convention of London, October 31, 1861* (Philadelphia: University of Pennsylvania Press, 1966), pp. 122-215, 517-20. See also Thouvenel to Mercier, Paris, 6 Nov. 1861, AMAE, CP, E-U, 125: 184-85, no. 30; Mercier to Thouvenel, Washington, 25 Nov. 1861, *ibid.*, fol. 219-25, no. 70; Mercier to Thouvenel, Washington, 3 Dec. 1861, *ibid.*, fol. 246-52, no. 72.

indirect imperialist effort, since the loan would be secured by a lien against Mexican territory:

> The truth is, unless I am mistaken, that if [Seward] could have responded frankly to the powers' proposal, he would have said that North Americans customarily think of themselves as Mexico's natural heirs, that they were keeping a jealous watch over that inheritance, and that the Washington government could not, without irritating public opinion, agree to anything which it thought could hinder it in the pursuit of its claims.[7]

Henri Mercier recognized America's long-standing and emotional interest in Mexico. He neither approved nor liked this interest, but he recognized it and saw no legitimate reason for France to add to her troubles by trying to subvert it. Unfortunately for everyone, his views, unsolicited, did not prevail.

THE GROWING FRENCH INVOLVEMENT

There was nothing in early 1862 to calm Mercier's apprehension about the affair of Mexico. As before, he was not especially consulted by the policy-makers in Paris nor was his ambassadorial role very crucial. All the same, he kept at the issue and threw what weight he could against the enterprise. The many imperial motives for pushing on in Mexico are part of a well-known story, as are the ultimately sounder motives for withdrawal. Among these latter, the

[7] Mercier to Thouvenel, Washington, 9 Dec. 1861, *ibid.*, fol. 274-76, no. 74. See also F. W. Seward to Dayton, Washington, 4 Nov. 1861, State Dept. Corres., France, Instructions, xvi, 83-84, no. 79; and Dayton to Seward, Paris, 6 Nov. 1861, State Dept. Corres., France, Dispatches, li, no. 74.

It is the thesis of Warren F. Spencer and that French involvement in Mexico created a desire in France to maintain friendly relations with the United States (Case and Spencer, pp. 455-56, 498-99).

opposition of the Washington government, that is, of American power, tradition, ideology, and nationalism, was to be triumphant. Mercier's repeated warnings about America's disgust must have had influence within his government, but his advice was as clearly fruitless as it was prudent.

Following the conclusion of the Tripartite Convention, the debt-collecting expedition had got under way in December of 1861. Great Britain's participation was nominal in deference to the strained Anglo-American relations caused by the pending *Trent* episode; the larger Spanish and French forces were directed by General Don Juan Prim and Admiral Jurien de la Gravière respectively. English reticence grew when a Spanish force of six thousand landed at Vera Cruz early in December—a larger, earlier move than London had wished. In January this reticence grew into alarm when the French emperor announced his intention to increase his force. Simultaneously rumors began to circulate of the Archduke Maximilian's willingness to accept a New World throne.

Mercier was interested, perhaps hopefully so, by the early Spanish landing. As he saw it, it was Spain's participation which most disquieted the Americans.[8] Thouvenel, however, had a different picture to draw for him: the French force was being augmented, and French involvement might have to transcend debt-collection.[9]

Dayton kept Seward well informed on all the public and semisecret developments. By early March of 1862 the American secretary had heard that France would back Maximilian, that Franco-Spanish friction had developed from General Prim's ambition to put a Bourbon on the Mexican throne, and that the rightist and pro-French General Almonte had left Paris for Mexico. "You will be satisfied I

---

[8] Mercier to Thouvenel, Washington, 6 Jan. 1862, AMAE, CP, E-U, 126: 3-13, no. 79. See also Bock, pp. 293-403.

[9] Thouvenel to Mercier, Paris, 6 Feb. 1862, *ibid.*, fol. 127, no. 5.

think at no distant day," concluded Dayton, "that money or the recovery of debts was not the great object that took France and Spain to Mexico. If you offer to pay or secure those debts you will not stay their course."[10] Meanwhile the Senate had taken up the idea of backing Juárez' debt payments—the Corwin treaty—and had passed a resolution against it.[11]

As Mercier noted sourly to Prince Napoleon, "It is not for me to say if . . . the advantages outweigh the disadvantages."[12] But he said it nevertheless, and brought in friends of the court to buttress his brief: "All my colleagues, and especially Lord Lyons, agree entirely with me about the trouble with the United States to which the allied powers would expose themselves by helping to set up a Mexican monarchy."

Mercier, who had lived in Mexico as a young attaché, could not understand what value his government might place on such a prize. "With the elements currently in Mexico," he argued, "I do not think it possible to establish a government worthy of the name under any form whatever. They are the most ungovernable of people, without necessities, slow moreover, and lacking industry, all the more so since they have been corrupted by a half-century of constant anarchy." Add to this such further factors as their ethnic variety, and the picture was not an easy one; and this, Mercier said, was also the opinion of the best-informed American Southerners. Furthermore, Mexico needed immigration if she were to develop; but immigrants were apt to demand a great deal of political liberty as an

[10] Dayton to Seward, Paris, 21 Feb. 1862, State Dept. Corres., France, Dispatches, LI, no. 117, also in *For. Rel. U.S.*, 1862, p. 317. See also Dayton to Seward, Paris, 13 Feb. 1862, State Dept. Corres., France, Dispatches, LI, no. 113.

[11] See *Lincoln Works*, ed. Basler, V, 109.

[12] Mercier to Prince Napoleon, Washington, 24 Feb. 1862, AMAE, MD, Papiers Thouvenel, XIII, 431-36.

inducement to leave home—another argument against a Mexican monarchy. Of course, the country could be reduced to colonial status again and go on as a supplier of raw material, but what European country would want to take on this responsibility? After this far-ranging discourse Mercier ended a bit lamely by admitting that there might be other "European considerations" which could influence Thouvenel's decisions.[13]

On 3 March 1862, Seward sent out a circular letter on Mexico which established American policy as suspicious, restrained forbearance.[14] To Europe—as to the Latin American diplomats who urged the United States to keep Europe out of the New World[15]—he professed to be sure that nothing beyond debt-collection could possibly be in the wind. It hardly needs saying that this was a pose; the United States, in the middle of a Civil War, preferred not to notice the challenge of Europe.

At this same time Mercier reported home that the United

[13] Mercier to Thouvenel, Washington, 28 Feb. 1862, *ibid.*, fol. 437-39.

[14] Seward to Dayton, Washington, 3 March 1862, State Dept. Corres., France, Instructions, XVI, 118-21, no. 121. See also J. Fred Rippy, *The United States and Mexico* (New York: Alfred A. Knopf, 1926), pp. 258-60; and A. R. Tyrner-Tyrnauer, *Lincoln and the Emperors* (New York: Harcourt, Brace & World, 1962), pp. 47-49.

[15] In January, Seward was approached by Federico L. Barreda, shortly to become Peru's minister to the United States (Castilla government), and urged to call a hemispheric conference on Mexico. Some weeks later, Federico Astaburuaga of Chile joined his voice to Barreda's. But Seward, for the same reason that he would not say "Monroe Doctrine" in public, continued to feign detachment, even when Barreda went ahead and held a conference in Washington at which Chile, Mexico, New Granada, Peru, and the Central American republics were represented. On 4 April, this conference, in an obvious gesture of support for Washington, issued a draft convention calling for nonrecognition of the C.S.A. and resistance to European encroachment (Robert W. Frazer, "Latin-American Projects to Aid Mexico during the French Intervention," *Hispanic American Historical Review*, XXVIII [1948], 377-88).

States would probably do nothing about the affront of a Mexican monarchy, just as she had reacted humbly in the *Trent* matter, and for the same obvious reason. This early in the game, Mercier seems to have felt that a United States governed by Northerners might really care less about Mexico than had the old regime of Buchanan.[16]

Throughout March Mercier was impressed by Seward's quiet, which even extended to the question of monarchy itself. "Mr. Seward," he wrote, "has become very calm on the question of Mexican monarchy because he is persuaded it is an abortive enterprise. If events prove him right, you know that unless you were really opposed, I for my part would not be very sad."[17] As Seward said to Mercier when the subject of "monarchical arrangements" came up: "Although there was good reason to think that the emperor welcomed such projects in the beginning, I was sure that His Majesty, once he was better informed of the complications involved, would have to renounce them."[18] And even when Seward, in early April, surprised Mercier by expressing concern about a Mexican throne, Mercier chalked it up to the secretary's desire to placate Congress and keep the record clear.[19]

In the next six weeks of 1862 the Mexican venture took a decisive and fateful turn, one which Mercier had feared. Britain and Spain withdrew from the expedition in April, and on 5 May the French force was administered a slap by Juárez' army at Puebla. Mercier, before the military picture was clear, kept hoping that something would extricate his country from the mess, perhaps the quick establishment of

[16] Mercier to Thouvenel, Washington, 3 March 1862, AMAE, CP, E-U, 126: 192-207, no. 88.

[17] Mercier to Thouvenel, Washington, 31 March 1862, AMAE, MD, Papiers Thouvenel, XIII, 443-45.

[18] Reconstructed language. Mercier to Thouvenel, Washington, 8 April 1862, AMAE, CP, E-U, 127: 9-23, no. 94.

[19] *Ibid.*, fol. 10-11.

a government under General Almonte.[20] And he remained mildly optimistic, not that anything good would come of the Mexican venture, but that France would somehow get out of the "mud" before it was too late: "If we achieve our objectives," he wrote, "you will be getting some blasts from here which, I hope, will not do much damage. It is not present, but future complications I fear. I would thus prefer it if we could avoid becoming involved."[21]

In the year between the French defeat of 1862 and the French victory of 1863, Mercier returned to the Mexican imbroglio several times. Especially when writing to Prince Napoleon, whose Northern sympathies Mercier knew well, he connected the Mexican involvement with the possible role of France as a mediator in the American Civil War: "When the moment for a solution arrives, and God grant it be soon, I cannot say yet what part we can play. Our expedition in Mexico has greatly [diminished] the confidence we formerly enjoyed."[22]

Mercier was more ready to support the installation of Maximilian von Habsburg than he was to approve a French involvement. Perhaps he saw the one as a substitute for the other. Here, as in all other areas of his interest, Mercier was first and foremost a defender of French interests. He was consistent in warning against a protracted Mexican involvement which would end in Franco-American bitterness.

Before leaving Washington for his 1862 vacation Mercier had spoken very sharply to Tassara, the Spanish minister, about the sloppy Spanish performance in Mexico. He urged

[20] Mercier to Thouvenel, Washington, 12 May 1862, AMAE, MD, Papiers Thouvenel, XIII, 452-53.

[21] Mercier to Thouvenel, Washington, 26 May 1862, *ibid.*, fol. 454-56. Korolewicz-Carlton says that the Mexican imbroglio helps to explain Thouvenel's supposedly less vigorous opposition to intervention in the months ahead; that is, it was now part of French policy to keep America from reuniting and ending the Mexican venture (Korolewicz-Carlton, pp. 122-24).

[22] Mercier to Prince Napoleon, New London, 4 (?) Aug. [1862], Mercier Family Papers.

the Spaniard to help France make a success of the Maximilian idea, saying that only a monarchy could save Mexico (by preventing the Indian majority from submerging the Spanish population) and that Maximilian was a Mexican, not a French, candidate.[23] In New London, fortified by a conversation with Admiral Reynaud, who was just up from Vera Cruz, Mercier again addressed the foreign minister:

> As for the people, they are as unfriendly to us as possible, and we can rely only on ourselves to arrive in Mexico City. . . . Setting up a government is . . . a very chancy operation and one which can take us far afield. We are taking a great risk of not regaining our expenses. In this case why not do as the Americans did? They had grievances; they made war on Mexico, and, for their damages . . . they took provinces. I understand perfectly that since the conditions are not the same, provinces could be an embarrassment for us; but we would sell them to the United States for ready cash, as Napoleon sold Louisiana to them. In this way . . . we might possibly succeed in facilitating peace between North and South. . . . Give a little thought to this scheme. . . . I have not had time to think it all out thoroughly. You will throw it into the wastebasket if that is all it deserves. . . .[24]

Presumably that is just what Thouvenel did with this midsummer night's dream, this Zimmermann note in reverse. The mind boggles at the thought of France seizing, say, Sonora and Chihuahua and then offering to sell them to America as a sort of bait for reuniting the sections. Mercier, who had opposed the French intervention from the outset, was still anxious that France make out well finan-

---

[23] Mercier to Thouvenel, Washington, 23 June 1862, AMAE, CP, E-U, 127: 253-68, no. 105.

[24] Mercier to Thouvenel, New London, 29 July 1862, AMAE, MD, Papiers Thouvenel, XIII, 479-83.

cially now that the damage was done. In selecting this financial issue for discussion, Mercier again revealed his tendency to concentrate too much on the economic facet of any given problem. In this respect his province-selling suggestion resembles his common-market proposal for ending the American Civil War.

MEXICO AND AMERICAN PUBLIC OPINION

Mercier had special reason in early 1863 to regret the Mexican involvement. The publication of Napoleon III's note to General Forey, French commander in Mexico, helped touch off a bitter debate in the United States about the French threat to American security. As we have seen, Mercier and France were already under fire in the American press as a result of the publication of Mercier's correspondence of 1862 and Mercier's conversation with Horace Greeley. The emperor's note helped to worsen the climate of Franco-American relations. It appeared in the newspapers on 9 February:

> We have an interest in the Republic of the United States being powerful and prosperous, but not that she should take possession of the whole of the Gulf of Mexico, thence command the Antilles as well as South America, and be the only dispenser of the products of the New World.
>
> If . . . Mexico maintains her independence and the integrity of her territory, if a stable Government be there constituted with the assistance of France, we shall have restored to the Latin race on the other side of the Atlantic all its strength and its prestige. . . .[25]

Mercier's difficulty would have been that much greater had the Yankees known the full extent of the emperor's

[25] Napoleon III to Forey, Fontainebleau, 3 July 1862, translation, *New York Times*, 9 Feb. 1863; for the original, see *LJ*, III (1862), 190-91.

ambition: one of his notions was a grand and fragmented design for all of North America in which a French-oriented Mexico would take her place beside the "United States," the Confederate States, and the Western States.[26]

Even as Americans read how the "Latin race" was going to recover its prestige, General Forey was organizing the strong reinforcements which the emperor had sent over. This French build-up produced a reaction in Washington. On 19 January, Senator McDougall of California introduced a resolution calling the French venture a violation of international law and a threat to the United States and to freedom everywhere. The resolution concluded "that it is the duty of this Republic to require of the Government of France that her armed forces be withdrawn from the territories of Mexico."[27]

Seward, of course, had long since abandoned the idea that war with a European power might somehow help to preserve the Union. Preserving the Union was always his chief aim, and for almost two years now he had been straining every muscle to prevent a European complication precisely so that the United States might go on living. He took a dim view, therefore, of the McDougall resolution. So did Senator Sumner, chairman of the Senate's committee on foreign relations, and it was this which effected the tabling of the resolution in early February.[28]

Whatever the benefits which the French government foresaw in Mexico, it knew well that the expedition was

[26] "Note on the Affairs of Mexico and the United States, January 21, 1863," cited in Kathryn Abbey Hanna, "The Roles of the South in the French Intervention in Mexico," *Journal of Southern History,* xx (1954), 3-21.

[27] *Congressional Globe,* 37 Cong., 3rd sess., p. 371 (19 Jan. 1863). See also James Morton Callahan, *American Foreign Policy in Mexican Relations* (New York: Macmillan Co., 1932), p. 289; Mercier to Drouyn de Lhuys, Washington, 27 Jan. 1863, AMAE, CP, E-U, 129: 54-57, private, also in Mercier Family Papers; La Gorce, IV, 309-10.

[28] Mercier to Drouyn de Lhuys, Washington, 6 Feb. 1863, AMAE, CP, E-U, 129: 79-81, no. 136.

souring relations with the United States and helping to thwart mediation. Though he shared the emperor's wish to see a conservative, "Latin" regime in Mexico, Mercier never had approved of France's direct involvement. He returned to this theme in the midst of his thoughts on ending the Civil War:

> You will already have noted that those who think it their business to gain time and to work against us, never omit to join our views to the expedition in Mexico in order to distort them. The expedition . . . has always been very unpopular and has become much more so since the letter to General Forey where the emperor made so little of that famous Monroe Doctrine. . . . Surely we do not have to let ourselves be troubled by this outcry, but neither would I want to despise too much the warnings which one can take from it.[29]

There is no question any more about the altered diplomatic position of France vis-à-vis the United States. Things had moved rather far from the *Trent* affair, from the time, that is, when France, speaking as a disinterested but benevolent friend, could represent international law and order. By intervening in Mexico the emperor had managed the neat trick of alienating both Britain and the United States. The entente was a shambles. And whatever the outcome of the Civil War, the future was bleak enough for any regime that French bayonets might finally install in Mexico City. It must follow that a reunited America would not long tolerate that regime; and though the Confederate States might take longer to move, the emperor must have known that it was precisely the Southerners and the Polk-Buchanan Democrats who had annexed Texas and coveted Cuba. The

[29] Mercier to Drouyn de Lhuys, Washington, 24 Feb. 1863, *ibid.*, fol. 148-52, private, also in Mercier Family Papers.

"Latin race" had few real friends in either Washington or Richmond.

Richmond, in fact, had been given a rather sharp jolt along these lines in the summer of 1862, and imperial France would now discover what imperial Germany learned in 1917—that Americans were extraordinarily sensitive about Texas. The public rehearsal of the affair began on 17 January 1863, when some Confederate documents, captured from a would-be blockade-runner off Charleston, were published in the Northern press. The effect of this publication was to curdle Franco-American sentiment even more. For the incident itself, however, we must go back to the previous August.

On the eighteenth of that month a man named Benjamin Théron, French and Spanish consular agent in Galveston, wrote a letter to Governor Percy Lubbock of Texas. Would not Texas be better off as an independent country, Théron asked, and would the governor favor him with a reply "to guide me in my political correspondence with the governments which I have the honor to represent"?[30]

Théron should have suspected what would happen next: Lubbock sent word to Jefferson Davis. As luck would have it (or it might have been some casual sort of co-operation) a similar incident took place some weeks later right in Richmond. There a M. Tabouelle, Alfred Paul's chancellor of the consulate, wrote to Senator Oldham of Texas and obtained some statistics, undoubtedly big and impressive, about the Lone Star State. Seeking perhaps to be courteous in the obvious manner, Tabouelle made some remark about Texas being large enough to go her own way. When Secretary Benjamin was informed and added Tabouelle to Théron, he thought he had uncovered a French plot to de-

[30] Quoted by the French consul: Alfred Paul to Thouvenel, Richmond, 12 Oct. 1862, AMAE, Correspondance politique des Consuls, E-U, XII, 132-35, unnumbered.

289

tach Texas. After all, the French minister to Mexico, Alphonse Dubois de Saligny, had been in charge in Texas in 1844 when France and Britain tried to prevent her annexation to the United States. With Mexico in French hands, the Rio Grande would be a truly vital frontier of the New France—or so Benjamin saw it. The secretary ordered the expulsion of the two consuls. Tabouelle was able to get a reprieve by pleading innocent, and Théron, by procrastinating and falling ill, was able to stay in Galveston till 1864 when he died.[31]

Meanwhile the whole matter had been aired in the North and equally resented there. The federal government, of course, was sure that Texas and Maine were inseparable; that, in fact, was mainly what the Civil War was about, and had Paris really been trying to detach Texas, there would in all likelihood have been a Franco-American war. Drouyn de Lhuys himself brought the matter up with Dayton and issued a most categorical denial, but not in time to prevent the *New York Times* from featuring Texas in its brief anti-France, anti-Mercier campaign. Right over its blast of 20 February 1863 at "the French Minister at Washington," it ran "Designs of France in America," in which the Théron affair was bracketed with the emperor's letter to Forey about Latin resurgence in the New World.[32]

Seward reacted as calmly to this turbulence as he did to all the other winter storms of 1863. He told Dayton that the

[31] For general coverage of the Texas incident, see Carland Elaine Crook, "Benjamin Theron and French Designs in Texas during the Civil War," *Southwestern Historical Quarterly*, LXVIII (1965), 432-54; and Bonham, *Studies in Southern History and Politics*, pp. 102-03.

[32] For the captured documents, see *National Intelligencer* (Washington), 17 Jan. 1863. For Drouyn de Lhuys's denial, see Dayton to Seward, Paris, 13 Feb. 1863, State Dept. Corres., France, Dispatches, LIII, no. 269, also in *For. Rel. U.S.* 1863, II, 711-12. The *Times* articles are in *New York Times*, 20 Feb. 1863.

United States did not think France guilty; that was for the published record.[33] Privately the secretary seems to have remained on his guard. In July he supported the move to send a Union expedition into western Texas, partly because he feared a French coup.[34] Rumors of French designs on Texas and Louisiana persisted into the fall and were insistently denied in Paris.[35]

THE TRIUMPH OF 1863

Mercier had said that if the French achieved their Mexican objectives, he feared future complications. It was a full year after the 1862 defeat before any of the French objectives could be said to have been achieved, and this achievement brought with it just the complications that Mercier had feared. On 19 May 1863 the French finally took Puebla, and on 10 June they entered Mexico City. General Forey and the French minister Saligny first organized a provisional Mexican government under General Almonte; then, on 10 July 1863, an assembly of notables convened. The assembly's decision was for a monarchy under Maximilian von Habsburg.

Despite all this, the Mexican venture remained vastly unpopular in France; the victories of May and June were

[33] Seward to Dayton, Washington, 2 March 1863, State Dept. Corres., France, Instructions, XVI, 342-43, no. 308, also in *For. Rel. U.S.*, 1863, II, 716.

[34] *Lincoln Works*, ed. Basler, VI, 354-55, 355n.

[35] See Drouyn de Lhuys to Mercier, Paris, 13 Sept. 1863, AMAE, CP, E-U, 130: 189-90, no. 21, also in *LJ*, IV (1863), 123-24; Dayton to Seward, Paris, 9 Oct. 1863, State Dept. Corres., France, Dispatches, LIII, no. 361, an extract of which is in *For. Rel. U.S.*, 1863, II, 789-90. Théron's story was that in writing to Lubbock he had merely been gathering material for a book (Théron to Méjan, Galveston, 4 Feb. 1863, AMAE, Correspondance politique des Consuls, E-U, XIV, 177, no. 495; Crook, *Southwestern Historical Quarterly*, LXVIII [1965], 441).

hailed primarily because they seemed to permit an early withdrawal.[36] Mercier seems to have felt that way too, the more so because of danger from the United States:

> We have just learned of the fall of Puebla; and I cannot refrain from expressing to Your Excellency all the joy I feel at this news which will be welcomed with so much satisfaction by the emperor and by France, and which will put an end to those speculations against us which American ill-will, fed by all sorts of false rumors, liked to entertain. In the United States more than anywhere else the success which our arms have just achieved is bound to produce an impression favorable to our influence.[37]

If Mercier meant by that that French power in the New World would somehow be able to push America into ending the Civil War, he was surely too optimistic. Seward suspected something of the sort and knew how to meet threat with threat:

> We cannot think so unkindly of the Emperor of the French as to believe that his recent success in Mexico would influence his judgment upon a question so entirely independent of the merits of his war against that republic, and at the same time so profoundly interesting to the United States.[38]

Mercier was involved in the spring of 1863 in an incident of considerable importance related to Mexico. It all began

[36] Case, *French Opinion on U.S. and Mexico*, p. 310; Nancy Nichols Barker, "The Influence of the Empress Eugénie on Foreign Affairs of the Second Empire," doctoral dissertation, University of Pennsylvania, 1955, pp. 187-88.

[37] Mercier to Drouyn de Lhuys, Washington, 2 June 1863, AMAE, CP, E-U, 130: 101-05, no. 154. The last three words were added as an afterthought.

[38] Seward to Dayton, Washington, 8 July 1863, State Dept. Corres., France, Instructions, xvi, 399-400, no. 368.

with an interesting historico-geographical coincidence: in two adjacent countries, Mexico and the United States, there were civil wars being waged simultaneously, with France so heavily involved in one that she dominated the conservative side. At various points along the Rio Grande these wars had the chance to touch each other in some way or other, but geography singled out the importance of Matamoros, Mexico, and Brownsville, Texas, two towns opposite each other where the river empties into the Gulf. From Washington's point of view, goods shipped into Matamoros were in good order so long as nothing worthwhile crossed the river into Confederate-held Texas. For Paris it was the other way around: goods bound for the Confederacy would have to worry about Union cruisers but were otherwise unexceptionable so long as they did not enter Matamoros and aid Juárez. It was a situation fraught with possibilities, especially for enterprising merchants.

Charles Wilkes of *Trent* fame steamed into this situation, and the results were inevitably disconcerting. On 25 February 1863, Wilkes, aboard the *Vanderbilt*, stopped and seized the British merchantman *Peterhoff* near the Virgin Islands. Wilkes reasoned that since the *Peterhoff* was bound for Matamoros, her cargo must be intended for Brownsville and the Confederacy. He conducted his prize to New York, and Anglo-American tension mounted sharply until a United States court declared against Wilkes and released the *Peterhoff*. In observing this situation, Mercier was struck by Seward's conciliatory gesture in having the ship's mail delivered unopened to the British consulate in New York— this despite the fact that an examination of the mail might have revealed the *Peterhoff*'s real destination.[39]

The capture of the *Peterhoff* alarmed a great many peo-

---

[39] Mercier to Drouyn de Lhuys, Washington, 5 May 1863, AMAE, CP, E-U, 130: 49-53, no. 148. See also Mercier to Drouyn de Lhuys, Washington, 25 May 1863, *ibid.*, fol. 85-88, no. 153.

ple, including Lloyd's of London, which began refusing insurance coverage to ships bound for Matamoros. Certain shippers then got the bright idea of appealing to Charles Francis Adams, the Union minister in Great Britain, for certification that their cargoes were not bound for the Confederacy but only for Mexico. In one particular case Adams, to his ultimate keen embarrassment, granted the request. Two characters named Zirman and Howell came to him in April with such a request. They bore letters of introduction from prominent Americans, and Adams saw no reason not to write a letter, addressed to Admiral S. F. Du Pont, which would help them obtain insurance. Unfortunately Zirman showed the letter a bit too widely, a copy of it was published, and Adams became the butt of a considerable outcry. British merchants wanted to know by what right the American minister thought he could approve or disapprove shipping ventures and how this precedent would affect their own Matamoros trips.[40]

But this was only the beginning of the problem, for in approving the Zirman–Howell expedition, Adams had ostensibly helped to supply Juárez and had done it "with pleasure," all of which was now part of the published record and was read with interest in Paris. There Drouyn de Lhuys wondered greatly if this represented some sharp anti-French shift in American policy or some kind of Yankee underhand shrewdness. He called in Dayton and then wrote a long letter to Mercier rehearsing the whole affair so that Seward would be properly accosted with Adams's performance:

[40] Adams to Seward, London, 18 and 23 April 1863, State Dept. Corres., Great Britain, Dispatches, LXXXIII, nos. 383 and 384. Appended to the former is a copy of Adams to Du Pont, London, 9 April 1863. See also Baron Gros to Drouyn de Lhuys, London, 22 April 1863, AMAE, CP, Angleterre, 724: 71-76, no. 56; and La Gorce, IV, 361-62.

In giving Messrs. Howell and Zirman the letter which they solicited, . . . Mr. Adams must have realized the cooperation which he was giving to an enterprise of war contraband which he knew was being undertaken against us; there would be, therefore, reason to ask ourselves by what oversight the minister of a friendly power was led to favor in this way acts overtly directed against France. . . . It is with pleasure that he learns the aim of the intended enterprise. The sending of arms and munitions . . . becomes legitimate as soon as it is intended to benefit the enemies of France.[41]

Even before receiving this, Mercier went to see Seward about what Adams had done. Seward was apologetic and said that Adams must have been duped by those letters of introduction and should have known that only he, Seward, could write such a letter for it to have any effect on policy. Mercier was able to supply Drouyn de Lhuys with a little background on "General" Zirman. He had known him in Madrid twenty years earlier where Zirman claimed to be an agent of Prince Metternich; when "Captain" Zirman fled after getting into some sort of scrape, the French arrested him at the border. In 1862 Mexican "Admiral" Zirman turned up in Washington, and it was Mercier's intervention which stopped Congress from commissioning him as a Union general! Finally, Mercier showed that he had already anticipated the foreign ministry's thought: "I would like to know what Mr. Seward would say if our ambassador in London recommended to our cruisers that they let a ship pass bound for Matamoros with

[41] Drouyn de Luhys to Mercier, Paris, 23 April 1863, AMAE, CP, E-U, 130: 38-40, no. 10, also in *LJ,* IV (1863), 115-18. See also Dayton to Seward, Paris, 24 April 1863, State Dept. Corres., France, Dispatches, LIII, no. 301, also in *For. Rel. U.S.,* 1863, II, 729-31. For another account of the Zirman–Howell affair, see Case and Spencer, pp. 517-21.

contraband of war on the pretext that this contraband was destined for the Confederates rather than the Mexicans."[42]

When Mercier presented Drouyn de Lhuys's protest, then, Seward could only repeat his apologetic interpretation. In writing Dayton he admitted that France had a right to an explanation, and the French foreign minister pronounced himself satisfied with the outcome. Slidell had rather hoped that the whole business would lead to Mercier's recall, but he had to report that such was not the case.[43]

Before the Zirman–Howell affair, Seward had given an interesting hint to Mercier, more interesting and clever than practical. He suggested that the French navy consider blockading the port of Matamoros in order to cut off Juárez' supplies; the real aim, of course, was to keep out Confederate-bound goods which were being sent across the Rio Grande into Brownsville.[44] When Drouyn de Lhuys heard that, he told Dayton that the extra strain on the French navy would probably make such a move impossible—a cute way of telling him that Paris had no intention of pulling Washington's chestnuts from the fire.[45]

Seward was embarrassed at how concrete his hint had become by the time it came back to him from Dayton via

[42] Mercier to Drouyn de Lhuys, Washington, 5 May 1863, AMAE, CP, E-U, 130: 46-48, private, also in Mercier Family Papers.

[43] Mercier to Drouyn de Lhuys, Washington, 8 May 1863, AMAE, CP, E-U, 130: 54-58, no. 149, an excerpt of which is in *LJ*, IV (1863), 121; Seward to Dayton, Washington, 8 May 1863, State Dept. Corres., France, Instructions, XVI, 370-75, no. 341, also in *For. Rel. U.S.*, 1863, II, 735-37; Drouyn de Lhuys to Mercier, Paris, 4 June 1863, AMAE, CP, E-U, 130: 108-12, no. 14, the relevant part of which is in *LJ*, IV (1863), 121-22; Slidell to Benjamin, Paris, 12 June 1863, *ORN*, 2nd ser., III, 806-07.

[44] Mercier to Drouyn de Lhuys, Washington, 21 April 1863, AMAE, CP, E-U, 130: 32-33, no. 146.

[45] Dayton to Seward, Paris, 8 May 1863, State Dept. Corres., France, Dispatches, LIII, no. 305. See also Drouyn de Lhuys to Mercier, Paris, 14 May 1863, AMAE, CP, E-U, 130: 74-76, no. 13.

Mercier and Drouyn de Lhuys. Dayton's letter, which Seward had to forward to Sumner's committee, was especially troubling; politicians unfriendly to the secretary would be glad to know that he had suggested a French blockade against Juárez! Seward therefore wrote a strong denial, claiming that Mercier had misunderstood him.[46]

MERCIER'S SECRET PLAN

Mercier's last summer and fall in the New World were a time of insistent rumor and speculation about the ultimate settlement of the Mexican problem and the ways in which such settlement might affect the American Civil War. As forces under General Bazaine wrestled with Juárez' guerrillas, the French extended control of Mexican territory. By the first of the new year this included most of the land between the capital and San Luis Potosí on the north and Guadalajara on the west; the country between Vera Cruz and the capital was solidly in their hands. At the same time a delegation from the conservative assembly of notables arrived in Austria, saw Maximilian at Miramar, and begged his acceptance of the Mexican crown.

Lincoln and Seward, working as one man since April of 1861, hewed steadily to the line that the United States could not afford a war with France so long as the Civil War continued. It took some doing for them to mollify the ultra-nationalists in Congress who wanted a harder line against France. Senator Sumner, for example, who previously had been almost friendly with Mercier, lashed out at Napoleon III in his famous (and interminable) foreign-policy speech of 10 September: "Trampler upon the Republic in France— trampler upon the Republic in Mexico—it remains to be

---

[46] Seward to Dayton, Washington, 23 May 1863, State Dept. Corres., France, Instructions, XVI, 383-84, no. 348, also in *For. Rel. U.S.*, 1863, II, 740. See also Mercier to Drouyn de Lhuys, Washington, 24 May 1863, AMAE, CP, E-U, 130: 81-84, no. 152.

seen if the French Emperor can prevail as trampler upon this Republic."[47] Seward wrote to congratulate the senator, his comment all tact and politics: "You are on the right track. Rouse the nationality of the American people. It is an instinct upon which you can always rely, even when the conscience that ought never to slumber is drugged to death."[48]

In September such elements as the Théron incident in Texas, the emperor's known sympathy for the South, his dream of a Latin block to American expansion, and the success of his army in Mexico gave rise to such speculation that Dayton felt he had better inquire at the foreign ministry. Was France about to recognize the South, he wanted to know, and had Paris and Richmond already agreed that Texas and part of Louisiana be given to France or Mexico? Drouyn de Lhuys brushed aside such wild rumors and countered with his own equivalent: was the United States about to threaten France in an official note, to conclude an alliance with Russia, to send a fleet to Vera Cruz? With all these rumors sharply denied, Franco-American relations relaxed a little, at least on the official level. Mercier gave Seward a copy of Drouyn de Lhuys's dispatch, and Seward had it published.[49]

In all sincerity Seward wanted France to know what a corner she was getting herself into in Mexico. America, he said, knew that Mexican public opinion favored a domestically organized republic over a French-inspired monarchy.

[47] Charles Sumner, *Works*, 15 vols. (Boston: Lee & Shepard, 1875-1883), vii, 327-471.

[48] Quoted in *ibid.*, p. 478.

[49] Drouyn de Lhuys to Mercier, Paris, 13 Sept. 1863, AMAE, CP, E-U, 130: 189-90, no. 21, also in *LJ*, iv (1863), 123-24; for the translation, see State Dept. Corres., Notes from the French Legation, xxi, also in *For. Rel. U.S.*, 1863, ii, 836-37. See also Dayton to Seward, Paris, 16 Sept. 1863, State Dept. Corres., France, Dispatches, liii, no. 347, and *Evening Star* (Washington), 24 Sept. 1863.

American civilization would ultimately foil attempts by foreign powers to control the hemisphere and the United States deemed republicanism among its neighbors as necessary to its own safety.[50]

Mercier, who saw as confirmed his fears that Mexico might muddy relations between France and America, had his own thoughts about this. In a dispatch to Drouyn de Lhuys he first sized up the American situation, then dropped a hint about Mexico—and about his perennial maladjustment to life in the United States. The peace faction, he found, was taking some encouragement from the relative lull on the battlefield, the fact that the Union momentum seemed gone, and the efforts of peace-candidates Vallandigham and George Woodward to win the governorships of Ohio and Pennsylvania. In spite of this, Mercier noted, Washington seemed unconcerned about the secret peace organizations in the West.

Then Mercier returned to an earlier theme and pressed his request for permission to come home on leave:

> A prisoner whose chains had been removed would feel less relieved than my poor wife, who since her arrival has not stopped suffering from homesickness. . . . I tell you that apart from any personal consideration, I feel a serious need to come and talk with you about our interests in America. By dint of reflecting on those interests and on the best way to make the circumstances serve them, I think I am on to a path which could lead us to arrangements at once most secure and best designed to resolve the Mexican question whether the Archduke accepts or refuses the crown.[51]

[50] Seward to Dayton, Washington, 26 Sept. 1863, State Dept. Corres., France, Instructions, xvi, 451-58.

[51] Mercier [to Drouyn de Lhuys], New York, 10 Oct. 1863, Mercier Family Papers. The fact that no copy of this letter exists in the archives of the foreign ministry probably means either that Mercier

Whether or not he could make the circumstances solve the Mexican problem, Mercier at least thought that the Mexican problem could be used to solve circumstances, namely the circumstance of his own exile. To a foreign minister caught up in the Mexican mess, Mercier hinted that he had a way out, but he would have to be allowed home to reveal it.

Mercier's Mexican plan sought to unite the Mexican and the American questions. Sometime during the last week of October he broke down and revealed the plan to Drouyn de Lhuys. Any state as big and as liberal as the United States, he said, was bound to crack up sooner or later anyway. Four score and seven years was about all anyone could sensibly expect from it. But economic union was something else again:

> Granted, then, that political division and economic unity offer a solution at once possible and desirable, . . . I ask myself if we should not seek to extend this principle to Mexico and if a tariff union between this country and North America . . . would not be of a sort to resolve some of the great difficulties which the establishment of a Mexican monarchy must encourage.[52]

This, then, was the plan which Mercier had first thought so worth the ministry's while that Drouyn de Lhuys would grant him a leave just to hear it. It was an ill-conceived effort to make a common market solve two of the century's thorniest problems of nationality and state sovereignty, problems which at the moment were causing men to kill one another in Virginia, Tennessee, and South Carolina—

---

never sent it or that Drouyn de Lhuys considered it so personal that he put it aside.

[52] Mercier to Drouyn de Lhuys, Washington, n.d. Oct. 1863, AMAE, CP, E-U, 130: 219-22, private.

and in Mexico. Mercier never would accept the most compelling fact that had been staring him in the face for almost three years: Americans—some of them, enough of them—cared more about national wholeness than they did about prosperity, or even life for that matter. Finally, Mercier could not explain how the marvelous benefits of free trade with the South and with Mexico would induce Washington to accept not only Maximilian but also Jefferson Davis.

As a climax to three and a half years of reflection upon Mexico, Mercier's secret plan is in poor taste. But if we take all of his Mexican thinking into consideration, his record must be accounted good. Despite the fact that Paris declined to consult him on the 1861 three-power intervention and even delayed informing him of it, Mercier made sure he was heard. "The American people," he said, ". . . will be made to see in this resolution an eagerness to take advantage of their difficulty which will be very irritating to them."[53] Nothing occurred in the next six years to justify a retreat from that unassailable judgment. The irritation kept growing, veered directly against France, and almost exploded into a Franco-American war.

Though the term was not yet in use, what Mercier was saying was that Mexico was in the American "sphere of influence." As a French nationalist Mercier did not particularly like that fact, but he recognized its importance, and he knew the ultimate outcome of any protracted European stay in Mexico. With all the other difficulties current between France and America, difficulties whose happy resolution was his solemn responsibility, Mercier saw no sufficient reason for France to be in Mexico. When it became evident to him in 1862 that Britain and Spain were out of the game and that France would push on alone, Mercier grew more alarmed. To Thouvenel and to Prince Napoleon

[53] Mercier to Thouvenel, Washington, 22 Oct. 1861, *ibid.*, 125: 151-63, no. 66.

he specified the kind of sorry reward France might expect —trouble from the United States, trouble from a poverty-stricken and ungovernable Mexican people. It is hard to say just how courageous Mercier was in his persistent criticism. The fact of his persistence is in his favor, but he may have been careful not to go too far, and he conceded that "European considerations" might overbalance his own arguments against the venture. Seward's calmness on this subject went far to relieve Mercier's mind, but Mercier still went on record with Thouvenel as hoping the enterprise would prove abortive.

On the specific point of installing the house of Habsburg in Mexico, Mercier was less adamant. He welcomed the victory at Puebla in 1863 as a proof of French power, but his acceptance of the plan to crown Maximilian was probably grounded in his desire that France obtain a way out of the affair. To non-French critics like Seward, Mercier was always ready to defend the French course of action. Feeling less at ease with Drouyn de Lhuys than he had with Thouvenel, Mercier was apparently less ready in 1863 to unburden himself of his thoughts. His overreliance on tariff union as a panacea for the ills of the hemisphere betrayed him into concocting a secret formula for Mexico, a formula which was partly designed to obtain permission to come home and explain it. We can credit Mercier, then, with astute judgment of the Mexican involvement and correct assessment of its probable outcome. It is less clear, however, that he had the confidence and perseverance to carry on the dialogue vigorously into 1863. The unbelligerent attitude of Washington and the hope that Maximilian's entry would prepare the exit of France help to explain this change.

Throughout 1863, then, Mexico was an increasing vexation to anyone as interested in good Franco-American relations as was Mercier. There were other problems, of course, and the relative quiescence of the intervention issue tended to underline their individual importance. We may now return to Mercier's diplomatic activity in the spring, summer, and winter of 1863, an activity which touched upon a number of international difficulties.

CHAPTER XI

A Sea of Troubles

MERCIER'S LIFE IN CORCORAN'S HOUSE

FOLLOWING the Georgetown fire, his trip to Richmond and his summer vacation, in the fall of 1862 Mercier accepted the offer of William W. Corcoran to live in his luxurious "H" Street home. By moving the legation into this house, the French minister risked adding to the mounting criticism of his own supposed Confederate leanings. From a purely personal viewpoint, however, the opportunity to live in one of Washington's most notable buildings was a blessing indeed, and Mercier undoubtedly hoped that it would ease his wife's burden of exile.

The house was brick, in three stories, with one-story wings on each side of the main structure. One of the wings contained the famous Corcoran art collection, which after the war was removed to its own museum; the other included an arched driveway leading to the garden and the stable area.[1] Prince Napoleon during his 1861 visit had stopped at the house. His reaction was not very favorable: ". . . Anglo-American style, large, but overdone and in rather bad taste; lovely greenhouses and gardens. . . ."[2] From Mercier's point of view the location was ideal—right opposite Lafayette Square, within easy walking distance of the

[1] The author is indebted for this information to Mr. and Mrs. David E. Finley of Washington. Mrs. Finley, née Eustis, is the granddaughter of George Eustis and Corcoran's daughter Louise.
[2] Prince Napoleon's diary, p. 263.

State Department and the White House. Near at hand were such buildings of the Virginia-dynasty era as the Tayloe–Cameron house, Dolly Madison's Cutts–Madison house, the Decatur house, and the British legation; the last two, like the White House, were designed by Benjamin Latrobe. The Corcoran house must have been highly prized, for Lyons let it be known that he wanted it should Mercier return to France.[3] Many of the diplomatic corps, in fact, were tenants of Mr. Corcoran; Mercier and especially Baron Gerolt of Prussia were his friends as well.

As the Merciers took up their rooms on "H" Street, Corcoran sailed for France, where his daughter Louise and her husband George Eustis had spectacularly preceded him. Exactly what went on in Paris of a politically interesting character is hard to determine, but the natural course of family affection bound Corcoran and the Eustises together and with them Eustis's employer, John Slidell. Beyond that, Slidell's daughter Matilda married into the famous Erlanger family, the banking house which handled the 1863 Confederate loan. In 1866, with Corcoran back home but the Slidells still in exile, Matilda's sister Rosine recalled those troubled but pleasant days on the rue de la Ville l'Évêque. "Papa and I went there a few days since . . . ," she wrote, "and I assure you it seemed quite dismal not to find our mutual friend, Mr. C. by the fireside, not to hear the little ones prattling and toddling about, and not to see Loulie's merry face."[4]

---

[3] *Guide to the Architecture of Washington, D.C.,* pp. 73-77. On Lyons and the house, see Hyde to Corcoran, n.p., 3 Nov. 1863, Corcoran Papers.

[4] Rosine Slidell to Corcoran, n.p., 1 Dec. 1866, Corcoran Papers. There was an even more striking indication of Corcoran's activities in early 1865 when Duncan F. Kenner of Louisiana came to Europe as part of Benjamin's last wan effort to obtain foreign help. Kenner went to Paris where he met both Mason and Slidell: "When they came together, Mr. Kenner, seeing that W. W. Corcoran was in

Corcoran's friend, business associate, and factotum Anthony Hyde looked after his property and interests for the
duration of the war. He had reason to fear that Corcoran's
unsatisfactory attitude toward the Republican government
might yet do him in. Rumors circulated—for example, that
Corcoran had helped finance the *Alabama*—and Hyde
wished that his friend had met "the demand made before
you left, humiliating as it was,"[5] which was probably a suggestion that he take an oath of allegiance. But Corcoran
managed a safe return in 1865, and he spent his later years
in dignified and munificent patronage of his beloved Washington. He became, in fact, a friend of the Grants.

Hyde's reports to Corcoran throw some light on the domestic side of Mercier's last year in the United States, but
the light is fitful, and the glimpses it provides are fleeting.
There are Mercier and Gerolt deciding how the coal in
the cellar is to be divided. There is Stoeckl asking Corcoran's gardener for the loan of some plants and being
politely refused. There is Hyde brushing off a tax collector
with the statement that Corcoran's plate is now being used
by the minister of France (the brush-off was later redressed
by the Treasury Department, and Hyde paid the tax). There
is Hyde again, worried about government confiscation and
giving Mercier the key to one of Corcoran's closets in which
are concealed some stocks. There are the Merciers giving a
large party. And there is the elusive Cécile-Élisabeth pre-
siding gently and leniently over the Irish servants.

---

the room, said: 'I was directed to show my instructions to Mr.
Mason and Mr. Slidell and to no one else.' But the latter gentlemen
informed him that he could safely proceed in the presence of Corcoran as he was their confidential adviser" (William Wirt Henry,
"Memoranda of Kenner's Narrative," quoted in James Morton Callahan, *The Diplomatic History of the Southern Confederacy* [Balti-
more: Johns Hopkins University Press, 1901], pp. 264-65).

[5] Hyde to Corcoran, New York, 14 May 1863, Corcoran Papers.

The servants, in fact, are a good part of Hyde's fussy correspondence. Just before Mercier rented the house, with Corcoran away in New England, Hyde was required to prosecute one of them for petty larceny. Daniel his name was, and after he was apprehended in New York and brought back to the capital, the hardware room of the "H" Street house disgorged a cache of sugar, preserves, cigars, champagne, and a picture of Mrs. Eustis, apparently on the way to being stolen! Earlier this same Daniel had put something into Corcoran's soup, not poison, but something bad-tasting, in an effort to make his pilfering easier by getting the cook fired. When Mercier took over the house, his own steward, a friend of Daniel's, caused an equal amount of trouble.

One difficult addition to the Mercier ménage was a Miss Anne Fletcher, whom Corcoran had apparently met some time before and had hired as a housekeeper when her ventures as a schoolmistress and maker of army shirts had failed. The Merciers' first impression of her was highly favorable, but conflict soon developed between Miss Fletcher and the steward. Hyde at first sided with Miss Fletcher and suspected the steward of taking graft, by taking money, for example, from both Mercier and the gardener for the gardener's room. Later, however, he set Miss Fletcher down as "overzealous." According to her, the Merciers were too good natured and lenient about such things. Trouble of this sort continued right up to the time that Mercier left America.[6]

All that aside, the important aspect of Mercier's residence on "H" Street was the fact that his landlord was in France and was a friend of John Slidell and the Erlangers. In some ways Mercier seems to have been a little imprudent about this. Frequently, at Mercier's own suggestion, Hyde sent

[6] The above information on domestic matters is taken from the letters of Anthony Hyde to William W. Corcoran in Corcoran Papers.

his letters to Corcoran via the "house," i.e., the legation. Sometimes these letters were directed to the Paris banking firm of Vandenbroeck Brothers, and sometimes to Corcoran's Paris house. At one point they were not getting through, and Mercier suggested that Corcoran inquire for them at the foreign ministry.[7] In May of 1863 a box for Corcoran, containing some important but unmentioned material, was smuggled out of the country with the cloak and dagger help of the French legation and the French consulate in New York.[8] Despite all this, Corcoran and Mercier came out of their association relatively unscathed.

For two months or so in 1863, i.e., from the end of February to the spring military crises, there was something like a disengagement in Franco-American diplomacy. Mercier's reports were as interesting and informative as ever, but they seem somehow detached and quiet when compared with his earlier dispatches. He found the South as determined as ever to be independent,[9] but in contrast to the situation at the beginning of the year, the population of the North now seemed equally set upon reunion. "That is to say," he reported, ". . . that a new obscurity envelops the end of the war and that we can no longer count on anything except unforeseen events to dissipate it."[10]

Once more it was Britain which came to the fore as the Union's chief worry. The *Alabama* and *Florida* depredations had hit New York shippers hard. Now it was the Confederacy's ironclad rams, a-building at Liverpool, which were striking something like terror into Northern hearts. Mercier got that directly from Senator Sumner, but still the min-

[7] Hyde to Corcoran, Washington, 29 Dec. 1862, *ibid.*

[8] See Riggs and Co. to Hyde, New York, 2 May 1863; Hyde to Corcoran, Washington, 4 May and 30 June 1863, *ibid.*

[9] Mercier to Drouyn de Lhuys, Washington, 20 March 1863, AMAE, CP, E-U, 129: 228-29, private.

[10] Mercier to Drouyn de Lhuys, Washington, 7 April 1863, *ibid.*, 130: 8-11, no. 143.

MR. SEWARD AND THE FRENCHMAN.

M. MERCIER. "He have trow down his Glove. Sall I peek it up? hein! Ah! by Gar! no—it is too moch big. I like better to fight wit de little Mexican."

Harper's Weekly, 11 April 1863.

309

ister felt that no Anglo-American war would result. Somebody would back down before things got to that point.[11]

Washington's decision to go ahead with national conscription raised some hope of reinvigorating the peace movement,[12] but it was the arrest of Clement Vallandigham which most intrigued Mercier. On 1 May the famous congressman made a speech at Mount Vernon, Ohio, in which he accused the administration of shedding needless blood for the liberation of Negroes while enslaving whites with violations of their civil rights. The government, he said, should have accepted France's offer of mediation. Ambrose Burnside, who had been shelved in Ohio after Fredericksburg and the January "mud march," arrested Vallandigham, denied him habeas corpus, and had him tried by a military court which sentenced him to confinement. President Lincoln, embarrassed, commuted the sentence and exiled the congressman behind Confederate lines, whence he later made his way via Canada back into Ohio. Mercier saw some hope for peace in Burnside's foolish severity: "As for the party of peace in the North, it was only waiting for an opportunity to come back on stage, and General Burnside has just provided it by having Mr. Vallandigham arrested. This excess of zeal on the part of a military authority has made a very lively impression."[13]

As always, the political and diplomatic situation depended upon military events, and with the return of spring there were events enough. In the West the very continuity of Confederate life depended on a stretch of the Mississippi River between Port Hudson on the south and Vicksburg on the north—the only stretch left to the Southern army and

[11] Mercier to Drouyn de Lhuys, Washington, 7 April 1863, AMAE, CP, E-U, 130: 8-11, no. 143.

[12] Mercier to Drouyn de Lhuys, Washington, 11 May 1863, ibid., fol. 62-69, no. 150.

[13] Randall and Donald, p. 303; Mercier to Drouyn de Lhuys, Washington, 19 May 1863, Mercier Family Papers.

therefore the only link between the eastern and western halves of the would-be nation. Here Ulysses S. Grant had been probing, dodging, and finally thrusting at Vicksburg to the utter confusion of Confederate General John C. Pemberton. On 22 May the long siege of Vicksburg began. Mercier reported the Union victory six months prematurely and thought that it had made any "peaceful transaction" that much less likely.[14]

In the East things were different. The attack of the iron-clads on Charleston failed, and the Army of the Potomac made one more unsuccessful effort to get around Lee. General Joe Hooker led them in this third attempt to push beyond Fredericksburg. A great many Americans died that first week of May, among them Stonewall Jackson, whose exploits in this battle of Chancellorsville did much to make it a vast Union defeat. Hooker joined Burnside, Pope, and McClellan in failure. Mercier found that this time the Union was reacting calmly; the North was hardened now, he said, and still confident; peace seemed further off than it had after Fredericksburg.[15]

To Mercier "peace" always meant a negotiated settlement which in all likelihood would begin with Northern recognition of the South's independence. That the North would simply slug on, crushing the South with hammer blows, freeing the slaves and fastening national sovereignty like a vise on Southern states seemed to him a tragic prospect. He could not see how such a settlement could last: surely the South would be too resentful ever to give her allegiance willingly to the national ideal, and surely freed slaves

[14] Mercier to Drouyn de Lhuys, Washington, 25 May 1863, AMAE, CP, E-U, 130: 85-88, no. 153.

[15] Mercier to Drouyn de Lhuys, Washington, 11 May 1863, *ibid.*, fol. 62-69, no. 150. Mercier referred to the battle of Chancellorsville as "Fredericksburg," but his meaning is clear enough from the context and date of his dispatch.

and white Americans would be incapable of living together in harmony. These basic premises made Mercier ever expectant of some development, if only the 1864 elections, which would break the logjam and bring the only kind of peace he thought viable. Viewing the Civil War from such premises, Mercier still was objective enough to record his surroundings with a great degree of accuracy. His comments in the wake of Chancellorsville are a tribute to that objectivity.

On 30 and 31 May, the legislative elections were held in France. To a body of 261 representatives, the opposition elected 32, about half of them republicans. This was a smaller number than would have been elected had the government not backed its official list with massive, pervasive aid; it was a significant increase over the opposition in the previous legislature. A slight but significant degree of political liberalization is part of the explanation for this, but the economic slump of 1862 was perhaps a more pressing factor. The American Civil War, therefore, played some part in the opposition's moral victory. Seward had his own interpretation of the election results:

The alternating reaction of liberal principles and rigorous ones in France comes sooner or later to be the chief subject of study for every representative of our Country who sojourns there. . . .

Mr. Mercier seems to estimate the respective conflicting forces in Paris by the same scale that you have assumed. I cannot doubt that the republicanism of France has derived some strength from violence done by real or seeming Imperial organs to the cause of republicanism in America. What has happened may prove beneficent to both countries, if it shall cause our civil war to be regarded in France less with regard to the material or commercial interests which are affected, and more with reference to the social and political questions which have been brought by reactionists to the test of battle.[16]

American leaders, even Buchanan, had always seen it that way: America stood for civil liberty and representative government, and if the federal government could not now hold its country together, freedom would suffer everywhere. The Civil War was many things to many people. To Mercier it was a senseless and brutal waste of life. To Seward and to Lincoln it was a fight for the dignity of ordinary men.

LETTERS OF MARQUE

This was a period of relatively minor irritants, for example the Northern threat to begin commissioning privateers. Though Seward had earlier offered to adhere to the 1856 Declaration of Paris, the governments of Britain and France had seen through the ruse and had declined to assist the United States in suppressing Confederate corsairs. Both North and South, therefore, were free to issue letters of marque. By the end of 1861, the Confederacy had found that the armed merchantman was a useless weapon, primarily because European countries would not open their ports to captured prizes. With the South, devoid of a regular navy, it was at least understandable that she would resort to this classic American means of naval retaliation. With the North, on the contrary, there was no such ready explanation. In fact it was emotional pique more than anything else which brought on this threat, and the pique was primarily Seward's.

The very fact that the South had almost no commercial ships afloat would preclude the success of a Northern pri-

[16] Seward to Dayton, Washington, 20 June 1863, State Dept. Corres., France, Instructions, xvi, 392-93. The extracts in *For. Rel. U.S.*, 1863, ii, 745-46, do not include the sentence about Mercier.

vateering campaign. Cruisers like the *Alabama* had nothing to fear from corsairs. That left neutral shipping, and here Seward himself was anxious not to be misunderstood: he told Dayton to make it clear in France that it had not yet been decided whether the president should use his authority, and that even should that decision be affirmative, every effort would be made to prevent harm to "friendly" nations.[17]

That left the question of "unfriendly" nations. It was surely Great Britain which was the main object of Seward's ire. The *Alabama*, built at Birkenhead near Liverpool, was taking a serious toll of Northern commercial shipping, and Seward seems to have thought that a threat to use privateers could help prevent a recurrence. Mercier speculated about other motives:

> Basically, I think, his chief aim is to engender war fever and to satisfy the chamber of commerce of New York. Moreover, I think there would be a perfectly legitimate way to prevent its being implemented; this would be to declare that in such a case France and England would open their ports to belligerent corsairs and their prizes. To judge by the exploits of the *Alabama*, nothing more would be needed to make it possible for the South to destroy the North's commerce and thus to bring about peace.[18]

The bill authorizing letters of marque became law on 3 March, but in fact the president never did issue such a let-

[17] Seward to Dayton, Washington, 20 Feb. 1863, State Dept. Corres., France, Instructions, xvi, 340-41, no. 304, also in *For. Rel. U.S.*, 1863, II, 713.

[18] Mercier to Drouyn de Lhuys Washington, 24 Feb. 1863, AMAE, CP, E-U, 129: 148-52, private. For an indication that Seward was chiefly trying to stop further outfitting of Confederate warships, see Seward to Dayton, Washington, 24 April 1863, State Dept. Corres., France, Instructions, xvi, 365-68, no. 336, also in *For. Rel. U.S.*, 1863, II, 723-33.

ter, an eloquent proof of the measure's inanity. Mercier found Seward's fondness for the move quite inexplicable and noted that the secretary's colleagues and even Senator Sumner were against the idea.[19] Drouyn de Lhuys greeted the threat with a shrug, blandly stating that even should the United States go ahead with it, Franco-American commercial relations need not be disturbed.[20]

POLAND

Thouvenel had given Italy and Mexico as two good reasons for France not to become involved in the American Civil War. Almost coincidental with the French approach of 9 January 1863, there was yet another reason why a negative response from Washington would find Paris too preoccupied elsewhere to indulge in much resentment. On 22 January a Polish revolutionary committee, fruit of an ancient nationalism and of the rising expectations engendered by Alexander II's slow reforms, declared war against the czar. Even before the French government had made its decision to intervene diplomatically, it was well understood that this most poignant fight for national self-determination would fully engage the attention of Napoleon III. For along with Woodrow Wilson, the emperor was probably the most consistent champion of that difficult national principle in the last two hundred years. Just as Seward's rejection of the 9 January overture became known in Paris, Dayton was reporting that "the insurrection of Poland has driven American Affairs out of view for the moment." And Judah Benjamin realized well that recognition by France was temporarily out of the question.[21]

[19] Mercier to Drouyn de Lhuys, Washington, 30 March 1863, AMAE, CP, E-U, 129: 251-54, no. 141.

[20] Drouyn de Lhuys to Mercier, Paris, 2 April 1863, *ibid.*, 130: 4-5, no. 7.

[21] Dayton to Seward, Paris, 23 Feb. 1863, State Dept. Corres., France, Dispatches, LIII, no. 276, also in *For. Rel. U.S.*, 1863, II, 713-

There were a number of ideological applications and parallels possible between the January rising in Poland and the American Civil War. On the one hand, Poland and the Confederacy could both be viewed as nationalities seeking legitimate self-determination. In that case the right of Abraham Lincoln to fight the Civil War was no greater than Alexander II's right to rescind his Polish reforms. One contemporary stated that Prince Napoleon and others had warned Napoleon III that if he recognized Poland, he would have to recognize the Confederacy too for the sake of consistency.[22] Like all comparisons, however, the parallel of Poland with the Confederacy could not be taken too far. Whatever an "American" was in 1863, it was plain that one language was spoken from the Great Lakes to the Rio Grande, and that the states between had voluntarily joined the Union and had never enjoyed a medieval or early modern history apart from that Union. The case of Poland was rather different, for a separate language and a separate past differentiated Poles from Russians in striking fashion.

On the other hand, the Americans of the North might well identify with Poland rather than with Russia. Self-determination, after all, had always been a logical extension of the American dream, that dream of which the Lincoln government claimed to be the only rightful heir. Supposing, then, that Washington sympathized fully with this latest example of a nation's seeking to determine its own future, was there anything to be *done* about it? This was an old question in American history, one going back as far

---

14; Benjamin to Slidell, Richmond, 24 March 1863, Eustis Papers, also in Richardson, II, 436-39. For a general treatment of the Polish revolt as it affected America and France, see Harold E. Blinn, "Seward and the Polish Rebellion of 1863," *American Historical Review*, XLV (1940), 828-33, and Case and Spencer, pp. 399-400.

[22] A. Dudley Mann to Benjamin, Brussels, 13 March 1863, Richardson, II, 436-39, no. 41.

as the Latin American revolutions in the 1820's, back even to the French Revolution. One school of thought—or better, perhaps, one occasional tendency—had called dramatically for some kind of diplomatic intervention in the common cause. The other, more "realistic," school can be summed up in the neat phrase of James Monroe relevant to the Latin Americans in the early part of their revolution: "If they cannot beat Spain, they do not deserve to be free." Even apart from the fact that America had its own problems in 1863 and could scarcely be expected to aid Poland, the attitude of the Lincoln government was affected by a whole conservative, "realist" tradition of interpreting the American dream. In this view America was the exemplar, not the defender, of political freedom; or in other words, "If they cannot beat Russia, they do not deserve to be free."[23]

By April the French emperor was ready with his proposal. As with his gentle probes into the American illness, it was long on talk and short on action, and it managed to annoy the existing government without materially helping the revolution. As Drouyn de Lhuys notified Mercier, France was conferring with England and Austria with a view to presenting joint "reflections" to St. Petersburg. Others were being invited to go along: "We call for the official adhesion of the different Governments, and we like to be persuaded that they will willingly defer to the wish which we express to them, either by addressing to the Court of Russia a communication similar to ours, or by presenting to it analogous considerations." Appended was a copy of the French note to Russia in which the Polish bloodshed was deplored and the fighting was held to "disturb the relations of Cabinets, and provoke the most regrettable complications." The liberal czar, finally, was asked to recommend a solution which would place Poland "in the conditions of lasting peace." As

[23] For another discussion of the Polish revolt and American diplomacy, see Woldman, pp. 157-59.

instructed, Mercier sent all this over to Seward for his consideration.[24]

Now it was America's turn. It was certainly not from an ideological basis only that Seward spoke—no more than was the case with the emperor, the czar, or anyone else involved. France, for one thing, was genuinely concerned about the brave Polish fight, but she also realized that if the United States could be edged into alienating Russia, there would be that much less reason to fear a Russo-American entente. Seward was genuinely committed to a policy of noninterference, but he also realized that Russia was Washington's only major diplomatic friend and that the opportunity was there to read France a lesson in staying out of other countries' concerns. With all this and more in mind, the secretary rose to the occasion.

He began by thanking Napoleon III for his kind invitation, and he expressed the Union's warm approval of this French overture. Since Alexander II was such a liberal emancipator, he continued, he would probably answer the overture "with all the favor that is consistent with the general welfare of the great state over which he presides with such eminent wisdom and moderation." But American participation was out of the question. George Washington himself had inaugurated the traditional policy of nonentanglement, even in the face of a treaty with France. Ever since then the United States had consistently rejected participation in joint diplomatic ventures and would do so now.[25]

France suffered a sharp diplomatic defeat as the czar,

[24] Drouyn de Lhuys to Mercier, Paris, 23 April 1863, no. 8, and Drouyn de Lhuys to the Duke of Montibello, Paris, 16 April 1863, translations, State Dept. Corres., Notes from the French Legation, xx; for the French versions see AMAE, CP, E-U, 130: 34-37.

[25] Seward to Dayton, Washington, 11 May 1863, State Dept. Corres., France, Instructions, xvi, 376-80, no. 342, also in For. Rel. U.S., 1863, ii, 737-39. See also Mercier to Drouyn de Lhuys, Washington, 11 May 1863, AMAE, CP, E-U, 130: 62-69, no. 150.

with Bismarck's aid, cracked down hard on the Polish revolt. The countervailing power of a great land-empire was
too much for the aspirations of French prestige. In America
a similar land-empire was at the moment distracted, and
this distraction was proving a boon to French aspirations
in Mexico.

All sorts of possibilities remained for the ultimate outcome of that distraction. General Lee might be able to
capitalize on Chancellorsville and launch a decisive counter-
blow. Something like that, in fact, was already afoot. After
a month of fruitless maneuvering, the Confederate army was
again marching north, marching into Maryland, north even
to the Pennsylvania line. Tracking it steadily was the much-
abused Army of the Potomac, walking fast, hour by hour
and day by day, back through friendly towns. The army
had a new commander now, Meade having replaced the
chastened Hooker. But the army had been through a lot
since McClellan, and the commander no longer mattered
so much as the army's will to win.

On the evening of 30 June, in a little town south of Gettysburg, Union Captain Strong Vincent sat quietly on his
horse, watching his men stride by in the moonlight as the
music played and the flags waved. "There could be worse
fates," he said, "than to die fighting here in Pennsylvania,
with that flag waving overhead. . . ."[26]

The Union Army versus the Roebuck Motion

The French proposal of 9 January 1863 had been so mild as
to seem superfluous, but it was well enough known that it
did not reflect all of the emperor's thinking. Despite the
risk of war with the United States, Napoleon III stood
ready to recognize the South if such a move could be a
joint one with Great Britain. That had been true the pre-

[26] Bruce Catton, *Glory Road* (New York: Pocket Books, 1964),
p. 283.

vious fall, and it had remained true all through the winter
and spring of 1863. There was always the chance that some
new development, economic or military, in the New World
or the Old, might move the Palmerston cabinet to reverse
its decision, but so far, even after Chancellorsville, there
had been no such development.

The Union defeat in Virginia, however, with word of a
successful Confederate counterattack expected daily, helped
to trigger the famous Roebuck motion, a renewed flare-up
of intervention fever which gave a special urgency to the
duties of General Lee and General Meade as they approached each other in southern Pennsylvania. Toward the
first of June in London, James Mason was visited by William S. Lindsay, the shipowner and member of Parliament
whose conversations with Napoleon III had played a part
in his unsuccessful intervention proposal the previous year.
With Lindsay came a fellow businessman and legislator,
John Arthur Roebuck, whose size and pugnacious personality had earned him the nickname of little "Don Roebucco."
The "don" and Lindsay wanted Mason's views about
whether they should again move for recognition of the
Confederacy.[27]

On 18 June in the Tuileries, John Slidell was granted another imperial interview. The emperor again said that the
South should be recognized but that only Great Britain
could afford enough help to France in the event of a naval
war with the United States. Warming to the subject, Napoleon told Slidell that he would be glad to receive Roebuck and Lindsay, that he would discuss recognition
with his advisers, and that he might himself propose recogni-

[27] James M. Mason, *The Public Life and Diplomatic Correspondence of James M. Mason*, ed. Virginia Mason (Roanoke, Va.: Stone
Printing and Manufacturing Co., 1903), pp. 412-14. For another
account of the Roebuck affair, see Case and Spencer, pp. 408-26.

tion directly to Lord Palmerston.[28] Roebuck and Lindsay saw the emperor shortly thereafter at Fontainebleau and were encouraged to go ahead with their motion. Accordingly, Roebuck rose on 30 June in the House and proposed that the queen enter into negotiations with other powers with a view to recognizing the Confederacy.[29] The battle of Gettysburg began within hours of Roebuck's speech.

Palmerston returned from a sickbed as the debate wore on, and at his urging it ended on 13 July with Roebuck's withdrawing his motion. Had the resolution come to a vote, it would certainly have been lost by a wide margin; even Gladstone had opposed it. A few days later word came of Gettysburg and Vicksburg; most Englishmen continued to feel that Britain would do well to abstain from the American tragedy.

For Mercier's benefit, with one eye on Seward, Drouyn de Lhuys sent an official version of what had been happening. According to this, the emperor had declined Roebuck's invitation to take the lead in proposing recognition, alleging as reason the declared negative attitude of the British cabinet; and he had not authorized Roebuck to announce his support on the floor of the Commons. He had said, however, that he would be glad to join in should Britain take the initiative. Roebuck's version, then, was held inaccurate on key points.[30]

---

[28] Slidell to Benjamin, Paris, 21 June 1863, Richardson, II, 514-17.

[29] The Austrian ambassador kept abreast of events: "Mr. Roebuck and Mr. Lindsay came directly to Fontainebleau in order to ask the Emperor whether it was true that his Majesty would no longer interfere in the affairs of America. The Emperor—as is his custom—allowed himself to be somewhat carried away and to say more on this subject, perhaps, than he wanted to. . . .

"M. Drouyn de Lhuys has not concealed from me his despair over the indiscretion committed by his Master" (Richard Metternich to Rechberg, Paris, 1 July 1863, quoted in Tyrner-Tyrnauer, pp. 85-86).

[30] Drouyn de Lhuys to Mercier, Paris, 8 July 1863, AMAE, CP, E-U, 130: 147-48, no. 17.

While all this talking and writing preoccupied western Europe in the first week of July, the American agony reached a crisis and a turning point. General Lee, who had begun his northern sweep mostly with food and supplies in mind, could see the wider implications by the time he reached Pennsylvania. Like Mercier, he now felt that a victory might revivify the Northern peace movement and bring on a negotiated settlement.[31]

On the morning of 1 July, across the rolling hills west of Gettysburg, Pennsylvania, units of the Union cavalry first sighted a Confederate column walking toward the town. For three days, then, on Wednesday, Thursday, and Friday, there occurred a battle, a meeting of men such as the New World had not yet seen, the whole building irregularly toward the climactic point of General Pickett's charge. When it was over, Robert E. Lee, self-composed, quiet, perhaps already aware of the future, ordered a retreat. Once again, as had been the case with Antietam, a Union victory had just coincided with a European peace move. But there was more. On Saturday, 4 July, General Pemberton at last surrendered the city of Vicksburg, Mississippi. With the simultaneous fall of Port Hudson, the Confederacy was now cut in two. As Union General Banks wrote to his wife, "You can tell your friends that the Confederacy is an impossibility."[32] It was the eighty-seventh anniversary of American independence.

Mercier, who had not yet left for his annual vacation in New England, had been concerned about his family's safety when the two armies marched north and had ordered the *Gassendi* as a safety measure.[33] As the great drama un-

---

[31] Catton, *Never Call Retreat*, p. 160.

[32] *Ibid.*, pp. 205-06.

[33] *Evening Star* (Washington), 3 July 1863. Lyons decided against a parallel British move: it might annoy Seward, and in any case he could always climb aboard the French ship (E. D. Adams, II, 176n.).

folded, however, he relaxed, concentrated upon observation, and then left for the Rhode Island shore:

> The Washington government has . . . every right to attach the greatest importance to the success which has just crowned its efforts; and it is certain that, with the possible exception of the fall of New Orleans, there has never been a more damaging blow to the Confederate cause since the beginning of the war.[34]

Between Mercier and Seward there seems to have been some misunderstanding about how things stood and what was now to be done. According to William Seward:

> After hearing the news of the defeat of the insurgents at Gettysburg, and the surrender of Vicksburg, Mr. Mercier called upon me and congratulated me upon the events, and declared without reserve that he regarded these disasters as fatal to the insurrection. He tendered me his good offices to the extent of suggesting to his Government that they should cause the insurgents to understand that they could no longer look to it for recognition, saying that such a suggestion was due to them as well as to the United States upon considerations of friendship and humanity. I did not accept the overture, although I thanked him cordially for making it. My only reason for waiving it was that an acceptance might possibly be construed into a willingness to invoke foreign influence in our domestic conflict.[35]

One can only speculate about this unusual statement. Nothing in Mercier's correspondence of this period shows that he thought the South was about to die, though it is

[34] Mercier to Drouyn de Lhuys, New York, 15 July 1863, AMAE, CP, E-U, 130: 149-53, private.

[35] Seward to Dayton, Washington, 10 July 1863, State Dept. Corres., France, Instructions, XVI, 401-02, no. 369.

possible that momentarily he did think so. Mercier's known propensity for reacting strongly to military shifts would also support this possibility. Again, on the point about telling the South not to look for European recognition, there is no such suggestion in Mercier's correspondence, unless one wants to speculate about ulterior meanings of broad, general statements. He certainly knew that his government would not act without England, that England showed no signs of acting, and that the time was not ripe in any case and might not be for some time to come, if ever.[36] Telling all this to the South would merely be stating the obvious. In any event, Dayton was briefly elated about Mercier's supposed change of mind: "If Mr. Mercier should make the suggestion to this Government, . . . it would be most serviceable to us. They have at all times relied much upon his representations and will do nothing, I think, without his assent and concurrence."[37]

The correspondence on the Roebuck motion reached Washington after Mercier had left. For Seward the news was a chance to write two more essays on the indestructibility of the Union, fairly unassailable essays in the light of Gettysburg and Vicksburg.[38] Mercier saw no reason to rush back to the capital.

On 21 July in New York, Mercier had a long conversation with John C. Fremont, whom he had first met two years earlier in St. Louis. At Fremont's invitation, Mercier summed up the situation as it seemed in mid-1863. He admitted that the North had the power to force the country back together, but he still thought the cost too high—destruction, Southern

[36] Mercier to Drouyn de Lhuys, Newport, 29 July 1863, AMAE, CP, E-U, 130: 177-79, private, also in Mercier Family Papers, where someone has wrongly dated it "15 July."

[37] Dayton to Seward, Paris, 30 July 1863, State Dept. Corres., France, Dispatches, LIII, no. 329.

[38] Seward to Dayton, Washington, 17 and 29 July 1863, State Dept. Corres., France, Instructions, XVI, nos. 374 and 380.

bitterness, and an insoluble racial problem. The great thing was to preserve as much as possible of the principles which had made America great:

> Among these principles, integrity [of territory] is undoubtedly one, but it need not be given more importance than it deserves, and to hold on to it exclusively would certainly mean sacrificing others which can be considered much more important. In this connection, the matter of conscription is already a serious warning.

In other words, the deprivation of liberty which Americans were undergoing was not worth the holding of the South. With the draft riots in New York less than three weeks in the past, both discussants had a very concrete reference for that argument.

If the Union would settle for sovereignty over the North's twenty million people and a common market with the South, he continued, a lot of problems would be avoided. Slaves in the new United States could be emancipated gradually, and the Confederacy would be left with the really serious racial problem. At present the North could make a good treaty with the South, but in a little while the interests of the Republican party might make the war something of a political necessity for the administration.

Fremont was struck by these observations, or at least Mercier thought he was. But Mercier saw no clear hope that anything much would happen; the Republicans and war Democrats would go on clinging to "territorial integrity," at least until the latter began to see that peace was their best chance to beat the Republicans.[39]

A month of relaxation brought Mercier no more optimistic prognosis about the duration of the war. It would probably go on for over a year, he thought, i.e., until the

[39] Mercier to Drouyn de Lhuys, New York, 22 July 1863, AMAE, CP, E-U, 130: 158-72, no. 161.

presidential election. European intervention was out of the question in view of Britain's firm decision not to move. And from Downing Street itself there was renewed confirmation of that: Sir Henry Holland, Palmerston's personal physician, was in Newport, and he said that neither government nor public would do anything except watch the American war.[40]

COTTON AND TOBACCO

Since the spring of 1862, i.e., since the fall of New Orleans, Mercier and Lyons had made repeated efforts to obtain cotton with the help of federal authorities. Mercier had been pessimistic about the possibilities of this approach even before that time, and nothing in the months after did very much to relieve his gloom.

Admiral Farragut could see part of the problem himself as his ships approached New Orleans—the burning cotton which had been fired when he passed the forts down river. The burning of stored cotton remained a major problem, and a good deal of what was not burned was destroyed by exposure. Studies bear out the extent of the difficulty: in 1862 about a million and a half bales of cotton were produced in America as against four and a half million the previous year. France imported only 271,570 bales in 1862 and 381,539 in 1863, the 1861 figure having been 624,600.[41] French efforts to develop substitute sources yielded little,[42] so it remained crucial that the South would retain her

[40] Mercier to Drouyn de Lhuys, Newport, 1 Sept. 1863, AMAE, CP, E-U, 130: 182-85, private, also in Mercier Family Papers.

[41] Arthur L. Dunham, "The Development of the Cotton Industry in France and the Anglo-French Treaty of Commerce of 1860," *Economic History Review*, I (1928), 291. See also Owsley, *King Cotton Diplomacy*, p. 46, and John Christopher Schwab, *The Confederate States of America, 1861-1865, A Financial and Industrial History of the South during the Civil War* (London: Charles Scribner's Sons, 1901), p. 279.

[42] Earl S. Pomeroy, "French Substitutes for American Cotton, 1861-1865," *Journal of Southern History*, IX (1943), 555-60.

cotton crop until her independence should be recognized. Public opinion in France mounted sharply against the American war in the fall of 1862, a development closely connected with the peace overtures of November and January, and Thouvenel himself had to travel incognito in some manufacturing areas.[43]

From the moment he first heard about New Orleans, Mercier was skeptical about its importance for getting cotton. Seward and the cabinet tried to be obliging, and it was soon clear that the Union would not insist on a prior withdrawal of Europe's recognition of Southern belligerency. In the first week of May 1862, he could tell Mercier that postal communication was already open, and in the second week that the port was open to trade.[44]

But the news of burning cotton reinforced French uneasiness. Perhaps, as Mercier heard, it was Washington's purpose to throw the onus upon the South; surely the South deserved a good part of it. But in tracing responsibility for Europe's suffering, Mercier also came back to the North—specifically to the new confiscation law. This second confiscation act, passed on 12 July 1862, declared forfeit the property of broad categories of people. Foreign merchants could scarcely be expected to buy cotton if the transaction might be held illegal under the new act. One of the provisions stated that a Southerner who within sixty days took an oath of allegiance to the United States could thus immunize himself against confiscation. Moderates like the secretary of state and the president, who had threatened

---

[43] Case, *French Opinion on U.S. and Mexico*, p. 257; Dayton to Seward, Paris, 22 April 1862, State Dept. Corres., France, Dispatches, LI, no. 141.

[44] Mercier to Thouvenel, Washington, 28 April 1862, AMAE, MD, Papiers Thouvenel, XIII, 446-47; Mercier to Thouvenel, Washington, 6 May 1862, AMAE, CP, E-U, 127: 85-105, no. 98; Mercier to Thouvenel, Washington, 12 May 1862, *ibid.*, fol. 123-39, no. 99. See also *LJ*, III (1862), 129-30.

to veto the bill, were embarrassed by the new legislation; in fact it remained pretty much of a dead letter as Attorney General Bates, with Lincoln's approval, moved conservatively to the prosecution. For his part Seward stressed the oath-taking provision to Mercier; the secretary was still seeking to be optimistic and to put the blame upon the South.[45]

In the last analysis the federal government was powerless anyhow, even apart from the damage done by the confiscation act. There simply was not enough cotton, nor were there enough Southern planters willing to waive the Confederacy's cause. Northern actions, designed to punish Confederate sympathizers and to choke off foreign specie from the South, only served to underline that basic situation. Mercier tried, but felt there was little he could achieve:

> I am forever preoccupied with the question of cotton. . . . Mr. Seward shows a constant good will which I believe quite sincere, but he is not qualified to express his views decisively, and the cabinet is afraid that the hard money we would put into circulation will bring, as the expression goes, aid and comfort to the enemy; then there is always the problem of doing more for foreigners than for American nationals. To sum up, I am very much afraid that we can attain our end only by some general measure which could be considered a preliminary to peace.[46]

In November the federal government tried a new tack. Cotton would now be seized rather than bought in Southern areas under Union control; it could then be sold where the hard money would not aid the Confederacy. Owners be-

[45] Mercier to Thouvenel, Washington, 27 June 1862, *ibid.*, fol. 272-76, no. 106, also in *LJ*, III (1862), 134-35; Nevins, *The War for the Union*, II, 145-46; Randall and Donald, pp. 284-85 .

[46] Mercier to Thouvenel, New London, 29 July 1862, AMAE, MD, Papiers Thouvenel, XIII, 479-83.

yond the definitions in the confiscation act would be compensated, others would not. Lyons and Mercier went twice
to confer with Seward about this, on 19 and 20 November.
They were sour and reticent as Seward must have expected
they would be, for he seems to have been embarrassed by
the new regulations. Mercier dubbed them rigorous and
insisted they ought not be applied against French cotton-
holders. Seward tried to assure him that only Americans
were affected. Mercier added the obvious: the new system
would all the more encourage Southerners to burn cotton
as the Union army approached their neighborhoods. When
it heard the plan, Paris agreed with Mercier.[47]

The year 1863 saw some lessening of the economic burden
upon Europe. French cotton imports, as we have seen, rose
by approximately 100,000 bales over the 1862 figure. In
part this was owing to increased imports from India, which
began in 1862 and gave some relief by the following year.
In any case, the unemployment wave in French textiles
crested in May 1863, which is not to say, of course, that
unemployment ceased to be a bitter problem.[48]

Tobacco was a similar problem, at once more direct and
more specific, though less massive, in its effect; for in
France, tobacco was a state monopoly, marketed through
the government's own tobacco "Régie." The importance of
America to this operation can be gauged from the fact that
up until 1861, shipments from the United States accounted
for three-fourths of all the tobacco consumed in France.[49]

[47] Mercier to Drouyn de Lhuys, Washington, 21 Nov. 1862, *LJ*,
III (1862), 149; Drouyn de Lhuys to Mercier, Paris, 11 Dec. 1862,
ibid., pp. 149-50; Lyons to Russell, Washington, 21 Nov. 1862, *Sessional Papers*, LXXII (1863), 55-56, no. 49; Bates, *Diary*, p. 266. See
also Case and Spencer, pp. 380-81.

[48] Schwab, p. 279; Dunham, *Economic History Review*, I (1928),
295; Blumenthal, *Franco-American Relations*, pp. 154-55.

[49] Blumenthal, *Franco-American Relations*, p. 104. A specific segment of the harvested crop, stored in Richmond and claimed by the
Régie, became the subject of one of the Civil War's most intricate

As French consul in Richmond, Alfred Paul assumed an unusual set of duties during the Civil War; Richmond's being the seat of government created situations which at times made Paul look like a minister to the Confederacy. For the better part of three years the French tobacco occupied a good deal of this consul's time; from first to last it was his special area. By May of 1862 he had at least convinced Benjamin to set the tobacco beyond the pale of future destruction should McClellan reach the Richmond suburbs and conflagration begin in the city.[50]

One of Paul's tobacco-related duties was to keep Henri Mercier interested in the problem. Tobacco, it will be remembered, was thought to be one of Mercier's main reasons for making his trip to Richmond in 1862. This mistaken idea was partly a cover-story and partly a result of Paul's known concern about the matter. It did not reflect any passionate worry on Mercier's part.

In the spring of 1863, a Confederate court ruled that the tobacco might be shipped to France. That was the end of the court's problem but only the beginning of the diplomats' work. Now it would be up to the Washington administration to see about the blockade, and with some hope of federal complaisance, Alfred Paul came to Washington in

---

negotiations. Some 2,260 hogsheads, about one-third of the total, had been purchased by the Messrs. Rothschild of Paris and August Belmont & Co. of New York in 1861. This purchase came to the attention of John Slidell shortly after his arrival in Paris in 1862. He certified to Richmond that the Rothschilds had proper title and thus helped keep the tobacco from being confiscated by the Confederacy as the property of a Northern firm (Slidell to Hunter, Paris, 19 Feb. 1862, Eustis Papers, also in Richardson, II, 189-90). For the tobacco story see Case and Spencer, pp. 525-44.

[50] Bonham, "French Consuls in the Confederacy," *Studies in Southern History and Politics*, pp. 86-88. Paul had reason to fear Benjamin's attitude. The previous month the secretary had briefly suggested seizing the tobacco in retaliation for France's retaining the Confederate ship *Rappahannock* at Calais (*ibid.*, pp. 91-92).

June and conferred with Mercier. Mercier agreed to co-operate fully in trying to get the necessary federal permission. Accordingly he sent off a note to Seward, accompanied by Paul's statement of the question, in which the amount of tobacco was given as 10,000 hogsheads.[51]

Though the Erlanger Confederate loan, secured as it was with Southern cotton, made permission for shipping cotton hard to get, the bad feeling did not rub off onto this negotiation, at least not where Seward was concerned. The secretary had a hard time trying to convince Gideon Welles, however, the man under whose jurisdiction the blockade fell. Welles at first flatly refused to go along but was later ordered to do so by the president. By 9 July, Paul and Mercier had their permission.[52] It seems odd, somehow, that the president and cabinet should have settled this matter while Hooker was being replaced and Lee's men were walking into Pennsylvania.

Welles's main concern was the integrity of the blockade. Once a major exception were granted, he feared, English and even American requests would flood in. Welles also seems to have had some feeling against France and Mercier: "No improper concessions will be made by me to France or her Minister."[53] The secretary had reason to fear, for Benjamin saw in this federal move a chink in the whole wall of Union ships. He alerted Slidell to the possibilities:

I shall send you official evidence of the passage of the first ship through the blockade under the federal permit, and it need only be communicated to some of our

[51] Paul to Drouyn de Lhuys, Washington, 19 June 1863, AMAE, Correspondance politique des Consuls, E-U, xv, 60-61, no. 77; Mercier to Seward, Washington, 20 June 1863, State Dept. Corres., Notes from the French Legation, xx.

[52] Welles, *Diary*, I, 338-40, and II, 9-10; Paul to Drouyn de Lhuys, New York, 9 July 1863, AMAE, Correspondance commerciale, Richmond, v, 291-92, no. 345.

[53] Welles, *Diary*, I, 340.

friends in New York to be used there in behalf of the neutral claimants of captured vessels and cargoes, to give infinite trouble to the enemy's Government.[54]

Seward did have to credit Welles's objections on one important score, namely the chance that Britain might use the French permission as a reason for seeking others of her own. The secretary, in fact, was being a little cautious; as of 1 September he had not yet put anything important into writing. But all seemed to go smoothly nonetheless. Drouyn de Lhuys got the English cabinet to forswear any complicating move, and Lyons even tried to help things along with Seward.[55] Meanwhile, the French went ahead with plans to get the tobacco down the James River to City Point and have it loaded aboard a French warship.[56]

By the second week of September, however, it was abundantly clear that some foreign object was jamming the diplomatic gears. Mercier had already heard rumors of what that object was, and when he got back to Washington, he heard it straight from Seward—Mexico. As far as he personally was concerned, Seward said, he credited the French assurances about Mexico and was anxious not to have too much to do with Juárez. But the state of American public opinion precluded any big concession like the permission to ship tobacco. Mercier found Seward's whole approach quite friendly; appreciating it as such, he thought it best

---

[54] Benjamin to Slidell, Richmond, 4 Aug. 1863, Richardson, II, 541-43, no. 21.

[55] Lyons to Seward, Niagara, 25 Aug. 1863, appended to Mercier to Drouyn de Lhuys, Newport, 1 Sept. 1863, AMAE, CP, E-U, 130: 182-85, private. See also Drouyn de Lhuys to Paul, Paris, 6 Aug. 1863, AMAE, Correspondance commerciale, Richmond, V, 294-95, no. 108; Mercier to Seward, Newport, 27 Aug. 1863, State Dept. Corres., Notes from the French Legation, XXI.

[56] Mercier to Seward, Newport, 3 Sept. 1863, private, State Dept. Corres., Notes from the French Legation, XXI.

not to press the matter of the tobacco any further for the moment.[57]

The *Régie* tobacco, therefore, was not to be dealt with in isolation, nor was it connected only with the blockade; it was a pawn in a much larger game of chess. When France allowed the Confederate warship *Florida* to be repaired and provisioned at Brest, when word came that Confederate ships were being built at Nantes and Bordeaux, the tobacco seemed destined to remain in Richmond, unsmoked, unchewed, and unsniffed. But when Paris ordered those ships detained, the doors were suddenly reopened. On 10 November 1863, President Lincoln formally ordered that any *Régie* tobacco bought before 4 March 1861, the date of his inauguration, might be shipped through the blockade.[58]

Mercier and Seward then got down to cases and put together an "informal convention," dated 23 November, covering the details of how the tobacco should be loaded and shipped, the whole to be completed in five months.[59] Washington was especially anxious that there be no inadvertent recognition of the Confederate authority. Article II of this convention incorporated the cutoff date specified in the president's order—which brought to light a whole new set of problems. It now appeared that only 1,500 of the whole 6,500 hogsheads had actually been bought before that date. On 11 December, Seward readily approved the shipping of the 1,500 hogsheads, i.e., that part of the tobacco which had been bought by the house of Hüffer and conveyed to the *Régie* before March of 1861. He would have to see

[57] Mercier to Drouyn de Lhuys, Washington, 14 Sept. 1863, AMAE, CP, E-U, 130: 191-97, no. 162.

[58] Lincoln, *Works*, ed. Basler, VII, 8.

[59] For the text of this Seward–Mercier convention, see *ORN*, 2nd ser., III, 1128-30.

about the rest. Mercier, meanwhile, wrote to Paul for more information about dates of sale, and it now developed that there was even some question about the Hüffer tobacco: the pre-March agreement, if any, had apparently been informal.[60]

Mercier's chief interest in the whole affair was to maintain good relations with Seward and between France and the United States. Paul, of course, had had to concentrate more specifically on tobacco. In handling this new embarrassment, Mercier was painfully honest, sending a copy of Paul's most recent report to the State Department. As Paul explained the Hüffer purchase to Mercier:

> I contented myself, in my report, with saying that the *contract of auction* had been made before the war and the blockade, which is true, and I refrained from mentioning the rest.[61]

On top of everything else, the whole confused matter had become a public controversy in Richmond. Somehow a copy of the Seward–Mercier convention of 23 November had been leaked, and merchants in Richmond were angry about the special consideration being given to the French tobacco, which they insisted had been bought after 4 March 1861. In the circumstances Paul felt that nothing

[60] Mercier to Seward, Washington, 10 Dec. 1863, Notes from the French Legation, xxi; Seward to Mercier, Washington, 11 Dec. 1863, Notes to the French Legation, vii, 289; Paul to Drouyn de Lhuys, New York, 15 Dec. 1863, AMAE, Correspondance commerciale, Richmond, v, 330-31, no. 359.

[61] Paul to Mercier, n.p., n.d., New York?, 20 Dec. 1863?, State Dept. Corres., Notes from the French Legation, xxi. Emphasis added. This note is the French original and was apparently unaccompanied by a covering note from Mercier. Seward was away from Washington just before Mercier left. It is probable that Mercier met him in New York just before embarkation and gave him Paul's note. See Seward to Dayton, Washington, 4 Jan. 1864, State Dept. Corres., France, Instructions, xvi, 498-501, no. 452.

could be done until the cutoff date was liberalized up to, say, 15 July 1863.[62] Somewhat incongruously, Drouyn de Lhuys's enthusiastic thanks for the Union's friendly gesture arrived just at this point. Mercier, who was about to leave for France, had word sent ahead that he would explain the new delay when he got there.[63]

Mercier, therefore, did not play a direct role in the next complicated act of this involved play. It may be synopsized briefly. Seward got the plot back on course with one of his —and the president's—periodic displays of international generosity. "This government is satisfied," he said, "that the Imperial Government is disposed to practice not only strict neutrality in our civil war, but also to extend to this government all the comity that shall be consistent with that relationship." The cutoff date would be rescinded, and all *Régie* tobacco might be on its way[64]—so stated by presidential order of 7 March 1864. When Grant's spring campaign in Virginia threatened to interrupt the shipment and push it beyond the five-months expiration date (23 April), that date was pushed forward.[65]

But it was Benjamin's turn to balk, for Ulysses S. Grant was in Virginia now. Like Burnside and Hooker, Grant had tried to get past Robert Lee in the Fredericksburg-

[62] Paul to Mercier, n.p., n.d., State Dept. Corres., Notes from the French Legation, xxi.

[63] Mercier to Seward, Washington, 22 Dec. 1863, State Dept. Corres., Notes from the French Legation, xxi; Paul to Drouyn de Lhuys, New York, 29 Dec. 1863, AMAE, Correspondance commerciale, Richmond, v, 339, no. 362. See also Dayton to Seward, Paris, 25 Dec. 1863, State Dept. Corres., France, Dispatches, LIV, no. 390, also in *For. Rel. U.S.*, 1864, III, 11.

[64] Seward to Dayton, Washington, 4 Jan. 1864, State Dept. Corres., France, Instructions, xvi, 498-501, no. 452.

[65] Lincoln, *Works*, ed. Basler, VII, 229; Paul to Drouyn de Lhuys, New York, 14 March 1864, AMAE, Correspondance commerciale, Richmond, v, 357-58, no. 367; Seward to Dayton, Washington, 21 April 1864, State Dept. Corres., France, Instructions, xvii, 49, no. 533.

Chancellorsville–Wilderness sector; like them he had failed; but unlike them, to the joy and thanks and cheers of his army and of Abraham Lincoln, he had gone on from there, had taken the right-hand turn coming east from the Wilderness, and had gone south. Nothing would ever be the same again. As Confederate Secretary of State Judah Benjamin knew, in contemplating Grant the South was staring at death as a nation. Europe had not recognized the Confederacy and never would. In such circumstances, the secretary's waspish reaction to Alfred Paul's renewed request was understandable.

Two French warships and two French-leased British merchantmen were off City Point when Paul went to see Benjamin about final clearance. The secretary demanded to see the Seward–Mercier convention—had he not read it already the previous December?—and expressed or feigned utter astonishment when he read it. Here was a foreign government, the United States, daring to write regulations for Confederate ports, saying who could and could not come ashore, providing for foreign (American) laborers to load the vessels.[66]

In the confusion caused by this sudden reversal, one ship did get away with some of the long-aging tobacco, but the best part of it stayed in its Richmond storehouses and was still there in April of 1865. Paul, Mercier, and Seward had done their best, but the *Régie* had little to show for their efforts.

CONSULS AND THE CONFEDERACY

This was not the first time that Benjamin had taken offense at a supposed insult to the Confederacy's sovereign status.

[66] Benjamin to Paul, Richmond, 24 May 1864, *ORN*, 2nd ser., III, 1125-28. See also Paul to Benjamin, Richmond, 26 May 1864, *ibid.*, pp. 1130-33; Benjamin to Paul, Richmond, 30 May 1864, *ibid.*, pp. 1134-35.

Since no state on earth recognized that status formally, it is not surprising that there were difficulties. Nothing was more designed to cause such difficulties than the consular system. The exequatur—i.e., the official authorization to a consul from the government of the country within which his duties lay—was the nub of the problem. Which government, and what country? The Confederacy began, realistically enough, by recognizing the exequaturs which had been issued by the United States prior to the outbreak of the war. Consuls so empowered were allowed to go on functioning in Richmond, Charleston, New Orleans, and other Southern cities.

Problems arose whenever a consul had to be replaced, for the Confederacy would scorn any exequatur issued in Washington, while Britain and France did not dare to ask Richmond for such a document: the implied recognition of Confederate sovereignty could lead to a break with the United States. So far as France was concerned, the trouble began in Charleston, where Belligny of the Bunch–Belligny affair had been consul at the outbreak of war. Here the Baron de St. André had replaced Belligny in December of 1862 with no fuss and without benefit of anyone's exequatur.[67] Benjamin had called upon St. André for an explanation, and when St. André told him that he was only a temporary replacement, Benjamin let him remain, thinking that Belligny would soon return.[68]

Matters drifted along that way until the spring of 1863. In late April, with Charleston in danger of Union capture, St. André returned to France. Not wishing to leave French subjects in Charleston without an official representative, Mercier and his consul general in New York, the Marquis

[67] The *Almanach de Gotha* for 1863 lists St. André as consul in Charleston (*Almanach de Gotha, annuaire diplomatique et statistique* [Gotha: Justus Perthes, 1863], p. 326).

[68] Bonham, *British Consuls*, p. 221.

337

de Montholon, arranged for Arthur Lanen, who was one of Montholon's aides, to go to South Carolina. As they might have expected, this stirred up the whole exequatur business, i.e., the whole issue of Confederate sovereignty.[69]

Benjamin got the word from General Beauregard, military commander in South Carolina. This time he decided to accept no face-saving explanation: Lanen would not be regarded as a "temporary" replacement for the long-gone Belligny. What made this seem more imperative to Benjamin was Lanen's commission from Montholon, drawn up on Mercier's authority, in which Lanen was promoted to acting consul without, of course, any permission from Richmond. Not only did the Confederate authorities refuse to recognize Lanen's position, but on 10 June 1863, the Richmond state department issued a note forbidding direct contact between consuls in the South and anyone, even ministers, in the North. This was a logical corollary of Southern independence, and Benjamin probably hoped it would keep London and Paris thinking about recognition of the Confederacy.[70]

Lanen was part of the reason for this decree of 10 June, but the Confederacy was having problems with the British consuls too, notably Frederick J. Cridland in Mobile and George Moore in Richmond. Moore was expelled on 5 June, five days before the decree, for his vigorous opposition to the drafting of assumed British subjects. Mercier

[69] Mercier even took the trouble to notify Seward, an exactly proper move but one which would have infuriated Benjamin had he known about it. Officially, of course, France still recognized Washington's authority over all thirty-four states (Mercier to Seward, Washington, 30 April 1863, State Dept. Corres., Notes from the French Legation, xx).

[70] Bonham, "French Consuls in the Confederacy," *Studies in Southern History and Politics*, pp. 94-95, and *British Consuls*, p. 221; Owsley, *King Cotton Diplomacy*, p. 478; Benjamin to Slidell, Richmond, 10 June 1863, ORN, 2nd ser., III, 792-95, no. 18.

offered to have Alfred Paul take charge of the British consulate in Richmond, but Lyons declined the offer, fearing that Benjamin would oppose such an arrangement for the same reason as he objected to Lanen's appointment, namely that it was ordered by a representative to a "foreign" country.[71] The Confederate decree explains Paul's trip to the North in the fall of 1863: Benjamin gave him permission on condition that he not go to Washington, but should he contact Mercier some other way, that could be winked at.[72]

The climax of all this consular trouble came on 7 October 1863 with the expulsion of the British consuls from the Confederacy. The immediate issue was an antidraft incident in Savannah, Georgia; but the broader background suggests it was part of an overall anti-British policy stemming partly from the basic attitude of the English cabinet and specifically from the detention of the Laird rams. Mason had already been ordered by Benjamin to leave London. Inevitably France emerged as the Confederacy's only strong potential friend, and this in turn explains why Benjamin permitted Lanen to stay in Charleston and function as acting consul. In November 1863 the secretary partially withdrew the order forbidding consuls to contact anyone in the North: letters to Paris could now be routed through Washington and New York.[73]

Insofar as Mercier had any jurisdiction in the South, it was resented and opposed by the Confederate authorities.

[71] Lyons to Russell, Washington, 16 June 1863, *Sessional Papers*, LXII (1863), 383-84, no. 13; Randall and Donald, pp. 506-07.

[72] Paul to Drouyn de Lhuys, New York, 3 Sept. 1863, AMAE, Correspondance commerciale, Richmond, v, 305-08, no. 349.

[73] Paul to Drouyn de Lhuys, Richmond, 23 Nov. 1863, *ibid.*, fol. 315, no. 355. On the expulsion of the British consuls, see Bonham, *British Consuls*, pp. 210-58. On the approval of Lanen, see Bonham, "French Consuls in the Confederacy," *Studies in Southern History and Politics*, p. 95. On Mason's withdrawal, see Benjamin to Edwin De Leon, Richmond, 17 Aug. 1863, American Jewish Archives, Cincinnati, Papers of Edwin De Leon.

This resentment was muted, however, because of the larger insults offered by the British and because of Great Britain's opposition to recognition of the Confederacy. In this context it was a sign of the Confederacy's diplomatic bankruptcy when Benjamin reacted in such a sharp and anti-French manner during the 1864 tobacco negotiations.

THE NEW YORK STATE EXCURSION

One of the more remarkable efforts which William H. Seward made to impress and attract foreign powers occurred in August of 1863. It was vacation-time; the Washington heat, the success at Gettysburg and Vicksburg, the failure of the Roebuck motion, and a desire to confer with Justice Samuel Nelson of the Supreme Court on draft-law issues all dictated for Seward a trip home to Auburn in upstate New York. Perhaps there was something "typically American" in Seward's idea of mixing a little business with pleasure; in any event, he invited the diplomatic corps to go along with him and see something of the country.

In one of his first dispatches after arriving in the United States, Mercier had said he was going to tour major cities and educate himself for his new post. In fact he had gone to Newport and rested. Mercier had seen more of the country than most of his colleagues, but that was largely thanks to Prince Napoleon's trip in 1861. For the rest it was mainly the Washington–New York–Newport circuit for Mercier as for most diplomats.

Mercier was already in Newport and probably joined the party in New York City on Saturday, 15 August. He may also have seen Montholon, who left for home on the *Scotia* on 12 August. A special car on the Hudson River Railroad took the diplomats up the Hudson and Mohawk Valleys, through Albany and Schenectady, to Sharon Springs, where they stayed over Sunday. On Monday and Tuesday they visited Utica, Rome, and Syracuse, and spent one night at

Mercier and His Diplomatic Colleagues near Seward's Home. From *Harper's Weekly*, where the figures were identified as follows: 1. William H. Seward. 2. Baron De Stoeckel. 3. M. Molina. 4. Lord Lyons. 5. M. Mercier. 6. M. Schleiden. 7. M. Bertinatti. 8. Count Piper. 9. M. Bodisco. 10. Mr. Sheffield.

Cooperstown, a stop which featured a sail on Otsego Lake. At Trenton Falls they posed for a group picture, an impressive enlargement of which is on the cover of *Harper's Weekly* for 19 September 1863. On Wednesday evening they arrived in Auburn, where the inevitable crowd greeted them. Seward and his home-town friends found room for everybody, and next day it was Fort Hill Cemetery, Auburn State Prison, and a ride on Owasco Lake in Seward's lifeboat.[74]

From Auburn the group went on to Buffalo and Niagara Falls, but Mercier was apparently not with them; he may even have missed the lifeboat ride on Owasco Lake. The minister was apparently sick more than once this summer, and illness forced him to miss part of the New York State excursion.[75]

SHIPBUILDING IN FRANCE

Mercier returned to Washington in the second week of September, primarily to hear Seward's annoyed comments on Mexico and how it prevented the expedition of the *Régie* tobacco.[76] He had apparently left Madame Mercier and the children at the shore and returned to fetch them, for on 1 October he was in New York, on his way back, when a telegram from Washington reached him. This time it was a serious and immediate crisis in Franco-American relations. Seward had proof that warships nearing com-

---

[74] The basic account is by Frederick Seward in *Seward at Washington*, II, 185-88 and *Reminiscences of a Wartime Statesman*, pp. 236-37. For newspaper coverage, see, e.g., *Courrier des États-Unis* (New York), 17 Aug. 1863, and *Evening Star* (Washington), 15 and 26 Aug. 1863; in the last-cited there is a reprint of an article in the *Auburn Advertiser*, 20 Aug. 1863.

[75] Mercier to Seward, Newport, 27 Aug. 1863, State Dept. Corres., Notes from the French Legation, XXI; Seward to Mercier, Washington, 31 Aug. 1863, *ibid.*, Notes to the French Legation, VII, 254-55.

[76] Mercier to Drouyn de Lhuys, Washington, 14 Sept. 1863, AMAE, CP, E-U, 130: 191-97, no. 162.

pletion at Nantes and Bordeaux were intended for the Confederacy. The controversy over the Laird rams at Liverpool had just ended with the capitulation of the British government. Now it was France's turn to take the brunt of real, unaffected American fear and anger.[77]

It had begun almost a year before, on 28 October 1862, when John Slidell had had his second interview with the French emperor. In the course of a conversation which touched on many things—mediation, recognition, armistice —Napoleon III had inquired about the South's lack of a navy. Slidell picked up the hint and asked whether the French police would watch too closely if the Confederacy tried to have ships built and armed. As Slidell recorded it, the emperor replied: "Why could you not have them built as for the Italian Government? I do not think it would be difficult, but will consult the Minister of Marine about it."[78]

Subsequently, however, the emperor drew back from direct connection with such a project. In January, Slidell was approached by M. L. Arman, shipbuilder of Bordeaux and deputy from the Gironde, a friend of Émile Erlanger and a man of many connections. When Slidell tried to sound out Drouyn de Lhuys, however, he met with a stiff "I know nothing," and Slidell's renewed effort to approach the emperor was indirectly rebuffed. Eugene Rouher, minister of commerce, was more cooperative, stating that the government would allow ships built in France to be armed. Despite the emperor's silence and Drouyn de Lhuys's annoyance, therefore, Slidell decided to go ahead. Accordingly, James D. Bulloch, the Confederacy's chief naval agent in

[77] Seward sent a note over to Treilhard and asked him to telegraph Mercier (Seward to Treilhard, Washington, 1 Oct. 1863, State Dept. Corres., Notes to the French Legation, VII, 266). For a full account of the shipbuilding crisis see Case and Spencer, pp. 427-80.

[78] Memorandum appended to Slidell to Benjamin, Paris, 28 Oct. 1862, Richardson, II, 345-51. See also Stern, p. 168, and Korolewicz-Carlton, pp. 189-93.

Europe, placed an order with Arman for four wooden cor-
vettes, each complete with a dozen mounted cannon. Chasseloup-Laubat, the minister of marine—who was married
to General Beauregard's niece!—promptly granted permission when Arman requested it.[79]

Arman found after he got started that he had to subcon-
tract for two of the wooden ships with M. J. Voruz of
Nantes. In May the Confederate government sent further
word that it was interested in ordering ironclads, and on
16 July, Arman began construction of two of these dangerous vessels. A month earlier, during their talk on the Roebuck motion, Slidell had even been able to get a renewed
verbal permission from Napoleon III.[80] By the end of the
summer, therefore, with the somewhat indirect but very
real permission of the emperor and two of his ministers, six
ships were being built for the Confederacy—despite the
Roebuck failure, despite Gettysburg and Vicksburg.

Thus with the Laird rams out of the way, France came
forward once more as the main concern of American diplomacy. The climax of this story began in Paris, on Thursday,
10 September, in the office of the United States consul, John
Bigelow. Here there came a Frenchman "of the Gascon
type," with news of ships being built at Bordeaux and
Nantes, and an offer to produce written proof that they
were intended for the Confederacy. On Saturday he returned with the documents, including a note from Arman
to Voruz acknowledging a check from Bulloch and impli-
cating the house of Erlanger. By the time Dayton had gone
over this evidence and readied it for Drouyn de Lhuys's
embarrassed inspection, the fate of the French-built ships

[79] Spencer, *Revue d'histoire diplomatique*, LXXVII (1963), 319-20;
Stern, pp. 215-16; Slidell to Benjamin, Paris, 4 March 1863, no. 28,
Eustis Papers, also in *ORN*, 2nd ser., III, 705-07.

[80] Memorandum appended to Slidell to Benjamin, Paris, 21 June
1863, Richardson, II, 514-17, no. 38.

was in fact sealed. No government unwilling to recognize the South was going to brazen its way past this.[81]

So it was that Mercier received the telegram on 1 October and hurried back to Washington. He presented himself at the State Department on Saturday morning, 3 October. Mercier must have expected to be given his passports for some unknown clash somewhere, for he was actually relieved when he found out what was bothering Seward. So far as is known, this was Mercier's first contact with the subject of shipbuilding, and he readily agreed to ask Drouyn de Lhuys to make an early decision about the ships. Before Mercier sent off his report to Paris, Seward received word that the ships would not be allowed to leave if they were really going to the American South.[82]

William L. Dayton was not a phrase-maker like C. F. Adams, and he did not threaten war in so many words. But Bigelow and he had laid their groundwork so well that the French authorities got the message loudly and clearly. For about three weeks after Drouyn de Lhuys received the evidence, the foreign ministry and the ministry of marine hedged and dodged. Chasseloup-Laubat tried to maintain that he really had thought the ships were going to fight pirates in the China seas. Drouyn de Lhuys, who knew less about the secret matter than Rouher,[83] could not

[81] Bigelow, *Retrospections*, II, 56-70; Clapp, pp. 203-05; Dayton to Seward, Paris, 11 Sept. 1863, State Dept. Corres., France, Dispatches, LIII, no. 344; Dayton to Drouyn de Lhuys, Paris, 22 Sept. 1863, *ibid.*, copy annexed to Dayton to Seward, 24 Sept. 1863, no. 350; Spencer, *Revue d'histoire diplomatique*, LXXVII (1963), 325.

[82] Mercier to Drouyn de Lhuys, Washington, 5 Oct. 1863, AMAE, CP, E-U, 130: 203-06, private, also in Mercier Family Papers. Seward let Mercier inspect the documents he had received from Bigelow (Mercier to Seward, Washington, 3 Oct. 1863, State Dept. Corres., Notes from the French Legation, XXI).

[83] Warren F. Spencer, *Revue d'histoire diplomatique*, LXXVII (1963), 325, concludes that Drouyn de Lhuys surely knew less than Rouher and possibly less than Chasseloup-Laubat.

order the detention of the ships immediately, nor did he do so fast enough to suit Dayton.[84] Finally, however, on 23 October, Dayton received the cooling and official word that the government had told Arman and Voruz not to arm the ships. Simultaneously, Drouyn de Lhuys notified Mercier of the happy outcome.[85] Some small difficulty remained as long as the ships were there and remained unsold to a neutral country, but basically the affair was over.[86]

The period from February of 1863 to the end of the year, i.e., the end of his American career, was a time of troubles for Henri Mercier but not a time of crisis. Once the exciting peace moves of January and February proved fruitless, Mercier at last began to detach himself from any immediate, practical concern about ending the Civil War. Northern peace agitation subsided sharply in the spring of 1863, and despite the inauguration of the draft in the summer, it did

[84] Dayton to Seward, Paris, 16 Oct. 1863, State Dept. Corres., France, Dispatches, LIII, no. 364, enclosing a translation of Chasseloup-Laubat to Drouyn de Lhuys, Paris, 12 Oct. 1863.

[85] Dayton to Seward, Paris, 23 Oct. 1863, ibid., LIV, no. 368; Drouyn de Lhuys to Mercier, Paris, 22 Oct. 1863, AMAE, CP, E-U, 130: 217-18, no. 22.

[86] On the aftermath of the shipbuilding crisis, see F. W. Seward, Seward at Washington, II, 200; Mercier to Drouyn de Lhuys, Washington, 9 Nov. 1863, AMAE, CP, E-U, 130: 223-25, no. 165; Spencer, Revue d'histoire diplomatique, LXXVII (1963), 328-29; Stern, p. 220; Seward to Dayton, Washington, 1 June 1864, State Dept. Corres., France, Instructions, XVII, 90-91, no. 568. As late as mid-1864 the ships had still not actually been sold, and Seward kept up the pressure that this be done. One ship, renamed the Stonewall, escaped the subsequent efforts made to keep it from the Confederacy. Before going to American waters it showed up in Spain for repairs where Mercier, now French ambassador there, received word from Drouyn de Lhuys to try to have it detained. Spain did nothing, but the Stonewall arrived in America too late to affect the war (Spencer, Revue d'histoire diplomatique, LXXVII [1963], 336-39; James D. Bulloch, The Secret Service of the Confederate States in Europe [2 vols.; London: Richard Bentley and Son, 1883], II, 54-55; Stern, pp. 335-37; Case and Spencer, pp. 466-79).

not threaten so seriously again. Seward's lofty, even patronizing rejection of the French armistice-talk suggestion underlined the government's continuing intransigence, and the Union victories at Gettysburg and Vicksburg sealed the fate of both the Roebuck motion and the Northern peace movement. Not that Mercier completely discounted the possibility of a negotiated settlement, however; his sights were now set somewhat diffidently upon the 1864 presidential election, that quadrennial hope of those who oppose what any American government is doing.

It was over two years now since Mercier had asked to be recalled whenever the American crisis abated sufficiently. The bloodiest part of the Civil War was still ahead, and in that sense the crisis had certainly not abated. But it was evident now that, barring some unexpected cataclysm, there would be no European intervention. Mercier was ready to go home.

CHAPTER XII

Last Weeks and Return

The Last Few Weeks

HENRI MERCIER had often requested permission to go home. The fact that this request was finally granted in December of 1863 corresponded to no particular, single event in the history of the American Civil War. Inevitably a number of matters were left in the air: Mexico and the *Régie* tobacco for instance. But the two major French efforts to intervene had failed, and Union victories and the abstentionist attitude of England had all but foreclosed the matter of intervention. Basically, therefore, there is a certain retrospective unity to Mercier's American career: he came as the old Union was breaking up; he watched the decisive years of battle and took part in the diplomacy they generated; he left after the great diplomatic question had been settled in the Union's favor. From this point on, Franco-American relations were mostly about Mexico, which was serious enough, but not of the same life-or-death order as the great question of Mercier's years in Washington.

The last weeks were crowded enough with this and that, but there is no overall unity to them. For one thing, the Russian fleet was in the country, and Mercier had to tell Paris how Americans were reacting to that. It was in September that the first units of Admiral Lisovsky's fleet passed the Battery on lower Manhattan; another fleet put in at San Francisco. Some editorialists leapt to the conclusion that America's great friend the Romanov emancipator was

348

sending moral and material aid to the Union cause. Gideon Welles was elated. "In sending them to this country at this time," he recorded, "there is something significant. What will be its effect on France and the French policy we shall learn in due time. It may be moderate; it may exasperate. God bless the Russians."[1] Under the circumstances, those rumors about an American alliance with Russia were understandable, and it was equally understandable that the "alliance" should be thought of as anti-French. Dayton and Seward were at pains to deny both rumors.[2]

Thanks to the frankness of his friend Stoeckl, Mercier knew better, knew that the trouble over Poland was at the bottom of it. But Mercier could not take Stoeckl's word completely at face value:

> My Russian colleague explains the arrival of this squadron by saying that in the event of a war with the maritime powers, his government wanted to put the ships out of harm's way which would be within range of their cruisers. But this explanation would not at all affect the ships which have come directly from Kronstadt. Therefore it is natural to assume, as is widely done, that the Russian government also had in mind some naval plan based on the eventual cooperation of the Americans.[3]

Actually no such worry was necessary. Russian fear of a British blockade and of ice adequately explains the presence of all the ships, and it is probable that no special "plan based on the eventual cooperation of the Americans" was part of the Russian decision, though New York and San

[1] Welles, *Diary*, I, 443.
[2] Seward to Dayton, Washington, 5 Oct. 1863, State Dept. Corres., France, Instructions, XVI, 460-63, no. 410, also in *For. Rel. U.S.*, 1863, II, 785-86.
[3] Mercier to Drouyn de Lhuys, Washington, 6 Oct. 1863, AMAE, CP, E-U, 130: 207-10, no. 163.

Francisco were eminently suitable neutral ports and the Lincoln government was glad to have the moral help implied by the visit.[4]

The American public lost its head a little over the Russian visit, but Mercier had seen the same thing happen when the Prince of Wales visited in 1860, and he was inclined to discount it, even after the mammoth subscription ball at New York's Academy of Music on 5 November.[5] On balance, then, Mercier's reports on the Russian visit, while properly suspicious, were reserved and accurate.

As valedictories, Mercier could contemplate the annual messages to their respective congresses delivered by President Lincoln and President Davis. Davis continued to hope, somewhat wanly, for some kind of help from France:

> It is not in my power to apprise you to what extent the Government of France shares the views so unreservedly avowed by that of Great Britain. . . . No public protest nor opposition, however, has been made by His Imperial Majesty against the prohibition to trade with us imposed on French citizens by the paper blockade of the United States, although I have reason to believe that an unsuccessful attempt was made on his part to secure the assent of the British government to a course of action more consonant with the dictates of public law and with the demands of justice toward us.

Lincoln stressed the positive side of things, congratulating the country on the detention of both the Laird rams and the Arman–Voruz ships. Mercier was struck by the confidence of President Lincoln and the mournful tone of Davis's

[4] Robin D. S. Higham, "The Russian Fleet on the Eastern Seaboard, 1863-1864," *American Neptune*, xx (1960), 49-61; Stern, pp. 232-34; Woldman, pp. 140-42.

[5] Mercier to Drouyn de Lhuys, Washington, 9 Nov. 1863, AMAE, CP, E-U, 130: 223-25, no. 165.

message: "In effect the encouraging presentation given by President Lincoln of the North's foreign and domestic affairs seems vindicated by the sorry picture drawn by President Davis of the situation in the South and by the bitter complaints which he addressed to Europe, more especially to England."[6]

In a larger sense, however, Mercier had heard a great word of summary and valediction some weeks earlier, for he had been invited to accompany President Lincoln to dedicate a cemetery. On the day before the dedication, Henri Mercier rode to Gettysburg in the president's railroad car along with Lincoln, Seward, Admiral Reynaud, Bertinatti, Nicolay, Hay, and about ten others. It was a pleasant trip through the autumn countryside, and at Gettysburg that evening the town was all excitement, speeches, and bands. The president had nothing but pleasantries for the serenade that stopped outside the Wills house to salute him, but next door Seward gave a little address to his audience, with some important but ill-phrased thoughts: "We owe it to our country and to mankind that this war shall have for its conclusion the establishing of the principle of democratic government." Seward's normal hoarseness kept most of his hearers from catching his words, but they got the drift of it.[7]

The next day was clear and beautiful. Mercier and the others got themselves into a big procession and all went up to the cemetery grounds to hear Everett's speech. John

[6] Davis to the Confederate congress, Richmond, 7 Dec. 1863, Richardson, I, 348-60; Lincoln to the federal Congress, Washington, 8 Dec. 1863, Lincoln, *Works*, ed. Basler, VII, 36-53; Mercier to Drouyn de Lhuys, Washington, 15 Dec. 1863, AMAE, CP, E-U, 130: 244-46, no. 168.

[7] Nicolay and Hay, VIII, 189-91; John Hay, *Lincoln and the Civil War in the Diaries and Letters of John Hay*, ed. Tyler Dennett (New York: Dodd, Mead & Co., 1939), pp. 119-20; *Evening Star* (Washington), 18 and 20 Nov. 1863.

Hay, later the coauthor of a reverent chapter on the affair, recorded it laconically enough at the time:

> In the morning I got a beast and rode out with the President's suite to the Cemetery in the procession. The procession formed itself in an orphanly sort of way & moved out with very little help from anybody & after a little delay Mr. Everett took his place on the stand— and Mr. Stockton made a prayer which thought it was an oration; and Mr. Everett spoke as he always does, perfectly—and the President, in a fine, free way, with more grace than is his wont, said his half dozen words of consecration, and the music wailed and we went home through crowded and cheering streets. And all the particulars are in the daily papers.[8]

One wonders how much Mercier understood of the morning's verbal torrent in a still unfamiliar language. Everett began, in fact, with the Greeks and went on with many other historical precedents and came two hours later to a peroration and a flourish. "The orator finished, and after the applause had died away the tall man in the black frock coat got to his feet, with two little sheets of paper in his hand, and he looked out over the valley and began to speak."[9]

It had been three years now since Mercier first learned about Abraham Lincoln, about the laborer and country lawyer who had been picked by his party without much in the way of visible qualifications. Mercier had talked that way before he met Lincoln. Afterwards, he mostly kept quiet: his dealings were almost exclusively with Seward, but his silence argues a certain amount of respect. Not many of the president's hearers that autumn morning knew that

[8] Hay, *Lincoln and the Civil War*, p. 121; see also Nicolay and Hay, VIII, 191-203.

[9] Catton, *Glory Road*, p. 359. That sentence is the book's last.

they were part of a great moral, human, and literary moment; if Mercier had any such insight, he failed to write it down. We must assume, then, that Mercier remained unconvinced, and that he went back to France still thinking that "American" was an economic adjective and had little to do with politics or philosophy. Had it all been in vain, the killing and all the rest? Mercier thought so. The president did not: ". . . the great task remaining before us . . . that these dead shall not have died in vain . . . that this nation, under God, shall have a new birth of freedom—and that government of the people, by the people, for the people, shall not perish from the earth." That is what Henri Mercier heard.

Mercier's actual leave-taking came upon Washington somewhat unexpectedly. What turned out to be his farewell visit with the president probably took place on 19 December during a White House reception which featured the officers of the Russian fleet.[10] At about the same time Mercier had a long final interview with Senator Sumner. As Welles got it, "Mercier said the Emperor was kindly disposed and at the proper time would tender kind offices to close hostilities, but that a division of the Union is inevitable. Sumner said he snapped his fingers at him and told him he knew not our case."[14] And the day before Christmas, Mercier spoke with Secretary of the Treasury Chase and discussed a proposal Chase had come up with for a decimal system of international coinage.[12]

Mercier probably received Drouyn de Lhuys's permission to come home "on leave" shortly before Christmas.[13] Treilhard had already been slated to return to Europe for re-

---

[10] *Lincoln Day by Day,* III, 228.

[11] Welles, *Diary,* I, 494-95.

[12] J. W. Schuckers, *The Life and Public Service of Salmon Portland Chase* (New York: D. Appleton & Co., 1874), pp. 395-96.

[13] See Mercier to Drouyn de Lhuys, Washington, 25 Dec. 1863, AMAE, CP, E-U, 130: 273, no. 169.

assignment, but since Geofroy was in Europe, Treilhard had to stay on in Washington for several more weeks. At the same time Dayton reported what Drouyn de Lhuys told him of Mercier's leave:

> He said that Mr. Mercier had repeatedly applied for a leave of absence on account of ill-health and that finally he had granted such leave. That, as a consequence, Mr. Mercier, with his family, would return to France at an early day, but would yet continue to retain his official position, as Minister at Washington.[14]

So rapid was Mercier's leaving that routine invitations from the State Department were still being addressed to him after he had left, and the newspapers reported his presence at the president's New Year's reception—at which moment he was actually at sea.[15]

It is clear by now that nothing could have induced Mercier to return to America once he had left. But for the record he was going home on leave. In view of the still-current rumors of imminent Franco-American difficulty, the foreign office undoubtedly decided that this story would cause the least speculation. The minister, Madame Mercier, Madeleine, Maurice-Henri, and their servants and effects arrived in New York on or slightly before 28 December. At noon the following day, Seward arrived from Washington en route to Auburn. It is probable, then, that he and Mercier saw each other in New York one last time, though it was not their last meeting on earth. The next day the Merciers boarded the *Australasian*. As the year 1863 faded into history, the year in which the United States freed the

[14] Dayton to Seward, Paris, 25 Dec. 1863, State Dept. Corres., France, Dispatches, LIV, no. 391.

[15] F. W. Seward to Mercier, 28 and 29 Dec. 1863, State Dept. Corres., Notes to the French Legation, VII, 297; *Evening Star* (Washington), 1 Jan. 1864.

slaves and fought her way back to national life, Henri Mercier sailed for France. For the second time in his life he was leaving the land of his birth and going home.[16]

MERCIER IN FRANCE

About the middle of January, then, Mercier was in Paris. He had a chance to go over everything with Drouyn de Lhuys, to greet Corcoran, to renew his acquaintances with both Dayton and Slidell. Dayton reported this:

> I have had the pleasure of seeing Mr. Mercier. That he is a frank and honorable gentleman I have no doubt, but I fear his report to this Government will do us no good. . . . He thinks it possible that we may suppress the insurrection, though he is by no means confident of this; that the coming spring will witness a fearful effort on the part of the South, and until that has passed he will not express a decided opinion on the question of our ability to overcome the rebellion. But admitting that we do succeed in this, his opinion is that our fierce dissensions and divisions will be such that the Union can never be reestablished.[17]

After that Dayton saw little of Mercier, and in fact the American was somewhat chagrined by this and wanted Seward to know it was not his fault. He indirectly heard later that Mercier was now saying that the South would fight so hard that the North could never win.[18] In April, Mercier went off on a yachting trip with Prince Napoleon.[19]

[16] *New York Times*, 28, 30, and 31 Dec. 1863; *Courrier des États-Unis* (New York), 30 Dec. 1863; Hyde to Corcoran, Washington, 28 Dec. 1863, 8 and 15 Feb. 1864, Corcoran Papers.

[17] Dayton to Seward, Paris, 26 Jan. 1864, State Dept. Corres., France, Dispatches, LIV, no. 406.

[18] Dayton to Seward, Paris, 1 April 1864, *ibid.*, no. 445.

[19] During these months Mercier played a supporting role in the effort of Senator William McKendree Gwin to colonize the Sonora province of Mexico with French help. Mercier got Gwin several ap-

In October 1864, Henri Mercier was named ambassador to Spain, and his American professional colleagues could now say those goodbyes which earlier would have been officially inappropriate. Dayton noted that the Madrid post was considered a promotion: "This advance in position is given him I am informed principally by reason of his satisfactory and useful service in the United States."[20] Seward had heard the news already and wrote to say congratulations:

---

pointments with Drouyn de Lhuys. The Sonora story is interesting and complicated but only tangential to Mercier's career. See Lately Thomas, "The Operator and the Emperors," *American Heritage*, xv (1964), 4-8 and 83-88; Evan J. Coleman, "Senator Gwin's Plan for the Colonization of Sonora," *The Overland Monthly*, 2nd ser., xvii (1891), 497-506; Bigelow, *Retrospections*, ii, 189-90 and 197-99.

Another Mexican-related problem of 1864 concerns the following question: did Mercier bring word from President Lincoln that if Maximilian refrained from recognizing the Confederacy, the United States would recognize Maximilian? Mercier may well have sent up such a trial balloon in Paris, though Slidell is our chief source for the story, and he had his own axe to grind: he had to explain to Benjamin why Maximilian would not see him during his stay in Paris. If Maximilian were hoping to assuage Washington, that would explain why he refused to see Slidell. Seward and Lincoln did tell Mercier that they would not encourage Juárez, and had Juárez' movement ended and French troops withdrawn, who knows but that they might have recognized Maximilian some day? Years later, in 1909, John Bigelow, through the then ambassador to France Henry White, tried to track all this down and discover whether Lincoln had ever been so soft on Maximilian. The Quai d'Orsay made a search for White but found no evidence for the charge. See Slidell to Benjamin, Paris, 16 March 1864, *ORN*, 2nd ser., iii, 1063-65, no. 58; Slidell to Benjamin, Paris, 2 May 1864, *ibid.*, pp. 1107-10, no. 60; White to Bigelow, Paris, 15 Feb. 1909, Bigelow, *Retrospections*, ii, 164-65; Mercier to Drouyn de Lhuys, Washington, 14 Sept. 1863, amae, cp, e-u, 130: 191-97, no. 162; Seward to Dayton, Washington, 21 Sept. and 23 Oct. 1863, State Dept. Corres., France, Instructions, xvi, 445-47 and 466-68, also in *For. Rel. U.S.*, 1863, ii, 774-75 and 798-99; Dayton to Seward, Paris, 21 March 1864, State Dept. Corres., France, Dispatches, liv, no. 438.

[20] Dayton to Seward, Paris, 14 Oct. 1864, State Dept. Corres., France, Dispatches, lv, no. 548.

I regret to learn from the journals this morning, that we are not to have the pleasure of seeing you here again, but as the transfer is doubtless in accordance with your own wishes, I cordially congratulate you upon it.

May I take this occasion to remind you that you were kind enough to promise to procure for me some good Burgundy before leaving France again? If you will do me the favor to ask your wine merchant to forward to me 10 or 12 dozen bottles, with his account for them, I shall be greatly obliged to you.[21]

Slidell in reporting the change was, as usual these days, sour:

This promotion is by some attributed to urgent recommendations of Prince Napoleon. . . . If this is true . . . the doubts I have heretofore expressed of the sincerity of M. Mercier's avowed Southern preferences are not unfounded, for the prince has always been a warm partisan of the Lincoln Government. . . . On the whole, we have no reason to regret the change.[22]

For a man whose supposed sympathy with the Confederacy had been fully discussed by American officials and the American press, that was an interesting epitaph to his Washington career. Slidell, at least, knew better than to call Mercier a Southern partisan.

MERCIER AND SEWARD: EPILOGUE

The close observer of Seward and Mercier receives a distinct impression that by 1863 at least, the two men understood each other very well. This was partly owing to their similar personalities and similar feelings about their work.

<hr/>

[21] Seward to Mercier, Washington, 19 Oct. 1864, Seward Papers.
[22] Slidell to Benjamin, Paris, 20 Oct. 1864, *ORN*, 2nd ser., III, 1125-26.

Neither man was a "natural" diplomat. Each was too out-going, too emotional, too flamboyant to be a Lyons, with his remarkable and consistent prudence, or a Dayton, too unsure of himself to go off on his own.

In Seward's case, as with other American secretaries of state, it was a matter of coming to diplomacy late in life. A man who has won election after election, has been governor, senator, and presidential aspirant, is not likely to be very reserved or self-effacing as a foreign minister. After 1 April 1861, Seward learned quickly, and in Lincoln he had a wise and considerate teacher. But enough of the orator-politician remained with Seward so that foreign representatives were never quite sure whether he meant what he said or not. Undoubtedly he used this quality, this bluff, precisely to keep Lyons and Mercier off balance, and in general he succeeded very well. Had Britain and France recognized the Confederacy, it is possible that the Union would not have gone to war against them. But no one could ever be sure.

With Mercier, in foreign service since his twenties, it was perhaps more a case of flamboyant personality combined with social insecurity. The unreserved, personal tone of his letters to Thouvenel reveal a sensitive, mercurial disposition. That he also was bothered by his bourgeois status is largely conjecture, but there is an oral tradition in the family that Cécile-Élisabeth felt she had married below her rank, which is plainly true. If Madame Mercier retained that thought, her husband must also have felt it. His trip to Richmond, his repeated requests for authority to intervene between North and South, might have been meant to make of himself a great historical figure, great in the eyes of his wife.

Seward and Mercier, therefore, each for different reasons, tended to be adventurous. As with Seward vis-à-vis Lin-

358

coln, so with Mercier vis-à-vis Thouvenel, the soldier of fortune was kept in check not only by the traditionally dry forms of professional diplomacy, but also by a patient, tactful superior. Position itself explains a lot: had Seward been president or Mercier foreign minister, they would probably have made the same decisions as Lincoln or Thouvenel. But by temperament and background, both Seward and Mercier were notably willing to take a chance.

By the autumn of 1863, something like real respect and friendship had grown up between the American secretary and the minister of France. "He is very wise" was one of Mercier's last comments on Seward, made in December of 1863.[23] How far that is from his earlier strictures! Seward, even in documents soon to be published, was equally generous:

> Mr. Mercier has returned to France for the winter. I have reason to believe that he has left us with kind and liberal sentiments towards the United States. Certainly, he bears with him the respect and good wishes of this government. The beginning of our unhappy civil war found him in close and intimate relations with the leaders of the insurrection. This could not well be a ground of surprise or of reasonable complaint . . . for those leaders were, until a very late hour in Mr. Buchanan's term, directors of the administration. . . . [Mr. Mercier's] bearing and his intercourse with the government are believed to have been frank and honorable.[24]

Later, when Dayton had reported the rumor that Mercier thought the North could not win, Seward, while stern, was still disposed to find explanations:

[23] Hay, *Lincoln and the Civil War*, p. 137.
[24] Seward to Dayton, Washington, 4 Jan. 1864, State Dept. Corres., France, Instructions, xvi, 498-501, no. 452.

This temper of his . . . has constantly been a subject of much speculation. It has generally been attributed to the sympathies which he naturally gave to those who are now insurgents, while they were yet . . . controlling the Government of the United States before the civil war broke out. But I fear that we are to look higher up for the source of Mr. Mercier's error. Whatever else may be said of him, he is a sincere partizan of the Imperial system established in France. We do not find it difficult to discover an antagonism in principle between that system and the Republican one under which this country is governed.[25]

On the night of 14 April 1865, Abraham Lincoln was assassinated. Secretary Seward was likewise attacked and escaped from death by stabbing only because of a brace he was wearing as a result of a recent fall. Mercier, now in Spain, reacted with shock and sorrow:

I was shaken by the news of the dreadful crime which has just brought trouble and sorrow to your country in the midst of her triumphs and her hopes. My sorrow was all the more intense since I supposed that you and your excellent son Frederick had met the same fate as your unfortunate president. I learn today that, thank God, you have escaped the assassins' blows, and I am greatly consoled by the thought that your country will not be deprived of your services at the moment when they can contribute so much to binding up her wounds. . . . You know well that the memory I preserve and always shall preserve of our long relations will never permit me to be insensible to anything which affects you, but in circumstances like the present, other sentiments are joined to those I convey to you,

[25] Seward to Dayton, Washington, 19 Feb. 1864, *ibid.*, no. 484.

sentiments which inspire me with a deep interest in the quick return of peace and prosperity to the United States.[26]

Peace and prosperity indeed returned, but Mexico, like a bad penny, kept turning up in relations between France and America. Seward worked manfully through 1865 and 1866 to prevent war with France; by 1867 the French were on the way home. Mercier wrote again, combining complaints with family chitchat:

> I am a little annoyed at you, may I say it as a real friend, because of your provocative attitude toward our affairs in Mexico. I have never been able to see the advantages of it from either the American or the Mexican point of view; for it was in no way necessary for you to make us give up an enterprise whose errors we already knew. . . . But in judging things from such a distance I might well be making a mistake. . . .
>
> You will doubtless learn with pleasure that the little Yankee who came to me in Washington has grown into the most lovable child in the world, and that he is our pride and joy. My wife is never in robust health, and as for me, I [live] quietly, and, thank God, at not too quick a pace, while often thinking of the long stay which I made among you. Please know, dear Mr. Seward, that it has left me the best of memories and a real and sincere friendship for you.[27]

The following month, his father-in-law having died, Mercier was given permission to assume the title of his wife's eminent family. Now he was Baron Mercier de Lostende. It was Mercier's lot to be near the center of his

[26] Mercier to Seward, Madrid, 28 April 1865, Seward Papers.
[27] Mercier to Seward, Madrid, 6 Jan. 1867, *ibid.* At some time after 1863 and probably after 1865, the Merciers had another son, Robert.

time's most awesome national crises—the American Civil War and the unification of Germany. The Hohenzollern candidacy to the Spanish throne became the subject of his work, and when it was done there was another war. On 10 September 1870, eight days after the capture of Napoleon III and six days after his government's formal end, Mercier left his post. He was fifty-three years old.

Seward was in retirement too, but unlike Mercier, his age was suited to it, and his health was in fact much broken. For two years he travelled to different parts of the world, and in 1871 came to Paris. Here he met the leaders of the new government and doubtless felt it to be a government conceived in liberty, with a right not to perish from the earth, a right fortified by a great civil war testing whether any government so conceived and so dedicated could long endure. In fact France had known such government for awhile under the old emperor, but nationalism and Germany had killed it nonetheless. Seward met Lyons, now ambassador to France, and Drouyn de Lhuys, Geofroy, and Montholon. His son Frederick records a long talk between his father and Drouyn de Lhuys. To him and to Lyons, Seward made that joking comparison, saying that Lyons, Mercier, and Hernando Cortéz were the three most impudent men in history:

> Hernando Cortéz when he proposed to Montezuma that he should . . . become the hostage in Cortéz's headquarters for the preservation of peace; Lord Lyons and Mercier, when, under instructions, they came together to the Department of State to announce an agreement between the British Government and the Emperor as to the course they should jointly pursue in regard to the American question.[28]

[28] F. W. Seward, *Reminiscences of a Wartime Statesman*, p. 425. For Seward's visit to Paris see *ibid.*, pp. 420-27, and Olive Risley Seward, *William H. Seward's Travels around the World* (New York: D. Appleton & Co., 1873), pp. 693-702.

Seward met Mercier too, but we know nothing of what was said beyond the fact that Seward was glad to see his old colleague.

Édouard Henri Mercier died in Clermont-Ferrand on Saturday morning, 16 October 1886, at the age of seventy. A few years later Madeleine died prematurely, but her mother lived on until 1917. At that time Mercier's son, "the Yankee," was serving as admiral of the French navy in the First World War. He fought beside Americans for an ideal of popular government which Woodrow Wilson had inherited from a long line of American leaders, including Abraham Lincoln. The American nation which Wilson headed, the nation whose dream he claimed to be furthering, was a large and powerful country, indivisible, successful. Wilson was born in Virginia.

Conclusion

Fʀᴏᴍ first to last it was a matter of defining "American." There had been tribes, cities, multitribal monarchies, empires, federations, confederations. And now there were nationalities and nation-states. Somehow the old way of personal subjection and loyalty within a definable boundary had become a part of one's being, one's "blood." By the time the United States was born, men were Frenchmen or Englishmen, not merely subjects of the French or English kings. And shortly after that, the very concept of being French not only survived the death of the Bourbons but throve and grew on it, so that the "fraternity" of being French became like a race or a breed. Modern nationalism, that is, issued from France. Some part of it had always been there, of course—language mostly, and mutual history. But now it was also a thing of the mind, a commitment to ideas of political right and freedom, ideas which had been current for centuries but which somehow seemed new in the context of the later Bourbon years. Being "patriotic" meant accepting some of those ideas, but it also meant being "French," and the others in Europe could be pardoned some confusion when French fraternity began to menace their liberty. So the defining went on, and people asked what is "German" and what is "Italian," and so on.

It was the same in America, but it was also different. Like a child seeking to define himself in opposition to his parents, the United States had begun and had continued in special relationship to England. Noah Webster notwithstanding, there was with Britain a mutuality of language, laws, and many other things which made the definition of "American" hard from the start. But there had also been that great Atlantic separation, those mutual economic interests among the states, that common fight against the Tory government. Mostly there was the "dream," the philosophical notion about human equality and political right; like the French ideology with which it was often compared, it was partly new but mostly old. And the dream had become more basic to defining "American" than any ideology anywhere else. There were French monarchists and French republicans, and few seriously claimed that the one was any more or less "French" than the other. But after a decade or so of independent life, "American monarchist" seemed almost a contradiction in terms. So central did the ideology become, that "blood" became somewhat irrelevant, and Germans and Irish alike could become American.

The idea that a people has the right to rule itself, a right to self-determination, was often read to mean that a nationality has such a right. Americans were apt to see themselves as exemplars of this ideal, and their hearts, if not their hands, went out to Latin America and to the Greeks and the Hungarians. But at the same time there were two very large, unsettled questions. First, what if a great segment of the United States should itself become a "nationality" and wish to assert a right to live alone? Second, what about the Negro slaves living in America? Ideology might transmute Germans and Irish, but could a Negro ever fully be an American?

By the time that Henri Mercier arrived in the United States, such questions were being posed with some sharpness. As an outsider he could view them with a certain detachment. And when it became apparent that a number of Southern states wished to determine themselves independently, he could see nothing so very wrong in that. American nationality, after all, was not a matter of "blood," but a precisely willed phenomenon of only some four score years' duration. Mercier's grandfathers knew a time when it had not existed. There seemed no pressing reason why, if one group of these people wished to separate from the others, they should not proceed to do so. Self-determination was part of the Americans' own ideology and, indeed, part of the French ideology as expounded by Napoleon III. As to the American constitution, Americans themselves disagreed about its meaning.

It is true, as Seward later said, that Mercier met some future Confederate leaders during 1860: Slidell, Benjamin, Maury, Trescot, and undoubtedly many others. But there is no need to worry at that point in order to explain Mercier's attitude toward secession. There was nothing in the American nationality or in American constitutional law which would compel a foreigner to accept the Lincoln thesis. The notion that America must remain one, so that government of, for, and by the people might prove viable, appealed very little to Mercier or to most other Europeans. From Mercier's viewpoint the democratic element in American government was directly responsible for demagoguery and corruption. What America needed was some order and direction. If America's brand of popular government were to be discredited by Southern secession, that was that.

James Buchanan knew, as Lincoln did, that secession would weaken the country and mock the dream. But despite that, even Buchanan felt that a determined state or section could not actually be forced to stay in the Union. Bad as national scission would be, a hard, bloody war would be much worse. An ideal of freedom which depended on bullets and bayonets seemed a contradiction. There were all shades of opinion for the minister of France to sample in 1860 and 1861 in Washington, and there is no need to single out the Slidells and Maurys in seeking to know who influenced him. Beside President Buchanan there were other Northerners with whom Mercier spoke. Stephen A. Douglas, though he stoutly defended the Union once war broke out, was already toying with the idea of a common market between the Northern and Southern states. Jesse Bright, friend of Corcoran and other pro-Southern leaders, was even more willing to see things go the Southerners' way. Even Senator Seward seemed willing to do a great deal in order to head off bloodshed, and when the abolitionist Horace Greeley spoke to him in 1863, Mercier knew that the need for peace was stronger than the need for unity. Mercier's more typical friends, the slave-owning Ridgleys, could certainly see no point in a war.

Slavery was at once the principal cause of the trouble and no cause at all. Until 1862 the Union government resolutely refused to tamper with this explosive question: it was a war to save the Union pure and simple. But the Union was in danger precisely because of slavery, that is to say, because of Negro slavery. Perhaps no motive for Southern separation was so forceful as the simple thought that without slavery the Negro must be accepted as a full human being, a fully accredited citizen with full rights as an American. On this point Mercier was in agreement with Americans South and North, many, perhaps most of whom could see no better than he how the two races could live side by side in harmony. His immediate reaction to the emancipation proclamation was outrage at what seemed to him to be an effort to start a servile insurrection in the South.

It is clear, then, that along with most Southerners and many Northerners, Henri Mercier was opposed to the North in its waging of the war. The idea that thousands of people should be sent to die in order to preserve anything so problematical as the American nationality and the American dream seemed obtuse if not worse. Mercier knew the strength of the United States; he may have realized that the relative power of France in the world would diminish

367

as America grew. But this thought played little if any part in his conclusions about the Civil War. For one thing, Mercier liked to think of America as a counterweight to Great Britain.

The issue which did most to bring France and the United States into confrontation, of course, was Mexico. Here Mercier was basically out of sympathy with the emperor's policy. Once it became clear that this policy was a settled plan, Mercier changed his tune a little and supported the idea of installing Maximilian. But he may have seen Maximilian as a way out for France. The notion that France should construct a Latin obstacle to American expansion appealed little enough to Mercier when compared with the danger of Franco-American conflict.

Mercier's first and overriding interest was the welfare of his own country. By late 1861 it was obvious that only peace in America could stave off severe economic hardship in France. In working for peace, then, Mercier thought himself not only sensible, human, and farsighted, but also patriotic and devoted to his country's interest. Most criticisms of Mercier come down to the assertion that he was not an American nationalist. To this charge he would cheerfully have pleaded guilty.

The question of secession, of the purposes and ability of Confederacy and Union, and of what Europe might do to shape the American future was most central to Mercier's American career. His first impression, taken largely from the affluent, moderate types of people he met in Newport that first summer, was that the South would not secede, that it was all a matter of who would control the Senate, and that it did not matter really whether or not Lincoln became president. By the time the election occurred, however, he knew that secession would take place. It was only a matter of time, he thought, before someone would ask him what France intended to do about recognizing the nascent polity.

Should France not set up steamship service with New Orleans as well as with New York, just in case? As conservative Europeans had been predicting since 1776, so Mercier saw it: the United States was about to dissolve, victim of its own democratic, republican institutions, of its slavery, its size, and its heterogeneity. To a Thouvenel whom he thought distracted by European concerns, Mercier sent word that America bore careful watching.

One of Mercier's beliefs was the strength of financial and commercial concerns to influence the course of political events. His syllogisms sometimes began with the premise that what was bad for the American economy might not be allowed to happen, that economic self-interest might triumph over all; his common-market proposal was a natural corollary of this reasoning. When New York commercial interests began to press for compromise in early 1861, therefore, Mercier tended to think that they might have their way. But he was no less confused than most other observers at that point, and Lewis Cass impressed him with his sour prediction that secession would indeed occur and would succeed. In dinner conversations with Douglas, Seward, and Crittenden, Mercier heard another view, determinedly optimistic. But he could recognize the note of special pleading there, and he knew that Paris was meant to hear, through him, that the Union would hang together. Instead he reported that the lower South was gone, that the border states might go too, should the North try to coerce the seceded states, and that the Republican administration could not compromise to the extent of reneging on its platform and accepting slavery in the territories. Even the plan to call a convention, he said, was bound to fail, if only because the government would have to face the issue of federal forts in the South before such a convention could save the situation. In making these pessimistic observations, Mercier proved a better prophet than Seward or Douglas.

As to what France might do about the new Confederacy, Mercier was certainly too sanguine in the early months of 1861. He apparently told L. T. Wigfall that there should be no difficulty about obtaining French recognition, and he said that France would simply wait to see what Washington might do—obviously Mercier thought the United States might itself recognize or at least tolerate the Confederacy. Lincoln's inaugural address did not seem to alter the picture much, and Mercier now recommended that he and Lyons be allowed to pick a moment *before* the outbreak of fighting when it should be clear that the Union was irreversibly done, a moment at which they would announce European recognition of the South. When we reflect upon this fact, then Seward's bellicose posturing in April and May becomes more understandable and more excusable. So well did Seward play his thundering role that, when Mercier received Thouvenel's statement of the French position, he was quite hesitant in approaching Seward, and he and Lyons delayed until 15 June their famous joint appearance at the State Department. That French position, of course, was the recognition of Southern belligerency, a middle ground which succeeded in maintaining neutrality without extending diplomatic recognition to the Confederacy. Mercier now felt that the war might not last beyond the summer and that in order to help end it, France should be ready with a common-market proposal, one which would grant the South her political independence and the North the economic advantages she desired.

By the fall of 1861 it was clear that the war might be a long one and that the blockade and the South's retention of cotton would cause severe hardship in Europe. Without recommending any immediate action, Mercier now emphasized the possibility of European intervention, an intervention which he thought should include, if necessary, diplomatic recognition of the South and the breaking of the blockade. Thouvenel spoke only of a special exception to the blockade to end the suffering in France, but Mercier went beyond this in his conversation with Seward and talked about intervention, albeit obliquely.

With the *Trent* affair out of the way, this diplomatic thread continued into early 1862. It was clear to Mercier that short of threatening war, Europe could do nothing until the outcome of McClellan's campaign against Richmond was known. How tenaciously might the South hold on should that campaign succeed? In one of the war's most startling diplomatic episodes, Mercier went personally to find out, and contrary to Seward's hope, the French minister came away from Richmond convinced that the South would fight on to the bitter end.

That end seemed close at hand in May, and Mercier concluded from what he saw at Yorktown that the North might win in 1862, and that in any event France should never become involved with the powerful might of the United States. When McClellan finally failed, however, peace talk began to rise in the North, and Mercier felt that it would reach a climax in the fall elections, at which time Europe might profitably stop the bloodshed by threatening intervention. Mercier and Thouvenel were of one mind that summer in their opposition to any immediate European initiative. But second Bull Run destroyed that agreement as Mercier, in the first week of September, came closer to saying "Act now." Even here, however, he qualified his recommendation, and he later said that had it been up to him he would not have acted before the elections. Antietam proved that second Bull Run had not really been fatal to the North, but despite Antietam Mercier interpreted the preliminary emancipation decree as a sign of Union desperation. Frustrated and angry, Mercier nevertheless could see that direct intervention would mean war with the United States. Accordingly he shifted his ground in late

371

September and began recommending a European call for American armistice, an armistice which might well have ended in Southern independence. Mercier had Thouvenel's own word for it that his dispatches helped generate the French proposal for a three-power armistice approach to Washington and Richmond. Even before he learned of Britain's (and Russia's) rejection, Mercier was already thinking that a solo French effort might stand a better chance of American acceptance in view of the continuing and strong Anglophobia in the North.

Early 1863 saw the climax of dissident peace sentiment in the North, and Horace Greeley saw to it that Mercier was kept excited in January and February. Mercier, again calling for discretionary authority to pick "the moment," recommended a French or Franco-Russian offer of mediation, an offer which could end, should the North reject it, in forcible European intervention. What Paris sent him was considerably less potent—a mere suggestion that Washington and Richmond talk peace without an armistice and without mediation. Seward patronizingly rejected this feeble plan, and Mercier, turning angry again, told Paris that any future effort should include an Anglo-French threat of force. That is to say, if threats were in order, Britain must come along too.

By the spring of 1863, however, a new Union offensive was in the making under General Hooker; Northern peace sentiment was beginning to decline; and France was no longer in the good graces of Northern officials or of Northern public opinion. The deepening French involvement in Mexico, the fear of French designs on Texas, and the publication of Mercier's 1862 correspondence all helped to create this depressing situation. Mercier continued to talk about a common market, but it was clear to him now that this side of the 1864 presidential election there was little that could be done about peace. The pattern of the war had now become clearer, so much so that Mercier did not even blink when Hooker was beaten at Chancellorsville; Gettysburg and Vicksburg only underlined the general situation. Mostly it came down to the same two factors which had been strongly operative from the start: the North was determined to fight on for territorial integrity, i.e., for the national life of the United States of America; and France, prudently unwilling to attack the United States alone, could do nothing so long as Britain remained aloof. After Gettysburg and Vicksburg Mercier might have seen, but could not see, that the South's cause was lost. At no time did he recommend, except in the most remote and hypothetical way, the one course which could have ended the war: European withdrawal of the recognition of Southern belligerency, European support of the Northern effort.

Henri Mercier was an affable man, and this quality stood him in good stead as he strove to perform his diplomatic duties. Both Seward and Lyons came away from their close association with Mercier convinced of his basic goodwill and reasonableness. His style in his dealings with Seward leaned heavily to conversation—informal, friendly, and, within limits, frank. It was in such an informal conversation with Seward, in the fall of 1861, that Mercier first broached the possibility of European intervention. Again, in September 1862, he told Seward that second Bull Run had just about proved the hopelessness of the Union cause. In both of these cases Mercier showed another of his qualities: his willingness to venture beyond the letter of his instructions. By nature he was a somewhat venturesome person; by training he had a diplomat's patience and reserve. Occasionally, as in the Richmond trip, his nature defeated his training. Beyond that, there was probably a desire to cut a great figure, a desire which may have stemmed in part from his bourgeois status and his wife's aristocratic connections. Repeatedly he asked for discretionary authority

373

to pick the moment for announcing European intervention; if this had led to anything, it might have been he who ended the Civil War, thus building himself up in his wife's eyes, and incidentally shortening their uncomfortable stay in the United States.

Mercier was notably observant, and his government was in general well served by the factual sections of his reports. His trip to Richmond was among other things a gold mine of correct information about Southern intentions, and, however unpleasant that information was to Northern supporters, it was nonetheless true that the South intended to fight on doggedly even should Richmond be captured.

Personally, Mercier was uncomfortable during his stay in the United States, though his pleas to be recalled were at least equally owing to his wife's wishes. As compensation for having to stay in Washington there was the fact that he was at the center of one of the most important events in modern history. It is not given to most men to participate in matters of that kind, and Mercier knew the importance of his work. Decent, intelligent, thoughtful, he consistently put French interests ahead of all others, ahead of the Anglo-French entente, ahead of American national purpose.

Henri Mercier stood for peace, for reasoned compromise, for French interests, for Franco-American friendship. That he failed to elaborate a formula which could perfectly express all these sentiments is not surprising. In fact such a task was impossible. For the United States to go on living as a nation so dedicated, the Civil War had to be fought and French interests had to be ignored. Those interests were deep and serious but neither deep nor serious enough to warrant a Franco-American fight. Given that fact, Mercier and France did all they could to end the Civil War. It was not, could not be, enough.

Bibliography

ARCHIVE SOURCES

Papers of James Buchanan. Philadelphia. Historical Society of Pennsylvania.

Papers of James Buchanan and Harriet Lane. Washington. Library of Congress. Manuscripts Division.

Papers of Salmon P. Chase. Philadelphia. Historical Society of Pennsylvania.

Papers of William W. Corcoran. Washington. Library of Congress. Manuscripts Division.

Papers of Edwin DeLeon. Cincinnati. American Jewish Archives.

Papers of George Eustis. Washington. Library of Congress. Manuscripts Division.

France. Paris. Archives du Ministère des Affaires étrangères.

Correspondance politique.

Angleterre:	Volumes 722
	724-726
États-Unis:	Volumes 123-130

Correspondance politique des Consuls.

New Orleans:	Volume 14
Richmond:	Volumes 12
	15

Correspondance commerciale.

Richmond:	Volume 5

Mémoires et Documents.

Papiers Thouvenel:	Volume 13

Paris. Archives Nationales.

Fonds Thouvenel.

Papers of Jessie Benton Fremont. Berkeley. University of California.

Papers of Sydney Howard Gay. New York. Columbia University.

Papers of James Hazen Hyde. New York. New York Historical Society.

Papers of Abraham Lincoln. Washington. Library of Congress. Manuscripts Division. The Robert Todd Lincoln Collection.

Papers of Henri Mercier. Dordogne, France. Archives of the Le Cour Grandmaison Family.

Papers of the Riggs Family. Washington. Library of Congress. Manuscripts Division.

Papers of William Cabell Rives. Charlottesville. University of Virginia.

Russia. Washington. Library of Congress. Manuscripts Division. Papers of the Ministry of Foreign Affairs. United States, 1860-1864. Papers of Édouard de Stoeckl.

Papers of William H. Seward. Rochester. University of Rochester.

United States. Washington. National Archives.
Archives of the Department of State.
Diplomatic and Consular Instructions.
Belgium: Volume 1
France: Volumes 15-17
Diplomatic Despatches.
Belgium: Volume 5
France: Volumes 47-55
Great Britain: Volume 83
Notes to Foreign Legations.
France: Volume 7
Notes from Foreign Legations.
France: Volumes 17-22

PUBLISHED SOURCES

Almanach de Gotha, annuaire diplomatique et statistique. Gotha: Justus Perthes, 1863.

Bates, Edward. *The Diary of Edward Bates, 1859-1866.* Edited by Howard K. Beale. *Annual Report of the American Historical Association, 1930.* Volume iv. Washington: U.S. Government Printing Office, 1933.

Belmont, August. *Letters, Speeches, and Addresses of August Belmont.* New York: privately printed, 1890.

Bigelow, John. *Retrospections of an Active Life.* 5 vols. New York: Baker & Taylor Co., 1909-1913.

Bonaparte, Prince Napoleon. "Voyage du Prince Napoléon aux États-Unis, 1861," edited by Ernest d'Hauterive, *Revue de Paris*, XL (15 Sept. and 1 Oct. 1933), 241-72 and 547-87.

Browning, Orville H. *The Diary of Orville Hickman Browning.* 2 vols. Springfield: Illinois State Historical Library, 1927 and 1933.

Buchanan, James. *Mr. Buchanan's Administration on the Eve of the Rebellion.* New York: D. Appleton Co., 1866.

Bulloch, James D. *The Secret Service of the Confederate States in Europe.* 2 vols. London, Richard Bentley and Son, 1883.

Butler, Benjamin F. *Autobiography and Personal Reminiscences of Major-General Benj. F. Butler: Butler's Book.* Boston: A. M. Thayer & Co., 1892.

————. *Private and Official Correspondence of Gen. Benjamin F. Butler during the Period of the Civil War.* 5 vols. Norwood, Mass.: Plimpton Press, 1917.

Carey, Henry C. *The French and American Tariffs Compared, in a Series of Letters Addressed to Mons. Michel Chevalier.* Philadelphia: Collins, 1861.

Chesnut, Mary B. *A Diary from Dixie.* Edited by Isabella D. Martin and Myrta Lockett Avary. Gloucester, Mass.: Peter Smith, 1961.

Clay-Clopton, Virginia. *A Belle of the Fifties.* Edited by Ada Sterling. New York: Doubleday, Page & Co., 1905.

Cowley, Lord. *Secrets of the Second Empire: Private Letters from the Paris Embassy, Selections from the Papers of Henry Richard Charles Wellesley, 1st Earl Cowley, Ambassador at Paris, 1852-1867.* Edited by F. A. Wellesley. New York: Harper & Brothers, 1929.

DeLeon, T. C. *Belles, Beaux, and Brains of the 60's.* New York: G. W. Dillingham Co., 1909.

Evans, Thomas W. *Memoirs: The Second French Empire.* New York: D. Appleton & Co., 1905.

Ferri-Pisani, Camille. *Prince Napoleon in America, 1861.* Bloomington: Indiana University Press, 1959.

————. "A French Visit to Civil War America," edited by Georges Joyaux, *American Heritage*, VIII (1957), 65-86.

France. *Documents diplomatiques (Livres jaunes).* 13 vols. Paris: Imprimerie impériale, 1860-1869.

――――. *Papiers et correspondance de la famille impériale.* 2 vols. Paris: Librairie L. Beauvais, 1872.

Great Britain. *British Sessional Papers, House of Commons (Blue Books).* Microprint edition edited by Edgar L. Erickson. 1861, volume LXV. 1862, volume LXII. 1863, volume LXXII. 1864, volume LXII.

Gurowski, Adam. *Diary.* 3 vols. Volume I: Boston: Lee & Shepard, 1862. Volume II: New York: Carleton, 1864. Volume III: Washington, D.C.: W. H. & O. H. Morrison, 1866.

Hay, John. *Lincoln and the Civil War in the Diaries and Letters of John Hay.* Edited by Tyler Dennett. New York: Dodd, Mead & Co., 1939.

Joinville, Prince de. *The Army of the Potomac, Its Organization, Its Commander, and Its Campaign.* New York: Anson D. F. Randolph, 1862.

Jones, John B. *A Rebel War Clerk's Diary.* Edited by Earl Schenck Miers. New York: Sagamore Press, 1958.

Lincoln, Abraham. *Collected Works.* Edited by Roy P. Basler. 9 vols. New Brunswick, N.J.: Rutgers University Press, 1953-1955.

Mason, James M. *The Public Life and Diplomatic Correspondence of James M. Mason.* Edited by Virginia Mason. Roanoke, Va.: Stone Printing and Manufacturing Co., 1903.

Perley Poore, Ben:. *Perley's Reminiscences of Sixty Years in the National Metropolis.* 2 vols. Philadelphia: Hubbard Brothers, 1886.

Raymond, Henry W. "Extracts from the Journal of Henry J. Raymond," *Scribner's Monthly,* XIX (1880), 703-10.

Richardson, James D., ed. *A Compilation of the Messages and Papers of the Confederacy, Including the Diplomatic Correspondence, 1861-1865.* 2 vols. Nashville, Tenn.: United States Publishing Co., 1905.

Russell, Lord John. *The Later Correspondence of Lord John Russell, 1840-1878.* Edited by G. P. Gooch. 2 vols. London: Longmans, Green & Co., 1925.

Russell, William Howard. *My Diary North and South.* 2 vols. London: Longmans, Green & Co., 1925.

Sand, Maurice. *Six mille lieues à toute vapeur.* Paris: Michel Lévy Frères, 1862.

Seward, Frederick W. *Reminiscences of a War-Time Statesman and Diplomat, 1830-1915.* New York: G. P. Putnam's Sons, 1916.

————. *Seward at Washington as Senator and Secretary of State.* 2 vols. New York: Derby & Miller, 1891.

Seward, Olive Risley. *William H. Seward's Travels Around the World.* New York: D. Appleton & Co., 1873.

Seward, William H. *The Works of William H. Seward.* Edited by George E. Baker, 5 vols. Boston: Houghton, Mifflin Co., 1884.

Sumner, Charles. *Works.* 15 vols. Boston: Lee & Shepard, 1875-1883.

Thouvenel, Édouard Antoine. *Le secret de l'Empereur, correspondance confidentielle et inédite.* Edited by L. Thouvenel. 2 vols. Paris: Calmann Lévy, 1889.

United States. *Congressional Globe,* 1860-1864.

————. *Foreign Relations of the United States.* Washington, D.C.: U.S. Government Printing Office, 1861-1864.

————. *Official Records of the Union and Confederate Navies in the War of the Rebellion.* 30 vols. Washington, D.C.: U.S. Government Printing Office, 1894-1927.

————. *The War of the Rebellion: A Compilation of the Official Records of the Union and Confederate Armies.* 70 vols. Washington, D.C.: U.S. Government Printing Office, 1880-1902.

Welles, Gideon. *Diary of Gideon Welles, Secretary of the Navy under Lincoln and Johnson.* Edited by Howard K. Beale. 3 vols. New York: Norton & Co., 1960.

NEWSPAPERS AND PERIODICALS

Courrier des États-Unis. New York.

Evening Star. Washington, D.C.

Harper's Weekly.

National Intelligencer. Washington, D.C.

New York Times.

New York Tribune.
Richmond Dispatch.
Richmond Enquirer.

HISTORICAL STUDIES

Ackerman, William K. *Early Illinois Railroads.* Chicago: Fergus Printing Co., 1884.

Adamov, E. A. "Russia and the United States at the Time of the Civil War," *Journal of Modern History*, II (1930), 586-602.

Adams, Charles Francis, Jr. "The British Proclamation of May, 1861," *Massachusetts Historical Society Proceedings*, XLVIII (1915), 190-241.

————. *Charles Francis Adams.* Boston: Houghton Mifflin Co., 1900.

————. "A Crisis in Downing Street," *Massachusetts Historical Society Proceedings*, XLVII (1914), 372-424.

————. "The Negotiation of 1861 Relating to the Declaration of Paris of 1856," *Massachusetts Historical Society Proceedings*, XLVI (1912), 23-84.

————. "The Trent Affair," *American Historical Review*, XVII (1912), 540-62.

————. "The Trent Affair," *Massachusetts Historical Society Proceedings*, XLV (1911), 76-148.

Adams, E. D. *Great Britain and the American Civil War.* 2 vols. London: Longmans, Green & Co., 1925.

Aldis, Owen F. "Louis Napoleon and the Southern Confederacy," *North American Review*, CXXIX (1879), 342-60.

Auchampaugh, Philip Gerald. *James Buchanan and his Cabinet on the Eve of Secession.* Lancaster, Pa.: Lancaster Press, 1926.

Bancroft, Frederic. *The Life of William H. Seward.* 2 vols. New York: Harper & Brothers, 1900.

Barge, William D. and Norman W. Caldwell. "Illinois Place-names," *Journal of the Illinois State Historical Society*, XXIX (1936), 189-311.

Barker, Nancy Nichols. *Distaff Diplomacy: the Empress Eugénie and the Foreign Policy of the Second Empire.* Austin: University of Texas Press, 1967.

Bell, Herbert C. F. *Lord Palmerston.* 2 vols. London: Longmans, Green & Co., 1936.

Beloff, Max. "Great Britain and the American Civil War," *History,* xxxvii (1952), 40-48.

Beyens, Napoléon. *Le Second Empire vu par un diplomate belge.* 2 vols. Paris: Plon-Nourrit & Cie., n.d.

Bill, Alfred Hoyt. *The Beleaguered City, Richmond, 1861-1865.* New York: Alfred A. Knopf, 1946.

Blinn, Harold E. "Seward and the Polish Rebellion of 1863." *American Historical Review,* xlv (1940), 828-33.

Blumenthal, Henry. *A Reappraisal of Franco-American Relations, 1830-1871.* Chapel Hill: University of North Carolina Press, 1959.

Bock, Carl H. *Prelude to Tragedy: the Negotiation and Breakdown of the Tripartite Convention of London, October 31, 1861.* Philadelphia: University of Pennsylvania Press, 1966.

Bonham, Milledge L. *The British Consuls in the Confederacy.* New York: Columbia University Press, 1911.

————. "The French Consuls in the Confederate States," *Studies in Southern History and Politics Inscribed to William Archibald Dunning.* New York: Columbia University Press, 1914.

Bragg, Jefferson Davis. *Louisiana in the Confederacy.* Baton Rouge: Louisiana State University Press, 1941.

Cain, Marvin R. *Lincoln's Attorney General, Edward Bates of Missouri.* Columbia: University of Missouri Press, 1965.

Callahan, James Morton. *American Foreign Policy in Mexican Relations.* New York: Macmillan Co., 1932.

————. *The Diplomatic History of the Southern Confederacy.* Baltimore: Johns Hopkins University Press, 1901.

————. "Diplomatic Relations of the Confederate States with England, 1861-1865," *Annual Report of the American Historical Association, 1898.* Washington: U.S. Government Printing Office, 1899.

————. *Evolution of Seward's Mexican Policy.* Morgantown: University of West Virginia Press, 1909.

Case, Lynn M. "La France et l'affaire du *Trent,*" *Revue historique,* ccxxvi (1961), 57-86.

Case, Lynn M. *French Opinion on the United States and Mexico, 1860-1867, Extracts from the Reports of the Procureurs généraux.* New York: D. Appleton-Century Co., 1936.

———. *French Opinion on War and Diplomacy during the Second Empire.* Philadelphia: University of Pennsylvania Press, 1954.

———. "La sécession aux États-Unis, problème diplomatique français en 1861," *Revue d'histoire diplomatique,* LXXVII (1963), 290-313.

——— and Warren F. Spencer. *The United States and France: Civil War Diplomacy.* Philadelphia: University of Pennsylvania Press, 1970.

Catton, Bruce. *Glory Road.* New York: Pocket Books, Inc., 1964.

———. *Never Call Retreat.* New York: Doubleday & Co., 1965.

Coleman, Evan J. "Senator Gwin's Plan for the Colonization of Sonora," *The Overland Monthly,* 2nd ser., XVII (1891), 497-519 and 593-607.

Connor, Henry G. *John Archibald Campbell, Associate Justice of the United States Supreme Court, 1853-1861.* Boston: Houghton Mifflin Co., 1920.

Corbin, Diana Fontaine Maury. *A Life of Matthew Fontaine Maury, U.S.N. and C.S.N.* London: Sampson Low, Marston, Searle, & Rivington, Ltd., 1888.

Crawford, Samuel Wylie. *The Genesis of the Civil War: the Story of Sumter, 1860-1861.* New York: Charles L. Webster & Co., 1887.

Crook, Carland Elaine. "Benjamin Theron and French Designs in Texas during the Civil War," *Southwestern Historical Quarterly,* LXVIII (1965), 432-54.

D'Harcourt, Bernard. *Diplomatie et diplomates, les quatre ministères de M. Drouyn de L'Huys.* Paris: E. Plon et Cie; 1882.

Donald, David, ed. *Why the North Won the Civil War.* Baton Rouge: Louisiana State University Press, 1960.

Dulles, Foster Rhea. *Prelude to World Power: American Diplomatic History, 1860-1900.* New York: Macmillan Co., 1965.

Dunham, Arthur L. "The Development of the Cotton Industry in France and the Anglo-French Treaty of Commerce of 1860," *Economic History Review,* I (1928), 281-307.

Eaton, Clement. *A History of the Southern Confederacy.* New York: Macmillan Co., 1958.

Einstein, Lewis. "American Secretaries of State and Their Diplomacy." Edited by Samuel Flagg Bemis. *Lewis Cass.* Volume VI. New York: Alfred A. Knopf, 1928.

Elliott, Charles Winslow. *Winfield Scott, the Soldier and the Man.* New York: Macmillan Co., 1937.

Evans, Elliott A. P. "Napoleon III and the American Civil War." Doctoral dissertation. Stanford University, 1940.

Fleming, Walter L. "Deportation and Colonization: an Attempted Solution of the Race Problem," *Studies in Southern History and Politics Inscribed to William Archibald Dunning.* New York: Columbia University Press. 1914.

Frazer, Robert W. "Latin-American Projects to Aid Mexico during the French Intervention," *Hispanic American Historical Review,* XXVIII (1948), 377-88.

Gavronsky, Serge. *The French Liberal Opposition and the American Civil War.* New York: Humanities Press, 1968.

Green, Constance McLaughlin. *Washington, Village and Capital, 1800-1878.* Princeton: Princeton University Press, 1962.

Hale, William Harlan. *Horace Greeley, Voice of the People.* New York: Harper & Brothers, 1950.

Hammond, Bray. "The North's Empty Purse, 1861-1862," *American Historical Review,* LXVII (1961), 1-18.

Hanna, Kathryn Abbey. "The Roles of the South in the French Intervention in Mexico," *Journal of Southern History,* XX (1954), 3-21.

Harris, Thomas L. *The Trent Affair.* Indianapolis: Bowen-Merrill Co., 1896.

Hauser, Henri, *et al. Du Liberalisme à l'imperialisme, 1860-1878.* 2nd ed. Paris: Presses Universitaires de France, 1952.

Hendrick, Burton J. *Lincoln's War Cabinet.* Boston: Little, Brown & Co., 1946.

Higham, Robin D. S. "The Russian Fleet on the Eastern Seaboard, 1863-1864," *American Neptune,* XX (1960), 49-61.

Holzman, Robert S. *Stormy Ben Butler.* New York: Macmillan Co., 1954.

Horner, Harlan Hoyt. *Lincoln and Greeley*. Urbana: University of Illinois Press, 1953.

Jacobsen, Hugh Newell, ed. *A Guide to the Architecture of Washington, D.C.* New York: Frederick A. Praeger, 1965.

John, Evan. *Atlantic Impact, 1861*. New York: G. P. Putnam's Sons, 1952.

Johnson, Allen. *Stephen A. Douglas, a Study in American Politics*. New York: Macmillan Co., 1908.

Jordan, Donaldson and Edwin J. Pratt. *Europe and the American Civil War*. Boston: Houghton Mifflin Co., 1931.

Kirwan, Albert D. *John J. Crittenden, the Struggle for the Union*. Lexington: University of Kentucky Press, 1962.

Klein, Philip Shriver. *President James Buchanan, a Biography*. University Park: Pennsylvania State University Press, 1962.

Korolewicz-Carlton, Richard. "Napoléon III, Thouvenel et la guerre de sécession." Doctoral thesis. University of Paris, 1951.

Landry, Harral E. "Slavery and the Slave Trade in Atlantic Diplomacy, 1850-1861," *Journal of Southern History*, xxvii (1961), 184-207.

Leech, Margaret. *Reveille in Washington, 1860-1865*. New York: Harper & Brothers, 1941.

Lonn, Ella. *Foreigners in the Confederacy*. Chapel Hill: University of North Carolina Press, 1940.

Lothrop, Thornton Kirkland. *William Henry Seward*. Boston: Houghton Mifflin Co., 1899.

Luthin, Reinhard H. "Abraham Lincoln and the Tariff," *American Historical Review*, xlix (1944), 609-29.

Lutz, Ralph. *Die Beziehungen zwischen Deutschland und den Vereinigten Staaten während des Sezessionskrieges*. Heidelberg: Carl Winter's Universitätsbuchhandlung, 1911.

———. "Rudolf Schleiden and the Visit to Richmond April 25, 1861," *Annual Report of the American Historical Association for the Year 1915*. Washington: U.S. Government Printing Office, 1917.

Maurain, Jean. *Un bourgeois au XIXe siècle: Baroche, ministre de Napoléon III d'après ses papiers inédits*. Paris: Librairie Felix Alcan, 1936.

Miers, Earl Schenck, ed. *Lincoln Day by Day, A Chronology, 1809-1865.* 3 vols. Washington: U.S. Government Printing Office, 1960.

Milton, George Fort. *The Eve of Conflict: Stephen A. Douglas and the Needless War.* Boston: Houghton Mifflin Co., 1934.

Nevins, Allan. *The Emergence of Lincoln.* 2 vols. New York: Charles Scribner's Sons, 1950.

————. *Henry White, Thirty Years of American Diplomacy.* New York: Harper & Brothers, 1930.

————. *The War for the Union.* 2 vols. New York: Charles Scribner's Sons, 1959 and 1960.

Newton, Lord. *Lord Lyons, a Record of British Diplomacy.* 2 vols. London: Edward Arnold, 1913.

Nichols, Roy F. "American Secretaries of State and Their Diplomacy." Edited by Samuel Flagg Bemis. *Jeremiah S. Black.* Volume VI. New York: Alfred A. Knopf, 1928.

————. *The Disruption of American Democracy.* New York: Macmillan Co., 1948.

Nicolay, John and John Hay. *Abraham Lincoln, a History.* 10 vols. New York: Century Co., 1890.

Ollivier, Émile. *L'Empire libéral.* 17 vols. Paris: Garnier Frères, 1895-1915.

Owsley, Frank Lawrence. "America and the Freedom of the Seas, 1861-65," *Essays in Honor of William E. Dodd.* Edited by Avery Craven. Chicago: University of Chicago Press, 1935.

————. *King Cotton Diplomacy.* 2nd ed. revised. Chicago: University of Chicago Press, 1959.

Pomeroy, Earl S. "French Substitutes for American Cotton, 1861-1865," *Journal of Southern History*, IX (1943), 555-60.

Randall, J. G. *Lincoln the President.* 4 vols. New York: Dodd, Mead & Co., 1945-1955.

Randall, J. G. and David Donald. *The Civil War and Reconstruction.* 2nd ed. revised. Boston: D. C. Heath & Co., 1961.

Rippy, J. Fred. *The United States and Mexico.* New York: Alfred A. Knopf, 1926.

Robinson, William Morrison. *The Confederate Privateers.* New Haven: Yale University Press, 1928.

Ruvigny, Marquis of. *The Titled Nobility of Europe, an International Peerage.* London: Harrison & Sons, 1914.

Scarff, John H. "'Hampton,' Baltimore County, Maryland," *Maryland Historical Magazine,* XLIII (1948), 96-107.

Schuckers, J. W. *The Life and Public Services of Salmon Portland Chase.* New York: D. Appleton & Co., 1874.

Schwab, John Christopher. *The Confederate States of America, 1861-1865, a Financial and Industrial History of the South during the Civil War.* London: Charles Scribner's Sons, 1901.

Sears, Louis Martin. *John Slidell.* Durham, N.C.: Duke University Press, 1925.

Sowle, Patrick. "A Reappraisal of Seward's Memorandum of April 1, 1861, to Lincoln," *Journal of Southern History,* XXXIII (1967), 234-39.

Spencer, Warren F. "Drouyn de Lhuys et les navires confédérés en France: l'affaire des navires d'Arman, 1863-1865," *Revue d'histoire diplomatique,* LXXVII (1963), 314-41.

Steiner, Bernard C. *Life of Reverdy Johnson.* Baltimore: Norman, Remington Co., 1914.

Stern, Philip Van Doren. *When the Guns Roared, World Aspects of the American Civil War.* New York: Doubleday & Co., 1965.

Tarbell, Ida M. *The Tariff in Our Times.* New York: Macmillan Co., 1912.

Taussig, F. W. *The Tariff History of the United States.* New York: G. P. Putnam's Sons, 1905.

Temple, Henry W. "The American Secretaries of State and Their Diplomacy." Edited by Samuel Flagg Bemis. *William H. Seward.* Volume VII. New York: Alfred A. Knopf, 1928.

Thomas, Lately. "The Operator and the Emperors," *American Heritage,* XV (1964), 4-8 and 83-88.

Trefousse, Hans L. *Benjamin Butler, the South Called Him Beast!* New York: Twayne, 1957.

Tyrner-Tyrnauer, A. R. *Lincoln and the Emperors.* New York: Harcourt, Brace & World, 1962.

United States. *Rhode Island, a Guide to the Smallest State.* W.P.A. Writers. Boston: Houghton Mifflin Co., 1937.

Van Deusen, Glyndon G. *Thurlow Weed, Wizard of the Lobby.* Boston: Little, Brown & Co., 1947.

——. *William Henry Seward.* New York: Oxford University Press, 1967.

Walpole, Spencer. *The Life of Lord John Russell,* 2 vols. London: Longmans, Green & Co., 1889.

Williams, Frances Leigh. *Matthew Fontaine Maury, Scientist of the Sea.* New Brunswick, N.J.: Rutgers University Press, 1963.

Willson, Beckles. *John Slidell and the Confederates in Paris, 1862-1865.* New York: Minton, Balch & Co., 1932.

Winters, John D. *The Civil War in Louisiana.* Baton Rouge: Louisiana State University Press, 1963.

Woldman, Albert A. *Lincoln and the Russians.* Cleveland: World Publishing Co., 1952.

Woodford, Frank B. *Lewis Cass, the Last Jeffersonian.* New Brunswick, N.J.: Rutgers University Press, 1950.

Index